YOUNG
THOMAS HARDY

Thomas Hardy aged 34 or 35.

Young
Thomas Hardy

by

ROBERT GITTINGS

An Atlantic Monthly Press Book

LITTLE, BROWN AND COMPANY · BOSTON · TORONTO

FIRST AMERICAN EDITION

T 05/75

LIBRARY OF CONGRESS CATALOGING IN PUBLICATION DATA

Gittings, Robert.
  Young Thomas Hardy.

  "An Atlantic Monthly Press book."
  1. Hardy, Thomas, 1840–1928—Biography—Youth.
I. Title.
PR4753.G5 1975   823'.8 [B]   75-5555
ISBN 0-316-31453-6

ATLANTIC–LITTLE, BROWN BOOKS
ARE PUBLISHED BY
LITTLE, BROWN AND COMPANY
IN ASSOCIATION WITH
THE ATLANTIC MONTHLY PRESS

PRINTED IN THE UNITED STATES OF AMERICA

Contents

87607

Illustrations

Frontispiece

Thomas Hardy, aged 34 or 35
from a photograph in the Dorset County Museum

Following Page 84

1. (*a*) The Heath, near Hardy's birthplace, with a distant view of Dorchester. (*b*) The old West Gallery, Stinsford Church (*both from sketches by Hardy in the Dorset County Museum*)
2. (*a*) Hardy's maternal uncles, William, Henery, and Christopher Hand (*from a photograph in the possession of Gertrude S. Antell*). (*b*) Thomas Hardy senior (*from a sketch in the Dorset County Museum*). (*c*) Hardy's aunt's husband, John Brereton Sharpe (*from a silhouette in the possession of Lloyd Brereton Sharpe of Ottawa, Ontario*)
3. Young Thomas Hardy, (*a*) aged 16, (*b*) aged 19, (*c*) aged 21 (*from photographs in the Dorset County Museum*)
4. (*a*) 16 Westbourne Park Villas, Hardy's home in London, 1863–1867 (*from an original sketch in the Graphic, 5 September 1925*). (*b*) Young Thomas Hardy in London, 1863 (*from a photograph in the Lock Collection*)
5. The Moule family, Fordington, Dorchester (*from a photograph in the Dorset County Museum*)
6. Hardy's mother and his cousins, the Sparks girls, (*a*) Hardy's mother, (*b*) Tryphena, (*c*) Rebecca, (*d*) Martha (*from photographs in the Lock Collection*)
7. Three capitals in Turnworth Church, designed by Thomas Hardy, 1869 (*from photographs by Clare Gittings*)
8. Two views of Weymouth as Hardy knew it, (*a*) The Promenade, (*b*) Sandsfoot Castle (*from prints in the Weymouth Local History Museum*)

Following Page 164

9. (*a*) Emma as Hardy first knew her (*from a miniature in the Dorset County Museum*). (*b*) Emma in middle age (*from 'The Young Woman' (1894) in the possession of James Gibson*)
10. The Cornish coast near Boscastle (*from a print in the possession of the author*)
11. Emma and Hardy during their courtship, August 1870 (*from sketches by Hardy and Emma Gifford in the Dorset County Museum*)
12. Thomas Hardy's annotations to his favourite passage, I Kings, xix, 11 and 12, in his Bible, 1859–1870 (*from the original in the Dorset County Museum*)
13. Thomas Hardy in 1875, sketched by Emma in her "honeymoon" diary (*from the original in the Dorset County Museum, enlarged*)
14. (*a*) Death-bed sketch of Hardy's uncle by marriage, John Antell, by his son, John Antell junior. (*b*) Sketch by Hardy for John Antell's tombstone (*both from originals in the possession of Gertrude S. Antell*)
15. Hardy's relatives (foreground) in the High Street, Puddletown (*from a postcard in the possession of Gertrude S. Antell*)
16. Thomas Hardy in his old age (*from the original sketch by Augustus John in the possession of James Gibson*)

Acknowledgement is made to the Trustees of the Thomas Hardy Memorial Collection in the Dorset County Museum for permission to reproduce the following illustrations from the Collection: *Frontispiece,* 1a, 1b, 3a, b, and c, 5, 9a, 11, 12, 13.

Acknowledgements

THOMAS HARDY'S secretive attitude towards biographers, set out in the first chapter of this book, means that any authoritative study must rely exceptionally on the gathering of materials from widely differing sources. The help I have received in this task leaves me greatly in debt to a vast number of people and institutions. All mentioned here have my deepest thanks. Any omitted by mistake have my profound regrets.

Space prevents more than a brief listing in most instances, but gratitude must make some exceptions. Chief among my personal helpers and encouragers, I must single out the Hardy scholar, James Gibson. This present book would have no real authority without his active and invariably accurate assistance. With invaluable generosity, Mr. Gibson placed at my complete disposal his unpublished Ms. variorum edition of all Hardy's poems. The time, labour, and trouble this has saved me are incalculable. He was the first to read and fruitfully criticize the draft of this book, to which he has provided two most significant illustrations from his private collection. In numberless conversations and discussions, he has given me the unique advantage of expert familiarity and friendly, informed criticism.

As will be seen from the notes, this study depends for much of its authenticity on the personal memories and knowledge of those related to Hardy, and still living in Dorset. Chief among these is my friend John Hardy Antell. His vivid family traditions, to which he always applies his own sound critical commonsense, have given a body and reality to Hardy's story that could not have come from any other source. Once more, his generosity has extended to long and friendly discussions, from which I have learnt much that would otherwise have remained obscure.

The three key institutions, whose staffs have helped me profoundly, are likewise local to Dorchester: the Dorset County Museum, the County of Dorset County Library, and the Dorset County Council County Record Office. To the skilful Curator of the first-named, R. N. R. Peers, M.A., F.S.A., F.M.A., I owe, like so many Hardy scholars, a gratitude that goes well beyond formal acknowledgement. His care, patience, and consideration for the exacting needs of scholarship have been exceptional, as have been those of his staff. Formal acknowledgement to the Trustees of the Thomas Hardy Memorial Collection in the

Dorset County Museum will be found elsewhere, but I am additionally grateful to Mr. Peers for providing such an efficient link with the Trustees. Secondly, K. Carter, A.L.A., County Librarian, and his friendly staff at the Dorset County Library have provided an invaluable service in meeting my many demands with continual, thoughtful, and expert help; I am most grateful. Finally, the County Archivist, Miss M. E. Holmes, M.A., and her knowledgeable staff have given me help far beyond the mere production of documents. This has extended to suggestions for sources, and corrections of my ignorance, which have notably enlarged the body of firsthand documentation on which a work such as this must vitally depend.

The list of other helpful institutions is a large one. It includes, in the first instance, my local West Sussex County Reference Library, its reference librarian, H. R. H. Harmer, A.L.A., who, with his staff, has smoothed many of the paths of research so willingly and efficiently. Other bodies who have given much assistance are the Berkshire Record Office; the City and County of Bristol County Libraries; the Bristol City Art Gallery; the Bristol Record Office; the British and Foreign School Society; the British Museum; the Curator of Rare Books and Manuscripts, Colby College, Waterville, Maine; the Librarian and Deputy Librarian, King's College, London; the Greater London Record Office; the St. Marylebone Borough Library; the City of Plymouth Public Libraries; the Public Record Office; the Principal and staff of the College of Sarum St. Michael, Salisbury; the Diocesan Record Office, Salisbury; the Master and Fellows, Trinity College, Cambridge; and the Weymouth Local History Museum. I should like to thank personally Mrs. Christina M. Gee, Curator, Keats House, Hampstead, for examining census returns and ratebooks, and Mrs. Anna Winchcombe of Hardy's Cottage for help with the Sparks papers.

As I suggested, this book benefits greatly from the willingness of people in the most varied circumstances of life and experience to help me with knowledge or memory of matters otherwise unknown to me. Among these, I should like specially to thank Miss Gertrude S. Antell of Puddletown, for her reminiscences of the Antell family, her fascinating family records, and her kindness in providing me with family illustrations, which I have fully acknowledged elsewhere; Miss Mary A. Blyth of the Moule family; Mrs. June R. Boose of Windsor, Ontario, for much information about the Sharpe family; Henry Gifford for family records; Sister Kathleen Hawkins, of La Retraite, Clifton, for putting me on the track of Hawkins family information; H. E. F. Lock for permission to use photographs from the Lock Collection, on loan in the Dorset County Reference Library; Miss K. M. E. Murray for permission to use two unpublished letters from Hardy to Sir James Murray; Kenneth Phelps for the interesting points raised in his letters; Michael Rawcliffe, senior lecturer in History, Stockwell College of Education, who has provided me with valuable entries and material from the College archives; the Misses Shepherd of Leigh-on-Sea, Essex, for their most delightful and instructive conversation about Dorset, and their kindness in allowing me to use some unpublished letters of their grandmother, Catherine Young Hawkins of Waddon; Miss Mary Stickland, also for her Dorset reminiscences and dialect readings, and particularly for her valuable memories of Hardy himself; J. C. Trewin for an authoritative note on the nineteenth-century playing of Rosalind; Mrs. Troyte-Bullock, present owner of Waddon; Dr. D. H. Twining, B.M., B.Sc., for medical information; and the Warneford Hospital Secretary and Mrs. Brenda Parry-Jones, Archivist, for making Hospital records available to me. I should also like to thank my friend David Driscoll for identifying an obscure reference in one of Hardy's early novels; Mrs. W. A. Dubben of Sydling for lively conversation and local anecdote; the Vicars of Hemington in Somerset, and Puddletown in Dorset, for allowing access to their parish records; and Mr. Butterworth of Puddletown School for access to the school logbooks.

The list of recognized writers and scholars on Hardy who have helped me is a long one. It must include Professor J. O. Bailey; Professor C. J. P. Beatty, with whom I have discussed details in his admirable thesis and in his edition of Hardy's architectural notebook; Evelyn Hardy, who first drew my attention to some errors and omissions in certain areas of Hardy biography; Desmond Hawkins, for ideas of great interest; Professor Michael Millgate; F. B. Pinion, for his splendidly meticulous comment on some biographical points; Professor R. L. Purdy, to whom I am very greatly indebted for kind permission to use his notes of conversations with Florence Hardy. There have also been many informal discussions with these and other workers in the Hardy field, from whom I have learnt much. It will be noticed that this book is dedicated to my friends and students at the University of Washington, Seattle. Among them, I wish to give special thanks to Sister Victoria Seidel, as friend, student, and Hardy scholar. Her work on Hardy's Literary Notebooks, in particular, filled many gaps in my own research, and she will recognize in the present book many happy parallels with our informal and always useful consultations.

My thanks must end with a few other personal ones: greatly, to my wife, Jo Manton, for her clear and professional editing of my rough typescript, and her knowledge of the Victorian scene; to our daughter, Clare Gittings, for advice on Dorset memorial brasses, and for taking the photographs of Hardy's work in Turnworth Church; and to my American publisher, Peter Davison, who first said I should write a book about Hardy. I should add that the author acknowledges assistance from the Arts Council of Great Britain.

To my friends
and students
at the University of Washington,
Seattle

1

Young and Old

THOMAS HARDY determined to set up a barrier against biography. Angered by biographical speculations in books published in his own lifetime, and always abnormally sensitive about any reference to his private life, he devised a scheme by which he hoped to silence future writers. This was to produce an apparently authoritative biography, to be published shortly after his own death, which could discourage any later writers. This book was to seem to be the work of his second wife; the fact that she herself was an author of stories for children gave plausibility to Hardy's plot. For what he planned was a most deliberate deception. He wrote his own life, or what he cared to tell of it, in the third person, to be passed off as a biography written by her. No author can have taken more care that the future should know only what he wanted it to know, in the two volumes of his *Life* published in 1928 and 1930.

Unfortunately for the success of this scheme, he did not always guard his tongue. An old man when he started it, in the natural lapses of old age, he occasionally said too much in conversation, and this in spite of a lifetime of extreme secrecy and reticence. In 1925 a nephew of Mark Twain, Cyril Clemens, visited him. In a sudden expansive moment, he said to Clemens:

> I intend to write my autobiography through my good wife. Each day I slant my memoirs as though my wife were writing them herself. After she has copied the day's stint on the typewriter, we hold a discussion, and she makes invaluable suggestions which are almost always immediately incorporated in the text. Then my original manuscript is given to the flames. Thus is insured absolute accuracy. My idea, of course, is to have the work appear after my death as a biography of myself written by my wife.

Nothing could have been more explicit. Clemens perhaps did realize that Hardy had not meant to give the secret away. He did not publish his account of this interview[1] until 1943, when Mrs. Florence Hardy herself had been dead for five years; he also may have coloured it by plagiarizing from recent sources, such as Sir James Barrie's reminiscences.[2] In his wife's lifetime, the scheme worked just as Hardy had hoped. When anyone questioned Mrs. Hardy how she came to know certain facts in the Life, she replied with perfect truth, but with considerable disingenuousness, that she had had them from her late husband's own lips.

Of course, when the true story of this process began to emerge, some twenty years ago, the result was the opposite of Hardy's intention. Although the publishers keep up to this day the fiction of Florence Hardy's authorship, and though many recent critics still praise the work as a unique insight into the writer, the feeling that the Life is, in some sense, a fake has made biographical speculation, often of the most lurid kind, run riot. A host of amateur investigators has appeared, eager to invent a new story, and quite simple statements have been given fantastic meanings.[3] Moreover, the mere fact that Hardy chose this way of presenting himself has caused, even among reputable biographers, a certain suspicion of his motives. Yet the origins of his scheme, so far as they can be traced, seem to have been relatively innocent. At some time in 1917, Mrs. Florence Hardy began to type what she called some "Notes of Thomas Hardy's Life . . . (taken down in conversations etc.) ". These fragmentary typescript notes[4] break off during the first half of the 1860s, and it is clear this method of setting down information about Hardy's early life proved both haphazard and unsatisfactory. This can be seen by the large number of obvious typing errors,[5] which invade the notes; one of these, in fact, helps to date, for the first time, when this mirror image of ghosted autobiography must have begun. The notes are usually headed by an approximate date for the events described, and by page 14 the typescript has reached the middle of April 1862, when Hardy first went to London. The next note is, however, headed "Last week in April 1917".[6] Mrs. Hardy, in a moment of domestic distraction, had obviously substituted the year when she was typing for the correct year in Hardy's early life. This whole process was then abandoned, a few pages later, for a much more systematic one by which Hardy actually wrote his own life in the third person, to be copy-typed by Mrs. Hardy as if it were her own composition. Later Hardy himself made alterations and additions in a form of disguised hand.

The system therefore may have started simply as a more efficient way of dealing with Hardy's reminiscences than dictating scattered notes. What has caused suspicion is the way Hardy developed this process. First, not only did he destroy his manuscript as fast as Mrs. Hardy completed the typescript of each passage;[7] he and she also destroyed the greater part of the letters, and excerpts from diaries and notebooks used by him in preparing his manuscript. This destruction far outlasted the writing of the Life. Hardy left instructions to his wife, and to Sir Sydney Cockerell, one of his trustees, to destroy anything left over, particularly anything relating to his early days. Hardy's gardener has left a record of the thoroughness with which he saw Mrs. Hardy burning letters and papers after her husband's death.[8] The second cause for suspicion is the obvious one that, in the book as published, whole areas of Hardy's life and experience are clearly omitted. An almost ludicrous example of this, which has been noted by some biographers, while others try to explain it away,[9] is that, if one were to believe the Life, Hardy had no contact at all with young women from the time he was sixteen to the age of twenty-nine, when he met his first wife. A brief mention of a girl by her initials, in letters to his sister Mary in 1863 and 1865, and an equally brief and generalized reference to flirtations at Weymouth in 1869, are all he allows his readers. No wonder eager speculators have rushed in to fill the gaps with their fantasies. Moreover, it has emerged that in quoting a letter to his sister Mary, apparently in full, Hardy left out[10] a short paragraph mentioning the name of a girl; and this was a girl whom Hardy, according to the girl's brother, at one time wanted to marry.[11] Here again, though, it would be unwise to believe all Hardy's omissions have to do with sexual or deeply personal secrets of his life. Probably the most powerful motive was some sort of snobbery. Not only, as has been pointed out, does the Life tend to raise the social status of his mother and father. He omits almost totally all his other close relatives, uncles, aunts, and very numerous cousins. The touchstone throughout seems to have been social class. Labourers, cobblers, bricklayers, carpenters, farm servants, journeyman joiners, butlers have no place in Hardy's memoirs, though he was related to all of these; nor, among women, do cooks, house-servants, ladies' maids, or certificated teachers, regarded in the nineteenth century as little better than servants. Snobbery has usually been laid at the door of Hardy's first wife. Yet one finds that in the 1880s, she was a sympathetic friend to Hardy's sister Mary, herself a certificated teacher, who poured out to the first Mrs. Hardy her grievance that "nobody asks me to dinner or treats me like a lady".[12] In fact it was Hardy himself who did not want to record the lives of his lower-class relatives.

The most powerful witness to this is what he himself called "The Hardy Pedigree", a genealogical table which he also drew up in his old age, while he was writing the memoirs.[13] The most striking feature of this family tree is the differing fullness with which he sets out—how accurately it is difficult to say—the various branches of his family. He gives elaborate attention to a branch only very remotely related to his mother, called Childs. According to Hardy, this Childs family eventually came to contain a certain number of professional men, particularly surgeons, and, as a culminating triumph, an Assistant Commissioner of Metropolitan Police. All this, taking up practically one half of the "Pedigree", is meticulously noted by Hardy, with special attention to any learned qualifications, MA, MD, FRCS, and so on. The other half of the Pedigree, which should have contained Hardy's really close relatives, is left virtually blank. Hardy had about thirty first cousins; but not one was in the learned professions, and none appears here. Other small supplementary pedigrees, which do mention a cousin or two, only name relatives with distinction outside Dorset, such as his second cousin, Nathaniel Sparks junior, Associate of the Royal College of Art and Fellow of the Royal Society of Painter-Etchers.[14]

Yet snobbery is too sweeping and easy a dismissal for Hardy's purpose. In early life he had to fight the massive social stratification of the Victorian age. Finally he broke through from one class to another; but one can only guess what violence this did to his own nature. To shut the door on a social past from which he had escaped became a compulsion in his later life. Nor were his motives merely those of social and class distinction, though these were powerful in the years when he was struggling for recognition, and he still remembered and resented them deep into the twentieth century. This strange record also reveals Hardy's reverence for learning. The gulf between someone with whom he could talk freely in an educated way, and one of his own background, who, however full of simple wisdom, could literally not speak the language which Hardy had acquired, haunted his mind. In novels, he might extol the instinctive rightness of the peasant; in life, he always sought the company of the educated. Again, one can only guess the conflicts this caused. Certainly this secret life of the mind, almost too intense at times for him to bear, is hinted in his almost prophetic markings in his Bible.[15] Text and annotation, in Hardy's hand, suggest that he regarded himself as some latter-day seer, unregarded or misunderstood by those nearest to him. Hardy's isolation is shown in the difference between himself and his brother Henry. Henry to the end—he died in the same year as Hardy—retained a broad Dorset accent and even broader and more expansive country manners. He frequently refused to use a watch, preferring, he said, to tell the time by the sun, even in an age of trains and buses.[16]

So, to regard Hardy's autobiography—for such it is—as some kind of elaborate and devious mystification for posterity, is to ignore all the human elements. Hardy was in his late seventies, when he began, and probably well into his eighties when he finished. Although his memory for minute details could be exceptional, there are obvious moments when it plays him false. As he confessed to a friend, he suffered at times during these years from an "overclouding" of his mind.[17] Then again, his always thin-skinned nature must have winced at some of these reminders from the past, and it is no wonder that he showed reticence in recording them. On 7 May 1919, he wrote that he had been "mainly destroying papers of the last 30 or 40 years, and they raise ghosts"; later in the same year he wrote of "the dismal work" it entailed. Again, the round-about phrasing he often used, which has sometimes roused suspicion, was an effect of old age. It was twenty years since he had written his last novel, and his prose style, always uncertain, had deteriorated. This can be seen in the awkward and pedantic alterations he made in his first wife's manuscript, *Some Recollections*, often ruining the scatter-brained spontaneity of her style.[18] He had confessed a loss of grip in maintaining the interest of *Jude the Obscure* twenty years before; now his idea of narrative had degenerated into a set of clumsily-connected anecdotes, often, it seems, chosen for quaintness or oddity rather than for relevance to the main themes of his life. In fact, this heavy hand sometimes gives an extra impression of honesty; it must be true, one feels, because it is so baldly written. Hardy writes his autobiography in the same style of commonplace naïvety as his letters. His style in both may be said, without much exaggeration, to be unconsciously that of the great comic book of the 1890s, George and Weedon Grossmith's *The Diary of a Nobody*. Hardy, in some of his unintentionally funny understatements, reminds one almost irresistibly of the Grossmith's lower-middle-class hero, Mr. Pooter; his references to his wife Emma, in particular, have an echo of Mr. Pooter's artless chronicle of the disasters of his dear wife Carrie. "E.'s shoulder, where the bicyclist ran into her, is practically well, though she occasionally feels twinges" is a typical passage from a letter.[19] It is matched by the autobiography's account of a visit to Guinness's Brewery: "On the miniature railway we all got splashed with porter, or possibly dirty water, spoiling Em's and Mrs. Henniker's clothes".[20]

The humourless and colourless pages of the autobiography almost always lack life, except where some flash of country anecdote or incident suddenly enlivens them, such as the brief dialogue between the street-preacher and the village girl, which ends by their going off into the woods together.[21] On the other hand, the lurid attempts of later writers to colour the story by fictitious means are even more misleading. Yet the life of the young Thomas Hardy meant even more than the early lives of most artists. "I have a faculty", he wrote, "for burying an emotion in my heart or brain for forty years, and exhuming it at the end of that time as fresh as when interred".[22] The most famous example of this process is one of his best-known poems, *In Time of "The Breaking of Nations"*, conceived during the Franco-Prussian War of 1870 and written during the First World War, about forty-five years later. The same is true of his later novels, and still more of the mass of personal poems of his old age. The death of his wife in November 1912 released a flood of memories, and the gates were opened still wider from 1917 or thereabouts by his attempted autobiography. His collections, *Moments of Vision* in 1917, *Late Lyrics and Earlier* in 1922, and *Human Shows* in 1925 are by far his largest publications of verse. Together they total 462 poems, one half of his published poetry. The greater part of this huge output of his old age deals with the remote past, either freshly written from the material and memories he was handling, or often quite specifically "from old notes" or "from an old draft". In these, the force of the far-off emotions he was re-experiencing broke through with startling effect. All his faults of style, sometimes painful and even on occasion faintly ridiculous, are transfigured or overcome by the deeply-felt personal urgency.

The true story of Hardy's early life is therefore essential to the understanding of some of his finest work. This cannot, however, be reached by treating his creative work as pure autobiography, and guessing at the early life by hints from the poems and novels. This is the way in which strange and far-fetched fictional accounts of the young Thomas Hardy have arisen. The only true method is to start from the facts of the life itself. Often these prove more strange and far more human than anything that has been invented. Only when we have these facts can we reverse the usual process, and explore some of the complexities and conflicts behind his mature work: to see this work, at least in part, in its relation to the life of the young Thomas Hardy.

2

Bockhampton and Puddletown

IN HIS old age, Hardy was obsessed with "the decline and fall of the Hardys", as he called it, the idea that his family had once been far more important than in his own lifetime—"so we go down, down, down". In point of fact, this was a delusion which led him to do less than justice to his own father. Thomas Hardy the father, so his son said, was too easy-going to make a success of his career as master-mason, and "did not possess the art of enriching himself by business".[1] The truth was the complete opposite; Thomas Hardy senior rose from very humble beginnings to make a considerable amount. According to family tradition, his grandfather, John Hardy, walked one day into Puddletown with his bag of mason's tools and little else.[2] In the year of his own eldest son's birth, Thomas Hardy was simply, like most of the Hardys, a self-employed mason; although he had recently inherited the goodwill of his father's trade, the actual cash in hand was negligible.[3] Ten years later, he had become a bricklayer, employing two labourers. Another ten, and he was for the first time designated master-mason, employing six men; while in 1871, he employed eight men and a boy.[4] He seems to have prospered even more in the next twenty years, until at his death in 1892 he had a personal estate of £850—£10,000 in modern terms—and real estate at West Stafford and West Knighton.[5] He had done extremely well for himself, while far from being careless or improvident, the Hardys had a local reputation for being close-fisted.[6]

Local tradition, it is true, still puts down much of the elder Hardy's success to the driving force of his wife, Jemima, and credits him with carelessness in behaviour of quite another sort. According to this, Thomas Hardy senior, a handsome and well-formed man, had a reputation for getting village girls into trouble. He seems to have met his match, though, when early in December 1839, Jemima Hand, a woman who, like himself, was in her late twenties, was found to be three months pregnant by him. She had been a cook for the Reverend Charles Fox-Strangways at Maiden Newton, and had been a servant in other Dorset houses, including probably Kingston Maurward House in Thomas Hardy's own parish of Stinsford.[7] She had also worked in Weymouth, and for a few months in London. She was herself the daughter of a servant,[8] George Hand, who had died many years before in 1822; but her mother, Elizabeth Swetman of Melbury Osmond, seems to have come from quite another social class. A yeoman farmer's daughter, exceptionally well-read, she found herself, after her misalliance with Hand, a penniless widow, disowned by her father, with seven children, three sons and four daughters, and a bitterness against what she regarded as undeserved poverty, lasting deep into her old age.[9] She and her offspring had no intention of letting Thomas Hardy senior shirk his duty; and he and Jemima Hand were married on 22 December 1839 at her mother's family church of Melbury Osmond. The witnesses were the husband of Jemima's eldest sister, James Sparks of Puddletown, and one of her unmarried sisters, Mary Hand. There were no Hardy witnesses.

Whatever Thomas Hardy senior was doing in this marriage, he was most certainly not marrying for money. He was, in plain fact, marrying into a family who had been brought up as pauper children on parish relief. His famous son, who must have known this fact very well, could not actually bring himself to say that his mother had been a pauper child. In his old age, he made a cryptic account of this,[10] and its effect upon his own mother:

> By reason of her parent's bereavement and consequent poverty under the burden of a young family, Jemima saw during girlhood and young womanhood some very distressful experiences of which she could never speak in her maturer years without pain.

This veiled account has led imaginative biographers to invent all sorts of sensational adventures for Jemima, imagining her to be a prototype of Tess of the d'Urbervilles, and even to have been seduced and borne illegitimate children. The plain facts, though harsh, make such fantasies unnecessary. From her father's death in 1822 until the accounts end in 1836, her mother, Betsy Hand, is shown as receiving monthly sums of money for herself and her children from the Poor Law Overseers of her parish of Melbury Osmond.[11] As each child went out to work, probably at the age of about thirteen, the dole lessened. A drop of some shillings in autumn 1826, when Jemima was thirteen, probably shows when she and one of her sisters went into service. Her mother seems to have gone on drawing a small dole, perhaps unofficially, all her life.[12] This, then, a maid-servant and one of seven pauper children, was the wife of Hardy's father.

He took her to live with his own widowed mother, Mary Head Hardy, in a house in the hamlet of Higher Bockhampton, in his parish of Stinsford. This house, a little more substantial than most cottages, had been built by his grandfather, John Hardy, at the beginning of the century, on land leased from the Morton Pitt family.[13] There were only seven other houses in the hamlet, which lay along a lane leading to the heath, known as Cherry Alley or Veterans Valley. The former service officers, who had given it the latter name, had almost all disappeared by this time, apart from one retired naval lieutenant. Nearly opposite Thomas Hardy senior lived his elder brother James, also a mason, with his wife and three sons, George, Walter and Augustus, and a twelve-year-old apprentice.[14] Thomas Hardy's house was the last on the south side of the lane, next to the heath, and it was here on 2 June 1840 that his eldest son was born. The labour was a difficult one, and nearly cost Jemima her life; the child itself appeared to be dead, and was thrown aside into a basket by the surgeon trying to save the mother, until the midwife exclaimed, "Stop a minute: he's alive sure enough!" He was at first extremely fragile, and seemed unlikely to be a normal child. After the birth of a daughter, Mary, in the following year, 1841, Jemima Hardy took her unmarried sister Mary Hand into the house, to help to look after her delicate son.[15] Her own mother at Melbury Osmond was too poverty-stricken even to come and visit—"pretty little fellow I love him so well to[o] . . . poverty separates chieftest friends".[16]

As it began to appear that Thomas would live and develop, his parents' relieved affection was concentrated on him. Each had much to give him. They were a handsome and attractive pair. Jemima, like all the Hand girls, had great vitality, and looked much younger than she was. From her mother she had inherited a passion for reading and had obtained some of her library of books. It is astonishing to find that her own favourite reading was Dante's *Divine Comedy*,[17] and it may be suspected it was at her suggestion that Hardy's godfather gave the seven-year-old boy a book on the Jews.[18] Although his sister Mary became a lifelong companion and confidante, his mother was like an elder sister to him. She combined, to an unusual degree, vivid independence, a lively sense of humour, and a sombre view of fate, all of which could be seen transmuted in her son. His more obvious inheritance at first was his father's ruling passion for music. Thomas Hardy senior's father, yet another Thomas Hardy, had built up a choir of instrumentalists in the parish of Stinsford. It consisted of himself on the violincello, with two of his sons, Hardy's father and uncle James, and their brother-in-law James Dart[19] on their violins. Though smaller than the band in the larger parish of Puddletown, and that of Maiden Newton, where Hardy's mother had worked, the Stinsford choir was reckoned the finest in the district. Hardy's father also sang tenor and played and danced country tunes, and was in great demand at dances. Music was Hardy's earliest delight; his first recollection was of being given a small accordion by his father on his fourth birthday. At the same age he remembered dancing endlessly to his father's country tunes, many of which moved him to tears; he could tune a fiddle when still very young, and soon learnt to play hundreds of country dances from his father's and grandfather's old music books. Church services at Stinsford combined for him the two passions of words and music. Isaac Watts's hymns provided him with one of the verse-forms he used till the end of his life, and the western sun shining on the Venetian-red wall-paper at home found the child Hardy reciting every evening "And now another day is gone". In church, he stared with relishing horror deep into the jaws of the marble skull on the tomb of the Greys. On wet Sunday mornings he used to wrap himself in a tablecloth for vestments, stand on a chair and read the Morning Prayer, with one of his boy cousins from across the lane responding as clerk, while his grandmother formed the congregation. Not all occasions were as solemn as these tales suggest. When he could walk across the heath to the neighbouring Puddletown, he and his mother disguised themselves in weird clothes, with cabbage nets pulled over their faces, and surprised one of her two married sisters there.[20]

When he was nine, his mother took him to visit her other sister, Martha Sharpe; she had married at Puddletown in 1841 John Brereton Sharpe, who became a farm-manager on the Marquis of Salisbury's estate at Hatfield,[21] while his brother, George Brereton Sharpe, had a medical practice in nearby Welwyn.[22] John Brereton Sharpe was Hardy's favourite uncle, a dashing figure, who, Hardy believed, had been in the Lancers,[23] and who is said to have been the model for Sergeant Troy in *Far From the Madding Crowd*. A letter from him[24] has the jocular, man-to-man tone of Troy. This visit to Hertfordshire was Hardy's first great adventure, and served to knit him even closer to his mother. She made the small boy her companion, in her own words, "for protection"; for, unlike most countrywomen of that time, she was apparently still extremely attractive at the age of thirty-five. One of his most vivid memories was of their stay in London on the way back. This was at an old coaching-inn, the Cross Keys at Clerkenwell. From his small bed in the attic, he watched his mother search the huge old closets of the room, in case any man were hiding there, before she put out the light.[25] His other memory, the brutality of men to the beasts in Smithfield Market, was one which coloured his thought, and many of his poems, for the rest of his life. A year before he died, he noticed with horror the cattle-trucks on the railway near his home.[26]

On this stay, he also found minor brutality when he went briefly to a school kept by a Mr. Ray at Hatfield. This school and the whole journey may have been a scheme by Jemima Hardy to wile her impressionable son away from a rival emotional influence. In 1845, when Hardy was five years old, the estate of Kingston Maurward in Stinsford parish had been bought by Francis Pitney Brouncker Martin. His wife, Julia Augusta Martin, was only a few years older than Jemima Hardy, but she was childless. She became, for some reason, obsessively fond of the small Thomas,[27] and later claimed to have taught him to read,[28] though Hardy put his own reading at what appears an earlier time, "almost before he could walk".[29] His mother told his sister Mary that at the age of three Hardy read a book, which still exists,[30] containing verses of the Cries of London, and published by March's Library, with brightly-coloured pages of illustration. At all events, Mrs. Martin seems to have treated him as still a baby, "to take into her lap and kiss until he was quite a big child". An emotional attachment grew between them, which has been seen as the origin of a constant theme in most of Hardy's early novels, sexual attraction reaching across class barriers.[31]

The small boy also played his part in one of Mrs. Martin's dominant interests. She was a devout Churchwoman, and, shortly after coming into Stinsford parish, she decided to provide it with a school, newly-built and run under the auspices of the National Society for Promoting the Education of the Poor in the Principles of the Established Church. This was Thomas Hardy's first school, to which he went on the formal opening of its new buildings in the autumn of 1848, though it seems to have started in temporary quarters earlier in the year. Here, as he says, he worked at Walkingame's Arithmetic, and did well in mathematics and geography. His mother, however, had ideas for her son's reading far beyond anything even Mrs. Martin's model school could provide. Perhaps following the example of her own mother, and almost certainly from the latter's library, she gave Thomas, in this first year at school, Dryden's translation of Virgil's *Aeneid*, Dr. Johnson's *Rasselas*, and a translation of St. Pierre's popular *Paul and Virginia*.[32] In this situation there was bound to be some emotional tug-of-war for the child. Hardy's admiration for his mother was strong, and they shared their lives closely; Mary, one year younger, was an exceptionally self-effacing child, and— most unusually for a rural family—there were no further children for the first ten years of Hardy's life. On the other hand, his feeling for Mrs. Martin was, as he afterwards said, "almost that of a lover". He used to make special water-colour drawings of animals for her, and sing her his favourite songs.

It seems likely, then, that the expedition to Hertfordshire was an attempt by Hardy's mother to defeat her rival, first by removing him physically from Mrs. Martin, and sending him temporarily to another school, then, when they came back, taking him from Stinsford school, and entering him at a school in Dorchester.[33] Hardy's own account of this shows obvious embarrassment; he tries to justify his mother by saying that Mrs. Martin should have guessed he was only being sent to her school "till sturdy enough to go further". Hardy's mother apparently failed to foresee the offence Mrs. Martin took at the choice of school. This was the school in Greyhound Lane, Dorchester, run by the British and Foreign School Society, a Nonconformist group. Mrs. Hardy had been attracted by the academic reputation of its headmaster, Isaac Last; like most of the inhabitants of Stinsford and Puddletown, she did not see a great difference between their Church services and those of the Chapel. Mrs. Martin, however, was a keen Churchwoman. This, apart from emotional ties suddenly broken, made her resent a Nonconformist school for her favourite pupil. The row between the two women is said to have lost work for Hardy's father on the Kingston Maurward estate,[34] though there is no evidence that he actually did work on the estate; it certainly did not prevent him from being paid for work at Stinsford Church, of which Mr. Martin was a churchwarden.[35]

The emotional effect on Hardy was deep, and he goes out of his way to record it. Mr. Martin ran the Kingston estate farm through one of the many Scottish servants he and his wife employed, George Singer, an Aberdeenshire bailiff.[36] He lost money eventually on it—perhaps some foreshadowing of the relationship between Farfrae and Henchard in *The Mayor of Casterbridge*. In spite of the disastrously wet summer of 1850, Francis Martin decided to hold a harvest supper, and to insure its success by inviting some non-commissioned officers from Dorchester Barracks to dance with the local girls. One of the girls, a small farmer's daughter, offered to take the ten-year-old Hardy, and he jumped at the offer as a chance to see Mrs. Martin again. She and her house-party arrived late. When she saw him, she exclaimed, "O Tommy, how is this? I thought you had deserted me!" The exhausted small boy burst into tears, and promised he had not deserted her. She gave him her husband's small niece as a dancing-partner, and little Miss Campbell, the daughter of a Naval officer, duly danced with the strange peasant boy; but the house-party did not stay long. Thomas was left for hours before he could extract the girl who had brought him from the arms of the soldiers, and get home to the rebukes of his parents. This must have accentuated the quarrel between the two women, for Hardy, in an unpublished note,[37] remembered that his mother "openly defied" Mrs. Martin. The stress of these incidents impressed him so deeply that in old age he could still recall "the thrilling 'frou-frou' of her four grey silk flounces when she had used to bend over him, and when they brushed against the font as she entered church on Sundays",[38] a memory he reproduced in exact detail in the short story, *The Withered Arm*. Even more strangely, in his eighties Hardy still indulged in day-dreams about imaginary love-passages which he believed might have occurred between them, if he had taken up the relationship in later life.

This childhood vision of life as lived by the rich and fortunate—even though Mr. Martin seems to have got tired of being a farmer, and left the district in 1853—had a profound effect. There was a great deal more contrast between this life and his own than Hardy afterwards cared to admit, and his over-insistence on his own father's independence, and the leasehold for life on the Bockhampton house,[39] was meant to distract attention from the huge social gap. Although small craftsmen like his

father were, as Hardy rightly insisted, in a different class from the ordinary labourer, the distinction was often tenuous, and the slightest slip
could cause social degradation. None of Hardy's writings admits, and no
book on him points out, that his eldest uncle, John Hardy, was an
ordinary labourer. This uncle, whom Hardy never mentions, but who
was born in 1803, married a labourer's daughter, Sarah Dart, in 1825.[40]
They had four children, Albert, Rebecca, Rosina, and Frederick John,
but all completely disappear round about the birth of the last child in
1835. The renewal that year of the lease of the Bockhampton home on
10 October prolongs it for the lives of his father and of his brothers James
and Thomas, but John is not mentioned.[41] One probable explanation is
that, like so many Dorset labourers who found themselves in difficulties,
he was forced to emigrate.[42] Though Hardy cannot have met him, he
was an example, very near at hand, of poverty and perhaps despairing
emigration in Hardy's own immediate family. The Martins of Kingston
Maurward, with their two manor houses, one Elizabethan, one Georgian,
and their careless squandering on farming experiments, must have
seemed like creatures from another planet, compared with Hardy's
home.

Hardy's silence about his uncle John also covers his aunts, Martha,
Mary Anne, and Jane Hardy.[43] It is possible that these, though living
in the same parish, were not well known to him in his outlying hamlet.
At any rate, they were not as familiar as the household of his uncle and
neighbour James. This had just undergone an addition and a loss—the
birth of a girl Theresa in 1843, and the death in 1844 of the twelve-year-
old Walter. Still more surprising is his silence about his mother's vivid
and varied relatives, the Hand family of Puddletown. His grandmother,
Elizabeth Hand, only moved there shortly before her death in 1847, and
he probably knew little of her except through his own mother; but as
soon as he could walk the two and a half miles across the heath to
Puddletown, he was introduced to a teeming society, in which many of
his relatives were well-known characters. This small town, for it was
considerably more than a village, was still practically medieval in its
way of life, neglected by absentee landlords and untouched by
eighteenth-century enclosure. It remained so throughout Hardy's
youth, until a new reforming squire in the 1860s and 1870s literally
cleaned up and rebuilt the place.[44] Perhaps because its medieval and
manorial character had been retained so long, it was a busy and thriving
little town, whose population increased steadily all through the
eighteenth century. In the 1820s it shot up from just under the thousand
to 1200, where it remained for decades while most Dorset towns suffered
severe depopulation. Puddletown was always a town of artisans and
small craftsmen, serving the farming community, but skilled and
independent of the fluctuations of agriculture. About one-third of the

town worked in trade, manufacture and handicraft, a very high proportion for a rural place.[45] It was reckoned a thriving spot to live; when James Sparks of Dorchester married Hardy's aunt, Maria Hand, in the late 1820s, he left his much larger home-town to carry on his profession of cabinet-maker in Puddletown among his wife's relatives.

These all belonged to the Puddletown Hardy knew and frequented in his first twenty years. Most characteristic among them, as inhabitants of the still-unreformed town, were his three uncles, Henery, William and Christopher, bricklayers. Long-limbed, sardonic, rough-mannered, quick-tempered, none of these three brothers, when Hardy first knew them, owned or leased his own cottage, but lived in rented lodgings.[46] Their fortunes varied, and sometimes rose, particularly Christopher's. Like his brother-in-law, Hardy's father, he ultimately made a success of the profession of mason, and his son and namesake afterwards went to school with Hardy. Yet heavy drinking, for which Hardy himself said Puddletown was then notorious,[47] prevented any of the Hands from getting as far as the Hardys. Christopher's drinking and knocking his wife about when she was with child distressed his own mother.[48] Two Hand sisters, Maria and Mary, had married craftsmen who owned their own homes by leasehold. Maria's husband, James Sparks, cabinet-maker, lived at the bottom of Mill Street, on a curve opposite the river that came to be known as Sparks Corner. He was well-connected, and one of his relatives had been a freeman of Dorchester,[49] while an older generation, leaving Dorchester, were country lawyers at Crewkerne in Somerset, and had acquired a coat of arms. His double cob-and-thatch faced the river Piddle, bounded on its other bank by one of the picturesque thatched walls typical of Dorset. The river, aptly named, was swift-flowing but far from healthy, having received, at the next corner higher up, the outgoings of the Old Cat, one of Puddletown's many public houses. The traditional saying, describing a Puddletown Sunday, still survives:

> Into Church,
> Out of Church,
> Into Cat,
> Out of Cat,
> Into Piddle.

The cottage itself was crammed to bursting with James Sparks's numerous family, and it is no wonder that Maria Sparks, Hardy's aunt, living in such surroundings, developed the slow consumption from which she died.[50] The eldest daughter, Rebecca Maria, had served an apprenticeship, and carried on a dressmaking business to supplement the family income, aided by her sisters Emma and Martha Mary as sempstresses. There was a son James, three years older than Hardy, and another Nathaniel, three years younger, while in 1850 yet another child was on the way.[51] The girls were lively, bustling, and attractive, though their mother kept a strict eye on them. Hardy was in and out of this household all his early life.

Another port of call was at his aunt Mary's in the High Street. She had married the cobbler John Antell, and though her children were much younger, she always had a welcome for the small Hardy, whom she had nursed through his delicate first years. Her husband was a wild and interesting character. Self-taught, he had dreamt of going to college, but poverty, hard work and drink had banished the dream. According to Hardy's second wife, he was partly—"but only partly"— the model for Jude Fawley in *Jude the Obscure*.[52] His self-taught Latin and his "great mass of black curly hair" certainly seem reproduced in Hardy's novel, and perhaps the manner of Jude's death; for his own, though at the age of 62,[53] is said to have been hastened by exposure through having spent the night in a ditch after a drunken bout. The savage alternations of Jude's life may well have been partly, though again "only partly", suggested by what Hardy came to know of the Antell household. On one drunken occasion, John Antell beat up his wife Mary, and blacked her eye. He had reckoned without her married sisters, Maria Sparks and Jemima Hardy. They in their turn beat him till he was forced to plead for mercy and swear he would not touch Mary again. Hardy had little need to go outside his own relatives for the brutal facts of rural life; yet, on the other hand, its dreams and ambitions, which he himself felt so early, were part of the same picture. John Antell's struggling genius descended through his family; a son John, who succeeded him in the business, wrote poetry of more than technical merit, had a talent for sketching and was a good musician.

Though the Sparks and the Antell familes were in the craftsman class, poverty was never far off; the former in particular, for all their family industry, never had a spare penny. Among real labouring families, the young Hardy saw worse than poverty; in the 1840s he actually knew a shepherd boy who died of starvation.[54] The Commons debates on the repeal of the Corn Laws in 1846 threw up a mass of information on the abject state of the Dorset peasantry. It was the subject of six special articles and much correspondence in *The Times*. Letters poured in, all confirming "the old story—7s. the average wages . . . the sexes of all ages inhabiting the same sleeping room" in the mud-floored, leaky and ruinous cottages,[55] and, as a labourer himself wrote, "young men and women living together like dogs".[56] Puddletown, not surveyed in *The Times* articles, was presumably better-off than most places; yet the average wage there of about 9s. a week—much less for single men— was too low for any decent life. There was a grumbling hopeless resentment against the gentry who opposed the repeal of the Corn Laws, and support, generally secret, for the Anti-Corn-Law movement. In 1846, the child Hardy heard enough to dip his toy wooden sword in the blood of a pig that had just been killed, and march about the garden shouting "Free Trade or Blood!"[57] His excitement had also been roused by seeing whoever killed the pig cut off a piece and eat it raw, in traditional propitiatory custom.[58]

Puddletown provided Hardy not only with a glimpse of the larger world, but, through his own relatives there, contact with broad and coarse social realities. As late as 1895, an indignant colonist, who had emigrated in the 1850s, wrote home to protest against the Victorian bowdlerization of the name of his native Piddletown.[59] If earthy humanity was to be found there, the walk home across the heath gave him the opposite extreme of mystery, poetry and fearful magic. Hurrying through the mists that came swirling up from the valleys of the Piddle and the Frome, along the bracken-covered heights, the fog itself seemed not so much an effect of the atmosphere, but an indefinable presence of sinister intent. Even in the ordinary winter dusk, he would suddenly run fast to escape his fears, roused by the movement of heath-pony or a deer or even an unfamiliar shape of bush.[60] Home was a re-assuring place of glowing rushlights and fireside; yet even the warm little house, with thick mud walls and long thatch-eaves, had attracted, by its isolation, strange history. Earlier in the century it had been a dumping place for smugglers, bringing their landings in from Ower-moigne or Lulworth; a whip-lash across the lower windows at nights would announce that some tubs had been temporarily stored. The lonely situation even encouraged them to come by day, in spite of the protests of Hardy's grandmother, which they countered by leaving her "a washing pan of pale brandy", to celebrate the birth of one of Hardy's uncles. They did not leave off until other houses began to be built, but the tradition lingered. When Hardy was a child, a gigantic woman known as Mother Rogers used to call at the door and ask if any of "it" was wanted cheap. Her hugeness was caused by bullocks' bladders slung round her hips, in which she carried the contraband spirits.[61] Another notorious visitor, though before Hardy's birth, was James Clase, otherwise Blue Jemmie the horse-thief, who stole the horse of a neighbour in the lane.[62]

The fascinating source of many of these traditions was, of course, Hardy's grandmother, Mary Head Hardy. Widowed in 1837, and in her seventies, she nevertheless managed the accounts of her son's business for the next dozen years,[63] and helped her daughter-in-law to keep a firm hand on the household. Born at Fawley, a village in Berkshire, in 1772, she never knew her father, who died in the same year. Her mother also died, perhaps in tragic circumstances, when she was only six and a half, and her memories of Fawley were so poignant that she never cared to return there.[64] How she got to Puddletown, where Hardy's grandfather seduced and then married her, is a complete mystery. Her stories and hints about her unhappy birthplace haunted her grandson so much that when his sister Mary had her first job at Denchworth in Berkshire, he urged her to visit Fawley and find out all she could about it.[65] Mary herself remembered their grandmother describing winters so snowy that she walked to church along the hedge-tops. Other traditions, folklore and legends clearly had their origin with this grandmother, who was thus the source of some of Hardy's most mysterious and moving poems and incidents in his novels. Tragedy seemed to follow her all her life; her husband was playing in the church choir one Sunday, and was buried on the next. Yet she remained, as Hardy remembered, gentle always.

On regular Sunday walks with his parents, they would take a more southerly track from the little wicket-gate across the heath to the silent pond, about a mile away, called Rushy Pond. According to legend it had been excavated by fairy shovels, and it was always a place of great significance for Hardy. Nearby, topping a further slope, was the tumulus group known as Rainbarrows, another favourite spot. Here Hardy's father would take a sweeping view with the telescope he always carried, and point out landmarks, including the houses where he was doing building work.[66] This habit, of taking a bird's-eye view of a whole area, stayed with Hardy all his life, like the mystical delight in high places which was most imaginatively expressed in his poem *Wessex Heights*. His father's easy-going enjoyment, contrasting with the more purposeful attitude of his mother, was something the small boy relished with a secret admiration. When his father died in 1892, Hardy wrote his name and date against the lines from *Hamlet*:[67]

> Thou hast been
> As one, in suffering all, that suffers nothing,
> A man that fortune's buffets and rewards
> Hast ta'en with equal thanks.

His father's enjoyment of nature was matched by his mother's extraordinary store of local legend and story. Together they filled Hardy's world with landscape and human dealing, the special blend that was to mark his poems and novels, so that emotion and place coalesce unforgettably.

The cottage home on the edge of the heath put Hardy into a companionship with all fellow creatures that never left him. Snakes and lizards flickered about the threshold, and even came into the house. When he was still a baby in his cradle, a large though harmless snake was found curled up with him as he slept. Heath-cropping ponies and deer looked in at the windows, and in the evening light the bats would fly in and out of the bedrooms. As he grew, he used to take a ladder and explore the thatch which was full of birds' nests; he went to sleep each night hearing small fluttering movements and subdued cheeping in the eaves. This characteristic close-up view of even the smallest living things, the sense of existing actually *with* them, never left him. As late as *The Dynasts*, written in his sixties, the field of Waterloo is seen as if by the tiny creatures that inhabit the battleground. With this went a sense of timelessness. He recalled distinctly an instance when, lying on his back in the sun, whose rays filtered through the straw of his hat, he decided that he did not want to grow up. His cousins George and Augustus were always talking of what they would do when they were men, but he "did not want to be a man, or to possess things, but to remain as he was, in the same spot", and only know his half-dozen friends and relations in the Higher Bockhampton hamlet. [68] As always, he felt more sense of identification with the dead than with the living, and used to pick up the flint arrowheads of stone age inhabitants of the heath, and ponder on these tokens of former life there.[69] He was perhaps over-quick to read horror into any situation. The two mysterious seated men, who terrified him once on Stinsford Hill, were probably merely smugglers, sitting on their contraband tubs to try and conceal them.

Stories of savage events were told him by his mother and father. These tales of their own childhood had a deep influence on the morbidly sensitive boy; it seems clear they had little idea how far these memories of a rougher and more brutal age, commonplace to them, would sink into the imagination of their small son. One story from each parent was recalled by Hardy long after, with a kind of amazed horror. His father's tale was of a hanging that had taken place when he himself was young.[70] He had witnessed the execution of four men, whose only crime was that they had been present when others had set fire to a rick. One of these was a lad of eighteen, so emaciated and half-starved that they had to put weights on his feet before they could break his neck. This story horrified Hardy more than any other; but his mother's tale, though again a country commonplace, must have seemed almost equally terrible, especially to an ultra-sensitive boy. She told him about a girl who had committed suicide, and whose burial she remembered as an event in her own childhood. The girl was buried on Hendford Hill, near Yeovil, at a cross-roads on a bleak hill-top. Few followed her to her unblessed grave. There was no coffin to carry her, and no wreaths, though one other girl threw flowers on the exposed body. When it was put into the grave, a stake was driven through it, before the earth was heaped over her, sloping up the sides of the stake like a prehistoric tumulus.[71] The parents left the thoughtful boy with impressions of human nature that darkened his youthful views of life, appalling and true.

Other stories of his own childhood at Bockhampton show him as a solitary introspective boy, much more in touch with the animals around

him than with the small group of fellow human beings. He was with his
father in the garden on a bitterly cold winter's day, when they noticed
a fieldfare, half-frozen. His father idly took up a stone, threw it in the
bird's direction, and hit it. The bird dropped dead, and the small boy
picked it up. It was as light as a feather, practically skin and bone,
starved. The memory haunted him to the end of his life. At another
time, he was crossing the ewe-lease on the way to Puddletown, which
was full of sheep; he decided to get on all fours himself and pretend to
eat grass, in order to see what the sheep would do. When he looked up,
they had gathered around him in a close ring, gazing at him with what
seemed astonished faces.[72] Poems of imaginative entrance into the minds
of dogs, cats, and even other animals, which he wrote later, all have this
in common, that they are not sentimental, though full of feeling. They
seem to be describing actual states of being and ways of life. This solitary
identification stayed with him, even though the next move he made was
away from Bockhampton, in the opposite direction from Puddletown,
to the larger and urban world of school in Dorchester.

3

Dorchester

DORCHESTER, in which Thomas Hardy went to school sometime in 1850,[1] was a town in a state of transition. The coming of the railway in 1847 is generally taken as a symbol of change. This change, however, was not so abrupt as Hardy himself afterwards made out. Stage coaches still raced into Dorchester along the main Puddletown road, half a mile from Hardy's home,[2] and local travel was still largely on foot or by carrier's wagon. Hardy's dramatic statement that the orally-transmitted folk-ballads were "slain at a stroke" by London comic songs on the arrival of the railway is to be doubted. The singing of "The Outlandish Knight" by the local girls at Mr. Martin's harvest supper was not such a last landmark as Hardy himself implied.[3] Much later, he still heard sung the cheerful bawdy ballad of King Arthur and his three sons, "three sons of whores", a favourite for a long time in the ale-houses of Puddletown frequented by his Hand uncles.[4] What killed the rough local ballads Hardy knew was Victorian respectability in the person of John Brymer, Squire of Puddletown. His mark can still be seen in the fearsome (though sanitary) Victorian Gothic terraces, designed by a firm of land surveyors from Shepton Mallett, which he put up in the 1860s and 1870s with pride of place for a new school, under a cricket-playing headmaster, and the Men's Reading Room of 1870.[5] Not only did this house London newspapers and magazines, but it became the centre for penny-readings of an improving kind. These were decorous entertainments, sponsored by Brymer and his ladies, and it was here that the inhabitants of Puddletown first heard the drawing-room ballads and the comic songs of London that Hardy deplored.

The same process in the county town of Dorchester a little earlier, in the 1850s, showed itself in the same two aspects, roughly building and books. The first affected Hardy's father, the builder, and the second Hardy himself, the boy and scholar. Benjamin Ferrey, pupil of the elder Pugin and fellow-student with the more famous younger Pugin, had already designed many churches, vicarages, and manor-houses in and around Dorchester. It was by coincidence that his new Town Hall appeared at the same time as the railway; yet his prolific output indicates a quickened tempo in building. Squires, farmers, and parsons, the latter often "squarsons", or landowning clergy, prospered on low wages and the high price of wheat, and were tempted to express themselves in bricks and mortar. It was a profitable time to be a builder; Hardy's father, in spite of his energetic wife's protests, had no need to seek work. Lying in the sun, and watching the grasshoppers from the thymy bank leaping over him,[6] he was confident that plenty of those needing his services would seek him out, as indeed they did. He worked on at least one of Ferrey's mansions near Stinsford, either Clyffe House to the north-east, or, more likely, Stafford House to the south-east.[7]

Dorchester's prosperity brought building orders to Hardy's father; to his son it brought newspapers, magazines, books, bookshops, and a variety of opportunities in education. The Dorchester directory for 1851 shows a remarkable number of schools, one of which Hardy's sister Mary also attended, two circulating libraries, and several bookshops. It was now possible to get London papers and periodicals, and the flood of Victorian books of popular education. Hardy as a small child had the habit of self-education. His fascination with the Napoleonic Wars had as much to do with a magazine, *The History of the Wars*, which he found in a cupboard at home, as it had with the handsome soldiers whom he had seen partnering the girls at Kingston Maurward.[8] On Christmas Eve 1849, he became the possessor of *The Boys' Book of Science* by John M. Moffatt,[9] and in the same year Walkingame's Arithmetic or *The Tutor's Assistant*.[10] His passion for solitary reading was noted by other pupils at both his schools. He was seen by neighbours at Stinsford, on his three-mile walk into Dorchester, as a solemn small boy, odd-looking and with a big head, carrying a full satchel of books.[11] His appearance and habits invited teasing, though not of a very severe kind. In South Street, Dorchester, was a shop, one step down from the street, kept by an old woman called Sally Warren. A country lad from Broadmayne used to throw Hardy's cap down the step, and watch Sally chase him with a broom when he went to fetch it.[12]

Dorchester itself provided a number of contrasts for a thoughtful boy. On the face of it, there was the busy and thriving atmosphere common to all county towns. The steep long High Street divided, at the point where Cornhill joined it from the south, into High East and High West Street. There were fairs in Cornhill itself, and the bustle of a weekly market. Handsome tree-planted Walks bounded the town still, and the fields came right up to what had been the old walls. Public buildings, many of them newly-constructed, like Ferrey's Town Hall, with its Corn Exchange on the ground floor below, gave an air of importance. The streets were full of farm-carts, in for the Saturday market, carriers' wagons, the neat dog-carts of the local residents, the carriages-and-pair of country gentry, each with coachman and footman. Dorchester was a garrison as well as a county town, its dash and colour enhanced by the brightly-uniformed artillery and cavalrymen. Military bands played in the Walks; military funerals, frequent in the crowded barracks, were accompanied by solemn music on the way to church, and brisk marches on the way back. Hardy's youthful confusion of the Dead March in *Saul* and "See the conquering hero comes" probably arose on one such occasion. Gun-carriages rattled out along the south-west roads, for exercises on the prehistoric slopes of Maiden Castle, and troopers would stand in their stirrups to slash with sabres at overhanging tree-branches as they went.[13]

The excitement and display of a military barracks stirred the civilian inhabitants; some of Hardy's most successful ballad poems, such as "The Dance at the Phoenix", are about the effect of dashing uniforms on the women. Rivalry affected the men too; demonstrations and riots were often spectacular. Until the late 1870s, the toughs of the town used to celebrate Guy Fawkes Night by rolling barrels of blazing tar down the steep High West Street, until a peaceful vicar managed to substitute a torchlight procession for this hair-raising tradition.[14] Anti-Catholic feeling was genuinely strong in a town that had suffered for Monmouth's Rebellion. In November 1850,[15] Cardinal Wiseman returned from Rome as Archbishop of Westminster, to effect, as he announced, the restoration of Catholic England. Feeling ran high in Dorchester, and a monster demonstration took place in Maumbury Rings, the Roman amphitheatre on the south edge of the town. Effigies of the Pope and the Cardinal were burnt, among insulting anti-Catholic tableaux. The ten-year-old Hardy was taken by his father to see this violent display; he was bewildered when, in the lurid flame-lit procession of men dressed as monks following the figure of Wiseman, the hood of one blew aside, and he recognized the face of one of the two workmen his father now employed.[16]

There were other still more violent elements in a county town that was also an Assize town with a hanging gaol, and where the hangman's cottage, with a loft where the rope was kept, was a mecca for prying boys. The sinister atmosphere when the Judge was sitting in Shire Hall, and High West Street was muffled with straw to deaden the clatter of horse-traffic, was not a matter of imagination. Although it was now over 150 years since Judge Jeffreys at his Bloody Assize had ordered wholesale massacre after Monmouth's Rebellion, the memory stayed; fascinated horror at cruelty lingered on in this little town. Stories of Jack Ketch, the brutal hangman who had actually executed Monmouth, were still told: how he used to march through the streets holding aloft the whipcord cat o' nine tails, with which he had lacerated his victims at the Dorchester Town Pump.[17] The horrible story of the burning of an alleged murderess in Maumbury Rings was also part of Hardy's folklore.[18] Very close to his own time were the savage sentences of transportation passed on the Tolpuddle labourers at Dorchester in 1834, only half a dozen years before he was born. Numerous whippings, "severe and private", were imposed for quite small offences during his own lifetime.

Transportation and unspeakable happenings in Tasmania and Australia were also part of Hardy's childhood. Dorset peasants were starving and despairing, Dorset magistrates punitive. A John Hardy of Wareham, probably no relation, has left a searing account of his experiences.[19] When this degrading punishment ended, it is an irony that the Dorchester district was brought face to face with its substitute. After protests by the colonies themselves, transportation to New South Wales and South Australia was ended in 1850 and to Tasmania in 1852,[20] while an attempt to ship convicts to Cape Colony nearly caused a revolt and had to be abandoned. Meanwhile the authorities, realizing that this country would now have to live with its own criminals, had already begun to build fortress-like single-cell prisons. Portland, begun in 1848, was one of the earliest purpose-built penal servitude prisons. Here, the convicts were to labour, after a term of solitary confinement, on the huge new breakwater enclosing Portland Harbour. The foundation stone of these works was laid by Prince Albert in July 1849, a visit to Dorchester remembered by Hardy and recorded in *The Mayor of Casterbridge*. The convict gangs hacked out rubble near the summit of the promontory, and lowered it to sea-level by wire-rope incline, a process later sketched by Hardy.[21] As the railway was extended to Weymouth in 1857, and a few years after to Portland itself, the faces of these men, dazed and brutalized by their previous solitary confinement, their grey uniforms marked with the Government broad arrow, became a familiar local sight. Warders in charge of gangs working on the road would make their men turn their faces to the wall when anyone drove by. This grim area aroused a morbid curiosity; sightseers made wagonette trips from Dorchester to Portland, and stood at certain points to watch the convicts in the stone quarries, creatures from another world.[22]

Hardy shared this ugly fascination. Many of his stories and poems deal with hangings, convicts, murders, and prisons. While these reflect his early environment and the history of the place where he was brought up, in adolescence, as will be seen, they took a more sinister turn. He also, of course, joined in the normal pleasures of schoolboys, watching with excitement when Mr. Curtis's fighting-cocks were let into the street from a cellar next to the Corn Exchange,[23] untroubled by reflections on the cruelty of the sport which came to him later. Isaac Last in the little school in Greyhound Yard was a strict disciplinarian, but was always pleased with Hardy; so were the other boys, since he was ready to help with their lessons. The habits of reading learnt from his mother carried him on at a tremendous pace; when he was twelve, and the family business flourishing, his parents arranged that he should be taught Latin as an extra. He was started on the old Eton Grammar with readings from Eutropius and Caesar, devised for himself a visual system for remembering the genders, and shot ahead. Earlier in the year 1852, he read a book of exploration, Bruce's *Travels in Abyssinia*.[24] At home he read the romances of the elder Dumas in translation, historical novels such as Harrison Ainsworth's *Old St. Paul's*, James Grant's *The Scottish Cavalier*, with G. P. R. James's works, and the plays of Shakespeare, though at that stage for the plots rather than for the poetry. *The Pilgrim's Progress* alarmed him so much that once, reading it on his way home from school, he felt convinced Apollyon would spring out from the dark trees overhanging the road.[25]

It was in the next year, 1853, that Hardy felt the benefit of Dorchester as a growing centre of education. Isaac Last's school belonged to a Nonconformist body, the British and Foreign School Society; he was a Congregationalist, and owed his appointment to the fact that the actual founder of the school, William Manfield, a local solicitor and landowner, was a Congregationalist too. Last was an ambitious teacher, whom ill-health had kept from going farther afield; but he determined to widen his scope in Dorchester. In 1853, therefore, he set up his own private fee-paying and partly boarding school. He was undoubtedly encouraged to do this by the very powerful Congregationalist colony in the Dorchester area. They nearly all, like Manfield himself, lived west of Dorchester, though one family, that of Wood, bought Athelhampton Hall, near Puddletown, founded their own Nonconformist school, and became rivals of Squire Brymer of Puddletown. This group of Congregationalist landowners, Manfields, Woods, Samsons and Homers, provided a body of backing for Last's further plans, and, incidentally, a lucky addition to Hardy's further education. At an ordinary British school, this would have ended at twelve or thirteen, unless he decided to go in for teaching himself, and stayed for another five years' apprenticeship as pupil-teacher. Now, with parental help, he could follow his master to the new school, continue his Latin, and prolong his school life.[26] In later life he was determined to regard the higher education afforded by Last's new "Academy" as some sort of equivalent of going to College. In an angry annotation to a book, which had described him as self-taught, he wrote that this was an "impertinent personality & untrue, as he was taught Latin & French at School and College".[27]

The driving force behind this continued self-improvement was, of course, Hardy's determined mother. She appears to have been as watchful over his moral development as she was over his intellectual growth. He and Mary felt the full weight of their mother's influence. Henry, born in 1851, and Kate, in 1856, seem to have been allowed to be easygoing; indeed, they were so different in later life as to appear, quite apart from the big gap in age, almost another generation. Two anecdotes show the values to which Hardy was expected to conform. Both also show him as the precocious one in a gathering of adults. At one of the local cottages, a live hen was put up as a prize, to be won by "raffling" —that is, throwing dice—at an entrance fee of twopence a head. Hardy, not much more than ten, joined the raffle. As he was almost a child, and the only one there, he was made to throw first, the superstition being that the first thrower was the least likely to win. To everybody's consternation, including his own, the three dice all came down the same number, in gambling terms "a pair royal" and the highest possible throw. Even worse than having ruined the sport was his reception at home when he arrived with the unwanted bird. As he remembered it, "The event was considered such a direct attempt by the devil to lead one of tender years to ruin that I was forbidden to gamble any more—& as a matter of fact, never did".[28] The incident, which helped him with the dicing scene in *The Return of the Native*, resembles one a year or so later, connected with his fiddle-playing. He was beginning to play outside the family circle at village weddings and dances. His mother strictly told him that he must never accept any payment, but on one occasion his hosts insisted, and a hatful of four or five shillings was given. Hardy had been longing for a book in a Dorchester shop-window, and bought it with the forbidden money.[29] The mother refused to see any good in the volume, a book of sports and pastimes, *The Boys' Own Book*. Hardy, however, stored it in his long memory, and later extracted from it Sergeant Troy's method of treading water and Farmer Shiner's technique for catching bullfinches for two of his early novels.[30]

Last and his Academy gave Hardy a full curriculum of mathematics and Latin, and the master rewarded his progress and good behaviour by giving him a prize at Christmas 1854, *Scenes and Adventures at Home and Abroad*, and at midsummer 1855 Beza's Latin Testament. Mrs. Hardy supplemented his school education by subscribing to Cassell's *The Popular Educator*, and, the habit once formed, persuaded him to continue spending his pocket-money on these improving issues.[31] He had already acquired several Cassell's publications, such as *Lessons in Latin*, and *The Illustrated Magazine of Art*.[32] Perhaps luckily, her second boy, Henry, claimed attention, and she seems to have begun to relax her exclusive affection; for though Hardy did not make schoolboy friendships, and always hurried home, avoiding other boys, he began at fourteen to have an interest in girls. Seeing a pretty girl riding in the South Walk, near school, he showed the susceptibility that was always to mark him, and fell for her for a whole week, until the sight of her riding again with a young man ended his fantasy.[33] The incident was recorded forty years later in exact detail in his novel *The Well-Beloved*.

It was from about this time, in fact, that Hardy later recalled a whole bevy of Stinsford village beauties, each one with her special charm, and all a few years older than himself. The leading lady in his memory was a beautiful creature with bay-red hair, Elizabeth Bishop. She was the daughter of the Stinsford gamekeeper, Joseph Bishop.[34] She fascinated Hardy sufficiently for him to immortalize her after many years in a delightful ballad-like lyric *To Lizbie Browne*: the difficulties of rhyme and rhythm in the name Bishop had naturally been too much for him. Next on the list[35] was Emily Dart, whom Hardy remembered for what he called "her mere prettiness". He might also have recollected, though he does not say so, that she was an illegitimate relative of his. She was the bastard daughter of Rebecca Dart, younger sister of Sarah Dart who had married Hardy's uncle, John Hardy.[36] Next came Rachel Hurst; Hardy noted "her rich colour and vanity, and frailty, and artificial dimple-making", which he copied into the character of Arabella in *Jude the Obscure*. Finally, there was a girl with blonde curls, Alice Paul.[37]

Nothing seems to have come of these temporary attractions. At the age of fifteen there was a typically negative but more long-lasting event. The largest farmer in Stinsford parish, as distinct from landowning gentry, was Stephen Toghill Harding, of Stinsford Farm, a holding of over 400 acres.[38] Hardy's father had done building work for him. As a churchwarden, Stephen Harding had allowed the strange learned boy to join the vicar's two sons as a Sunday School teacher to the slow-witted though often very pretty rustic girls of the parish. It was another matter when the young Hardy began to be smitten by one of Harding's own six daughters. This was Louisa, a cheerful, lively round-faced girl, just over a year younger than Hardy. There is no knowing if she felt anything for him, but to her family he was, for all his precocious learning, just another village boy; Louisa was forbidden to respond to his obvious glances, and his murmured "Good evening". He seems to have hung about her for years, gazing at her in church, at Stinsford and when she went to finishing school at Weymouth, and even trying to meet her when he came home during his first year in London. This totally negative encounter caused him to write several poems on her death in 1913, to seek out her grave anxiously in his own old age, and in his youth to moon about singing the air "How oft, Louisa" from Sheridan's *The Duenna*.[39] It was part of the curious psychological tendency in Hardy always to prefer a remote relationship to a close one. It may be allied to his dislike, from boyhood, of anyone touching him. He mentioned that his school-friends first found this out, and thought that no one else had. In fact, in a gossiping small town like Dorchester, where every hint of eccentricity was noticed, everyone observed how Hardy, to the end of his life, always walked in the road, regardless of traffic, to avoid brushing against passers by on the pavement, and how servants were instructed never to help him on with his coat.[40] In his old age, outdoors, friends were careful to drop a shawl lightly over his shoulders, avoiding contact.[41]

The picture of Hardy's adolescence, so far as it emerges from these scattered anecdotes, suggests a strangely divided personality. He seems to have been very susceptible emotionally, yet at the same time fearful and nervous of physical contact. Mental precocity forced him into the company of his elders, with what often must have been bewildering results. Some of this bewilderment shows in his account of one of the dominant passions of his boyhood, his fiddle-playing. His reminiscences in old age[42] take on the oddly evasive tone which he almost always adopts over topics of deep significance to him. The Stinsford church choir of instrumentalists had closed down when Hardy was only two, and he never knew his father as a church musician; but Thomas Hardy senior was still in great demand for weddings, dances, and festivals, and from an early age Hardy himself went with him as a player. His own account shows curious overtones. He says it is strange that his mother, so ambitious for his purely intellectual development, allowed these performances, then adds "Possibly it was from a feeling that they would help to teach him what life was", an odd motive for a woman who had objected to innocent dice-throwing. On the other hand, he says his father, whom he always portrays as so easy-going, objected strongly to Hardy coming to such gatherings, though he failed to carry his point with his wife, "as he himself had not been averse to them when young". Perhaps this set of non-sequiturs about his parents, in which mother and father seem to reverse their usual roles, conceals some adult use of the boy for their own purposes. With an infant son, Henry, Jemima Hardy was house-bound again for the first time in ten years. She no longer had the help of her sister Mary Antell, now coping herself with a violently temperamental husband and four young children, John, George, Francis, and Mary (known, like her mother, as Polly). On the other hand, Mr. Hardy was still attractive and youthful-looking, blue-eyed, dark-bearded, and handsome. Moreover, his reputation among the girls was not forgotten, and even the county ladies, for whom he worked, found him charming. Was Mrs. Hardy's real motive in letting her son accompany his father to insure the latter's good behaviour and not-too-late return home? No doubt many of these dances were innocent lively fun as Hardy always makes out, especially when local gentry attended them. He and his father were remembered playing at the West Stafford house of Mr. Floyer, when the squire joined the dance, "up the sides and down the middle".[43] Yet village gatherings were not always under such control. If squire and parson were not present, or had left, and particularly at "Club" meetings got up by the villagers themselves, dancing could develop into the one relief in their hard-pressed lives, drunken and animal love-making. As *The Times*'s correspondent on the life of the Dorset labourer confessed, "scenes are enacted which can at least rival, if not exceed, the disgusting orgies of antiquity".[44] Hardy himself found suitably explicit classical allusion when he wrote in *Tess of the d'Urbervilles* of "Lotis attempting to elude Priapus, and always failing".

The boy was highly emotional where music was concerned, and these occasions excited him beyond measure. At one party his hostess had to seize his bowing-arm to make him stop, in case three-quarters of an hour of playing a favourite dance, "The New-Rigged Ship", should actually harm his health. The late journeys home had their incidents too; on one he was terrified by what appeared to be a white human figure without a head. His father, more used to such late-night sights, found it to be a drunk man in a long white smock-frock, leaning against the bank with his head on his chest. The boy had to help his father guide and push this apparition to its own cottage-door, where the man's wife pounced on her husband and knocked him down.[45] These were introductions to life that his mother can hardly have bargained for. The unconcealed love-making after the dance must have been tumultuous for the reserved adolescent boy. One incident in his puberty has come down to suggest this. Many of these dances and entertainments were at the homes of friends and relatives, and, in any case, the young Hardy was always in and out of the cottages of his Puddletown cousins. Mary Antell, in spite of her demanding family, welcomed the boy she had nursed, but his chief port of call was the home of his other aunt, Maria, at Sparks Corner. This busy but improvident family was reorganizing itself to deal with continued lack of money. The birth of yet another daughter, Tryphena, on 17 March 1851, had meant a fresh mouth to feed. It was uneconomic for the two middle daughters, Emma and Martha Mary, to continue helping their eldest sister Rebecca in her dressmaking business, when they could both be out and earning. Accordingly, sometime in the 1850s, both left home to go into domestic service, Martha Mary, the smarter of the two, to London, and Emma somewhere in Somerset; but the boys, Jim and Nat, were still around as companions for Hardy. Rebecca, with her own business and her mother's bouts of ill-health, was virtually head of the Sparks family. The Hand girls of all generations had strong family likeness, and with maturity Rebecca greatly resembled her aunt, Hardy's mother. This is perhaps part explanation of what happened. At the Christmas Mummers' rehearsal at Sparks Corner, while drink was flowing in the unofficial beer-barn next door, Thomas started making violent approaches to his older cousin Rebecca. He was caught and there was a family scene. The Sparkses, who had witnessed the enforced marriage of Hardy's parents, suspected that the boy might take after his father. All members of the Hand family were apt to flare into quick temper, women as much as men; Hardy's own mother had shared in the beating-up of her brother-in-law, John Antell. Maria Sparks, Rebecca's mother, is said to have shown the door to young Hardy and forbidden him the house. Though this did not last—his early twenties saw him visiting Nat Sparks at Christmas[46]—it was a severe shock to his adolescence.

What this shock, or perhaps something of the same nature, meant to him, is contained in another cluster of hints by Hardy himself:[47]

> His immaturity [he wrote] . . . was greater than is common for his years, and it may be mentioned here that a clue to much of his character and action throughout his life is afforded by his lateness of development in virility, while mentally precocious.

Part of the difficulty in interpreting exactly this "clue" is the term "virility". Other usage by Hardy seems to confirm that he means the dictionary definition, "the capacity for sexual intercourse". In another part of his autobiography, he makes an amount of satisfied play with the fact that he was a founder member of the Rabelais Club, instituted in 1879 by Sir Walter Besant as "a declaration for virility in literature". It is clear that the Club equated "virility" with the portrayal of sex in literature, but Hardy, perhaps wishfully, seemed to associate it with sex in life. A subconscious envy of notoriously "virile" and sexually potent public men remained with him all his life. In his old age, he recorded a dream of his,[48] which could be the theme for endless psycho-analytical study. In this, he saw himself climbing a ladder, carrying a baby, which he was trying to put with great difficulty into a hay-loft. He wrote

> My endeavour was to lift it over the edge of the loft to a place of safety. On the loft sat George Meredith in his shirt sleeves, smoking; though his manner was rather that of Augustus John. The child was his, but he seemed indifferent to its fate, whether I should drop it or not.

The association of Hardy's efforts with the indifferent onlooking of a spectator, who mingles in himself two of the most generally-known sexual symbols of their time, George Meredith in the nineteenth century, Augustus John in the twentieth, need not be stressed.

Hardy's own analysis of his sexual "virility", written at about the same time as this dream, does seem to indicate that he developed sexually very late, if indeed he developed at all. His voice was always considered to be very quiet, though not as noticeably as that of Sir Edward Marsh, a well-documented case of total lack of sexual development after mumps complicated by German measles.[49] The evidence with Hardy is too fragmentary for any final judgement; yet delayed or imperfect physical development is quite consistent with sexual curiosity, an attraction to the idea of love without the power to fulfil it. Hardy's continual speculation about almost every woman he meets, and his apparent habit of passing from one to another virtually without conscious volition, suggests such a pattern.

Whether the experience with Rebecca Sparks was really traumatic, or whether in fact there was some more general physical condition, the age of sixteen, up to which Hardy himself said he was "a child", was in many ways a turning-point. His own and his mother's ambition had added French to his intellectual attainments. At fifteen he had been given a text-book, *A Stepping Stone to the French Language*, and acquired a French dictionary and teacher, the French governess from the school in Dorchester attended by his sister Mary.[50] On the other hand, his father, though finding money for the extra fees, could see no exact profession for his bookish son, apart from a vague idea that he might enter the Church. Chance and the building boom provided the next move. Hardy's father was engaged to restore Woodsford Castle, a fortified fourteenth-century manor-house, a few miles across the Heath to the south-east of Bockhampton. While with his father, Hardy met the architect, John Hicks of Dorchester, who noticed the boy's all-round ability, and suggested he should help with a survey, as a test. According to Hardy,[51] Hicks then offered to take him in an apprenticeship. Hardy's mother, whom perhaps recent events made anxious her son should be settled away from Puddletown, struck a favourable bargain over the premium. She managed to knock down Hicks's original suggestion of £50 (he usually took £100) to £40 for ready money. So, a month after his sixteenth birthday, Hardy started as an architect's apprentice in John Hicks's office at 39 South Street, Dorchester.

4

Apprenticeship

UNTIL his apprenticeship in 1856, there is no instance of Hardy writing either poetry or prose. In the previous December, he had copied in pencil, on the inside of the door of the grandfather clock at Bockhampton, the homely and sentimental verses by the Manchester poet, Charles Swain, *The Old Cottage Clock*;[1] but original composition seems to have been outside his thought. As for prose, his sole experiment had been the second-hand exercise of writing, for the village girls he taught in Sunday School, their love-letters to Army sweethearts in India. This may have brought him close to human emotions, since India was a dangerous place to be on the eve of the Mutiny; but, once again, it was hardly an original form of composition. Hicks's office in Dorchester, though, was an exceptionally literate place for a young man who already had a stock of reading in his head. The architect himself was very well-educated; the son of a country rector who had been a classical scholar, he was widely read, and allowed his apprentices plenty of time for their own reading outside their architectural studies. Hardy's fellow-apprentice, Henry Robert Bastow, was also well-educated. A handsome, cheerful-looking youth, a year or so older than Hardy, he had been to school near London, and had literary and scholarly interests, and religious ones too. Bred as a Baptist, he became convinced of the doctrinal necessity of adult baptism, and, in fact, was baptised during the time of their apprenticeship,[2] probably on 2 September 1858, when he joined the Baptist Church at Dorchester.[3] Lively intellectual and religious arguments and discussions took place between the two apprentices, in which their master Hicks himself joined. It is likely that Hardy found assistance for his part in these by buying two books, George Campbell's *Philosophy of Rhetoric* and Richard Whately's *Elements of Logic*, both of which he marked heavily.[4]

In the atmosphere of friendly rivalry in Hicks's office, and the lighthearted competition on points of learning and literature, Hardy came naturally from apt quotation and construing of classics to trying his own hand at writing. His first effort was as anonymous as the love-letters he was writing for the Stinsford girls, and has not survived. It was a skit for a Dorset paper in the form of an imaginary letter from the clock which had formerly stood over the Dorchester Alms Houses, and which had been taken down for repairs. The success of this adolescent piece of humour, which, Hardy claimed, caused the clock to be restored to its proper place,[5] indicates the lines along which his mind already worked. Letter-writing, thanks to his village practice, came easy to him; so did a clever boy's humorous misuse of quotation, and the adoption of a disguising persona. His effort was perhaps suggested by someone else's contribution earlier that year, in March 1856, another mock letter containing some of the excruciating puns fashionable at that period, and signed "The Wareham Town Pump".[6]

Another less imaginative form of prose-writing also occupied his apprenticeship time. He wrote for the *Dorset Chronicle* accounts of the numerous church restorations carried out by Hicks. These were all anonymous, but it is likely that Hardy wrote about St. Peter's, Dorchester, in both 1856 and 1857, the churches at Rampisham (10 March 1859) and Powerstock (3 November 1859), St. Mary's, Bridport (19 July 1860), the church at Combe Keynes (29 August 1861), and the newly-built churches at Athelhampton (2 January 1862) and at Bettiscombe (3 April 1862).[7] None of these contributions, if they are Hardy's, rises above the standard of competent prose. It is certainly likely that the two articles on St. Peter's, Dorchester, are his, since he definitely worked on the chancel east window and on the north vestry himself. The architectural plan signed by him still exists, and hangs in the church.[8]

His imagination, however, was strongly stirred in other directions which show the peculiar bent of his adolescent mind. Shortly after he started his apprenticeship with Hicks, Hardy attended a public hanging, and, as it appears, was very close to the gallows, which was put up high above the entrance to Dorchester Gaol.[9] It was, moreover, the hanging of a woman, who had killed her husband in a crime of jealousy, which had so many mitigating circumstances that they nearly brought a reprieve. Indeed, if she had not maintained almost to the last her husband had died from a kick from his horse, instead of, as she finally confessed, a blow from her hatchet, public sympathy might have persuaded the Home Secretary to leniency. The woman, Elizabeth Martha Brown, was nearly twenty years older than her husband, John Brown, who had been a fellow-servant with her. He had married her, according to gossip, for money, and the couple had lived at Birdsmoorgate, near Beaminster. She had caught him making love to a local woman, and had a violent quarrel late at night, during which he struck her with his tranter's whip. She retaliated with the wood-chopper, killed him, and then tried to conceal the crime.

This sensational story was well known, and a large crowd turned out in the early morning drizzle on 9 August 1856. Her handsome appearance, younger than her years, and her lovely hair, added to the morbid curiosity. So did her utterly calm behaviour, though her own vicar, a national authority on oriental languages but with a passion for capital punishment, chose to regard this as callousness. After shaking hands with the prison officials, she walked firmly to the scaffold, and seemed to show no fear. Even Calcraft the executioner showed nervousness. Since it was some time since he had executed a woman in public, he forgot to tie her dress so that she should not be exposed as she swung, and had actually to reascend the scaffold to do this. The execution was even the occasion of a leading article in the *Dorset County Chronicle* advocating the abolition of the death penalty.

It is clear that the sixteen-year-old Hardy, instead of going straight to Hicks's office that morning, got himself a good place to view this sight. In a crowd of three or four thousand, his favoured position close to the gallows can hardly have been an accident. He was so close that he could actually see her features through the rain-damp cloth over her face. It made an impression on him that lasted until old age.[10] The nature of that impression offers a somewhat disturbing insight into his mind as it then was. The well-remembered occasion had for him distinctly sexual overtones. He wrote in his eighties, in words whose unconscious tone is barely credible, "what a fine figure she showed against the sky as she hung in the misty rain, and how the tight black silk gown set off her shape as she wheeled half round and back", after Calcraft had tied her dress close to her body. For one ardent watcher at least, the hangman's would-be humanitarian action had created an additional excitement.

Even Hardy seems to have realized that these reminiscent delights were abnormal, for he added the excuse, whenever he wrote of this, that he was very young at the time.[11] The second Mrs. Hardy, assiduous to present her famous husband in a good light, wrote of the pity that he had been "permitted" to see such a sight—though he seems to have gone entirely at his own volition—and added "It may have given a tinge of bitterness and gloom to his life's work". This verdict hardly accounts for Hardy's obvious sense of enjoyment and anticipation, followed by a sensation of calm that seems to give the whole experience a sexual character. As for its effect on his life's work, or at least upon his most famous novel, another account, perhaps the most telling and circumstantial, certainly does suggest a deep impression with extraordinary personal overtones. On 2 November 1904, *The Sketch* printed the following paragraph.

Mr. Neil Munro tells a curious story of the origin of Mr. Hardy's "Tess". When Hardy was a boy he used to come into Dorchester to school, and he made the acquaintance of a woman there who, with her husband, kept an inn. She was beautiful, good and kind, but married to a dissipated scoundrel who was unfaithful to her. One day she discovered her husband under circumstances which so roused her passion that she stabbed him with a knife and killed him. She was tried, convicted, and condemned to execution. Young Hardy, with another boy, came into

Dorchester and witnessed the execution from a tree that overlooked the yard in which the gallows was placed. He never forgot the rustle of the thin black gown the woman was wearing as she was led forth by the warders. A penetrating rain was falling; the white cap was no sooner over the woman's head than it clung to her features, and the noose was put round the neck of what looked like a marble statue. Hardy looked at the scene with the strange illusion of its being unreal, and was brought to his complete senses when the drop fell with a thud and his companion on a lower branch of the tree fell fainting to the ground. The tragedy haunted Hardy, and, at last, provided the emotional inspiration and some of the matter for "Tess of the D'Urbervilles".

Hardy cut this out and pasted it into a scrapbook, which was marked "Personal".[12] He crossed out and altered the sentence suggesting he knew Martha Brown and also the erroneous account of the Browns' profession; but he then headed the cutting with the word "Corrected", and made no further alteration. This shows that the story, apart from slight details such as the exact murder-weapon, was accepted by him as generally a true picture. Years later, he himself repeated the story, almost exactly, to a young visitor "with a sort of gaiety".[13] He emphasized again the weird effect of the woman's features showing through the execution hood. "That was extraordinary", he commented in the later conversation. Yet the most significant detail is one found in this newspaper account only. Munro, a serious journalist and novelist, who would hardly invent at this point, records that Hardy "never forgot the rustle of the thin black gown the woman was wearing". The rustle of a woman's dress had enormous sexual meaning for Hardy. It will be remembered that when he recalled his feeling for Mrs. Julia Augusta Martin, which, he himself said, "was almost like that of a lover"[14] he paid special attention to "the thrilling 'frou-frou' of her four grey silk flounces when she used to bend over him", and even recollected the same sound having an effect on him when she came into Stinsford Church on Sundays. There can be hardly any doubt that hanging, and particularly the hanging of a woman, had some sort of sexual meaning for Hardy, which remained powerfully in his thoughts to the end of his life. This account hints that it supplied at least part of the emotional power of his best-known novel.

The sense of suspended animation at the moment of execution, and the feeling of anticipation, both virtually sexual in character, were again shown by Hardy quite soon after, at the next Dorchester execution. This was one which he clearly took great and extraordinary pains to witness. Almost exactly two years to the day after the execution of Martha Brown, another public hanging took place at Dorchester Gaol. The hanged person was a young man called James Seale, and his crime was a specially horrible one, the apparently motiveless murder of an inoffensive and deformed young woman of twenty-three, Sarah Ann Guppy. The murder and trial attracted a good deal of attention, and a broadsheet was printed, giving full details.[15] The date fixed for the execution was Tuesday, 10 August 1858. Hardy, far from being appalled by the execution he had witnessed just two years before, noted the coming event with interest and anticipation, as his own remarkable memories show:

> One summer morning at Bockhampton, just before he sat down to break-fast, he remembered that a man was to be hanged at eight o'clock at Dorchester. He took up the big brass telescope that had been handed on in the family, and hastened to a hill on the heath a quarter of a mile from the house, whence he looked towards the town. The sun behind his back shone straight on the white stone facade of the goal, the gallows upon it, and the form of the murderer in white fustian, the executioner and officials in dark clothing and the crowd below being invisible at this distance of nearly three miles. At the moment of his placing the glass to his eye the white figure dropped downwards, and the faint note of the town clock struck eight.
>
> The whole thing had been so sudden that the glass nearly fell from Hardy's hands. He seemed alone on the heath with the hanged man, and crept homeward wishing he had not been so curious.[16]

What may well seem so strange about this narrative is the almost total lack of horror at the hanging itself, and the fate of the hanged man. Hardy is disturbed not by the event nor the moral and social ideas connected with it, but by his own sensations at the moment, and his own isolation. "He seemed alone on the heath with the hanged man" suggests almost a pleasant kind of horror, and he only half-heartedly rebukes himself for having been so "curious"—itself a monumental understatement for his eager early-morning dash out on the heath. There is no doubt that he treasured the moment morbidly, since it is surely the basis for one of the weirdest incidents in his first published novel, *Desperate Remedies*. For plot purposes, Hardy had to make his heroine suddenly lose her architect father. Almost any kind of death would have done for her orphaning; but he chose to let her see, at a distance, her father abruptly drop to his death from a scaffold round a church tower. These two scaffold scenes, the execution and the accident, are described in almost the same way. There is no doubt Hardy was remembering the hanging when he wrote the novel.

This suggests an early thread of perverse morbidity in Hardy, some-thing near abnormality. That he developed normally may be due to new and powerful intellectual influences. When Martha Brown went to the scaffold, the prison chaplain, Dacre Clemetson, was too overcome to go with her. Instead, with firm steps, walked a tall, handsome clergyman, known to Hardy through his mother as the preacher she had most admired in Dorchester in the days of her youth. His name was Henry Moule.

The Reverend Henry Moule, Vicar of Fordington, had just won, in dramatic circumstances, his battle to be accepted by the parishioners of that teeming parish in southern Dorchester. The son of a Wiltshire banker, he had been in another Dorset parish before coming to Fordington in 1828, but his views and actions had brought him into head-on collision with the Dorchester locals. A strong preacher, he attacked the morality of places like the well-named Cuckold Row in the parish; his ear for music made him critical of the church choir. Finding the vicar interfering with both morals and music, his Dorchester flock conducted a long-drawn-out war with him. Each Maundy Thursday night, they marked Easter Festival by uprooting the vicarage railings and garden shrubs, and his children were jeered at in the streets.[17] Nor was he any better liked by the gentry, who decided, at a Hunt meeting, he must be a Methodist. This went on for the best part of twenty-five years, until the sensational year 1854 changed him from a villain into a kind of folk-hero. This was the year of the third great cholera epidemic, when another type of folk-hero, Dr. Snow of London, forcibly demonstrated his theory that the disease was water-borne by taking the handle off the pump in Broad Street, Soho. Henry Moule's action in the Dorchester outbreak was similarly dramatic. He moved single-handed among his dying and diseased parishioners, burning clothing, cleansing and comforting, absolutely without fear. Realizing that his church itself might be a focal point for infection, he held instead open-air prayers.[18] From that moment he could do no wrong for them, and both his sermons and his church singing were loyally supported.

Not only his physical bravery, but also his moral courage and social conscience won their hearts. Fordington, by an historical anomaly, was part of the Duchy of Cornwall, of whose Council Prince Albert was then President. At the height of the cholera outbreak in London, the Home Secretary found himself faced with the disease in the huge Millbank Prison. Since Dorchester lay remote from the public eye, 700 prisoners and their warders were evacuated to the Dorchester Cavalry Barracks, which was now vacant because the Crimean War had taken the troops. This was in West Fordington parish. The poverty-stricken homes there, long neglected by the Duchy, took in the prisoners' washing, and the clothes polluted the primitive water-supply. Moule was so moved by this administrative crime that he boldly wrote no less than eight letters direct to Prince Albert about the responsibility of the Duchy in this matter, and had them published in the following year. To see someone respectfully but firmly putting the plain fact of appalling housing and disease in their parish to the Prince, who had passed through cheering crowds in Dorchester five years before, was a revelation, never forgotten.

From being objects of derision, Henry Moule's children now shared their father's popularity, a dynasty of local heroes. They were themselves an impressive race. Seven sons[19] (one child had died in infancy) seemed to carry on their father's ideals of scholarship and service. Two became missionaries in China (one of them a Bishop there), one a country vicar. On the scholarly side, Handley Carr Glyn Moule was, first, Fellow of Trinity College, Cambridge, and then for nearly two decades Bishop of Durham. Charles W. Moule was Fellow and finally President of Corpus Christi College in the same university. Horatio Mosley Moule was a member of Queens' College, while Henry Joseph Moule, after a life of travel, found an ideal home for his strong archaeological interests in the curatorship of the Dorset County Museum in Dorchester.

It is not quite clear how Hardy got to know the family, nor which member he knew first. It was probably the last-named, Henry Joseph, since they were drawn together by water-colour painting, which the sixteen-year-old Hardy, after his childish efforts to please Mrs. Martin, was now taking up seriously. Henry Joseph Moule was an accomplished water-colourist, and Hardy first remembered him, in about 1856, standing by while Hardy sketched,[20] and criticizing freely, in a way common to the Moule family. Yet though they remained friends for nearly fifty years, it was one of his younger brothers, met in 1857, who had the greatest influence on Hardy.

This was Horatio Mosley Moule, usually known as Horace. Regarded by his brothers as the most brilliant of the family, his career suggests tragic inner tension and intellectual contradiction. He had first gone to Trinity College, Oxford, as a scholar in 1851, but had left in 1854 without a degree. In that year he matriculated at Queens' College, Cambridge, yet went down some years later with the Hulsean Prize (1858) but still no degree, and was not actually awarded his B.A. until 1867. According to what was virtually his obituary,[21] he was, however, a fine classical scholar. Whatever the reason for this curious record, it was a symptom of something deep-laid. Many large nineteenth-century families produced one member in each generation who was impaired physically, mentally, or merely temperamentally; the history of the Giffords, the family of Hardy's first wife, shows something of the same pattern. It is likely that there were some depressive elements in Horatio's make-up, quite apart from the disappointments of his academic career and even more disastrous personal events. At some undefined time, he started talking suicide in fits of depression; he also tried to ward off these fits by drinking. It became an open secret with his relatives that he sometimes slept with a razor under his pillow, to be removed by them secretly.[22] He was the typical casualty of an outwardly successful and happy family.

There is no doubt, though. that whatever his temperamental handicaps, Horace Moule was a brilliant and inspiring teacher. This was officially recognized during a short spell (1865–68) as assistant master at Marlborough but unofficial, personal tributes are even more explicit. The chief of these came from his youngest brother, Handley Moule. He wrote[23]

> My dear brother Horace had a hundred charming ways of interesting and teaching me, alike in scholarship and in classical history. He would walk with me through the springing corn, translating Hesiod to me. He would draw a plan of ancient Rome with lines of pebbles on the lawn . . . Wonderful was his subtle faculty for imparting, along with all due care for grammatical precision, a living interest in the subject-matter, and for shedding an indefinable glamour over all we read.

This was the man who took virtual control of Thomas Hardy's life in the year 1857, not only as a teacher but as a friend. He gave Hardy, some time in this year, *Elements of Experimental and Natural Philosophy . . . for the use of Youth and Schools* by Jabez Hogg, and inscribed it "from his friend Horace".[24] This was intellectual food of a not much more elevated kind than the encyclopedic, self-improving volumes Hardy was still buying for himself, such as *Things Not Generally Known, Familiarly Explained* by John Timbs, and G. A. Mantell's *Wonders of Geology*, both purchased the following year.[25] Yet is was clearly in these friendly and intimate rambles in the fields round Dorchester[26] that Hardy breathed, just as described by Horace Moule's brother, a new world and atmosphere.

Many of Hardy's later references to Moule are laconic and formal; he is merely "a scholar and critic of perfect taste".[27] Such phrases carry little hint of the emotional inspiration Moule provided at these first meetings. There is, however, a later poem which seems to catch this moment with feeling and insight. It is called "An Experience" and addressed to "My friend", the term which Hardy always reserved, in other poems, for Moule.[28] This little-known poem has puzzled the few critics who have noticed it, one of whom[29] exclaimed in bewilderment that it suggests "an incident during a picnic". Hardy's totally exclusive use of the word "friend" for Moule, and the poem's likeness to the prose description by Moule's brother of Horace's effect on younger pupils, make it certain that here we have Horace Moule as he first appeared to the youthful Hardy.

> Wit, weight, or wealth there was not
>   In anything that was said,
>   In anything that was done;
> All was of scope to cause not
> A triumph, dazzle, or dread

To even the subtlest one,
> My friend,
To even the subtlest one.

But there was a new afflation—
> An aura zephyring round
> That care infected not:
It came as a salutation,
> And in my sweet astound,
> I scarcely witted what
> Might pend,
> I scarcely witted what.

The hills in samewise to me
> Spoke as they greyly gazed,
> —First hills to speak so yet!
The thin-edged breezes blew me
> What I, though cobwebbed, crazed
> Was never to forget,
> My friend,
> Was never to forget!

This fresh world of experience was given intellectual shape and back-bone by an altogether new type of reading. There is no instance, until now, of Hardy reading any weekly periodical other than the highly provincial and parochial *Dorset County Chronicle*, with its recital of farmers' meetings, rick fires and sale prices. In 1857, according to his own account, and certainly under Moule's influence, he began to read regularly a leading London weekly. This was *The Saturday Review*, and it had a determining effect on many of his basic attitudes and beliefs; he was still reading it seventy years later. Much of Hardy's peculiar mental approach can be found in its pages, and Horace Moule's introduction to this paper was deeply significant for Hardy's outlook on life. No dramatic fantasies are needed to explain Hardy's scepticism and criticism of human affairs, if one studies the files of this magazine, to which he was introduced at such a susceptible time of adolescence, and by such a winning personality.

The Saturday Review, founded in 1855, was one of the most brilliantly-written journals of its time. It was said, with something of an élite snobbism, that a writer for it who had not first-class honours at Oxford or Cambridge was a distinct rarity. Its chief task was to expose, in all fields, the hypocrisy and smug sentimentality of a large part of Victorian morals and manners, and to lash out at the smothering woolliness of most middle-class conventions. "There is no such thing," it announced, "as what is vaguely called absolute morality." It believed that social evils were, in the main, accentuated by social inequality. It declared that landlords were responsible for rural immorality, and that the two-roomed cottage was productive of incest to a degree that could hardly be conceived. In a leader called "Sweet Auburn" on 14 March 1857, just when Hardy began to read it, it took the lid off the sentimental middle-class view of village life in withering sentences.[30]

At the same time, the social criticism of *The Saturday Review*, though it bitterly exposed hypocrisy, was, in the main, intensely conservative. This was so much Hardy's attitude in most of his novels that it clearly corresponded with his early reading of this magazine; he accepted social inequality with little more than an ironic shrug. Alec d'Urberville has the power, and Tess Durbeyfield has not. When she usurps that power in despair, and kills him, society takes over and kills her. Hardy has his famous final comment, but he does not suggest any change in the nature of a society that can exact this ending. The same is true of the view of religion that he also imbibed, perhaps rather more slowly, from the *Saturday*. All forms of religious excess were criticized by the magazine, mainly for their intolerance of other forms; but no one religious position was ever defended. Equally, it attacked the vast revivalist meetings, the sensational tactics of popular preachers, and Anglo-Catholics and Roman Catholics alike. It was accused, naturally enough, of being an irreligious paper; but, it claimed, it only attacked those who made religion intellectually impossible for the modern man to accept. This reply was very much that which Hardy was later to make, in answer to criticisms of such novels as *Tess* and *Jude*. The Church, in all its aspects, he claimed, had not kept pace with modern life and modern intellectual developments; yet like the *Saturday*, he hardly gave any practical suggestion as to how the Church should perform this change.

What emerges from the pages of the *Saturday*, for all the verve and hard-hitting style of the writing, is an essentially negative attitude. The comment on the *Saturday*, made by Walter Bagehot in 1860, put this account of its purely negative nature in telling form:

> We may search . . . for a single truth which it has established, for a single high cause which it has advanced, for a single deep thought which is to sink into the mind of its readers. We have, indeed, a nearly perfect em-bodiment of the corrective scepticism of a sleepy intellect.

"Corrective scepticism" is exactly the phrase one can apply to an aspect of Hardy's own work, especially some of the early novels, when the reading of the *Saturday*, and its exposition by Horace Moule, was still fresh in his mind, to be introduced into the novels in pieces of some-what naïve digressive comment on life. In his first published novel, *Desperate Remedies*, what Hardy calls, rightly enough ,"a depressing picture of married life among the very poor of a city" is introduced by the quite unnecessary piece of cynicism, "Mrs. Higgins was the wife of a carpenter who from want of employment one winter had decided to marry". At the other end of the social scale, there are the paraders in

Rotten Row in *A Pair of Blue Eyes*, who "bear on their faces, as plainly as on a phylactery the inscription 'Do, pray, look at the coronet on my panels.'". Such destructive comment on human habits stayed with Hardy obsessively even among the far more sympathetic analyses of character in his later novels; in *Jude* one gets the absurd equation that all married people look miserable, so happy faces show no marriage has taken place. The *Saturday* habit of exposing pretension and sham often left him with nothing but a negative outlook to put in its stead.

It is clear, too, that Hardy soon absorbed Horace Moule's own habits of mind. One of the earliest prose studies by Moule appears in a little book of proceedings of a Dorchester intellectual society, which held its meetings at his father's vicarage.[31] An essay on Patriotism, just after the Crimean War, sets out to deflate the usual idea of patriotism as a military or militant virtue. There is a better way, not to die but to live for one's country, and to follow "the highest and best fulfilment of my duty to God and my neighbour". Hardy's own poems, both in the Boer and the First World War, explore this idea; it is those at home who have to go on living, who show what may be called true patriotism. Yet *how* they are to go on, he does not suggest.

These, and other such attitudes of mind, the young Hardy learned from this unofficial tutor, eight years older than himself, whose sensitive, almost feminine face shows him to be as attractive physically as he was mentally. Hardy was not the only pupil of Moule at this time. One of the many schools in Dorchester that took more advanced pupils was that of the Dorset poet, William Barnes, next door to Hicks's office in South Street. Knowing Barnes to be a philologist as well as a poet, Hardy, in some of his linguistic arguments with his fellow-apprentice Bastow, used to call on him to settle points of grammar, and triumph when the elderly schoolmaster-poet came down, as he generally did, on Hardy's side. Though Barnes was not one of Horace Moule's literary society, he had been an honoured guest there, and had contributed an original poem to its proceedings. Among the youths then at Barnes's school was one about a year younger than Hardy, Thomas William Hooper Tolbort. He possessed a passion and an ability for languages, which naturally found encouragement from Barnes; but there seemed no outlet for this gift in Dorchester, and he was apprenticed to his uncle, James Froud, a chemist in High East Street. At this point, Horace Moule took a hand in the making of his future, as he was doing with Hardy, but to an even more decisive effect. Impressed by Tolbort's gifts and hard work, he persuaded him to sit for the Oxford Local Examination. Tolbort took first place out of 900 candidates, and later went on to do as brilliantly in the entrance examinations for the Indian Civil Service.[32] Moule's walks in the fields with these two youths led him to see the more academic boy as a natural success for the new system of competitive entry, which was introduced by the Indian Civil Service Act of 1853. He did not, as yet, see as clearly what his other bright but not so narrowly-talented apprentice-pupil might eventually do with his passion for self-improvement. Besides, Hardy, rather healthily, also read popular thrillers such as Goldschmidt's *The Jew of Denmark*, which he purchased on 14 October 1857.[33]

In fact, Thomas Hardy's world was far more varied and broad-based than that of the usual bookish provincial boy. He recognized this when, looking back, he described it as "a life twisted of three strands—the professional life, the scholar's life, and the rustic life, combined in the twenty-four hours of one day".[34] He would read his copy of the *Iliad*, Greek text with Latin interleaved, from six to eight in the morning out at Bockhampton, then walk into Dorchester and work at Gothic architecture all day, and then rush off with his fiddle under his arm, often with his father and uncle James, to play at remote village festivals till dawn. Sometimes the bookish element was uppermost, as when he caught himself soliloquizing in Latin during his evening and morning walks to and from Bockhampton.[35] Yet his feet were kept on the earth by the human scene around him, the fund of human experience at home, among relations in Puddletown, and the events of the neighbouring villages.

One such experience was the death of his father's mother in the year 1857. She had meant much to him, and her stories were an enduring memory, deeply felt and demonstrated in a later poem to her, *One We Knew*. One hot thundery summer in his childhood, she had said casually, "It was like this in the French Revolution, I remember".[36] Now her death was almost certainly the seed of his first effort at original poetry. The form this took was also almost certainly determined by his new intellectual guide, Horace Moule. Moule, like nearly all vicarage children, wrote himself in a sort of sub-Wordsworthian style, lyric or blank verse. Hardy did not buy himself a Wordsworth until some years later, but he caught the style faithfully from his friend, and perhaps from actual reading with him, since his lines are much more exactly in the Wordsworthian manner than many imitators. However imitative and literary, their observation of the country scene gives them a reality that breaks through the conventional description and sentiment. Their ending, when he imagines his grandmother talking of her life when she first came to live in the newly-built house at Higher Bockhampton, has his own sympathetic identification with all forms of wild nature, and a foretaste, however immature and derivative, of what he might later achieve as a poet.

> Our house stood quite alone, and those tall firs
> And beeches were not planted. Snakes and efts
> Swarmed in the summer days, and nightly bats

Would fly about our bedrooms. Heathcroppers
Lived on the hills, and were our only friends;
So wild it was when first we settled here.

The voice from the past, and particularly one from a recently dead woman, always the most powerful inspiration for Hardy, is earliest heard in this, the very first of his numerous poems, and by no means the least successful among them.

5

Religion

THOMAS HARDY described himself as being in his early twenties still "quite a pink-faced youth".[1] This is certainly borne out by photographs. Even more striking in their youthfulness are the two photographs taken in Dorchester at sixteen and nineteen, while he was still apprenticed to Hicks. For all his frock-coat, portfolio and knotted cravat, these show an almost boyish creature, like a child dressed in adult clothes.[2] The exceptionally slight figure and schoolboy face remind one of portraits of Swinburne. Nothing could be a greater contrast with the typical Dorset man, broad-shouldered and barrel-chested, rural·yet shrewd, walking town and village to the present day. Among these people in Dorchester, Puddletown or in his own parish, young Hardy must have appeared like some changeling, an innocent in a rough, practical world.

Hardy's is so much the traditional look of the fresh-faced Victorian curate that one can see why friends and relatives assumed the precocious boy would go into the Church. The times were certainly ripe for a youth of intelligence, even if self-taught, to think of ordination. Earlier, in the 1820s, one out of three beneficed clergy was an absentee from at least one of the livings which he held; but by the 1840s, reform had halved this number. A flood of money for church building had begun, and by 1858, over 3000 new churches had been built in fifty years, a process from which, as we have seen, Hardy's builder father had benefited. Church organization was reformed; in 1835 the Ecclesiastical Commission was set up by Sir Robert Peel, absenteeism became illegal, and there were other strenuous efforts for improvement, both public and private. In 1854, a leader of the Church commented that "It is a very rare thing to see a careless clergyman, a neglected parish, or a desecrated church".

Yet this good work, and the optimism it engendered, had received a devastating blow in the year 1851, when statistics about church attendance in England were gathered. In 1851, at the first thorough Census of Population,[3] a census of church attendance was also taken. It proved that on Sunday, 30 March 1851 only 7,261,032 out of a total population of 17,927,609 had gone to any form of religious service.[4] The general message was plain. In an outwardly worshipping Christian country, less than half the adult population went to church or chapel. The percentage of Church of England worshippers who actually went to church on this last Sunday in March, as compared with that of other denominations, was only fifty-two per cent to forty-eight per cent.[5] Not only was England merely half Christian, it was only one quarter orthodox and Anglican. This underlined a difference between church and chapel, which Hardy himself was to point out from his own observation, not many years later. "There are two sorts of church people," he wrote in his notebook, "those who go, and those who don't go: there is only one sort of chapel people; those who go."[6] This proverbial fact, numerically demonstrated in the 1850s, was the second blow to the pride of the Church of England, just when young Hardy might have thought of turning his talents to the ministry.

In one sense it might have seemed an ideal time for the Church to welcome a promising young recruit. There had been a huge leap in population. In the fifty years since 1801 the population in England and Wales had actually doubled; the growth in urban manufacturing areas had been phenomenal. A whole new race had grown up as heathens, hardly knowing the name of Christian belief. This was a challenge which the Church in the 1850s certainly tried to meet. Not only did it provide even more buildings; it set itself to man them. The 1861 Census, ten years later, showed nine clergy for every eight of the previous census; the reclamation of one's fellow-countrymen to Christ took on the nature of a crusade for many young men.

Yet there were limitations, imposed largely by the older and more conventional clergy. Bishops were on the look-out for any lowering of standards. Many required of ordination candidates not only a specialized training in a theological college, but also a university degree. The standard guide for any youth intending to enter the ministry was John James Blunt's *The Duties of a Parish Priest*; published posthumously in 1856, it went into four editions in five years.[7] Blunt, a Cambridge professor of divinity, assumed that all the men for whom he wrote had been well-educated at some university, and even that most of them were likely to be the sons of clergy. His typical parson is of the same social class as the squire, sharing many of his duties and attitudes. He is a learned man, who can read and study the Hebrew and Greek texts, and expound their meaning to his unlearned and simple congregation. An observant foreign visitor at this time noted[8] that "The clergyman . . . is a gentleman, often by birth and fortune, almost invariably by education."

This was far from Hardy's background; in fact, it is remarkable that until the age of twenty-five he still considered entering the Church.[9] Markings in his treasured copy of *The Popular Educator* seem to show that he took special interest in the regulations for entry into the University of London, which had provisions for "self-taught students".[10] Thomas Hardy senior, though, was already paying for his daughter Mary to attend Miss Harvey's School in South Street, and to prepare to enter Salisbury Training College for teachers. The expense of sending his elder son on a much longer course of education would have been far beyond his means, though Hardy himself liked to think his father could have afforded it,[11] and the project of his going to a university does seem to have been at least discussed.

Legend says that Hardy, about this time, actually applied for candidacy for the Christian ministry, and was rejected on the ground of his humble origins. There is no evidence at all for this unconfirmed oral tradition. Even if he had applied to the Bishop of Salisbury, any rejection would more likely have been for his technical lack of formal education rather than any matter of class. Walter Kerr Hamilton, Bishop of Salisbury, who established one of the new theological colleges there in 1861, was more likely to reject candidates on educational grounds than for any ungentlemanly qualities. A manuscript note from him can be taken, though conjecturally, as implying a certain disapproval of the number of non-graduates then, as he says, "pressing into H. orders".[12] The legend that Hardy suffered some sort of snobbish rejection is really derived from his own bitter and sarcastic remarks about the clergy in some of his novels, and particularly some short stories. A Bishop of Salisbury (Melchester) is pilloried and made a fool of in *Two on a Tower*. Perhaps the most unpleasant character in all Hardy's works is the egregious and cruel young snob who becomes a clergyman in *The Son's Veto*, which Hardy seems to have considered his best short story, and in which the horrible youth, Randolph, is probably drawn from his wife's nephew, Walter Randolph Gifford.[13] The passage most quoted to illustrate what are supposed to be his own experiences is from another very unpleasant story, *A Tragedy of Two Ambitions*.

> To succeed in the Church, people must believe in you, first of all, as a gentleman, secondly as a man of means, thirdly as a scholar, fourthly as a preacher, fifthly, perhaps, as a Christian—but always first as a gentleman.

It is perhaps significant that these two stories were produced when Hardy was conceiving and writing *Tess of the d'Urbervilles*, in which the gentlemanly Angel Clare and his clerical family—though allegedly based on Hardy's friends, the Moule family—behave so cold-heartedly to their social inferior, Tess herself. Yet these were not necessarily Hardy's feelings some thirty years before in the 1850s and early 1860s. He had experience, through the Moule family as they appeared to him then, of clergy who were far from setting themselves apart from the parishioners. His particular friend was not even a graduate, though he had been to two universities; this may have disqualified Horace Moule for the ministry, though he wrote a prize religious essay and an excellent text-book, *The Roman Republic.*

It is also untrue that Hardy suffered at this time the dramatic loss of faith which was such a feature of the lives of well-educated people in the mid-Victorian era. The two books generally taken to mark this revolution in the spiritual life of England are Darwin's *Origin of Species*, published in November 1859, and, perhaps even more immediately influential, the symposium entitled *Essays and Reviews*, which came out in the following year. Both, in their various ways, struck at the literal acceptance of Bible teaching and biblical infallibility. *Origin of Species* argued a process of evolution through natural selection instead of a divine creative act; *Essays and Reviews* largely subjected the Bible to the latest methods of textual and interpretive criticism. Out of its seven contributors, three, Baden Powell, Mark Pattison, and Benjamin Jowett, were the most powerful.[14] Powell, on the study of the evidence of Christianity, ruled out all ideas of miraculous intervention; Pattison, on the tendencies of religious thought in England, provided a brilliant analysis of the changing history of belief in the last 150 years; Jowett, with his slogan of "interpret the Bible like any other book", provided a standard of criticism which, for all its reverence, seemed to many a trenchant criticism of the Church itself.[15]

Hardy himself was impressed by these essays, and discussed them on his walks in the fields with Moule;[16] but there is no evidence that they changed in any way his own habits of worship or belief, at this very early stage. Though the evolution controversy was pushed into prominence by the famous clash between Thomas Huxley and Bishop Wilberforce at the British Association meeting at Oxford in June 1860, the idea that there was a definite conflict between science and religion took several years more to spread; it was not until May 1864 that *The Times* first had a leading article on the topic.[17] Similarly, the full agitation about *Essays and Reviews* was delayed until February of the same year, when a judicial committee of the Privy Council decided that what two of the contributors taught was not inconsistent with the formularies of the Church of England.[18] It was only in the mid-1860s that the struggle between new thought and old faith became acute; and this is the reason that up to the summer of 1865, Hardy could still think of a career in the Church for himself. It should also be noted that his virtual *vade mecum*, the *Saturday Review*, did not touch *Essays and Reviews* for a year after it was published, and then only did so to play down its revolutionary nature.[19]

Hardy's continuing orthodoxy at this time is best illustrated by the facts that at Easter 1861 he acquired and began to annotate copiously both a prayer book and a Bible of his own, and that on 27 September the same year, he got for similar purposes a copy of John Keble's popular pocket-book of Christian verse, *The Christian Year*, which consisted of poems specially designed for every Sunday and Holy Day throughout the Church calendar.[20] From these three books, it is evident Hardy was a punctilious church attender, not only at Sunday morning and evening service, but on most important Saints' days, sure evidence of his upbringing "in High Church principles".[21] Almost his first act after buying *The Christian Year* was to go, two days later, to the Feast of St. Michael and All Angels at Fordington Church, and to record the fact against Keble's verses for that festival. His pencilled annotations were, in fact, very seldom doctrinal or interpretive, and certainly not in any way questioning. Many in his prayer book and *Christian Year* form a kind of diary of the church services he attended, the actual church and the dates of attendance. We can therefore trace for at least the next two years, 1861–63, and often much later, just where Hardy was on any particular Sunday or church festival. His record for these years bears out his own statement that "he knew the Morning and Evening Services by heart including the rubrics, as well as large portions of the New Version of the Psalms".[22] What he meant by this new version was the metrical version by Brady and Tate, included at the back of the prayer book; this had a vital influence on him, both as an expression of religion in memorable form, for which it was designed, and also as a basis for his schooling in the twin arts of music and poetry.

In fact, though Hardy was an exceptional attender at church all through the 1860s, as these meticulous records show, the result was not any increase in belief—this could hardly have been greater—but a greater awareness of words and of the music associated with such words. Words, with Hardy, were never solely literary; they were almost always linked to a remembered and familiar tune, undivided. This is his real strength as a lyric poet; his poems are hardly ever formal exercises on the page, but contain the most subtle modulations, stresses, and changes, entirely reminiscent of musical composition. These variations, with their dramatic breaks in rhythm or emphasis, are used with almost infallible skill when they underline emotional states. This is what makes Hardy consistently our most moving lyric poet. His markings in his copy of the Brady and Tate "New Version" of the psalms[23] show again and again how a poem was identical in his mind with a tune. Often these tunes are named as those sung, as he notes, by the "Old Stinsford Choir", and appear in the music-books of his grandfather, father, and uncle. Psalm 16 was sung to the tune called "Frome", Psalm 23 to "Shirland", Psalm 78 to "Cambridge New", Psalm 106 to "Wilton", and Psalm 133 to "Lydia". Nor were words and music associated only with church-going; some were favourites for home singing by his mother. Psalm 16 and its tune are marked "Mr used to sing this", and the words do seem to express some of the stress of her upbringing and character:

> Protect me from my cruel foes,
> And shield me, Lord, from harm,
> Because my trust I still repose
> On thy Almighty arm.

The grim Psalm 53, denouncing God's enemies, was also a favourite with Mrs. Hardy, according to her son.

Although the emotional timbre given by the old psalter tunes must have been deeply stirring as they filled the rafters of the country church, the words themselves provided by Brady and Tate were little more than commonplace versification. Inspiration of a different and far more genuinely poetic sort came from John Keble's *The Christian Year*. From September 1861, Hardy followed these weekly poems for Sundays and Feast Days. They were the work of a considerable poet, whose best can stand comparison with the religious poems of Herbert and Vaughan, especially some of their openings:

> O for a sculptor's hand,
> That thou might'st take thy stand,
> Thy wild hair floating on the eastern breeze,
> Thy tranc'd yet open gaze
> Fix'd on the desert haze,
> As one who deep in heaven some airy pageant sees.

Again, in the autumn poem for the twenty-third Sunday after Trinity:

> Red o'er the forest glows the setting sun,
> The line of yellow light dies fast away
> That crown'd the eastern copse: and chill and dun
> Falls on the moor the brief November day.

One critic compared the poems to the paintings of Gainsborough. Admittedly, few lived up to such beginnings. Many are from the start a kind of sub-Wordsworth. Wordsworth himself is said to have wished he had written them, though with characteristic reservations.[24] Yet the book was phenomenally popular. When Hardy purchased his copy in 1861, over eighty editions had been printed since its first appearance in 1827. Its main appeal was to people of all sorts who found its poetry easy and its sentiments orthodox; yet, in fact, both were based on the concealed power of Keble's scholarship, which had made him "the first man in Oxford".[25] It was just the book for someone like Hardy, with reverence for learning and a taste for literature, but with an unsophisticated background.

What held most fascination for Hardy was the variety of technique and form. Keble was no innovator; but he was a tireless experimenter with forms already tried and proved by the known masters of English verse, Spenser, Milton (especially his Nativity Ode), Wordsworth himself, and the seventeenth-century lyricists. His own lectures as Professor of Poetry at Oxford stressed the use of complicated metrical devices. Hardy's debt to Keble in his own later poems is not only in verbal half-memories, like the "bright hair flapping free" of his lyric to his first wife; it also lies in his ceaseless lyric invention. We may compare the two poem-openings by Keble just quoted with the last verse of Hardy's *Later Autumn*:

> Spinning leaves join the remains shrunk and brown
> > Of last year's display
> > That lie wasting away,
> On whose corpses they earlier as scorners gazed down
> > From their aery green height:
> > Now in the same plight
> > They huddle; while yon
> > A robin looks on.

The technique is virtually the same. What is different is the emotional charge generated in the Hardy poem. Although *The Christian Year* followed a much-loved young sister's sudden death, Keble's ingenious verses lack intensity of emotion.

Hardy's markings of favourite passages in his Bible seem to be of a different nature. These have the air of being chosen not for poetical or religious reasons, but because they had some personal application. Two passages are marked again and again, one in the Old Testament, one in the New. The first is among the verses in the First Book of Kings, chapter 19, which describes how Elijah came to hear the voice of God in the wilderness:

> And he said, Go forth and stand upon the mount before the Lord. And behold, the Lord passed by, and a great and strong wind rent the mountains, and brake in pieces the rocks before the Lord; but the Lord was not in the wind: and after the wind an earthquake; but the Lord was not in the earthquake:
> And after the earthquake a fire; but the Lord was not in the fire: and after the fire a still small voice.

Hardy marked this passage retrospectively for 1859 and 1860, and thereafter for every year up to 1864, and again in 1870.[26] It is, as he also noted, the first lesson at evensong on the ninth Sunday after Trinity, occurring in August. He made special mention of it during his first summer in London, in the year 1862.[27] His second favourite passage was the fifteenth chapter of the First Epistle to the Corinthians, which was the second lesson at evening service on the Tuesday in Easter Week,[28] and which he marked at various times and at various dates in April when he heard it. It is also, of course, the chapter on resurrection, read at the service for the burial of the dead.

Regular church attendance, the association of Biblical texts with himself and his personal life, the learning by heart of both the "Metrical Psalms" and *The Christian Year* poems, all suggest a young man of such high seriousness that the Church would be his natural home. On the other hand, Hardy had other interests and talents; his time in church was not entirely occupied in worship, as can again be seen in those little volumes, the Prayer Book and *The Christian Year*. On the fly-leaf of the first-named, during some service at Stinsford in 1861, Hardy occupied himself by making a sketch of a labourer friend of the family, William Bishop, dressed in his church-going Sunday best.[29] At a similar place at the back of his copy of *The Christian Year* are little sketches of a woman in a bonnet and a man, almost certainly his own mother and father, since the woman has the distinctive Roman nose Jemima Hardy inherited from her own mother.[30] Hardy was often reduced to impending giggles by the face of his vicar, which, he noted, had the clerical peculiarity of always seeming to be on the verge of a smile, even on the most solemn occasions.[31] Hardy's human interests and his sense of the ridiculous were saving graces in a young man whose intellectual growth might have made him a prig. These interests themselves were not, however, without their religious side. Robert Bastow, Hardy's companion in Hicks's office, following his own adult baptism, urged the doctrine strongly on Hardy, and advised him to be baptised too. He put the case for adult baptism as against the Anglican baptism of infants so strongly that Hardy actually came to discuss this with his own preternaturally smiling vicar.

The Vicar of Stinsford, the Reverend Arthur Shirley, was obviously bewildered by the weird and earnest young man. Nothing in his Oxford training had prepared him for such a question, nor had his own upbringing. He came from a well-known county family in Warwickshire, and his nearest brother had just commanded the Connaught Rangers in the Crimean War.[32] Grasping hopefully at the set reading he himself had done at Christ Church, some thirty years before, he produced for Hardy a copy of Richard Hooker's *The Laws of Ecclesiasticall Politie*. Somewhat mystified, Hardy ploughed through the eight books of this Anglican classic, but found nothing in it to his purpose. He had still less luck when he appealed to a curate of another parish; all that the latter was able to lend him was a handbook on the Sacraments of the most elementary kind.

Finding so little help from the clergy of the faith in which he himself had been so thoroughly brought up, Hardy characteristically struck out on his own, and got hold of as many notes and books about Infant Baptism as he could lay hands on. Though he found himself appalled by the feebleness of their arguments for infant christening, he decided to stick to those of "his own side". These, he still believed, were those of the Anglican Church, although, he later confessed, at some cost to his intellectual conscience. He and Bastow then went at it hammer and tongs, until Hicks's wife, in her drawing-room over their office, would send down imploring them not to make so much noise.[33] Bastow called to his aid the two Aberdeen University sons of the local Baptist minister, Frederick Perkins, who could quote in the original Greek from the required texts in the New Testament. Faced with this challenge, Hardy bought himself on 7 February 1860 the latest edition of Griesbach's text, which he had seen advertised as more accurate than his older one, and sat up at night studying this to confute his opponents.

Whatever the controversy did, it gave Hardy a scene in a later novel. The Scots father of the two young Perkinses appears in *A Laodicean*, where the arguments over infant baptism are faithfully rehearsed. Hardy was impressed by the character of these people, and their stubborn Scots virtues. His feeling that they were right on adult baptism was countered by a certain narrowness in their views, however much he grew to admire them as people. He even rejoiced when he caught them deserting their strict principles, and in his old age related with some malicious glee how, on one occasion, they had forgotten about a prayer-meeting when Cooke's popular Travelling Circus paid a visit to Dorchester.[34]

This friendly religious controversy also stimulated Hardy's further study of Greek. He had already learnt the rudiments from the companion volume to the old Latin Eton Grammar he had studied under Isaac Last. This second publication was Clement Moody's Greek Eton Grammar, first published in 1852. Hardy, in schoolboy fashion, showed his delight in the unfamiliar Greek characters by transcribing his name in them, Θωμὰς ʿΑρδυ.[35] Now, far beyond such adolescent delights, he sat with Bastow on summer evenings on the gate of the enclosure of Kingston Maurward ewelease, comparing notes and readings of the Greek Testament, and even deserting Homer for the pleasure of more advanced scholarship.[36] This pursuit was broken late in 1860, when Bastow finished his term of apprenticeship, and hearing of the building boom in Australia, went to seek his fortunes as an architect there. Without the stimulus of controversy, Hardy went back to his more general classical studies, and a letter from Bastow, in May 1861, lamented enviously that while Hardy was reading Homer, his former companion, now in Tasmania, had not touched a Greek book since he emigrated. Hardy's *Iliad* once more became daily reading, and as at this time he started to lodge in Dorchester near the office, so as not to waste time on walks home, he got through a prodigious amount of study in his spare moments.

He had renewed his apprenticeship to Hicks for a longer term than the original three years, but what should be his next move? He was obviously a promising architectural pupil, but his learned interests surely indicated a larger sphere. Should it be the Church, fortified by his recent study, and might that be preceded by a university career, to which his basic grasp of the classics could be directed? It was natural in such questions to consult his local link with these middle-class worlds, the Moule family of Fordington. Early in June 1860, he heard the head of that family, the Reverend Henry Moule, preach in his fluent extempore way on the text from the Book of Job, "All the days of my appointed time will I wait, until my change come".[37] Hardy's habit of applying biblical texts to his own life made this an occasion he remembered for the rest of that life, still recalling the vicar's intonation in his own extreme old age. Was this a sign that he should passively wait for the signal from God, whatever it might be? On the other hand, he had a ready aid and adviser in his particular friend among the vicar's sons, Horace, now living at home in Dorchester.[38] Notes dating from about 1860 show a close friendship between the two, in spite of their different social background.[39] Moule addressed him as an equal, gave him books, including a translation of Goethe's *Faust*, and even borrowed for him from the Cambridge University Library.

Yet Moule's decision, when Hardy put the question to him was clearly a surprise. Hardy had enquired, in his roundabout way, whether he should not now read some Greek plays, Aeschylus or Sophocles, as a preparation perhaps for a university career? Moule advised against this. His opinion, which Hardy says was given reluctantly, was that Hardy should press on with the architectural career, for which his parents had provided the money. Since Hardy's father could probably not have afforded university fees, this was sound worldly advice. Yet it also seems to show that Hardy, in spite of early promise, was not an exceptional scholar. Moule had backed young Hooper Tolbort's leap from his social class into the Civil Service, seeing the boy had something special to offer the larger world in his gift for languages. He did not see Hardy as a pure scholar in the same light. It is difficult to know how he put this, but something may be gathered from later advice to Hardy by another member of the Moule family, Charles Walter. A dozen years later, when Hardy was hesitating whether to go all out for a career as a novelist, he consulted this brother. C. W. Moule quoted[40] from Coleridge's *Biographia Literaria* to suggest "that literature will be most efficiently pursued by those who are tied down to some regular employment, official or professional". Some dictum of this nature (which, incidentally, poor Coleridge never managed to follow in his own life) may have been the basis of Horace Moule's advice in 1861. Hardy, he said, should not try to branch out into a life of scholarship or a career in the Church, but stick to his trade, as architecture then was. Psychologically, Hardy was young enough and hero-worshipping enough to obey, just as he notably disobeyed the other Moule brother a dozen years later. At the latter time, he was urged and encouraged by his future wife. Now he had no one to give him courage in his own vocation. When his change should come, to use the words of the Vicar of Fordington's text, it would come from inner conviction alone.

6

London

A few months before his death, Thomas Hardy declared that if he had his life over again, he would prefer to be a small architect in a country town.[1] Now, in 1861, at the age of twenty-one, he might well have had that prospect. Mr. Hicks was to die in eight years' time; Hardy could have succeeded him, and set up a profitable local combination of architect and builder with his own brother Henry, who seemed destined to follow their father. In actual fact, his mind was in a ferment. He was strangely learned, emotionally immature, pious and vaguely ambitious. His darker patches of sexual fantasy are perhaps hinted by a retrospective entry in his prayer-book. In spring 1860, he visited his sister Mary at her training college in Salisbury, and first saw Salisbury Cathedral. He noted the fact,[2] and then put a cross against verse 9 of Psalm 119; "Wherewithal shall a young man cleanse his way: even by ruling himself after thy word." He underlined the words "ruling himself"; but he also underlined, later in the psalm, "My soul breaketh out . . . My soul melteth away".

What move, if any, should he make? The examples among his own immediate friends and relations were not encouraging. His fellow apprentice, Bastow, seemed slightly disillusioned in Tasmania. Those of his family who had tried a move had little to show for it. His sister was pursuing her usual unobtrusive way at Salisbury, and was soon due to pass on to her life's role of certificated teacher, after a blameless college career. His cousins, James and Nathaniel Sparks, had gone to be carpenters, one to London, the other to Rode in Somerset; neither, in the event, ever made any money, though the latter eventually supplemented his wages by doing some violin repairs.[3] Of their elder sisters, Emma Sparks, in service at a house in Somerset, had married on 14 August 1860 Thomas Cary, the improvident carpenter son of a small Somerset farmer. It was possibly on a visit to them in March 1861 that Hardy made a sketch, which still exists, of Glastonbury Abbey.[4] They had settled in the hamlet of Faulkland, near the Mendips, and in August 1861 Emma produced the first of a brood of children, whose mouths eventually proved too many to feed. Failure, ruined health, emigration, and death a month or so after landing in Queensland were to be her lot.[5] Her smarter sister, Martha Mary, was away from home as an upper servant, and seemed likely to better herself, while the youngest Sparks girl, Tryphena, was doing well at the little Nonconformist school at Athelhampton, under its conscientious bachelor head-teacher, Mr. Holmes. Though only eleven, she showed enough intelligence to hope to follow her cousin Mary Hardy, and train as a teacher, the one legitimate way for a working-class girl to break through social and economic barriers. Apart from this, the rest of the Antells, Hands, and Hardys stayed where they were. Hardy's dashing aunt, Martha Sharpe, had also succumbed to frequent child-bearing and the hardships of emigration, dying at Paris, Ontario, on 28 August 1859 at the age of only forty-two. The Planet Ruler, an itinerant astrologer, had prophesied "she would have a large family, travel, and so on".[6] This had come tragically true.

Nothing suggested it would be to his own advantage to move; yet early in 1862, he determined to do so. It is impossible to say what made him feel that his "appointed time", in the words of the Vicar of Fordington's text, had come. Horace Moule may have relented so far as to advise him to seek a wider sphere in architecture, and perhaps combine it with literary interests. One of the books Hardy was reading under his influence was Walter Bagehot's literary studies, *Estimates of Some Englishmen*, and in January 1862[7] he gave Hardy a copy of the newly-published *Golden Treasury* anthology of lyric verse. Its editor, Francis Turner Palgrave, was the art critic of *The Saturday Review*, Hardy's weekly reading, for which Moule himself was beginning to write. The inscribed copy evidently had both literary and sentimental associations. Folded into it was a large skeleton leaf and, later, a printed cutting of Moule's own poem, *Ave Caesar*. A second and more dubious reason for Hardy to seek his fortune outside Dorchester is the story that he had just proposed marriage to a girl in the Mantle Showroom there, and had been rejected.[8] The girl, Mary Waight, was seven years older than him. The story of this proposal, and of a signed photograph of Hardy, was handed down in her family; but there is no confirmation of its truth, nor, if true, that it had anything to do with Hardy's move to London. More to the point, Hardy's father was in favour of the move, and his connection with house-owners and architects might help. He obtained from one of the former, described by Hardy as "a gushing lady", whom, presumably, the elder Hardy had charmed, a letter of introduction to Benjamin Ferrey. Hardy's other introduction, probably through his master, was to John Norton of 24 Old Bond Street, a friend of Hicks, who had been associated with him in Bristol before their ways parted, one to Dorchester, the other to London.[9]

On the Sunday before Easter, 13 April 1862, Hardy sang in Stinsford Church

> Lord, hear my prayer, and to my cry
> Thy wonted audience lend;
> In thy accustomed faith and truth
> A gracious answer send.

On Maundy Thursday, 17 April, he was in lodgings at 3 Clarence Place, Kilburn, where he spent his first Easter in London.[10] In his pocket was the return half of a ticket, from Paddington to Dorchester. He was ready to retreat if the adventure proved unsuccessful.[11] His landlords were a middle-aged couple called Allen, with three sons, the eldest, a GPO letter-carrier, being about Hardy's age.[12]

Hardy's unfledged appearance, his youthful and abnormally boyish expression, were evidently plain to see. "Wait till you have walked the streets a few weeks and your elbows begin to shine, and the hems of your trousers get frayed as if nibbled by rats," he was told. "Only practical men are wanted here." To his prospective employers he looked an innocent abroad as he ventured, the following week, into the West End. Benjamin Ferrey, at 1 Trinity Place, was polite about Hardy's father, whom he remembered, but had nothing to offer the son. Nor had John Norton; but rather than see such a mother's boy tramp the streets, he offered his office as a place to practise drawing, even though he had no actual vacancy. To this protective kindness, Hardy owed his first real job. When he presented himself on Monday, 28 April to Norton, he was told of a lucky encounter at the Royal Institute of British Architects. Norton had been asked by Arthur Blomfield if he knew of a young Gothic draughtsman who could restore and design churches and rectories; he packed Hardy off then and there to apply. On the following Monday, 5 May, Hardy found himself starting work in Blomfield's drawing-office at 8 St. Martin's Place.

For such a provincial adolescent as Hardy, this was a plunge into the very deep end of sophistication. The regular opening remark at the office, "Any spice in the papers?", recorded by Blomfield's own nephew twenty years later,[13] was already typical in 1862. The Thomas Hardy who punctiliously attended St. Mary's, Kilburn, and St. Stephen's, Paddington, was to find church architecture conducted in an atmosphere very far from "churchy", as he described himself. The two or three architectural assistants, of whom Hardy was one, and the half-a-dozen articled pupils, were left very much to their own devices, in a bustling office, whose Principal was usually away, supervising work on site. Blomfield had a fashionable practice, charged a stiff premium, and his pupils were public school men from the upper classes; Etonians were not unknown. Little or no formal instruction was given, either on the theory and history of architecture, or on applied construction. It was a kind of free-for-all plan-producing factory, full of distractions, high spirits, and horseplay.[14]

The character of the office in which Hardy found himself was that of its Principal. Arthur Blomfield was the son of one Bishop, and brother of another. He was now thirty-three years of age, brilliant, handsome, witty, a first-rate amateur actor, singer, and water-colour painter. He

had unbounded energy and humour; at Trinity College, Cambridge, he
and his older brother had been nicknamed Thunder and Lightning.[15] A
famous oarsman and a well-travelled man, he was immensely sought-
after, both professionally and in society. Ultimately, this was to his dis-
advantage. He took on too many commissions, left too much to his
assistants, and a great deal of his work became a matter of mechanical
repetition, a stale hash of his early ideas. In the high Gothic revival of
the 1860s his work does not stand the test, like that of Street, Butterfield,
and others. Yet at this time his reputation was probably at its height.
He was President of the Architectural Association, founded in 1847 to
promote original ideas and to foster the training of young architects; at
its meetings, papers were read and new designs freely criticized in
healthy competition. Blomfield appreciated youth, and it is to his credit
that he could recognize something in the diffident and uncertain West
Country lad, so reserved and unsure of himself. It was the beginning of a
mutual liking, and a friendship of many years. Hardy later paid tribute
to his influence at this time, and to others who, in spite of their mistakes,
"were really artists just awakening and feeling their way".[16]

The unguarded tone of the office, the racy talk and doings of the
public school and university men there, were poles away from Hardy's
previous experience. The strict upbringing of puritanical women, the
doctrinal discussions with Bastow and the Perkinses, the homely
provincial Church of England chat at Fordington Vicarage could hardly
prepare him for this raffish company and their London ways of life. One
of the pupils battened on to him to borrow money, which he could ill
afford, and in later life even went so far as to forge Hardy's signature on
a cheque.[17] All had a façade of worldly-wise experience. Hardy's sole
hint of the sophisticated pleasures of Town had been gained from a
fellow-apprentice during his first years at Hicks's Dorset office. This was
a young man with the Dickensian name of Herbert Fippard, son of a
Dorchester grocer and draper,[18] who had been on trips to London. Four
years older than Hardy, he had demonstrated the delights of London
society by whistling and dancing the latest quadrille in the office, while,
in Hardy's words, "embracing an imaginary Cremorne or Argyle
danseuse".[19] The memory of Fippard's action in Hardy's retentive mind
now sent him off eagerly to the Argyle Rooms in Great Windmill Street
and the Cremorne Gardens in Chelsea, where his childlike face must at
once have attracted attention; for the girls there, disguised by Hardy's
euphemism of danseuse, were all prostitutes, and their clients moneyed
men of pleasure, prepared to spend, in modern terms, at least fifty
pounds a night. A French visitor in this year described the Argyle
Rooms as "a kind of lust-casino".[20] An English diarist wrote that in
Cremorne Gardens on Sunday, 25 May 1862, "there was hardly an
innocent face among the women, or a noble one among the men", while

a mill-girl from Bolton, who visited the Gardens in June, roundly exclaimed "It's no fit for respectable lasses".[21] The respectable old age of Thomas Hardy caused him to muffle this experience: but it flickers in the ending of an otherwise decorous poem, *Reminiscences of a Dancing Man*, written in his restless fifties:

> Whither have danced those damsels now!
> Is Death the partner who doth moue
>   Their wormy chaps and bare?
> Do their spectres spin like sparks within
> The smoky halls of the Prince of Sin
>   To a thunderous Jullien air?

The office-talk was similarly startling; the morning cry of "Any spice in the papers?" can seldom have gone unanswered. Hardy himself said that the conversation was about notable courtesans, Cora Pearl, "Skittles", and Adah Isaacs Menken,[22] the powerful equestrienne of Astley's, who fascinated Swinburne, and performed her sensational ride as Mazeppa in a vest and shorts that made her appear naked.[23] His memory as an old man, however, somewhat telescoped the years. In 1862, the first two ladies had deserted London for more profitable conquests in Paris, while Menken, beloved by the literati as much for her quite professional poetry as for her apparent nudity, had not yet left her native America. Another lady he mentions, Agnes Willoughby, had in fact just hooked a rich husband and retired in triumph. What must have struck Hardy, though, was the class nature of the talk he heard. Many upper-class Englishmen, including clergy, kept a well-established lower-class mistress, and the fantasy-talk of the office made free with these names. An even greater shock for a provincial in London was to see the widespread and open street prostitution. At this exact time, it was estimated, there were no less than 80,000 prostitutes in London, many of them children.[24] One could be accosted twenty times in a short stroll along the Strand or Haymarket. A gentleman walking after dark in Pall Mall would be seized by a prostitute, and offered *fellatio* then and there.[25] Other women would promise to behave like dogs in every detail.[26] "The Social Evil", as it was popularly called, was the subject of a current show at a place Hardy also visited, the Cider Cellars in Leicester Square, where it packed the house. In a mock trial, the notorious "Lord Chief Baron" Renton Nicholson, having settled himself with a cigar and brandy-and-water, would "try" a case of prostitution, with girls and bawds represented by male actors; when the last ounce of indecent humour had been extracted, this was succeeded by more-or-less nude *poses plastiques* with real girls.[27]

The fact that Hardy, in spite of his architectural occupations, found time to be drawn into such places shows how much good sense there had been in John Norton's feelings that he should on no account be left idle in London. Even the innocent and outwardly respectable places he also frequented had their rough side. One of these was the popular Evans's Supper-Rooms, in an underground hall in Covent Garden. Here, it was possible to find two drunk and incapable clergymen waiting for a third who, when he arrived, proved even more drunk than they.[28] Observation of the clergy on the loose in London may have begun Hardy's gradual disillusion with the goings-on of Ministers of the Church. It was in this year that a West End bawd told Henry Mayhew, with rather charming diffidence, that "although we mustn't mention it, we hooks a white choker now and then, coming from Exeter Hall".[29] Yet perhaps more than drink or prostitution, it was sheer poverty that would impress a youth, who had already been trained to observe this in a county of huge differences between rich and poor. Here the contrast was even more apparent. The monogrammed carriages in the Park, which Hardy later satirized in *A Pair of Blue Eyes*, passed within 'a short distance of the human flotsam and jetsam, mere bundles of hopeless rags, sleeping out like beasts, men and women, in the dirt.[30] Quite apart from these work-less down-and-outs, many working men and women were so scarred by hard labour that they had features more like animals than humans. Maids of all work and the dustwomen, who swept the mounds of refuse off the streets, had hands so calloused that the dead skin could be cut away as a blacksmith would pare the hooves of a horse.[31] Brawny milk-women carried pails on a huge wooden yoke that bent their shoulders and rubbed them raw.

As always with Hardy, however, morbid curiosity into the seamy side, and horror at the hideous aspects of human life, were balanced by his insatiable intellectual pursuit of knowledge and self-improvement. The artistic and scientific side of a great metropolis drew him like a magnet. The chief draw, as always in his life, was music, and here the office had something positive to offer. Choral and church music was one of Blom-field's passions, and he had formed an office choir, into which Hardy was at once welcomed as an accurate though not strong tenor. Slack times in the office were used for practising glees and catches, aided by the Principal's own powerful bass, and Hardy records Blomfield's remark, "If you meet an alto anywhere in the Strand, ask him to come and join us".[32]

London also gave Hardy a chance for professional musical experience on an unlooked-for scale. It was the era of the great sopranos. Adelina Patti had just begun a career that was to stretch into the twentieth century, Therese Tietjens was at her best, and Christine Nilsson, the Swedish soprano, was also just beginning. Hardy heard all three, and others, in the operas of Rossini, Donizetti, Verdi, Meyerbeer, and Bellini. With a musical young man from his lodgings, he went to the newly-rebuilt Opera House, Covent Garden, and to the Queen's Theatre, Haymarket, Vanbrugh's original building, then known as the Royal Italian Opera House, two or three times a week. He was so enthusiastic about Italian opera, particularly the broad and beautiful melodies of *Il Trovatore*, that he bought himself a second-hand fiddle, and practised transcriptions of the famous arias with his lodging-companion, who luckily was an adequate pianist. English opera also offered a company performing at this time, where Hardy heard William Vincent Wallace's *Maritana* and Michael William Balfe's *The Bohemian Girl*. The work of these two Irishmen gave Hardy an opportunity to hear the failing voice of William Harrison, a moving and even painful experience.[33] By contrast, the drama was less of a passion for Hardy, though he saw Charles Kean and his wife Ellen Tree in Shakespeare at the Princess's Theatre, and was still able to enjoy, at the Haymarket, the actor-dramatist John Baldwin Buckstone, a comedian whose voice off-stage set audiences laughing[34] before he even made his entrance.

An even stronger passion was Hardy's obsession with the acquisition of knowledge and information of any kind. He afterwards said that one of his motives for going to London at this time may have been that the world fair or Exhibition was opening there early in the summer of 1862, and his movements in his first six months in London seem to support this. He went down to see it at the Cromwell Road for an hour every evening after work, two or three days regularly every week, and every now and then spent half a day there.[35] Shadowed by the death of its patron Prince Albert, the International Exhibition of 1862 seemed to many people only a pale reflection of the Great Exhibition of 1851. Unable to bear the contrast, the Queen herself had taken her widow's weeds to Balmoral on the very day it opened. Yet in the six months before it closed on 1 November, it drew almost exactly the same number of people as its famous predecessor, and showed the material progress of the past ten years. There was a comprehensive photographic exhibition, reflecting what was now the latest craze; William Morris exhibited furniture, and his firm was commended for its medieval design; the machinery section, mostly from the North of England, with cotton operatives from Lancashire and Yorkshire, was extremely popular. Exotic items included jewellery from an Egyptian tomb, astonishing in its modern appearance.[36]

Undoubtedly, one of the chief attractions of this Exhibition for Hardy was the excellent art galleries there. In Dorchester, he had practically never seen a painting, and his visual imagination had to rely on the black and white reproductions in Cassell's *Illustrated Magazine of Art*.[37] Now the Exhibition gave him not only the best from previous Royal Academy shows in the modern English section, but a particularly strong collection of French, German, Flemish, and Dutch paintings. It stimulated Hardy's new interest in art, already in full career from the permanent exhibitions in London, and reinforced by his methodical study. He and his room-mate at Kilburn, known to us only by the enigmatic initials P.S., were reading Ruskin's *Modern Painters* at this time, though it was not for another year, on 12 May 1863, that Hardy made a systematic précis in one of his earliest notebooks of all the European schools of painting, ancient and modern. He rounded off these regular visits by going to the reading room of the South Kensington Museum, only a short distance away, and at that time housed in iron sheds known to Londoners as the Brompton Boilers; here he could do an evening's reading before catching the horse omnibus back to Kilburn Gate.[38] It was pleasant, too, this summer to show his sister Mary round London, taking her to the Exhibition and to the theatre.

In these first few months of Hardy's new pursuits in London, he also promised himself to renew an old loyalty; he may even have hoped that his fresh veneer of sophistication might cause it to develop in surprising directions. He had often thought about Julia Augusta Martin, who had caused such an emotional upheaval in his childhood, before she left Stinsford in 1853. In the nine years since he last saw her, the Martins had established themselves in London intellectual society. Francis Pitney Brouncker Martin had not wasted his time as a landowner at Kingston Maurward, though Hardy hints he lost money on the home farm.[39] An M.A. of Wadham College, he was an amateur scientist and meteorologist. The disastrous wet and stormy year of 1850, when the Kingston harvest supper had been such a traumatic experience for young Hardy, had been the scene of a series of experiments by the Lord of the Manor. During the wild and windy April that had ushered in the season, Mr. Martin had observed the weather minutely from a spot "about 16 miles North of Portland Lighthouse, in the open air, on a high commanding situation".[40] This was almost certainly Hardy's own favourite vantage-point of Rainbarrows on the heath, where the whole circuit of the horizon could be viewed. Here he made exact calculations, which seemed to show a constant pattern of atmospheric currents. He had been instructed in meteorology by Major-General Sir William Reid, who had developed a circular theory of hurricanes and published a book on it.[41] Mr. Martin now extended his purely local observations in Dorset by collating numerous log-books of ocean-going ships in files of the Board of Admiralty. He had easy access to these, since his wife's father and grandfather had both been admirals, and indeed the former had suggested this study.[42] He emerged with, in his own words, "a settled conviction that . . . THE LAW OF STORMS is Universal, Semper, Ubique, et ab omnibus".[43] He demonstrated this theory in a book privately printed at Kingston House in 1852, which claimed to show a system by which the

main storm tracks of the North Atlantic could be charted, their course
forecast, and shipwrecks obviated; and though a companion volume,
which he announced, on the Indian Ocean was apparently never printed,
his original volume gained him scientific notice when he came to London
in 1853. In 1857, he was elected a Fellow of the Royal Geographical
Society, his proposer being none other than the President of the Royal
Society.[44] As for his wife, she had a fashionable connection with
literature of the day in her much-younger cousin, Hamilton Aidé, a
most popular if now-forgotten novelist. It was on the doorstep of this
distinguished pair that Hardy found himself standing one summer day
in London. One does not know if he had done his homework, and read
Mr. Martin's treatise. It is tempting to see the observations of the
heavens by the young astronomer in *Two on a Tower* as some parallel to
Mr. Martin's activities—he was at least five years younger than his wife.
Again, though Hardy certainly did not need a rich amateur meteorologist for his knowledge of the Dorset weather, the strange fluctuations
of the path of the storm in *The Hand of Ethelberta*, which the heroine
watches as "typical of her own fortunes", have their likeness to some
of Mr. Martin's exact descriptions. At all events, when the door of 14
Bruton Street opened, it was a pleasure for him to see William Henry
Adams, the butler from Blandford whom he had known in the Kingston
Maurward days.[45] He at least was unchanged. "But", as Hardy afterwards remarked in mock-comic dismay, "the lady of his dreams—alas!'
Hardy's reminiscences here adopt the obliquity of reference that always
afflicts him when any topic becomes acutely embarrassing. One can only
guess that this reunion of the young man of twenty-two and the lady of
fifty-two was somehow like the eventual meeting of Ellen Terry and
Bernard Shaw, and even more disparate as to age. Hardy implies that
she was very much "altered", being now in her early fifties, and that she
was embarrassed by meeting "a young man of over twenty-one, who was
very much of a handful in comparison with the rosy-cheeked, innocent
little boy she had almost expected 'Tommy' to remain."[46] On the other
hand, on his own evidence, he was still absurdly youthful-looking, and
extremely innocent. He did not respond to her invitation to come again
to her house, though he still had day-dreams of love-passages with her.[47]
It is more than probable that much of the embarrassment was on his
side, and had to do with her social status, even more obvious in London
than it had been down in Dorset. His flight from her, cloaked by his off-
hand remarks about his own "fickleness", may have been a panic
action, and may indeed have lost him some of the professional advantages he needed as an architect. Her cousin, Hamilton Aidé, was not
only a popular novelist; he was a lifelong friend and exact contemporary
of Hardy's boss, Arthur Blomfield.[48] To be in Mrs. Martin's "set" would
have given Hardy the social entrée that he afterwards said he lacked in

his profession. At all events, any such opportunity was soon lost; for the Martins gave up their London house a year later.[49]

That it was some sort of flight is suggested by another incident later in the summer. One of Hardy's many girl cousins, Martha Mary Sparks, was now a ladies' maid in Paddington.[50] Early in August, Hardy sought her out, and took her for an evening to the International Exhibition.[51] The setting was not by any means a purely cultural one, in spite of Hardy's insistence on self-improvement. The fountains wafted a highly-scented spray all over the passers-by, the French Court was adorned with "two lifesize female figures, . . . in which bronze for the limbs & alabaster for the garments are combined in a manner quite unique".[52] Crowds gathered before the Tinted Venus, a piece of coloured sculpture by the veteran John Gibson, pupil of Canova and Thorwaldsen. Hardy had a romantic setting in which to entertain a young woman of his own class. According to her own brother,[53] he became attracted by her, just as he had been by her elder sister Rebecca, and more deeply. He even, at some unspecified time, wanted to marry her, but her mother barred the way. Martha herself was nearly six years older than Hardy; but this was perhaps part of the attraction. All the girls had the features of the Hand family, and therefore of Hardy's own mother. More than most mother-fixed youths, Hardy was falling in love with his own mother over and over again, in a physical and consistent way that was a typical part of his almost literal-minded nature. Besides, at this time Martha represented a welcome break in the alarming class-barriers of London.

We should know more about these aspects of Hardy if we could possibly find means to interpret the extraordinary "Diagrams shewing Human Passion, Mind, & Character—Designed by *Thos Hardy*. 1863". In these tree-like and snake-like pencilled constructions, often like designs by William Blake, it seems clear that the Passions are central, the pith of the whole growth. As the three elements come together, "Impossible Monster of the Will", "Impossible Monster of Intellect", and "Impossible Monster of the Passions", the last-named seems to gather itself into some kind of nuclear cluster. After an amalgamation of all three, there is a section marked "Moral Harmony", which then seems to produce various "Affectives Dominant", such as Friendship, Love, Ambition, and so on, of which only one, the Familial, appears to be adorned in any way, with curious-looking fruiting buds or flower-heads. Whether this really represents Hardy's intense familial sense, even to the exact interpretation of his apparently automatic reaction of falling in love with his cousins, is extremely difficult to say; but some such clue may very well lie in this strange exercise, which he evidently thought worth preserving among his notebooks,[54] though it may also be his attempt to reproduce pictorially "The Passional Tree" from a book known to him, *The Passions of the Soul* by Charles Fourier.[55]

We are on more certain ground in the events of his life that concern the "affectives" of friendship and of ambition. Both these received an addition in November 1862. In this month, his friend Horace Moule was admitted to the Middle Temple, and could be expected more in London.[56] Indeed, he had visited Hardy the previous August, and taken him out to dinner at the Old Hummums Hotel in Covent Garden, where he used to stay while in Town.[57] Also in November, Hardy himself was elected a member of the progressive Architectural Association, proposed by Blomfield, its president.[58] He had decided to enter for the silver medal of the Royal Institute of British Architects, and had chosen to write his essay "On the Application of Coloured Bricks and Terra Cotta to Modern Architecture", the title being picked from the four set by the Council of the R.I.B.A. for their annual competition.[59] It is possible that Blomfield, who had just built a church at Shoreditch of red, yellow, and blue bricks, guided his choice, and helped his work,[60] while he himself continued to gather material for it from his reading in the South Kensington Museum. Early in 1863, too, Blomfield's expanding practice made him move office; and by February, Hardy, the other assistants, the pupils, with masses of drawings and papers, were in 8 Adelphi Terrace. A few weeks later,[61] Hardy moved his own lodgings. The far side of Kilburn was proving too distant for his many activities. He went to 16 Westbourne Park Villas, in the parish of St. Stephen, a church where, from some of his earliest weeks in London, he had attended services.[62] Though it was still a fair way, he could now walk to the office. The exact reason for his choice of lodging is not known. One curious feature in this choice is that Westbourne Park Villas was, at that time, a fairly select social area, and not the row of Paddington lodging houses it later became. Only at the far end, a long distance away from No. 16, had the lodging houses just begun to sprout. Otherwise it was a street of middle-class professional people, civil servants and stockbrokers, or retired ladies and gentlemen living on investments.[63] There was a flourishing school for young gentlemen. No. 16 did not apparently normally take lodgers, and the owner seems to have been a gentleman of independent means. One possible clue is that the house next door, No. 18, contained an elderly architect, Richard Armstrong, and his son, who was an architect's pupil, though not one of Blomfield's. There is the curious fact that the father, and later the son, did architectural work for a brother of the new owner of Kingston Maurward House.[64] No. 16 was a pleasant, countrified semi-detached villa, with a small oak tree in the front garden.[65] Hardy must have found considerable comfort in his new digs; but he seems also to have found considerable loneliness, lacking the fellow-lodgers of a normal lodging-house: no more duet-playing and mutual reading.

7

Self-help

THE new office was an instant success. Larger and south-facing, it also afforded exhilarating surroundings. Hardy drew and studied just inside the easternmost window on the first floor. When he felt idle, he went out on the iron balcony and looked along the river below. The natural shores of the Thames were not yet obscured by the new Embankment, though the works were due to start. Wharves and shipping still made the West End of London like some West Country sea-port. There was even one small dock, just below where he stood, an old quay by the side of it with some eighteenth-century buildings. These contained a little counting-house and a range of sheds with rough blackened timber and old dun-coloured tiles. Casks and kegs heaped the quay, and brightly-painted barges with reddish-brown sails lay at anchor.[1] With its sailor-like men coming and going, it could have been Weymouth. Hardy described it with enthusiasm to his sister Mary, now in her first teaching post at Denchworth village school, near Wantage in Berkshire.

The new quarters had their effect on the assistants and pupils in the office, now more light-hearted than ever. These cheerful iconoclasts scrawled caricatures on the white marble mantelpieces, with which the brothers Adam had provided the elegant rooms. An extreme splinter-group of the philosophical radical movement, the Reform League, had its offices on the ground floor below. Well-known left-wing characters could be seen coming and going. The architectural pupils, "Tory and Churchy" as Hardy said, decided to torment these worthies. They resorted to one of the oldest schoolboy ploys, letting down, on a string, little bits of paper inscribed with ironical and ribald satire to dangle on the heads of the reformers. The joke went so far that they eventually had to apologize to the secretary, though the matter was kept from Blomfield's ears. Hardy, a reader of the right-wing *Saturday Review*, and himself never keen on doctrinaire reform, seems to have enjoyed this upper-class activity.[2] His closer companions, though, were two young men from Benjamin Ferrey's office nearby, named Molsey and Paris. They were perhaps more of his own social class, and he lunched and dined with them frequently at Bertolini's Restaurant in St. Martin's Street, a picturesque old house with sanded stone floors.

He was, of course, intensely busy. The result of the R.I.B.A. prize essay competition was due to be announced some time in March 1863.

In the meantime, he decided to put in, by the twenty-seventh of that month, a design for a prize offered by William Tite, the architect of the Royal Exchange, who was largely concerned with the plans for the coming Embankment. The set subject was a design for a country mansion. With memories of his father's work, and his own memories of Kingston Maurward revived by his encounter with the former Lady of the Manor, Hardy found this a congenial task. A grandiose scheme, which still exists, very neatly drawn on a page in his notebook, may represent his entry. It indicates his interests that a very large library leads off the spacious entrance-hall. Ironically, on the page opposite he drew plans for "Labourers Cottages—4 under one roof at £80 each".[3]

As usual he was reading intensely, and enjoying discussions with Horace Moule, when the latter came up from Dorchester to eat dinners at the Middle Temple. Moule was suffering from one of his periodic attacks of nervous depression, which he put down to overwork and wrong hours, though the causes may have been deeper. He was now contributing regularly to *The Saturday Review*, and was also preparing a topical lecture to deliver in Dorchester, based on former Princes of Wales and marriages with Danish princesses.[4] Hardy's entry of Princess Alexandra's name in his copy of *The Christian Year* shows that the forthcoming royal wedding was much in his mind too.[5] A tremendous procession through the streets of London was planned for the actual day of the wedding, 10 March. The public, kept short of such occasions for over a year by the Queen's determined and prolonged mourning, responded hysterically. The crowds got out of hand, and Hardy had a lucky escape. He left the Mansion House area before the greatest crush there began. Spectators saw a woman carried out above the heads of the mass, and at first assumed she was drunk;[6] but she, and five others with her, proved to be dead. Hardy's friends, Paris and Molsey, were trapped here, and scarcely expected to get out alive. Hardy by that time had got back to the West End, having planned his walk in the reverse direction from most people. Even so, he was caught at the bottom of Bond Street, his waistcoat buttons torn off his small frame, and his ribs bruised before he managed to slip into a doorway out of the mob.[7]

By April he had received a boost to his self-esteem. Both of his current "*Ventures*", as Horace Moule called them, had succeeded. His design for the country mansion received the small Tite prize, and the R.I.B.A. awarded him their silver medal for his essay. He received this at the Institute's headquarters in Conduit Street from the hands of George Gilbert Scott. Hardy had studied Scott's own work on a visit in 1861 to Cattistock church,[8] where the London architect had added a south aisle with a polygonal apse in early thirteenth-century style, having found traces of an unusual medieval apse there already.[9] This presentation, on 18 May, was not without its ironic side. According to one authority, the judges' approval of this essay as "a very fair one" was accompanied by some criticism.

> The author of this essay has scarcely gone sufficiently into the subject proposed, and that portion referring to moulded and shaped bricks has scarcely been noticed.

They therefore could not recommend that the money prize of £10, which should have accompanied the medal, should be awarded. Hardy does, however, seem to have received some sort of consolation prize, in the shape of books on Gothic Architecture by Norman Shaw and William Nesfield.[10]

One does not quite know how this somewhat condescending verdict may have affected Hardy; in the reminiscences of his old age he takes care not to mention it. He does, however, say that at this point he began to be disillusioned with the type of architectural training he was getting, mere mechanical drawing: and, perhaps more significantly, that he had no ability for "pushing his way into influential sets", which might lead to a profitable practice. After a year in London, he was finding himself up against the class barrier that forms such a part of his earlier novels. Such was the snobbery in the professions at this time that he might have received the money prize without question if he had belonged to the right public school and university background; the judges felt free to teach a lesson to the unconnected young man from the country. At all events, Hardy dates from this time his return to literature and reading, which was in full swing by the end of the year. He had paid what was always for him a reviving visit to his sister Mary at Denchworth, and on 26 April had sketched her school there, nestling against the village church and graveyard.[11] Her simple admiration for a genius brother with his knowledge of Greek and Latin, a wonder she maintained till her old age, gave him the confidence his diffident nature always needed. According to his second wife, Hardy spent the smaller money prize which he was allowed to receive, the William Tite award of £3, on buying a set of Buckley's translations of the Greek dramatists in the Bohn Library series.[12] His annotations to these books belong to a much later date, but it does seem likely that here was the turning-point when Hardy took up again his systematic self-improving reading in all subjects. He bought the complete works of Shakespeare in a ten-volume edition, and by the autumn he was helping himself to take notes by teaching himself shorthand from Harding's *Universal Stenography*.[13]

Hardy, of course, turned in any matter of intellect to Horace Moule down in Dorchester, and the two kept up a regular exchange of ideas by letter. Moule was now writing steadily for the *Saturday Review*, and his application and conscientious reading made him a useful reviewer of all types of books. He did not adopt, except in minor details, the slashing and destructive style of the rest of the paper. His notices are always kindly and considered, if firm. In this, he is most unlike the character Hardy is sometimes said to have based on him, Knight, the literary critic in *A Pair of Blue Eyes*. For instance, Moule actually directed Hardy's attention to his review, on 21 February 1863, of the posthumous stories by Hugh Miller. Miller, like Hardy, was a working-class man, and a stone-mason who had literally carved out a reputation for himself with his geological essays, the classic *Old Red Sandstone*. Moule perhaps asked Hardy to look at the review because it contained a message for himself. "Self-education", wrote Moule sympathetically of Miller, "is probably, at the best of times, a great deal harder than most of us are disposed to imagine", though he goes on to chide Miller gently for having written too much. Another review by Moule, a fortnight later, which he also recommended to Hardy, was of a book on the claims of canal or railway to cross Panama; here the detailed background reading Moule had obviously put in was itself a lesson to Hardy.[14]

By June, therefore, Hardy was fully absorbed in the passion of self-education. His view of intellectual matters, which in some ways he retained to the end of his life, was that anything and everything could be learnt, if one used the right books and took enough trouble. Even style and technique in English literature was something which could be got up from a text book, as a schoolchild gets up set homework. One only needed to find the correct text books. He therefore applied himself to the popular books and anthologies of English literary extracts. Following the recommendations in these, he proceeded systematically to analyse the style of the leader-writers in *The Times*, and to send his conclusions to Horace Moule in Dorchester. Moule, perhaps a little alarmed by such sorcerer's apprentice activity, sent a reply,[15] striking a warning note which is of great interest when applied to Hardy's later work. While admiring these analyses, he did not feel they led to much real appreciation of style; such formulae only led to a superficial view. Real style lay in the thoughts of a writer, and a real appreciation of his style lay in a full understanding of his thoughts. One's own style likewise emerged from one's essential thought. He advised Hardy to take a subject, and then jot down every thought on it that occurred to him, "just *as* they occur", without any reference to logical order. Next day or next time, Hardy could arrange the thoughts into headings, and then have the basis for a piece of writing in which the prime motive had been thought, and not merely external style. His warning against inserting from others "some felicitous methods or phrases" was one which Hardy might have remembered more often when he began to write novels, in which odd bits of learned comparison or imagery are so often tacked on with ludicrous effect, destroying instead of completing the point he is trying to make.

Hardy was still very much Moule's pupil. The letters, with all their affectionate endings, are those of a university tutor to an undergraduate, and this correspondence was, as it turned out, Hardy's university. Early in the next year, 1864, the book that Hardy buys, though still in a sense another text book, is significantly titled *Thoughts from Latin Authors*.[16] Moule's advice on the importance of thought in literature was so well assimilated that, exactly two years after Moule's letter, on 2 July 1865, Hardy was applying its precepts to one of Moule's own heroes:

Worked at J. H. Newman's *Apologia*, which we have all been talking about lately. A great desire to be convinced by him, because Moule likes him so much. Style charming, and his logic really human, being based not on syllogisms but on converging probabilities. Only—and here comes the fatal catastrophe—there is no first link to his excellent chain of reasoning, and down you come headlong . . .[17]

Hardy's notes on Newman's *Apologia*, which still exist,[18] bear out how well he has mastered this method of reading and criticism. They almost entirely concentrate on the stages of Newman's thought, hardly quoting and extracting from any of his brilliance of style or phrase.

What was Hardy to do with this new burst of intellectual activity? It clearly made him less and less able to think of himself as an architect; although he went on at the office, he began to consider this only a nominal activity, "an awful imposter at that, really", he said later.[19] Moule began to suggest that Hardy might follow his own footsteps, and go in for some sort of mild journalism. It indicates his tutorial estimate of Hardy's mind that he never thought of Hardy as a fellow-contributor to the *Saturday Review*, that province of those with university privileges and attainments. An architectural critic, using his specialized knowledge, was one suggestion. Another, in a letter early in 1864,[20] was the rather mundane one that Hardy could turn a useful guinea by being the local correspondent for London affairs to some provincial paper, like the *Dorset County Chronicle*—"Yr. chatty description of the Law Courts & their denizens is just in the style that wd. go down". One may wonder how much Moule's informal tutorship both helped and hampered Hardy's development. On the one hand, there were certainly appreciation and encouragement: "I cannot say enough in praise of yr. analyses. They *must* do your head good". Yet, so often, there is the almost embarrassed tone of a mind adapting itself to a less able one. The letter which suggests the job of provincial journalistic correspondent for Hardy is mainly concerned with a text book exposition of how to use the subjunctive properly. Though it is clearly a reply to an enquiry by Hardy on this topic, the fact that Hardy could not decide without applying to his mentor shows lack of confidence. When Hardy himself plays the instructor to his sister Mary by commenting on Thackeray's novels, he writes[21]

> He is considered to be the greatest novelist of the day—looking at novel writing of the highest kind as a perfect and truthful representation of actual life—which is no doubt the proper view to take . . . People say it is beyond Mr. Thackeray to paint a perfect man or woman—a great fault if novels are intended to instruct, but just the opposite if they are to be considered merely as Pictures. Vanity Fair is considered one of his best.

The interest of these opinions lies in their diffident expression. Hardy was not writing for publication, nor in a letter that might be handed round. Yet the tone is as though someone were looking over his shoulder, and the frequent qualifications sound as if he were expressing not his individual views, but what he had been told was correct by someone else. "He is considered"—"if they are to be considered"—"is considered"—all these phrases seem to shift the burden of judgement into more experienced hands. Hardy's natural uncertainty was increased by the unseen censorship of habitually submitting his opinions to Moule.

Another very curious indication of the same diffidence is that, as far as can be found, Hardy in the 1860s never visited either Oxford or Cambridge. In the same letter to his sister, he notes that she herself has visited Oxford twice already from her Berkshire village of Denchworth, and remarks, with what sounds like affected casualness, "It must be a jolly place. I shall try to get down there some time or other". There is, indeed, a persistent legend that Hardy had a hand in the building of the Radcliffe Chapel at Oxford by Blomfield in 1864;[22] but on examination, there seems to be no evidence for this, and much to the contrary. Apart from people who say that he "must have" done so, because of the Oxford scenes in *Jude the Obscure*, the idea relies on a misreading of Hardy's introduction to this novel. He wrote, "The scenes were revisited in October 1892", with exact precision as to the month. In October 1892, he revisited the village of Fawley and its neighbourhood in Berkshire, where, in fact, many of the major scenes in the novel do take place. He did not visit Oxford, apparently for the first time, until June 1893.[23]

Nor did he visit Cambridge in the 1860s. He may not have liked to ask Horace Moule to take him to the scene of the latter's academic failure; but from 1865, he had an opportunity through another member of the Moule family. In that year, Horace Moule took over the post of classical master at Marlborough.[24] He did so in succession to his brother Charles Walter Moule, who left for Cambridge to take up a Fellowship at Corpus Christi College there. Charles Walter Moule was well enough known to Hardy to warrant a visit to that university too; but again Hardy did not go. For a young assistant in Gothic architecture to avoid either place suggests some feeling of social or intellectual inadequacy in Hardy. It may be that he was even now, in some sense, his own Jude, and that this feeling of mental inferiority was an unconscious legacy from Moule. Then, too, there was Moule's own position. In spite of his connections with both places, he still had no degree from either university. There was some element of Jude there too; and Hardy must have pondered on the strange anomaly of his friend's unsatisfactory career. Moule's own family loyally supported the idea that he was prevented from taking a degree for so long "by stiff mathematical requirements that were shortly to be modified".[25] Yet in actual fact, these requirements, similar to those that had prevented the poet Wordsworth from obtaining a fellowship, had already been abolished at Cambridge by the time Moule should have taken his degree.[26] There are already hints of a greater mystery in the life of this man, who had such a dominant influence on Hardy at this time, though their contact lessened with Moule's job at Marlborough. Busy at schoolmastering from 1865, Moule had time only for occasional visits to London, to stay at the New Hummums Hotel in Covent Garden, and to go to the neighbouring Opera House with Hardy.[27] His bouts of depression, drink, and suicidal thoughts were by now established;[28] but it seems possible that in 1865–66 a new and alarming fact also entered his life. This was probably not fully revealed to Hardy till much later, though the enigmatic early sonnet "A Confession to a Friend in Trouble" may refer to it. The shadowed life of the man who meant so much to him was an added cause for disillusion in Hardy.

The stress and uncertainty for Hardy of these years, 1863 and 1864, should not, however, be exaggerated, though it is significant that on 31 July 1863 he underlined the text, "The spirit truly is ready but the flesh is weak".[29] Dissatisfied and feeling his way, he still had much to satisfy him and keep him in a more healthy mood. One factor was the reinforcement of his home and his family. Hardy renewed his country roots by going home regularly every Christmas, as did many of his relatives, including his sister Mary. At Christmas 1863, he anticipated having "a bit of a lark" down in Dorset with her.[30] The lark included a great deal of visiting and gossip and drinking all around Stinsford and Puddletown. At Christmas 1864, Hardy spent the afternoon and evening of Boxing Day with his cousin Nathaniel Sparks, back from his carpenter's job in Somerset. The Sparks home was much as it had been before, and Hardy was clearly welcomed there, in spite of his earlier contretemps with Rebecca. The youngest daughter, Tryphena, was continuing to show promise at the Athelhampton school, where she had been a monitor, helping to teach the younger children, since summer 1862. A sampler which she had lately worked, showing all the counties of England and Wales, demonstrated that like her eldest sister Rebecca she was becoming a good needlewoman. Hardy also saw his other cousins, the Antells, and spent some time in the company of a young schoolmaster, Arthur Brett, who like himself and Mary was spending Christmas holidays in his native Dorset.[31] The restraining hand of Squire Brymer was as yet not too heavy on Puddletown, and public-house drinking and family parties were in full swing all over Christmas.

These family contacts were clearly more real to Hardy than the varied but somehow unsatisfactory life in London, what he himself called "the fitful yet mechanical and monotonous existence that befalls many a young man in London lodgings".[32] His life was always coloured not only by the living personal presence of relatives and friends, but by the mysteries and obscure, often horrifying hints from the past and the dead. It was only seven years since his paternal grandmother, Mary Head Hardy, had died in the Bockhampton house, with her strange and hardly spoken childhood history at Fawley in Berkshire. Now Mary Hardy, her namesake, was teaching at Denchworth, a few miles north of Wantage. The hamlet of Fawley lay due south of Wantage, tucked among the fine escarpments of the Ridgeway and the Berkshire downs. Early in May 1864, Mary Hardy, obviously prompted by her brother, set off to spend a sketching week-end there, and wrote him a full account.[33] She found it a pretty place, "up among the finest hills I ever saw. The people seem quite cut off from the rest of us . . . They are among the most original & hearty set ever could be I think". She questioned them, but could find no memories of her grandmother, though the name Head brought from the parish clerk a strange story of a farmer of that name in a nearby hamlet. He had left his bride on the day after their wedding, and was never heard of till he came back quite an old man and died at Fawley. This addition to the family mystery, and Mary's news that the old church was being pulled down and re-placed, sent Hardy himself there in the autumn. He made a small pencil sketch of Fawley old church,[34] similar to the drawing of Denchworth schoolhouse and church which he had made the previous year. Whether he had more success than his sister in finding their Head ancestors is uncertain. If he had, he would have found suggestions of a tragedy and an unexplained illegitimacy there, a hint of his grandmother's horror.

Family and personal history loomed far larger in his life than the general history of the world around him, even when this touched on essentially working-class issues, which might have seemed relevant to his own life. The only external event that seems to have excited him was, characteristically, the public hanging in 1864 of five men for piracy and murder.[35] The American Civil War of 1861 to 1865 finds not one single mention in all Hardy's writings; it is as if it had never occurred. Yet it was the subject on everybody's lips in all classes of society during these years. When the Lancashire mills were deprived, through the war, of raw cotton, over a million pounds relief was raised for the out-of-work cotton operatives, thought to be the largest sum ever contributed up to that time by voluntary effort. Yet none of this seems to have interested Hardy, nor even the whole question of slavery, although Horace Moule sent him in 1864 a pamphlet by the liberal reformer, Goldwin Smith,[36] a Christian Socialist document[37] of considerable power and rhetoric, condemning "that supreme tyranny of capital which makes its victims slaves".

Again in 1864, Garibaldi, the hero of revolutionary Italy, made his remarkable triumphal progress through London. According to one diarist,[38] this was "The greatest demonstration so far that I have beheld", and it has been said that up to the present time, there has never been another like it.[39] One great feature of this was that, as *The Times* said, it was "a working-men's reception from first to last".[40] Another was that it was almost incredibly orderly, and the police had nothing to do. The contrast with the murderous hysteria of the Royal wedding crowds a year before was amazing. There was neither drunkenness, theft, nor a single serious accident. It was perhaps the most successful and peaceful working-class demonstration in the whole of the century. Yet again Hardy ignores it totally.

It is possible that he was so absorbed in his own affairs that he was not there to see it. On the day that Garibaldi's ship entered the Solent, 3 April 1864, Hardy was at St. Peter's Church, Brighton.[41] In spite of quite unsupported conjectures that he was there to take the sea-breezes for his health,[42] his obvious architectural goal was this remarkable church itself, which Sir Charles Barry had designed—winning an open competition—when he was still under thirty. This was a natural source of inspiration for a young Gothic architect.[43] At this time, it still had the polygonal apse, similar to that which Hardy had seen in George Gilbert Scott's work at Cattistock. For all the deprecating tone of his reminiscences, it is clear that at this time Hardy was still taking his work as an architect seriously, even though it may have been becoming irksome. His notebook shows a full awareness of all the exciting new developments in the world of building, some of which were taking place only a short distance from the offices in Adelphi Terrace. The new Charing Cross Station which opened on 11 January 1864, obliterating the old Hungerford Market, was generally reckoned to be a disaster, and a gloomy forerunner of utilitarian buildings without any sense of beauty.[44] Yet the Strand Music Hall, afterwards the Gaiety Theatre, which opened further along the Strand nine months later, was quite another matter, and of great interest to Hardy. Its much-criticized design by E. Bassett Keeling had individuality, and a novel use of modern materials, influencing later building, and fascinating Hardy. Its roof was constructed of wrought iron and zinc, and its cast iron columns had copper foliations to their capitals. Hardy, who often passed it, copied a part of a description of it from *The Building News*, and noted minute details, in which comparatively new materials were used to cope with some of the stresses of traffic, dirt, and other hazards of modern life.[45] He paid special attention to the bedding of the coloured glass sheets, in their zinc frames, on to india rubber, "thus facilitating the removal of the glass for cleaning, overcoming the difficulty of expansion & contraction, & obviating by the india r. beds liability to breakage or vibration", while in another place,[46] he noted from *The Builder* the durable qualities of the zinc, "abt. 35 years". Here was utility and use of manufactured materials that did not have to be brutal or unaesthetic, an architecture that kept pace with both modern life and older values. This idea runs through all Hardy's novels to *Jude*, and is exemplified in *A Laodicean* (1880). In this novel, Hardy said, he put more of his past life than he had done in any other up to that time, and for his architect-hero he coins the term "technicist" to express his ideal, the union of the technologist and the artist.[47]

At the end of 1864, Hardy seemed to be at some sort of spiritual cross-roads. Still technically absorbed by architect's work, revived in self-improving literature; still "churchy"—he seems to record attending Communion in Westminster Abbey in summer 1863 and other churches in 1864—and perhaps slower to adopt advanced ideas than has generally been thought; still waiting for his "appointed time" and the "still small voice" of his favourite passages in the Bible; beginning, as he had written a year before to his friend Bastow, to consider "the pen as one of his weapons" in his "*struggle for life*".

8

Poetry

ON 21 SEPTEMBER 1864, Thomas Hardy had his head examined by a phrenologist. The "science" of phrenology, having had its heyday in the first half of the century, was now in decline, although it still had many advocates, notably George Eliot, Charles Dickens, and Harriet Martineau. It was categorized by Leslie Stephen as "popular with the half-educated", and indeed occupied much space in the type of self-educating journals read by Hardy. By the 1860s it was beginning to be rejected by scientists, and to fall into the hands of unqualified self-styled "professors". To one of these, Professor C. Donovan, M.A., 111 The Strand, Hardy submitted his bumps. He received a detailed report, long afterwards rescued by his mother from an old coat pocket. The three dozen "Faculties", into which the report is divided, animal, moral, and intellectual, often appear contradictory. It seems strange that those of Destructiveness and Constructiveness should both be "large". Among Hardy's intellectual faculties, it is interesting to note, Tune and Language are similarly labelled "large".[1] Although presumably the Professor did not know it, Hardy was on the brink of becoming an author.

On 18 March 1865, he contributed to *Chambers's Journal* a short humorous article, originally written to amuse Blomfield's pupils, entitled "How I Built Myself a House", for which he received £3. 15s. This little work, which has been heavily handled by some critics,[2] has great charm and is worth noticing. Parts of it are obviously imitative of his favourite writers of the day; the style of some of the opening sentences remind one of Thackeray, whose work Hardy had been recommending to his own sister:

> The new residence was to be right and proper in every respect. It was to be of some mysterious size and proportion, which would make us both peculiarly happy ever afterwards—that had always been a settled thing. It was neither to cost too much nor too little, but just enough to fitly inaugurate the new happiness. Its situation was to be in a healthy spot, on a stratum of dry gravel, about ninety feet above the springs. There were to be trees to the north, and a pretty view to the south . . .
>
> After a considerable time had been spent in these studies, I began to see that some of our intentions in the matter of site must be given up. The trees to the north went first. After a short struggle, they were

followed by the ninety feet above the springs. Sophia, with all wifely tenacity, stuck to the pretty view long after I was beaten about the gravel subsoil. In the end, we decided upon a place imagined to be rather convenient, and rather healthy, but possessing no other advantage worth mentioning . . .

This is very much in the manner of Thackeray's *The Book of Snobs*.

We were reading the passage lately at the house of my friend, Raymond Gray, Esquire, Barrister-at-Law, an ingenuous youth without the least practice, but who has luckily a great share of good spirits, which enables him to bide his time, and bear laughingly his humble position in the world. Meanwhile, until it is altered, the stern laws of necessity and the expenses of the Northern Circuit oblige Mr. Gray to live in a very tiny mansion in a very queer small square in the airy neighbourhood of Gray's Inn Lane.

As Hardy's effort proceeds to dialogue and character, the model is unashamedly Dickens. The client is taken by the builder's foreman up on the scaffolding to look at the chimneys:

Then a workman, with a load of bricks, stamped along the boards, and overturned them at my feet, causing me to shake up and down like the little servant-men behind private cabs. I asked, in trepidation, if the bricks were not dangerously heavy, thinking of a newspaper paragraph headed "Frightful Accident from an Overloaded Scaffold."
"Just what I was going to say. Dan has certainly too many there," answered the man. "But it won't break down if we walk without springing, and don't sneeze, though the mortar-boy's hooping-cough was strong enough in my poor brother Jim's case," he continued abstractly, as if he himself possessed several necks, and could afford to break one or two.

Yet there are individual touches of human observation which are quite Hardy's own. The swift financial calculations of the architect and his clerk, and his grasp of the lay-out of the building, so that "His professional opinions, propelled by his facts, seemed to float into my mind whether I wished to receive them or not" are all delicately and amusingly sketched. Over one human detail, Hardy was even more observant than he can have known. The plan of the house, when first marked out on the ground, looks so small, that although the clients "were told that houses always looked so", the wife insists the drawing-room must be lengthened. When Hardy architected his own house, Max Gate, just twenty years later, the rooms were found to be too small and dark, and extensions had to be built shortly after.[3] Even in miniature, Hardy already shows a grasp of human failings, including his own.

Hardy afterwards dismissed this small but successful exercise in comedy as "a trifle" and "unrepresentative".[4] The second description was not false modesty; for his mind was now set not on prose but on poetry. He was now evidently a kind of licensed literary feature of the office, a local pundit: a characteristic way for a shy youth to establish an individual position for himself. In this allowed character, he delivered half-hour orations on poets and poetry, whose burden was the superiority of poetry to prose; he even criticized Dickens, though at about this time, he was going to the great novelist's public readings. It is a mark of this new phase that in 1865 he began his own systematic self-education in poetry too. His markings in the *Golden Treasury* that Horace Moule had given him showed that what he mainly enjoyed were ballads and songs,[5] especially when they reminded him of his musical days in Dorset; Herrick's *Gather Ye Rosebuds* is annotated "My grandf[rs] song". There is also a habit, which was to become almost obsessive in his novels, that of comparison with well-known paintings. Against the lines from Gray's *The Progress of Poetry*,

> O'er her warm cheek and rising bosom move
> The bloom of young desire and purple light of Love

he made a note that they reminded him of an Etty nude, seen in the South Kensington Museum in 1863. He often was to quote the "purple light" in much this sense.

Such markings and stray preferences, however, were far too haphazard for someone consciously fitting himself to be a poet. In 1865, Hardy began what may be called his grand assault course on poetry. Like everything he did, it was thoroughly methodical; its concentration and detail remind one of another great self-educator of an earlier generation, John Keats. First, there were the basic tools of the trade. In quick succession, he bought *English Literature from Chaucer to Tennyson* by Henry Reed, P. A. Nuttall's *Standard Pronouncing Dictionary*, and, perhaps most practical of all, the *Rhyming Dictionary* by John Walker, edited and revised by J. Longmuir.[6] He is also said[7] to have possessed the recent *Manual of English Literature* by Matthew Arnold's brother Thomas. These were to be the guides to his new systematic ambition of reading and writing poetry. That he felt he needed such guides is shown by one of his markings in Reed's book. On page 11 of this work, there is the observation "It is a bewildering thing to stand in the presence of a vast concourse of books". Hardy put a marginal line alongside these words; they express the dilemma he faced.

Part of the trouble was the cost of this vast planned exploration of the poets. For Shakespeare, luckily, there were the cheap, popular seasons at Drury Lane. With one of Blomfield's more bookish pupils, Hardy managed always to be among the first in the crowded pit, leaning on the front barrier with only the theatre orchestra between him and the actors.[8] Here he saw *King John* and *Henry IV*, bringing to each play a good edition of the text, which he propped sideways in front of him to follow the speeches. In this way, he enjoyed the fine performances of Samuel Phelps, no longer actor-manager but still a great player, as Falstaff. If Hardy did not quite, like the architect-hero of his first published novel, "know Shakespeare to the very dregs of the footnotes", he certainly acquired a working familiarity with the text by this direct method. His later novels show a large number of references to both parts of *Henry IV*.[9]

Non-dramatic poetry was provided for him mainly by one of the many cheap editions of the time, Moxon's Popular Poets series. He had the works of Spenser, Milton, Herbert, and Thomson, with Butler's *Hudibras* and Percy's *Reliques*, in this handy form.[10] Of the Romantics, he bought and dated in this year an edition of Coleridge,[11] and he clearly already had an acquaintance with Wordsworth and Shelley through the *Golden Treasury*. Odd as it may seem, his annotations to these two are not matters of appreciation, but attempts to make their meaning clearer, a literal-minded way of treating poetry, which he retained to the end of his life.

There is no doubt, of course, that Hardy read Shelley at this time far more widely than in the limited selection of the *Golden Treasury*, though it was the lyric he annotated there, "O World! O Life! O Time!" that he later named as being one of the finest passages in all English poetry.[12] Hardy's first published novel is so packed with quotations from Shelley[13] that this poet must have been among his staple reading in the 1860s, just as a further burst of enthusiasm for his works in the 1890s left its mark everywhere in *Jude the Obscure* and in *The Well-Beloved*. J. M. Barrie, who saw and later owned the copy Hardy had used in his youth, said, "There are a hundred, a thousand, pencil marks on those two volumes that look now like love messages from the young poet of one age to the young poet of a past age".[14] Although Barrie may have been wrong in thinking all marks he saw were Hardy's youthful notes, since some passionate markings were probably inspired by Hardy's middle-aged fervour for Mrs. Florence Henniker, whom he called "the child of the Shelleyean tradition",[15] there is no doubt that Hardy read Shelley fervently in the 1860s too. He seems to have used two odd volumes.[16]

Luckily, one volume of Shelley that Hardy was reading in the 1860s still exists. It is a small one-volume edition, *Queen Mab and Other Poems*, bought and inscribed by Hardy in 1866.[17] His markings are numerous. Though many are linked with poetic appreciation, it is clear he is applying much of Shelley personally to himself and to his own life in London. Round the title of *The Revolt of Islam*, for example, he wrote the words "Hyde Park—morning", though one can only guess at the occasion prompting him. This poem, which remained an obsessive favourite all his life, clearly influenced his own work at this time. His marking of the heroine's resolution to share an "undivided tomb" with the hero is echoed in Hardy's poem "1967", written in the year 1867, although Hardy's imagery—"That thy worm should be my worm, Love!"—is that of Donne rather than of Shelley. His marking of *Prometheus Unbound* was specially extensive. In this, he paid detailed attention to passages of natural description, the exact effect of the interplay of natural forces, with which more modern appreciators of Shelley have been so concerned, the effects of wind upon water, of shadow upon light. These, continuously marked by him here, were afterwards used by him with the most complete mastery in poems such as *Beeny Cliff*. His final marking

> To love, and bear; to Hope till Hope creates
> From its own wreck the thing it contemplates

has much of the style and stoic philosophy of Hardy's own early poems.

As for Wordsworth, Hardy certainly bought a copy of his works during this time at Westbourne Park Villas;[18] but his reading of the famous preface to *Lyrical Ballads* seems to have come later. It does not seem that he was influenced yet by Wordsworth's theories of poetic diction, although in his middle age he wrote poems of an obviously Wordsworthian character, such as *The Widow Betrothed* and *A Sunday Morning Tragedy*. Although these later poems also remind one of Crabbe, whose works Hardy was reading in London, none of his own poems bears much resemblance, except perhaps in the "realism", which he himself said he learnt first from Crabbe.[19] On the other hand, his addiction to Scott as a poet dates from this time. He probably read him in another cheap edition, the one published by Routledge, and he set very high store by Scott's poems.[20] *Marmion*, in particular, became for him almost a touchstone for poetry, and it is somewhat surprising to find him afterwards using as a term of praise the astonishing statement that Homer "was very kin to *Marmion*".[21] His sympathy for Scott was probably heightened by the way the Scottish poet had retrieved the old Border ballads.

Among poets living and publishing in the 1860s, Browning is always cited as having the greatest influence on the early poems of Hardy;[22] but, on examination, this hardly seems to be so. Hardy's convolutions of style and syntax in these beginnings are peculiarly his own, and seem to owe nothing to Browning's daring effects of rhyme and grammatical order. Apart from two quotations from *The Statue and the Bust* in his first published novel, all Hardy's references to Browning come from much later in his life. So do those narrative poems which echo Browning in their abrupt and colloquial way of story-telling, and often in their choice of subject. Such are some of the historical poems that form a large part of Hardy's *Wessex Poems*, printed in 1898. The

earliest date to any one of this group, all clearly associated in style, is
1878. The only poem of the 1860s to show any marked influence by
Browning is the curious and unsatisfactory set of verses entitled *The
Two Men*. Here one has a typical Browning subject, the ironic contrast
between the careers of two schoolmates, and a typical Browning
opening stanza:

> There were two youths of equal age,
> Wit, station, strength, and parentage;
> They studied at the selfsame schools,
> And shaped their thoughts by common rules.

Its original title, *The World's Verdict: a morality rime*, also suggests
Browning; but apart from this, and perhaps the equally curious verses
written for Blomfield, *Heiress and Architect*, the influence of Browning
on Hardy's early poems seems negligible.

If Browning, among contemporaries, had little effect on him at this
time, still less had Tennyson. Yet poets for whom Hardy did have an
enthusiasm equally failed to affect his own style. In this year, 1865,
Swinburne's *Atalanta in Calydon* was published, and Hardy was one of
its earliest admirers. When this was followed in 1866 by *Poems and
Ballads*, Hardy used to walk from Westbourne Park Villas to the office
with a copy in his pocket, even reading it, as he said, "walking along
the crowded London streets to my imminent risk of being knocked
down".[23] In spite of this enthusiasm, and his indignation at the attacks
on Swinburne, which, as he also said, made his blood boil, there is not a
touch of Swinburne's style in his own work. He seems to have let the
liquid lyric gift wash over him in a tide of pure pleasure, without once
considering it as a model.

In actual fact, the one book of contemporary verse from which Hardy
seems to have learnt anything was George Meredith's *Modern Love*,
published in 1862. Hardy was unaffected in his admiration for this work
even when his own favourite *Saturday Review* launched its notorious
and violent attack on Meredith for writing it:[24]

> With the great literary error of *Don Juan* before his eyes, it was
> scarcely worth his while to commit the sickly little peccadillo of
> *Modern Love*.

It was probably the unfair abuse of this work, pilloried elsewhere as
"modern lust", that made Hardy give it special attention. It is certainly the major influence on Hardy's sonnets, which form at least half
of the poems he allowed to remain from these years in London. Yet even
here, there must be one reservation. Hardy's sonnets and the *Modern
Love* sequence have in common that both derive from Shakespeare.
Meredith disguised his debt by adding to his own "sonnets" two extra
lines, giving a breadth and rhetorical emphasis; he also—and here he

was followed by Hardy—used a variety of extended and non-Shakes-
pearian images, the type of language that, in its own day, could truly
be called "modern". It is sometimes the language of new, contemporary
thought—

> What are we first? First, animals; and next
> Intelligences at a leap;

More often it consists of similes which introduce a romantic and non-
Elizabethan touch into what seems a Shakespearian opening:

> Thus piteously Love closed what he begat;
> The union of this ever-diverse pair!
> These two were rapid falcons in a snare,
> Condemned to do the flitting of the bat.

Hardy, in his own sonnets, is not so skilful in escaping the purely
Shakespearian echo. These lines, written in the summer of 1866, could
have come straight from a Shakespeare sonnet:

> As common chests encasing wares of price
> Are borne with tenderness through halls of state,
> Their core their warrant,

One is instantly reminded of Sonnet 52:

> So is the time that keeps you as my chest,
> Or as the wardrobe which the robe doth hide,
> To make some special instant special blest,

Yet at other times he achieves, within the Shakespearian form, a
Meredithian freedom of imagery.

> Amid the happy people of my time
> Who work their love's fulfilment, I appear
> Numb as a vane that cankers on its point,
> True to the wind that kissed ere canker came:

or again, writing of an untoward thought,

> It goes, like murky bird or buccaneer
> That shapes its lawless figure on the main,

and, in some better-known lines in their earliest known version,

> Remembering that with me lies not the blame,
> That Sportsman Time but rears his brood to kill,

He also expresses the "modern" scepticism, common in Meredith:

> —Crass Casualty obstructs the sun and rain,
> And dicing Time for gladness casts a moan . . .

What certainly emerges, even from these smoother and more imitative
examples of Hardy's early poetry, is his intense and original treatment
of words. It is true that in what has been considered his most autobiographical novel, *A Laodicean*, he has a clumsy and jocular satire on

himself as a poet in his mid-twenties, when he describes his architect-hero's efforts at verse:

> For two whole years he did nothing but write verse in every conceivable metre, and on every conceivable subject, from Wordsworthian sonnets on the singing of his tea-kettle to epic fragments on the Fall of Empires.

Although the literal truth of the epic fragments on the Fall of Empires may be doubted, there is no doubt that, as he confesses elsewhere,[25] Hardy tried at this time to turn the Book of Ecclesiastes into Spenserian stanzas, an extraordinary task that fortunately defeated him before he had gone too far with it. In fact, the main tone of the surviving poems of these two years, 1865–67, is one of a fierce and determined individual concern with words. In this, they are unlike the early verses of any other writer. To be fascinated by words themselves is common with young poets; but to try and manipulate and vary them, until they form what is virtually a new language, is unique. Even Hardy's contemporary Hopkins, in poems written at this exact time, is not nearly as original, although drastic later revision to such poems as *Heaven-Haven* and *The Habit of Perfection* may make it appear that he was.[26]

Part of this determined originality can be seen in Hardy's copy of Walker's *Rhyming Dictionary*, which still exists.[27] Hardy not only took attractive rhyming words from the dictionary itself—"buccaneer", in the sonnet just quoted is probably one; he also set about enlarging the dictionary's list of rhymes with his own individual collection. These additions are interesting, first of all, in showing how he plundered for literary purposes the vocabulary of his own profession. A number of these are both architectural and "churchy". They include the words ogee, epistyle, peristyle, introit, and terce, the last further glossed by Hardy with the word "service" in brackets. The fact that he added some new words to existing lists of rhymes also gives an illuminating clue to his own pronunciation, which was not always in the standard English he afterwards claimed to use. "Groat" in his added annotation is given as a rhyme for "ought" and "bought". It is clear that he pronounced it "grought", as he had perhaps heard people do in Dorset.

In fact, the largest number of additional rhymes, recorded by Hardy as acceptable, are country or sometimes specifically Dorset words. It is clear that these were natural to him, and that he added them not as curiosities but for legitimate usage in his poetry. This is fully borne out in the paragraph, with which he prefaced, many years later, his first published book of verse:[28]

> Whenever an ancient and legitimate word of the district, for which there was no equivalent in received English, suggested itself as the most natural, nearest, and often only expression of a thought, it has been made use of, on what seemed good grounds.

This is the great difference between Hardy's poetic vocabulary and that of Barnes. Barnes is writing in a calculated dialect, observed by him as a philologist; this is why his Dorset poems, even at their best, have something of the air of an academic exercise. With Hardy, the use of a local word was, as he says, natural, and this is seen by the way he recorded such terms in his copy of the *Rhyming Dictionary*. Not all these terms, of course, were actually used in the poems of this date which have survived, attractive though some of them seem to us. One can only regret that he did not find use for "fellowfeel", meaning sympathize, or "palampore" for counterpane. On the other hand, the delightful "wanze" for grow pale, or decay, was effectively used by him in a much later poem, *The Beauty*.

It is true that sometimes, when he had used one of these words for a particular, and, as he would say, legitimate effect, he seems to have grown self-conscious and removed it in a later draft. An example of this is the first line of *The Temporary the All*, which begins *Wessex Poems*. This poem, although undated, seems obviously to come from the 1860s which it describes. For one thing, it is an essay in writing English Sapphics, a task almost as difficult as trying to turn Ecclesiastes into Spenserians, and typical of what Hardy tells us of his experiments at that period. It also uses a large number of local words, and, in fact, originally started with the line

Change and chancefulness in my bloothing youthtime

The bold oddity of "bloothing youthtime" appealed to Hardy in his early experimental stage, and in his *Rhyming Dictionary* he had added the word "Blooth", meaning bloom, to the rhymes there for "youth". When he came to print the poem thirty years later, however, Hardy seems to have felt he had gone too far in his first dashing enthusiasm, and substituted the innocuous but feeble "flowering".

What is perhaps most interesting of all, in the light it throws on one distinctive habit of Hardy's first poems, is the large number of words he added to the dictionary with what are, to us, unusual prefixes. Some are usages found in country places still. "Eachwhere", "everywhen" and especially "anywhen" can be heard today in south-west England. Less usual, possibly even in Hardy's own time, is his use of "fore" (with a hyphen) for "former". He added to the dictionary the words "fore-wife" and "fore-strife". Most significant for their use in the poems are the number of words he added with the prefixes "un" and "out", particularly the former. It seems clear from this that he did not regard the prefix "un" as implying a negative modification of the original word, but as the complete negation of it, and therefore an entirely separate word. In this sense, it is used freely throughout all his early poems. It appears again and again in the sonnets. "Unblooms" in the

1 (a) The Heath, near Hardy's birthplace, with a distant view of Dorchester

(b) The old West Gallery, Stinsford Church

Old West Gallery. Stinsford

2   (a) Hardy's maternal uncles, William, Henery, and Christopher Hand

(b) (left) Thomas Hardy senior

(c) (right) Hardy's aunt's husband, John Brereton Sharpe (possibly the original of Sergeant Troy)

(c) Aged 21

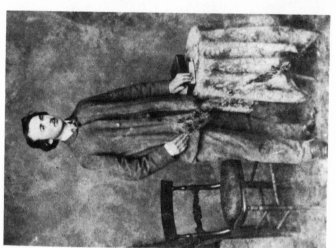

(b) Aged 19

(a) Aged 16

3   Young Thomas Hardy

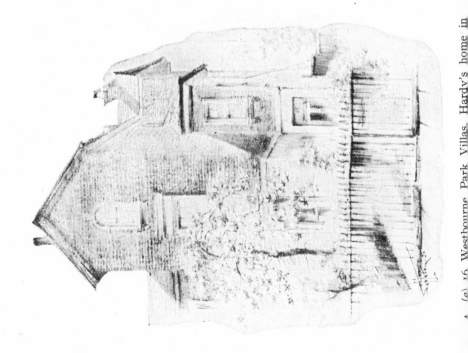

(a) 16 Westbourne Park Villas, Hardy's home in

5 The Moule family, Fordington, Dorchester; Hardy's friend Horace Moule against the centre window

(a) Hardy's mother (née Jemima Hand)   (b) Tryphena Sparks

6 Hardy's mother and his cousins, the Sparks girls

(c) Rebecca Sparks   (d) Martha Sparks

7   Three capitals in Turnworth Church, designed by Thomas Hardy, 1869

(*a*) The Promenade

8   Two views of Weymouth as Hardy knew it

(*b*) Sandsfoot Castle

sonnet *Hap* is used in the sense of "never blooms" (not of having bloomed and then having ceased to bloom). "Unknows" in the sonnet *At a Bridal* is used in the sense of "never knows": and there are many others. This most characteristic, and incidentally most parodied, aspect of Hardy's poetry is shown by his dictionary markings to be a totally natural form of expression in his own habitual mind.

It is true, of course, that he probably used this and similar forms to achieve an effect of terseness and brevity in his verse, and to avoid a Tennysonian lushness so popular at that time. Once again, this can be deduced from other books that Hardy was conscientiously reading and marking, in his poetic self-education. In his copy of the collected poems of Coleridge, bought in 1865, Hardy underlined in the preface a passage[29] where Coleridge attacks "the sleek favourites of fortune", and this probably includes in his mind those whose verse can also be regarded as sleek: for in his copy of Reed's *English Literature*, he took a passage quoted from one of those favourites of fortune of his own time, Elizabeth Barrett Browning, and wrote in the margin the critical comment "not terse enough".[30] Hardy, then, was drawn to uncompromising brevity and compression. It is the style in which nearly all his early poems are written; yet it is, as now seems, a style that was not self-consciously adopted, but derived from a language and usage natural to him. The only exceptions to this rule are the two surviving narrative poems of 1866. These tell a story in a much looser metre and style, and they are both, quite openly, in Dorset dialect. They are also both extremely funny. The humour and observation of his *Chambers's Journal* article have found their way into these riotous excursions into rustic satire, *The Ruined Maid* and *The Bride-Night Fire*. Both deal with familiar village-ballad figures, the seduced village-maiden, who has done very well out of the experience,[31] and the young girl who manages, by luck, to escape going to bed with an old husband.

It is as well to remember that Hardy's early verses contain these two delightful, successful and light-hearted story poems, since practically all the rest of his poems at this time are in some way flawed, and their tone almost universally sombre. Though there are fine moments in nearly every poem, each one has lines that show Hardy's inexperience at this stage. The line already quoted from the sonnet *Hap*,

> And dicing Time for gladness casts a moan,

is not only clumsy but obscure—one has to substitute "in place of" for the word "for" to make any sense of it.[32] Another powerful sonnet, *Discouragement*, has an odd cliché in the seventh line,

> Over her purposed genial hour a chill,

which has often been criticized.[33] The modernisms of Hardy's time do not always succeed. It is a little absurd that the creator of the universe, in the sonnet *To an Impersonator of Rosalind*, is credited with having had "telescopic sight". The pomposity of "junctive law", meaning marriage or love, spoils the close of another moving sonnet, *Revulsion*. In the lyric *Amabel*, which is itself something of an exercise in rhyming on the name of the title, one of Hardy's attempts is

> All find in dorp or dell
> An Amabel.

The obvious dragged-in rhyme of "dell" is accentuated by the odd archaic "dorp", a word probably got by Hardy from his newly-bought copy of Dryden.[34]

Yet out of these two years of trial and error, there emerged one almost totally perfect poem, one of the finest and most moving in the language. It often happens that in a cluster of early work, a poet will suddenly anticipate his more mature and assured style in a completely unforeseen way. One thinks of Keats's sonnet, *On First Looking into Chapman's Homer*, a swan among the ducklings of his first book of verse. In exactly the same way, Hardy's poem *Neutral Tones* stands out from the thirty-odd poems of 1865–67. It was written in his lodgings at Westbourne Park Villas in the later part of his two-year stint of verse, some time in the first half of 1867;[35] it therefore may be thought to have gained from the cumulative efforts of the previous two years. Yet, on any account, it is a startling achievement, in what, as far as can be gathered, is its first version.[36]

> We stood by a pond that winter day,
> And the sun was white, as though chidden of God,
> And a few leaves lay on the withered sod;
>   —They had fallen from an ash, and were grey.
>
> Your eyes on me were as eyes that rove
> Over tedious riddles solved years ago;
> And some words played between us to and fro
>   On which was more wrecked by our love.
>
> The smile on your mouth was the deadest thing
> Alive enough to have strength to die;
> And a grin of bitterness swept thereby
>   Like an ominous bird a-wing. . . .
>
> Since then, keen lessons that love deceives,
> And wrings with wrong, have shaped to me
> Your face, and the God-curst sun, and a tree,
>   And a pond edged with greyish leaves.

This poem is uniquely Hardy's own. It is true, though not previously noticed, that there are superficial resemblances with Meredith's *Modern*

Love poems. Hardy's poem, like these, is a sixteen-liner and has the identical rhyme-scheme. It also has the exact touches of observation that mark the poems of *Modern Love*. Its withered leaves

> —They had fallen from an ash, and were grey.

have some counterpart in Meredith's

> Her tears fall still as oak-leaves after frost.

The situation of the two lovers by the pond "edged with greyish leaves" has something of the same precision as the description of Meredith's lovers by the sea-shore.

> In hearing of the ocean, and in sight
> Of those ribbed wind-streaks running into white.

Yet one has only to read a few lines further in any of the Meredith poems to find such exactitudes dissolving into rhetoric and gesture, while Hardy remains true to the terse and moving sincerity that owes nothing to any model. Again, although the rhyme-scheme is the same, the shorter and more varied lines, which seem to flicker and play over the scene like the emotions of the unhappy pair, have the effect of speech, and the air of an actual happening—the eighth line, one of Hardy's early clumsinesses, was revised for publication. It is the first poem of a type Hardy made uniquely his own, the catching of a momentary incident in such a way that its emotional truth long outlasts the occasion. The influence of Meredith is certainly seen in Hardy's dialect poems, partly derived from similar ballad-poems printed by Meredith in his *Modern Love* volume; but the emotional charge of *Neutral Tones*, though recalling the *Modern Love* sequence, is essentially and typically Hardy's own.

9

Loss of Faith

T H E singular difference between *Neutral Tones* and any other poem by
Hardy in this period can best be seen by comparing it with a poem
written within a few months, *The Musing Maiden*. This is not a bad
poem; but beside the other, it appears a neat exercise in conventional
poetic ideas. Though pleasant and well-turned, every part is predictable,
and lacks that distinction which has made even the most selective
critics rank *Neutral Tones* with the finest of Hardy's lifelong poetic
output. Its title originally was *The Imaginative Maiden*, and the form
given here is, so far as can be judged, its earliest version, before revision
by Hardy for his publication in the posthumous *Winter Words*.

"Why so often, silent one,
Do you steal away alone?"
Starting, half she turned her head,
    And guiltily she said:—

"When the vane points to his far town
I go upon the hog-backed down,
And think the breeze that stroked his lip
    Over my own may slip.

"When he walks at close of day
I ramble on the white highway,
And think it reaches to his feet:
    A meditation sweet!

"When barges hence to London sail
I watch their outlines waning pale;
His window opens near the quay;
    Their coming he can see.

"I look upon the moon at night;
To mark the moon was our delight;
Up there our eyesights touch at will
    If such he practise still."

This, written at Westbourne Park Villas in October 1866, has many
of the attributes of the greater poem. It is exact and factually descriptive. The "He" of the poem is Hardy in his office at Adelphi Terrace.
He sees the "barges" and the "quay", just as Hardy did, looking down
on the Thames from his office window. "The hog-backed down" is an

accurate description of the Ridgeway, running along the hills above Weymouth, from which, as Hardy himself showed in one of his imaginative illustrations to *Wessex Poems*, the coastal vessels leaving Weymouth Harbour can be seen. These pictures are effectively organized, and so are the ideas associated with them. The idea that the same breeze may blow over the girl's lips that had stroked Hardy's lip in London was repeated, long after, in *Jude the Obscure*, where the boy Jude imagines that the breeze he is breathing, coming from the north-east, may have touched the face of his old schoolmaster in the streets of Oxford. The final stanza has a poetic conceit that reminds us how early Hardy, quite unusually for his time, was reading John Donne; the geometrical image of the lines drawn along the track of their two eyesights meeting in the same moon seems to echo *The Extasie*.[1] Yet the whole effect of this otherwise charming poem, perhaps likely to be associated with his own sister Mary rather than Louisa Harding, or some other village maiden, is one of a poetic exercise; nothing could be less like the deeply-felt and agonized *Neutral Tones*.

At all other stages of Hardy's career, emotional shock or personal upheaval heralds a new outburst of creative energy, and a new peak of achievement. It is worth, then, looking for some such happening in the years 1865 to 1867, to account for the depth and maturity of his 1867 production, *Neutral Tones*. The pointers are few, for of all the holocaust of his private papers in his old age, he seems to have been most active over those of this period; hardly a note survives. This in itself is no proof of intense emotion, but it may incline us to look in that direction. It would also be interesting to know in what exact year Hardy decided to disguise his preternaturally innocent and youthful face with the heavy dark beard he is found sporting by 1870. We may not be wrong to guess it was in these years, for the small evidence we have suggests that they were a time of intense searching and doubt about his whole personality.

One of the few personal notes from these years occurs on his twenty-fifth birthday. On 2 June 1865, he wrote:[2]

> My 25th. birthday. Not very cheerful. Feel as if I had lived a long time and done very little.
>   Walked about by moonlight in the evening. Wondered what woman, if any, I should be thinking about in five years' time.

His two concerns, career and women, significantly in that order, can be examined through the scattered traces he has left, mainly in those virtual diaries of his days, Bible, prayer book, and, to a lesser but important extent, Keble's *The Christian Year*. The external events of his life, few in 1865, apparently non-existent in 1866, appear in some more random brief notes, letters and later memories. In the middle of

July, there were two occasions he felt worth chronicling. He saw John Stuart Mill, who had been persuaded to stand as Liberal candidate for Westminster in the general election, speak in front of St. Paul's, Covent Garden. The political philosopher spoke somewhat above the heads of the crowd, which, Hardy says, was not "unimpressed by his words; it felt they were weighty, though it did not quite know why".[3] At about the same time, at the end of a walk from his lodgings to Harrow, he came across signs of another national event. Knots of people in doorways were discussing the disaster of the Matterhorn, when three men, two of them from Harrow, Lord Francis Douglas, Mr. Hudson, and Mr. Hadow, had been killed, only Edward Whymper surviving.[4] A third public event he recorded was the state funeral of Lord Palmerston on 27 October 1865. Blomfield obtained tickets for Hardy and a friend from the office named Lee, to have a complete view of the service from the triforium in Westminster Abbey. "I wd. not have missed it for anything", Hardy wrote to his sister Mary, sending her a map to show where the grave was, and where he himself stood.[5]

The two aspects of his birthday note on his life, his ambitions for himself and his relation with women, are charted even more sparsely, though in old age he attempted to put into words a curious episode connected with the first. His poems, sent hopefully to numerous magazines, had all come back. Not a single one was accepted. In some curious way, as he afterwards himself admitted, he rationalized these rejections by deciding that his architecture, of which he was swiftly tiring, could not be combined happily with poetry. A hint of his disappointment, and the attempt to shift the blame on to the circumstances of his life, runs through his notes at this time. He came up with the idea that poetry could be combined with a career in the Church. He plunged into theological study, and even wrote to a friend at Cambridge—possibly Horace Moule's brother Charles at Corpus—to ask for details of university matriculation.[6] This was a strange volte-face, since all the signs are that he was at this time falling away from the regular pious church-going of his earlier years in London. His favourite prophetic passage from the First Book of Kings remained totally unmarked for this year, 1865, and did not reappear in his Bible markings until a new love-situation brought it back in the year 1870. Indeed, in the throes of this idea, he actually attended Communion in Westminster Abbey on 5 July 1865—"a very odd experience, amid a crowd of strangers"—and went to church as late as 1 September;[7] yet it can be more than suspected that the collapse of this revived scheme to enter the Ministry had something to do with his love-life at this time late in 1865. The two aspects of his life, on which he had pondered, were thus connected.

The evidence for this connection between love of some woman and final loss of faith may seem tenuous, since it is derived from a single entry in one of his religious books. Yet one must remember how much these cryptic and abbreviated jottings always meant to Hardy, with his vision of himself as something of a nineteenth-century biblical prophet. Anything that occurs in the context of his annotations in any of his religious books has an importance beyond its laconic appearance. With Bible and prayer book now virtually abandoned, Hardy still went on marking his copy of Keble's *The Christian Year*. On the twenty-fourth Sunday after Trinity, which in 1865 was 26 November, Hardy carefully put the year and a heavy line down the margin of this stanza of Keble's verses:

> For if one heart in perfect sympathy
>   Beat with another, answering love for love,
> Weak mortals, all entranced, on earth would lie,
>   Nor listen for those purer strains above.

The moral of the poem is that since, Keble says, such earthly enchantments are so strong, one should avoid them to have true faith; but Hardy by marking so emphatically this particular stanza, seems to announce that he has found more satisfying the "one heart in perfect sympathy" with his own, and turned from the "purer strains above"; for he made no mark against the remaining stanzas of the poem, in which these "purer" pleasures are detailed.[8] Not many weeks later, Hardy marked with great emphasis this stanza from Shelley's *The Revolt of Islam*, describing the girl Cynthna's effect on the hero Laon:

> She moved upon this earth a shape of brightness,
> A power, that from its objects scarcely drew
> One impulse of her being—in her lightness
> Most like some radiant cloud of morning dew,
> Which wanders through the waste air's pathless blue,
> To nourish some far desert: she did seem
> Beside me, gathering beauty as she grew,
> Like the bright shade of some immortal dream
> Which walks, when tempest sleeps, the wave of life's dark stream.

Laon and Cythna, at the end of many cantos and stanzas of Shelley's poem, leave behind them triumphantly

>   the long array
> Of guards in golden arms, and Priests beside,
> Singing their bloody hymns, whose garbs betray
> The blackness of the faith it seems to hide.

It seems clear that Hardy was passing through some such extreme emotional experience just at this time, in which love for a kindred spirit, some woman in whom he felt complete sympathy, was associated with an abandonment of the faith of his upbringing, still more of his recent plans to become some kind of poetic clergyman.

It is likely the exact name of the girl will never be determined, so thoroughly did Hardy expunge this episode from nearly all his records. The one named girl he is known to have seen in London is his cousin the ladies' maid Martha Sparks; but she cannot possibly be the girl of his loss of faith. Quite apart from her strict religious upbringing in her own family at Puddletown, she appears as a devout believer at her mother's death there in 1868, three years later. Though very well-educated for her social class, there is no evidence that Martha had the intellectual sophistication any woman would need at that time to renounce conventional Christianity. Although Hardy certainly wanted at one time to marry her, until prevented by her watchful mother, the total absence of dates for this event makes any exact speculation impossible. It may even be that the affair of Martha Sparks, like the much earlier one of Hardy and her elder sister Rebecca, was over by this time, or at any rate fading away. Nearly all Hardy's impulses toward women were, on the evidence, extremely short-lived.

There was, however, one association with a girl in London which seems to have survived for some years, and to have been quite close, though here again the evidence is fragmentary. In two letters to his sister Mary, one on 19 February 1863 and the other on 28 October 1865 itself, Hardy mentions a girl, only referred to by her initials, H.A.[9] A survey of his markings in his Bible at this period shows only one mention of someone associated with London. This is his cryptic entry at the end of the first chapter of the first Epistle to the Thessalonians. It ends a page, at the foot of which Hardy has written "H. Lond^n". This cannot possibly be his friend Horatio Mosley Moule, to whose name Hardy's notes always give the full initials, H.M.M.

It is therefore reasonable to connect the "H. Lond^n" of Hardy's Bible with the H.A. of his letters to Mary Hardy. What emerges from these letters, though not much, does place her as someone well known to Hardy's sister, as well as to him. In the first letter, he mentions that she has been recently ill, and asks if she has written to Mary yet. In the second letter, when her relationship with Hardy had apparently lasted for over two and a half years, Hardy wrote to his sister at her cottage in the Berkshire village at Denchworth, where she was still teaching,

Will it be a good thing or will it be awkward for you if H.A. and I come down for Xmas day and the next?

The girl was evidently well known to Mary Hardy, as indeed were most of Hardy's friends whom Mary had met on her fairly frequent visits to London. What is remarkable is both that Hardy's association with the girl has lasted for so long, and has reached a stage when he is proposing to come away alone with her, even if they are to be chaperoned at the end of the journey by Mary. Unaccompanied journeys by two young people of opposite sexes were sufficiently remarkable then, as indeed Hardy's own early novels stress, to suggest that the relationship between Hardy and this girl was by now very close.

There are other suggestions of a close relationship, in Hardy's care that this visit should not be "awkward" for his sister. Mary Hardy adored her brother, and would never have complained at anything he did, even if she secretly disliked it. Hardy applied to her peculiarly reserved nature the verse he marked in his own prayer book, from Psalm 39, "I kept silence, yea, even from good words".[10] Knowing she would not complain even if the situation were awkward for her, through local gossip perhaps, he gives her every opportunity to make some excuse. The fact that H.A. was proposed at all for Mary's small cottage lodgings—her own sketch[11] shows how small they were—seems to show that she was of the same class as Mary. It is probable she was also a schoolmistress, the only type of girl of Mary's and Hardy's class at all likely to hold advanced or freethinking opinions at that date. Other professions for poor but educated girls were only just getting under way, if at all. The Working Women's College at 29 Queen's Square, Bloomsbury, had been open barely a year.[12] If this visit took place, and Mary, with her passive nature, was not likely to have prevented it, it was in the middle of a bitter winter. It is just possible that the bleak scene described in *Neutral Tones* may have happened at Denchworth, or more likely Fawley, the nearby home of Hardy's mysterious ancestors. The frozen pond at Fawley plays its part in *Jude the Obscure*. It may be the actual setting for the much earlier poem.

It does seem certain, though, that Hardy's loss of faith, connected with the influence of a woman, during these years in London, had a strong bearing on his hero and heroine when he came, in the 1890s, to write *Jude the Obscure*. Writing to Edmund Gosse in 1895, Hardy said, of his spiritual heroine, Sue Bridehead, that

> Sue is a type of woman which has always had an attraction for me, but the difficulty of drawing the type has kept me from attempting it till now.[13]

"Always" is a vague word; but it indicates an early experience of such a woman. None of Hardy's known early loves—for example, two and eventually three Sparks girls—resembles in the slightest way the intellectual Sue. Hardy, of course, combined many elements in his drawing of Sue, as he did, even more, in his portrayal of Jude; but one striking element in the early character of Sue is her rationalism and anti-Church bias. Hardy, in fact, ironically contrasts this with her money-earning employment, which is designing illuminated texts for churches, an idea left over from a minor theme he had used in *The Poor Man and the Lady*. Sue herself, however, is wedded to the new historical criticism of the Bible, which Hardy had found expounded by Jowett in *Essays and Reviews*. In pursuit of this, she makes herself what she calls "a *new* New Testament" on historical lines. She achieves this by chopping up the Epistles and Gospels, as she explains, "into separate *brochures*", and rearranging them into their probable order of composition, thus beginning the new book with the Epistle to the Thessalonians. It was against this Epistle that Hardy wrote, in his own Bible, "H. Lond^n"; it seems then more than likely that the London girl of the initials was responsible for this action by Sue Bridehead.

The character of Sue Bridehead was seized on by critics in the 1890s as representing "the New Woman" of that era, restless, intellectual and in some ways unfeminine. In reality, she is very much more what was called "The Girl of the Period" in the 1860s. The genuine New Woman of the 1890s was likely to have political affiliations with socialism, to play some part in opening the professions to women, and probably to have received some sort of university training. Sue is still back in a period some thirty years before that, when a band of enthusiasts in London ran *The Englishwoman's Journal*, and aired, for practically the first time, the independent views of women. The works of John Stuart Mill, whom Hardy had just seen on his way to be elected for Parliament, were their standard reading, and the editor of *The Englishwoman's Journal*, Bessie Rayner Parkes, wrote two long articles expounding his principles. By the 1890s, Mill was out of date, superseded by the new socialism; but Sue reads and quotes Mill even obsessively. "What do I care about J. S. Mill!" moans her poor husband, "I only want to lead a quiet life!" Sue's intellectualism is very much that of the 1860s; she is not attached to party politics, nor is she striving for male professional qualifications, nor economic independence. She accepts the very minor jobs then allotted to women.

Still more typical of the 1860s is Sue's own loss of faith, and the idea she finds as a substitute for it. She is never quite explicit about this; but, in fact, the terms she uses show her to be a follower of the Positive Philosophy of Auguste Comte, made fashionable in the 1860s among English intellectuals by Mill's exposition of it in the 1840s, and Harriet Martineau's two-volume abridged translation of it in the 1850s. In her religious arguments with Jude, Sue mocks him by using terms that would be familiar to any reader of Comte. When Jude is in his phase of studying to be a clergyman, as Hardy was in 1865, she ridicules the theology of Oxford which, she says, is anti-intellectual. She condemns Oxford and its orthodox religious beliefs as "a place full of fetichists". Here she is using the language of Comte, or rather of the Harriet Martineau translation. For Comte believed that mankind passed through religion in its early history, to arrive, via metaphysics, at scientific or "positive" philosophy, which was the "religion" of the future. He analysed, at great length, the history of religion itself, and found its origins in the "fetichist" superstitions of primitive tribes: hence Sue's expression. Sue then mocks Jude as merely himself being in a later era of Comte's tracing of religious history—"You are in the Tractarian stage just now . . . Let me see—when was I there?—In the year eighteen hundred and—". She thus shocks Jude, by assuming that, even in slow process, he will grow out of religion itself, as she has already done. Finally, like Comte, she believes in a secular "pantheon" of intellectuals, rather than one of saints.

In all this, Hardy is clearly modelling Sue, in her anti-religious, rationalist, and scientific "positive" phase, on a girl of the 1860s, and not on one of the 1890s when he was writing. By 1890, Positivism in England was virtually dead, except for small groups in London and in Liverpool. Although its handful of believers were constant to its general principles, it had been disastrously split in the 1870s into two groups, represented in London by those who congregated at Newton Hall, off Fetter Lane, and those who worshipped at the hall in Chapel Street, off Lamb's Conduit Street. For Comte, feeling the need for a spiritual element in his rationalist philosophy, had come in later stages of it to construct a system very like the Catholic Church, in which he had originally been brought up, with a hierarchy of scientists, philosophers, and humanists instead of saints—Sue's "pantheon"—and an actual worship of what was vaguely called "Humanity", with some sort of service resembling a Catholic Mass without Christ. This split the already tiny number of English positivists, never more than a few hundred, into two even smaller groups, those who stuck to the original "positive" philosophic principles, and those whose need for a substitute Christianity made them welcome the later more "religious" form of Positivism. No new intellectual woman in the 1890s would have been a positivist. Sue is, once more, a girl of the 1860s, and so perhaps, once more, the girl through whom Hardy, like Jude, lost his faith then.

The immediate result of this shadowy episode seems to have been for Hardy one of the utmost gloom, both personally and poetically. Poems of 1866, such as *At A Bridal, Postponement, Revulsion*, speak of obscure but bitter and disillusioning situations. A marriage takes place from which Hardy is excluded, so that the children he dreamed of for his own marriage will never be. Nature, he says, is indifferent,

If all such aimed ideals have such a close.[14]

It is also hinted that lack of money has been a stumbling-block to any marriage for himself. He was not

Born to an evergreen nesting-tree,

which, in his old age, he interpreted as meaning enough money to marry on.[15]   The sonnet *Revulsion* seems to mirror a mood in which all love-endeavour is so doomed that it is better not to love at all. How far these all apply to one love-affair, and whether all or any are associated with the girl of the enigmatic initials can perhaps never be finally settled, though the probability is that they are.

More certain is the concentrated gloom that seems to gather over all Hardy's doings in the year 1866. There are, of course, signs that he pursued many of his usual activities, and among these the passion for self-education and self-improvement intellectually was still dominant. On 10 October 1865, he entered himself to study French from seven to nine each Tuesday and Friday evening at King's College.[16] In this pursuit he spent two terms, lasting until March 1866. The head of these courses was Professor Alphonse Mariette, whose *Half-Hours of French Translation* was the set text. Hardy was actually taught by his assistant, M. Stièvenard, whose *Lectures Françaises* was also used. He liked Stièvenard, and remembered him well in old age,[17] though he recollected that "being also engrossed in English poetry, I did not do much in class". The fly-leaf of his copy of Mariette's book may show that his mind wandered both to architectural and personal matters. There is a shorthand note on an architectural problem, and both a map and a sketch of Weymouth, with the bulk of Portland Bill in the background.[18] The view of Weymouth, with ships in the bay, resembles the scene of one stanza of his 1866 poem, *The Imaginative Maiden*, and perhaps formed a basis for his later illustration in *Wessex Poems*.

As this suggests, his attention was taken up by his own emotional problems rather than any progress in education or career. The small number of notes that he allowed to survive all show a brooding introspection. Early in 1866 he wrote "A certain man: He creeps away to a meeting with his own sensations", and the "certain man" was presumably his ultra-diffident self. What these difficult "sensations" were may be indicated by the note which almost immediately follows:

> There is no more painful lesson to be learnt by a man of capacious mind than that of excluding general knowledge for particular.

This seems to hint at something more painfully personal than the experience of studying the minutiae of French grammar under M. Stièvenard. On 14 May, his despair had crystallized into a kind of Byronic world-weary resignation. On that day, he wrote the date against a stanza in Canto Three of *Childe Harold*:[19]

> Secure in guarded coldness, he had mix'd
> Again in fancied safety with his kind,
> And deem'd his spirit now so firmly fix'd
> And sheath'd with an invulnerable mind,
> That, if no joy, no sorrow lurk'd behind;

And he, as one, might 'mongst the many stand
Unheeded, searching through the crowd to find
Fit speculation; such as in strange land
He found in wonder-works of God and Nature's hand.

Within a week, he tried what the wonder-works of Man's hand and
Nature's would do for him, and made an expedition, on 20 May, to the
little village of Findon, underneath the Sussex Downs.[20] Here he made
a charming sketch of the Gothic church, nestling in trees, and seen from
the hills above, the spire backed by the deep leafage of early summer:
but another country visit on 6 June was not so happy. For some reason
he chose to revisit Hatfield,[21] which he had not seen since his three
weeks' stay there at the age of nine. In retrospect, all its associations
seemed sad. Whether this was because of his dead aunt, or whether,
more deeply, he now realized his mother had taken him there to break
him from Mrs. Martin, he now felt that he

regretted that the beautiful sunset did not occur in a place of no
reminiscences, that I might have enjoyed it without their tinge.

Hardy's Byronic attitude of a determined and lofty gloom finds typical
expression in an entry of 13 July—"A man's grief has a touch of the
ludicrous unless it is so keen as to be awful".

In actual fact, and perhaps healthily, his own grief took a slightly
ludicrous direction round about the turn of the year. He conceived the
ambition to write plays in blank verse; and as, unknown to him, Ibsen
had just been doing, he tried to get himself a job in the theatre. He
planned first to try a walk-on part in one of the big London manage-
ments, and obtained an interview with Coe, Buckstone's stage-manager
at the Haymarket. This does not seem to have been successful—Hardy
had scarcely the physique or extrovert personality for the stage—and
his one job came through a quite different source. The man who executed Blomfield's designs for church metalwork also did trick-scenery,
such as stage trap-doors, for pantomimes. Through him, Hardy found
himself in a walk-on part in *The Forty Thieves* at Covent Garden. The
result was far from giving him the desired education in dramatic verse.
Perhaps as might be expected, it led to a set of would-be serious though
definitely pantomime-type couplets describing a rehearsal, which he
later marked as not fit for publication. The frowsty atmosphere of the
empty theatre and the yawning actors in shabby clothes under a dim
works-light is quite well caught, though it breaks down as poetry when
Hardy tries to moralize about their private lives.

Hardy tended, in spite of his Byronic pose, to be innocently and
youthfully stage-struck. Contact with actors, and particularly actresses,
even from the level of one among (presumably) forty thieves, seems to
have had an effect on his always susceptible nature. There is a note of

this in his couplet on the leading lady, at the rehearsal, whose private life is, predictably, said to be "shady". This, and perhaps a reaction from the romantic majesty of his Byronic persona—"Remember", he noted on 18 February 1867, "that Evil dies as well as Good"—brought about something in April which reminds one how very young Hardy still was emotionally, in spite of experiences which may have been genuinely searing in themselves. He performed the typically youthful action of falling in love briefly with a very pretty though not very good actress. On 8 April, a great-granddaughter of the legendary Mrs. Siddons made her debut on the London stage. This was Mrs. Mary Frances Scott-Siddons, performing Rosalind in *As You Like It* at the Haymarket, adding as an after-piece some extracts from *Romeo and Juliet*. The reviews tended to concentrate, in the slightly suggestive way of much Victorian journalism, on her physique. *The Daily News* praised her "neat figure, pretty face", the *Daily Telegraph* noted she had "the advantages of a neat symmetrical figure" and "the external requisites" for the part, while the *London Review* said she "has a figure admirably suited to the part".[22] Her acting ability was discreetly soft-pedalled, and indeed seems to have been negligible.

What was obviously not negligible was her appearance in tights, in a part beloved for that reason by all right-thinking Victorian gentlemen. Hardy was no exception to the general taste, though, with his reading, he might well have reminded himself that her famous great-grandmother disdained such a costume. He saw her at a repeat performance on Saturday, 20 April, and the next day wrote a sonnet to her, which he followed with another. The sonnets revert to an earlier, immature technique and a much more youthful style and feeling. The second is full of romantic sentiment in such lines as

> When now the knowing you is all of me,

and in its idea that Hardy's world has been entirely changed by seeing this one performance of an actress who, apart from her figure, had little to recommend her except a certain "saucy" and "arch" delivery of her lines, and a number of free gestures and movements, which showed off her natural advantages. Perhaps he himself may have felt he had gone a little far, though physically he does not seem to have got even as far as the stage-door. Only a week later, his journal shows the solemn reflection that

> Had the teachings of experience grown cumulatively with the age of the world we should have been ere now as great as God.

The teachings of experience had certainly not advanced Hardy beyond an almost pathological habit of falling in love with each woman he encountered, particularly if there was something striking about the surrounding circumstance. His later encounter with the woman he was to marry showed how unusual and dramatic settings could work upon him, so that he literally did not see what he was doing. Stage glamour provided that factor in the affair of Mrs. Scott-Siddons, which was nevertheless so real to him that he was still writing about it twenty years later.

Nor, for all its obvious touch of absurdity, as the Byronic and, by now, surely bearded Hardy behaves like a lovesick teenager, should the whole matter be treated without sympathy. It may even be an indication of actual malaise in Hardy, an illness, part physical, part psychological, induced by the emotional and mental tempests that had clearly assailed him over the past few years. His five years in London were ending almost in breakdown. For one should never underestimate the part played by the loss of faith. Few of the Victorians were in the relatively happy position of Leslie Stephen, who said that he had never lost his faith, but simply found he had never had one. The majority would have endorsed Mark Pattison's poignant view. "Agnosticism", he wrote, "has taken away Providence as death takes away the mother from the child and leaves us forlorn of protection and love".[23] In such a state, for one reason or another, Thomas Hardy now found himself.

10

First Novel

WHATEVER the cause, by 1867 Hardy's health seemed to be seriously affected. This decline probably dated from sometime in the year 1865. In that year, he bought for himself a recent edition of *Modern Domestic Medicine* by Thomas J. Graham.[1] This was a standard home medical guide, "intended", as the title-page announced, "for the use of clergymen, heads of families, emigrants, etc.". In an earlier edition, it had been the stand-by of the Reverend Patrick Brontë, who relied on it for his own cures, though it had notably failed to check disease in his doomed family. Hardy marked heavily the hundred or more pages devoted to materia medica, containing notes of the chief ingredients of prescriptions; but nothing did him any good, and he grew shockingly pale and debilitated. The exceptionally wet and cloudy weather of the year 1867 did nothing to help, and the climax came in the dreadful month of July. The rainfall in that month was twice the average, and it must have been practically impossible to go out of doors. The first of Dr. Graham's general principles in Hardy's medical handbook read

> Remember that the restorative powers of nature are great, very great; and consequently many disorders will be cured by time, mild diet, cheerful conversation, rest, and pure air.

Arthur Blomfield seconded this advice by saying that Hardy should go into the country for a time; and at the crucial moment, Hicks of Dorchester, also suffering from ill-health, wrote asking for a good assistant. Hardy replied that he himself would come. A further draw was that his beloved sister Mary had just returned from Berkshire to teach at a Dorset school,[2] Minterne Magna, just north of Cerne Abbas, whose patron was the local landowner, Lord Digby. So, at the end of July, Hardy returned to Bockhampton. Admittedly, the weather in Dorset was no better than it had been in London. August and September were more than usually cloudy and wet, to be succeeded by one of the worst Octobers on record.[3] However, Hardy's country routine of walking each day in all weathers from Bockhampton to Dorchester soon had its effect. Health began to return. Dr. Graham's book had recommended, as well as fresh air, "the bitter ales of Bass and Allsopp", and according to local tradition, Hardy had been prescribed a bottle of milk stout a day.[4] As these simple remedies brought the colour back to his cheeks, his energy increased too. He began to think how he might impress the literary world as he had so singularly failed to do in the past two years. He decided to use the experiences he had accumulated. In Walter Bagehot's essays, he had read the description of Shakespeare as "a first-rate imagination working on a first-rate experience". This was to be his model; as he wrote,[5]

> He considered that he knew fairly well both West-country life in its less explored recesses and the life of an isolated student cast upon the billows of London with no protection but his brains—the young man of whom it may be said more truly than perhaps of any, that 'save his own soul he hath no star'. The two contrasting experiences seemed to afford him abundant materials out of which to evolve a striking socialist novel—not that he mentally defined it as such, for the word had probably never, or scarcely ever, been heard of at that date.[6]

Hardy entitled this *The Poor Man and the Lady,* and at first sub-titled it "A Story with no plot, Containing some original verses". He evidently hoped to include some of the poems rejected by journals during the past two years. This subtitle was abandoned, but when it came into the hands of publishers' readers, their main complaint was that it still had indeed "no plot".[7] As far as can be gathered,[8] the "plot" seems not so much non-existent as very naïve. The story was told in the first person by the Poor Man, the son of a Dorset labourer, named Strong, an obvious synonym for Hardy. Strong shows such promise at the village school that the squire and his lady, the Hon. and Mrs. Guy Allancourt, pay for him to be further educated as an architect's draughtsman. However, he and the squire's lovely daughter fall in love, and the squire banishes him to London. There he assists a leading architect, and makes such progress that he wins a prize, which, however, is withdrawn—a clear echo of the withdrawal of the money award to Hardy by the R.I.B.A. In spite of her father's disapproval, Strong and the squire's daughter consider themselves engaged, and write each other letters, until the squire forbids this also.

Strong, in his resentment, then adopts radical politics. The squire and his family come to London, and the daughter hears Strong make a socialist speech in Trafalgar Square. Offended by his sentiments, she breaks off their understanding; but shortly afterwards, the two find themselves at a public concert, Strong in the front row of the cheap seats, she in the back row of the expensive ones. They hold hands, and she invites him to call at the squire's London house. Through one of those accidents so common in Hardy's later novels, she is out when he calls. There is an angry scene with her mother, who faints. Strong pours water on her face, her rouge runs, and she is doubly angry. The squire has Strong thrown out, the family returns to Dorset, and the lovers cannot correspond. Strong hears, however, that the girl is about to marry, hurries to Dorset, and, the night before her wedding, has a meeting with her in the church. She confesses that he is the only man she has ever loved. She falls ill, and her father sends for Strong, but she dies. Strong designs her memorial, free of charge. There are other isolated incidents, whose position in the story is impossible to determine. There was a scene in Rotten Row, and one where a gentleman pursued his wife at midnight, and struck her. There was also the episode of an architect's mistress, who was a ballet dancer, but who also designed church furniture, a typical Hardy adaptation from his acquaintance with Blomfield's metal-smith who also made stage machinery.[9]

It is extremely difficult to say which of these incidents is autobiographical. Hardy already handled raw materials professionally, as in his later work, transposing sexes, names, relationships, and professions from people and incidents actually experienced into their artistic and fictional form. One example of this method seems actually to have occurred in this novel. Early in his work for Blomfield, Hardy assisted in the latter's commission for All Saint's Church at New Windsor; his sketch of Windsor Castle, dated 24 August 1862, may indicate a visit to the site.[10] On 21 November 1863, Hardy was present at the laying of the commemorative stone for this new church. The English Princess Royal, who in 1858 had married Prince Frederick William of Prussia, was there with her husband to perform the ceremony, and was handed a trowel by Blomfield, from which she got her glove daubed with mortar. She thrust the trowel back to Blomfield with a distressed whisper of "Take it, take it!"[11] This seems almost certainly to have been preserved in a scene between the architect hero and the heroine in Hardy's novel.[12]

Hardy had also evidently learnt the novelist's method of asking professional advice when he wanted a piece of specialized, technical information. At one time—though this may not have occurred in the completed novel—he wished his hero to become temporarily blind through overwork. More important, he wanted his heroine's midnight escapade in the church to result in an illness, which would be fatal, but which would leave her in command of speech and faculties to the last, presumably so that she could die still expressing her love for Strong. His copy of Graham's *Modern Domestic Medicine* gave him no sure guide on these points; but he remembered that on his boyhood visit to Hertfordshire with his mother, he had met his aunt's doctor brother-in-law, George Brereton Sharpe. Dr. Sharpe had made a switch in middle life from medicine to the church, and was now a vicar in Wales; but Hardy wrote off hopefully for information and advice, and in January 1868 he received a long and detailed reply.[13] His idea that the hero might go temporarily blind "from *continued* study late at night of small print or Greek characters" was confirmed. Dr. Sharpe then set himself to solve plausibly the problem of a naturalistic cause for the heroine's fatal yet conversible illness.

> For the young lady I think Haemorrage on the lungs beginning with a slight spitting of blood would be most suitable—it is less prosaically common than inflammation would be for your purpose.
> Haemorrage would very naturally follow the hurry and exertion—and if you like—external chill that the enterprise you name would entail.
> It also admits your object of perfect self-possession & consciousness till a sudden late flow of blood stops utterance and produces suffocation with the mind perfectly clear. . . .

Dr. Sharpe also added the warning, with which Hardy was to become familiar in the next few years, that it would be unwise to build any hopes of financial success on the work—"that is the lot of but few". However, he made the kindly remark, "I don't say it may not be yours", and enquired in a friendly way about Hardy's present whereabouts and doings. This letter, which Hardy kept for reference, is a reminder how even in this unfledged attempt, Hardy showed a serious concern to teach himself about every aspect of life, a continuation into his new life as a novelist of his deliberate self-tuition since boyhood, and his retentive memory for every useful source of information. The hero's temporary blindness "from *continued* study" formed a vital part of *The Return of the Native*, a decade later.

This one glimpse of his methods certainly suggests that much of the book, where it was not autobiographical, was carefully worked out from authentic sources now lost to us.

For instance, it would be fascinating to know more of the hero's radical politics, which Hardy saw as the unifying feature of the novel. He may well have got a hint for these from his cousin the carpenter, James Sparks of Windsor, described by his own brother Nathaniel Sparks as "a real loyal Rad".[14] If so, the accent should probably be on the word loyal. As has been said, politics is almost entirely absent from Hardy's own autobiography and notebooks; socialism, in the sense of economic and political socialism, hardly, if at all, appears. Although J. S. Mill had examined theoretical socialism twenty years before in his *Principles of Political Economy*, Hardy's early reading in Mill's works has probably been exaggerated; though he claimed himself to know the reformer's *On Liberty* "almost by heart" in the year 1865,[15] he did not apparently buy, read, and annotate his own copy until at least 1867.[16] From the plot, it would seem that the main emphasis was not on political socialism, but on what we should now call class-consciousness, expressed in crude satire of the ruling classes. It is clear that he overreached himself in some of this; the first publisher who read it mildly rebuked Hardy for the impossibility of the final idea in the novel, that the Hon. Guy Allancourt should be mean enough to rejoice at getting the hero's design for his daughter's tomb free of charge.

The main targets of satire were predictably those he saw attacked every week in his reading of the *Saturday Review*, namely "London society, the vulgarity of the middle class, modern Christianity, . . . and political and domestic morals in general".[17] In addition, there was probably some commonplace moralizing on the theme of countryman versus townsman. In the spring of 1869, when he still hoped the novel had a chance of being published, Hardy, down in Dorset, wrote in his notebook,[18] "One of those evenings in the country which make the townsman feel: 'I will stay here till I die—I would, that is, if it were not for that thousand pounds I want to make, & that friend I want to envy me.'". Similar touches of peasant cynicism appear in all Hardy's early novels and, no doubt, did in this one.

The story of the writing and the reception by publishers of *The Poor Man and the Lady* seems to have been more dramatic and interesting than the plot of the novel itself. Hardy noted with pride the distinguished *dramatis personae* of those who, in one way or another, had to do with his first immature attempt.[19] Once started, in the middle of August 1867, he wrote with great concentration, in the intervals of his architectural work for Hicks, only pausing for a flying visit to London in October to pick up the books and papers he had left there. In five months, by the middle of January 1868, he had finished the first draft. The fair copy took him just a week under another five months, and was finished on 9 June 1868. In all, with draft and fair copy, he must have completed nearly a thousand handwritten pages in under ten months, a steady rate which left him little time for anything else, though he records reading Browning and Thackeray in April, when he also took down the exact sound of the nightingale's song in the thickets outside the Bockhampton house.[20]

There then followed a pause of six or seven weeks, while he sent the completed novel to his mentor, Horace Moule at Marlborough. Moule's opinion has not survived, but he evidently liked it well enough to write Hardy a letter of introduction to the publisher Alexander Macmillan, which Hardy enclosed with one of his own. Moule's letter did not tell Macmillan about Hardy himself, and did not mention his age; but the publisher must have guessed he was dealing with a young man from Hardy's own letter.[21] It is typically youthful in its slightly hectoring tone, as Hardy tabulates, as if in some youth club debate, those considerations that had led him to write the novel: among them,

That the upper classes of society have been induced to read, before any, books in which *they themselves* are painted by a comparative outsider. . . .

That, nowadays, discussions on the questions of manners, rising in the world, etc. (the main incidents of the novel), have grown to be particularly absorbing.

Alexander Macmillan, who had succeeded his brother Daniel, the founder of the firm, on the latter's death in 1857, was well known for his good relationship with authors. For many years the firm ran a weekly social meeting with its contributors, and showed an understanding sympathy with their problems. Macmillan himself had come from a poor croft in Scotland, and a novel dealing with "rising in the world, etc." was likely to be of special interest to him. He showed this interest not only by reading it very carefully himself, but by sending it to a brilliant young man who had just become, while still under thirty, the editor of the *Fortnightly Review*. This was John Morley, whose own youth and radical views would bring him in sympathy with Hardy's novel. On 12 August, Macmillan wrote Hardy a long letter enclosing these extracts from Morley's opinions.

A very curious and original performance: the opening pictures of the Christmas Eve in the tranter's house are really of good quality; much of the writing is strong and fresh. But there crops up in parts a certain rawness of absurdity that is very displeasing, and makes it read like some clever lad's dream: the thing hangs too loosely together. There is real feeling in the writing, though now and then it is commonplace in form as all feeling turning on the insolence and folly of the rich in face of the poor is apt to sound: (e.g. p. 338). If the man is young, there is stuff and promise in him: but he must study form and composition, in such writers as Balzac and Thackeray, who would I think come as natural masters to him.

For queer cleverness and hard sarcasm—e.g. p. 280—a little before and after: p. 333–p. 352. For cynical description, half worthy of Balzac, pp. 358–9.

This last episode, "half worthy of Balzac" was probably the scene of the rouge on Mrs. Allancourt's face, both from its evident position in the manuscript, and from the fact that Macmillan himself in his own detailed criticism, did not mention it. In several other scenes he picked up Morley's suggestion of "a certain rawness of absurdity", and gently and kindly reasoned with the author about their unlikely nature. He also made a more general criticism, again in some detail, about the wholesale blackening of the upper classes, which, as he said, "falls harmless from very excess . . . It is inconceivable," he added, "that any considerable number of human beings—God's creatures—should be so bad without going to utter wreck within a week." He also very acutely noticed the *Saturday Review* style, natural to a young man who read it every week, and took up Morley's suggestion of the likeness to Thackeray. Yet he pointed the difference that while Thackeray only meant fun, "you mean mischief". He gave Hardy credit for great sincerity and for some excellent writing, and certainly showed no political prejudice; he singled out the Trafalgar Square speech for praise, "full of wisdom". He ended

> You see I am writing to you as a writer who seems to me, at least potentially, of considerable mark, of power and purpose. If this is your first book I think you ought to go on.

He had, in fact, been so impressed that he had decided to send the manuscript to another reader, "who knows more of the upper class than either" Morley or himself.[22]

This was almost as good as Hardy could have hoped, apart from instant acceptance; but after another month of waiting for the opinion of the other reader, whose name was never divulged, his natural impatience got the better of him. He wrote on 10 September, showing great respect for Macmillan's judgement. Taking the criticism of his scenes from fashionable life to heart, he wrote that he had been "hunting up matter for another tale, which would consist entirely of rural scenes and humble life". Yet he confessed he had not the courage to go on with it until he knew what was happening to *The Poor Man and the Lady*. His inner anxiety may be reflected in an entry in his notebook, "How people will laugh in the midst of a misery! Some would soon get to whistle in Hell!"[23] In the first week in December, he had a personal interview with Macmillan, who said that though he could not publish it, Hardy should have no difficulty in placing it with a firm such as Chapman and Hall; he gave Hardy an introduction to Frederick Chapman, to whom Hardy delivered the manuscript, slightly revised, in person on 8 December. There was the usual publishers' delay over the Christmas season, and on 17 January 1869, the agitated author once more left for London. The visit brought a friendly gesture from the book's first reader, John Morley, who offered to try and get him reviewing work with the *Saturday Review*—more than Hardy's friend Moule had ever done—but on 8 February Chapman's reader gave a report, which was less favourable than Morley's had been, though he put his finger on the same main weakness, the lack of plot; "you have not got an interesting story to work upon and thus some of your episodic scenes are fatally injured".[24] There was, however, a suggestion that Chapman and Hall would risk the book if Hardy paid the relatively small sum of £20 as guarantee against loss. Hardy agreed, and returned home with this partial success, and the experience of having seen the aged Carlyle in Chapman's Piccadilly shop. Yet still neither contract nor proofs arrived; and early in March he received a note asking him to meet "the gentleman who read your manuscript".

At this summons, enough to make any author nervous, Hardy went to London once more, and in a dusty back room at Chapman's office, was confronted with a tall, impressive, handsome and dramatic-looking person, who turned out to be none other than George Meredith. The novelist and poet, whose *Modern Love* sequence had influenced Hardy's own early poems, gave the young man an eloquent lecture, waving the manuscript in his hand. The gist was that while the firm was still willing to publish, he thought the book might be so heavily attacked by reviewers that it would handicap Hardy's future. He advised Hardy either to rewrite considerably, or, better, write a new novel with less social purpose and more art, taking care this time to give it plenty of plot.[25]

So Hardy returned once more to Dorset with the novel. He did not, however, at once take Meredith's advice. These two near misses had made him feel, as any author would, that it was worth trying one more publisher. His choice was a curious one for an author who had just been warned that his book might not be to the popular taste. William Tinsley of Tinsley Brothers was at that time the publisher of best-selling authors, including the vastly-popular Miss Braddon and the prolific journalist, George Augustus Henry Sala; his list was frankly on the lighter and more sensational side. However, Hardy sent him the novel, and once more suffered the pangs of waiting for a decision. By 8 June 1869, he was again writing for news of his manuscript, and offering to obtain another letter of introduction if necessary. Tinsley scrawled "Return" across this letter, but he did not mean an outright rejection. He put terms to Hardy for publication, through the negotiation of a friend of Hardy's, who may possibly have been either Moule or Morley. These evidently involved a much greater payment by the author than the £20 Chapman had suggested; and finally, on 14 September, Hardy wrote to say the terms were beyond him.[26] Two years in pursuit of success for this prose work had brought him the same result as the previous two years of poetry.

This recital of hope and rejection shows there was in Hardy, for all his basic timidity, a strong strain of obstinacy, and a determination to succeed against all odds. It was something he inherited from his mother, and shared with other members of her family, many of whom had ambitions to strike out for themselves. Maria Sparks, Jemima Hardy's sister, was like her, ambitious for her children, and resentful of anyone who seemed to stand in their way. She supported the idea that her clever youngest daughter, Tryphena, should, like the child's cousin, Mary Hardy, become a teacher. Tryphena had already taken the first step on this career by becoming, at the age of eleven in 1862, a monitor in the Nonconformist school at Athelhampton.[27] The next step was to become a pupil-teacher, but here the plan ran into difficulty owing to the small size of the school. It already had one pupil-teacher, and was too small to need another. In the late 1860s its average attendance was only sixty-one.[28] Squire Brymer was now well in control of Puddletown, and his "National" or Church of England school there had recently expanded into two large sections, one girls' and one boys'.[29] Although an earlier education at a Nonconformist school cannot altogether have recommended her to the squire, Tryphena was accepted late in 1866 as a pupil-teacher in the girls' section under Mrs. Sarah Ann Collins, Mr. Collins taking the boys. The job was arduous. Mrs. Collins's bad health, and unruly mothers—one called Tryphena a fool—saddled her with responsibility.[30]

Schools at this time were still organized under the somewhat unsatisfactory Revised Code of 1862, attacked by Matthew Arnold, among other things, for weakening the status and tenure of pupil-teachers. Under the Code, they were now employed and paid by the school managers, without indenture, instead of being apprenticed. Lacking the safeguard of an apprenticeship for a stated period, they were at risk of being arbitrarily dismissed, and could lose their jobs and have their careers ruined for trivial causes.[31] Tryphena, · however, satisfied her employers all through 1867, apart from a weakness in geography; this was a topic on which heads of local schools were sensitive, since the Inspector's report for that year in Dorset had commented that the subject was either not taught in schools or taught very poorly.[32] She did much better anyway than the pupil-teacher of the boys' section, Frances Dunman. Early in 1868, though, she ran into trouble. Mrs. Collins entered in the school log-book that she had "reproved pupil-teacher for neglect of duty" and added "parents very angry in consequence, & determine to withdraw her a month hence". One does not know what the "neglect of duty" was. One possible cause was that her mother's increasing illness gave Tryphena more work at home; Mrs. Collins herself, too, was heading for a breakdown that disabled her for the next three months. What is certain is that it cannot have been any moral cause.[33] H.M. Inspector of Schools, who examined the log-book, and must have enquired into the cause, specially named Puddletown School in this year as having a healthy moral tone.[34] Since the scene with Mrs. Collins, and Mr. and Mrs. Sparks's annoyance, would make further work under Mrs. Collins difficult, Tryphena was transferred to the boys' section of the school almost immediately, in exchange with Frances Dunman.

The quarrel with the school, however, was not made up—Tryphena's mother, though ill, had the quick temper for which all the Hand family were noted—and Tryphena then appears helping to teach at another school. This was the little school at Coryates, a hamlet under Blackdown Hill, east of Dorchester. The family of the local landowner, Catherine Hawkins, had a tradition that a relative of Thomas Hardy had taught there.[35] This cannot have been either Mary or Kate Hardy;[36] and, moreover, Tryphena, in a later letter,[37] showed an intimate knowledge of the people and places in this district, remote from her own home. She got the job, by a coincidence, through the same group of people who had backed Isaac Last's Academy, which Hardy had attended in his youth. This was the powerful group of Dorset Congregationalists. Coryates School, like the Athelhampton School Tryphena had first attended, was a "British" or Nonconformist school. It had been founded by Thomas Samson, whose friend and relative, George Wood, founded the Athelhampton school. Samson died soon after but Coryates school was now run by his elder unmarried daughter, Miss Elizabeth Samson of Upwey. Miss Samson was a frequent visitor of the Woods at Athelhampton.[38] After Tryphena's good record at Athelhampton, Miss Samson would willingly appoint her pupil-teacher at Coryates. The connection was lasting; Miss Samson was one of Tryphena's earliest visitors at the school where she had her first job after passing through college.[39] She also stayed with Miss Samson at Upwey during a later school holiday, an extraordinary privilege for a girl of her class; "don't you seem to see me with a servant behind my chair at meals?", she joked to her brother.[40]

One cannot tell how much Hardy saw or knew of his cousin while they were both battling out their careers in their various ways; but the most interesting link between Tryphena's story at this time and Hardy's later work is her connection with the landowner, Mrs. Catherine Hawkins. Tryphena shows a close and longstanding friendship with Mrs. Hawkins's farm bailiff, Robert Spiller, and his wife.[41] It is probable that she lodged in the Spillers' house while teaching at Coryates. Mrs. Hawkins was an enterprising young widow who, with Spiller's assistance, ran her own large farm of 525 acres.[42] The story of the farm managed by a young woman became a local legend; and it would even seem, from chapters 8 and 10 of *Far From the Madding Crowd*, that Bathsheba Everdene in the novel employed the same number of men and boys Catherine Hawkins did in real life at Waddon House. Hardy, when he came to write the novel, transferred the setting from Waddon to Puddletown.

This work, his first fully popular novel, was still some years in the future. At present all he had for his pains of 1867–69 was a novel which he had been advised not to print. Perhaps worse, the labour and anxiety of novel-writing seems virtually to have dried up his poetry. On 17 July 1868, he noted "Perhaps I can do a volume of poems consisting of the *other side* of common emotions", but nothing remains of this project. A month earlier, while Moule was reading the fair copy of *The Poor Man and the Lady*, Hardy sketched the plan of a narrative poem on the Battle of the Nile. This was not finished and has not survived. Nor has a lyric entitled *A Departure by Train*, written earlier in the year.[43] The only poem that has survived, from the middle of 1867 to the middle of 1869, is a draft *Song* dated 22 June 1868.[44] This is only interesting in showing how Hardy used to compose poems at this time. He later wrote to Edmund Gosse: "Many of the poems were temporarily jotted down to the extent of a stanza or two when ideas occurred, and put aside till time should serve for finishing them—often not till years after".[45] This *Song* demonstrates the process, though the draft shows more than "a stanza or two". The poem is in stanzas of eight lines each. Stanza 1 has only one and a half lines, and then "&c" and dots. Stanzas 2, 3, 5, and 7 are written in full, and then worked over with corrections, the last heavily altered. Stanza 4 is represented by the first two lines, and then dots, stanza 6 by dots only. The system seems to show that Hardy, at least at this time, "architected" a poem rather as he would a building, sketching the whole of the main outline, and filling in embellishments and details later. However, this is the only poem of his in any way associated with the date 1868; apart from the few instances mentioned, he does not speak of any others. This is not to say that his poetic observation failed him. In a poem obviously written much later, entitled *Life and Death At Sunrise* (*Near Dogbury Gate*, 1867), he recalls in chilling and exact detail one of the many thick foggy mornings of the grey October of 1867. All the evidence, though, is that his grapple with full-length prose narrative had temporarily silenced his poems. What it had not silenced was the inner voice which told him of his destiny as a prophetic creative writer.

11

Tryphena and the Sparkses

H A R D Y 'S secret mind in these years, including this inner confidence in his own destiny as a writer, is shown in a very curious and typical piece of personal evidence. This evidence is contained in the markings he made during the years 1868 to 1872 in his Bible and his prayer book. Compared with the prolific annotations of the years 1861 to 1864, these marks are very few. If the complete lack of annotation in the years between 1865 and 1867 does indeed show his loss of faith in this period,[1] it does not seem that there was any fervent renewal from 1868 onward. Rather, it seems likely that the return home to the familiar habits of childhood and youth had caused a revival of church-going and Bible-reading, but with none of the previous intensity of belief. One must, of course, guard against reading too much autobiography into all of these. Often, even when they seem most specific, the dates he added in the margin of the text simply indicate that this was part of the lesson or psalm for that day in the Church calendar, noted by him after some service, or reading of the appropriate passage. For example, he annotated verse 17 of chapter 4 of the Epistle of St. James, with what appears great exactitude, "Dec. 11 –70: 10.40 p.m." Yet this was simply part of the second lesson at evening service that day, and probably indicates no more than a late night reading or recall of that passage. Similarly, in his prayer book, the date "8.9.72" written above Psalm 41 indicates that this was one of the psalms for evening service on the eighth day of the month.

On the other hand, a few of Hardy's datings from 1868 onward do suggest an intensely personal application, quite unconnected with the Church calendar. The most striking of these is his dating of Job, chapter 12, verse 4, "I am as one mocked of his neighbour". Against this underlined passage, Hardy wrote "1868–71". What this meant in his personal life is expanded in a poem written much later, and called *In the Seventies*. He headed this poem with the Latin version of exactly the same passage from Job, and wrote

> In the seventies I was bearing in my breast,
>   Penned tight,
> Certain starry thoughts that threw a magic light
> On the worktimes and the soundless hours of rest
> In the seventies; aye, I bore them in my breast
>   Penned tight.

In the seventies when my neighbours—even my friend—
    Saw me pass,
Heads were shaken, and I heard the words, "Alas,
For his onward years and name unless he mend!"
In the seventies, when my neighbours and my friend
    Saw me pass.

In the seventies those who met me did not know
    Of the vision
That immuned me from the chillings of misprision
And the damps that choked my goings to and fro
In the seventies; yea, those nodders did not know
    Of the vision. . . .

Hardy, even in the poem, does not specify exactly what "the vision" was; but the dates in the Bible against precisely the same passage from Job which heads the poem show it was the inner consciousness of his own power as a writer through all his battles to become published during these years, starting with 1868, when he first sent a novel to a publisher, working through to 1871, when his first published novel, *Desperate Remedies*, finally appeared.

Other marked passages suggest a feeling of destiny in his work at this time; there seems no doubt that he had found encouragement in Morley's judgement that there was power in his writing, even though *The Poor Man and the Lady* had eventually proved unpublishable. Yet there are other notes which suggest that during his two-year struggle to get that novel accepted, there was also a struggle in his emotional and personal life. The exact nature of this conflict will probably never become completely clear; certainly, the exact order of events will always remain in doubt. At the same time, the general course of the emotional difficulties, in which Hardy now found himself, can be fairly well traced, in spite of the fact that it has become wildly confused by later guess-work, conjecture, and controversy.[2]

The situation involved his close relatives, the Sparks family of Puddletown, and, in the first instance, his mother's sister, Maria Sparks, born Maria Hand. Strong and strict, like all the Hand women, it was she who had held her family together and kept them to what she hoped would be profitable careers. Her last effort seems to have been her defiance of the Puddletown school over Tryphena, and her success in seeing her daughter settled as teacher in the British school at Coryates, early in 1868. During that year, her own health, never good, deteriorated alarmingly. Her husband, James, wrote on 29 August that she was "like a person in a decline",[3] and on 2 November she died. Through failing health, her driving force on her family had already lessened. Her easy-going husband had failed in his cabinet-making business, and was obliged to seek employment as a travelling journeyman.[4] His own health, in his late sixties, was unable to stand this, and in the next few years he complained of feeling so ill that he could hardly walk long distances to seek work[5] as a joiner. In fact, before many years, in 1874, he himself was to die sadly from an injury contracted at work, a poisoned wound in the hand resulting in erysipelas.[6]

With even less money coming in than usual, it was necessary for the Sparks children to have successful careers to help support their father. The two boys, James and Nathaniel, both like him struggling carpenters, and like him improvident, had nothing to send home from their respective jobs in London and Somerset. One daughter, Emma, also in Somerset, the hardest worker in the family,[7] was already submerged by numerous children and an unsuccessful husband, Thomas Cary. The eldest daughter, Rebecca, still managed her dress-making business in Puddletown; but with the decline in population there, and the drift to Dorchester at this time, she was not getting as much work as she had in the past.

There remained the family's two most promising members, Martha and Tryphena. Martha was now a ladies' maid in a good job in a new fashionable quarter of London, the freshly-built Prince of Wales's Terrace, Kensington, where she worked for a Mrs. Molineux at No. 16.[8] Petite, well-dressed and smart, she had profited by her employment, during which she had visited Paris and learnt French. Upper servants like herself, though not well-paid, could command better salaries than in the country, and with good references could expect steady employment. Even more promising was the future that lay before Tryphena. If she could complete her three years' of pupil-teaching, which had started in November 1866, pass an examination, and receive a testimonial of good conduct, she could qualify for a two year course at a training college. If she passed through this successfully, she could at once receive a salary as a teacher which might be as much as £100 a year or more.[9] This would lift her into a different social bracket from all the rest of her family, and she could find herself, in her twenties, earning far more than her own father in his sixties.

The question was, now that the tight rein of the mother was removed, whether Martha and Tryphena would stick to their promising careers, and particularly whether Tryphena would complete her next qualifying year from November 1868 to November 1869. In a later and grimly humorous poem, Hardy pictured the breaking-out of just such a family after their strict mother's funeral, when "Mother won't know".[10] He himself was now specially involved in the situation caused by his aunt's death. It was she who, when he was only a youth, had disapproved of his adolescent advances to Rebecca and shown him the door. It was she who when, according to her son Nathaniel, Hardy seriously wished to marry Martha, refused to allow the match and claimed that it was "against the law of the church" for cousins to marry.[11] What would be his action now that this uncompromising relative was removed? He could have taken up his hopes with Martha again; but it is impossible to tell what had passed between them by now, and whether either or both would have considered it. There is no evidence, and conjecture is useless.

What is certain is that Hardy became involved in some way with Tryphena. He was attracted again and again by the same type of woman, a replica of his own mother, with the striking features shared by all women of the Hand family. Tryphena, with her dark hair and eyebrows, fine eyes and strong, intelligent face, was a younger version of both Rebecca and Martha. From photographs, she seems to have had one quality not so apparent in their likenesses, a lurking sense of fun about her full wide mouth. In fact, her own letters show a lively, not to say broad type of humour. Writing to her brother Nathaniel in 1869, she added a mocking postscript, "How's your sweetheart old blow porridge Bibican?"[12] This rough term, obviously indicating some tendency in Nathaniel to blow hot and cold in his love affairs, also shows a certain shrewdness by Tryphena about human nature. In the event, Nathaniel Sparks did not marry his sweetheart, a girl called Annie Lanham, who had been a near contemporary at training college with Mary Hardy,[13] until almost the last possible moment, when she was already seven months pregnant.[14] Since her home was at Trowbridge,[15] only a few miles from where he worked at Rode, he had only his own dilatory nature to blame.

How deep was the attraction that Hardy felt towards this sequence of cousins? His almost passive preoccupation with the type rather than the individual suggests something less normal than any ordinary love-attraction. This involuntary pattern indicates that none of these attachments showed real strength and depth. It is a pattern remarkably repeated in Hardy's curious novel of his fifties, *The Well-Beloved*, in which the hero, Pierston, falls in love, again almost without volition, with three generations of girls, all with strong physical resemblances. In the large Sparks family, his three girl-cousins were so widely separate in age as to suggest three generations. The eldest, Rebecca, was over twenty-one years older than the youngest, Tryphena. One of the few, puzzled reviews of *The Well-Beloved* remarked that it seemed to present "a man who all his life is in love with love rather than any particular woman".[16] This could well be the verdict on Hardy himself during these attachments, whose extraordinary sequence lay behind the basic scheme of the later novel.

On the other hand, his impulse toward each girl seems to have been strong enough at the time, however little it was to last, for Hardy to express his feelings in a more normal way. Martha's brother witnessed that Hardy had wished to marry Martha; his own son reported this in a description of Tryphena, during which he remarked, "Thomas Hardy first wanted to marry Martha".[17] Then, so he writes, Hardy afterwards wanted to marry Tryphena; but with his rebuffs over Rebecca and Martha, Hardy is not likely to have expressed this wish until after the mother's death early in November 1868. His attachment to the youngest cousin, Tryphena, can probably be dated in 1869.[18]

It was helped by a change, during this year, in the circumstances of Hardy's professional life as an architect, or rather an "architeck's clerk", as he was described locally.[19] The prolonged negotiations over *The Poor Man and the Lady* had made his work for Hicks in Dorchester, as he admits, fairly desultory; but it entered into a new phase when, on 12 February 1869, Hicks himself died at the early age of fifty-three. Hicks's firm was taken over by G. R. Crickmay, A.R.I.B.A., who already had a flourishing architectural practice at Weymouth, with a contract for what was virtually a large middle-class housing estate in the Green Hill area of that town. Crickmay found that Hicks had a number of unfinished contracts for church restoration and re-designing still outstanding. In April, just after Hardy had received Meredith's advice not to publish *The Poor Man and the Lady*, Crickmay approached him for help over these commissions. The most urgent was for the large-scale conversion and expansion of an Early English church at Turnworth. Hardy took this on as Crickmay's assistant, and was left effectively in charge of many details of design. The rebuilding was financed by the Parry Okeden family, as a memorial to the late squire, the major part of the backing coming from his widow, Julia Parry Okeden. Hicks had drawn up a plan on 3 December 1868, which was not so much a restoration as an almost complete rebuilding. The whole of the old and ruinous church, except the tower, was to be demolished, and a new church built with the addition of a north aisle. The faculty for this was published on 7 May 1869, and on 13 May work started under Hardy's supervision, the specification having already been drawn up by Crickmay,[20] with what appear to be Hardy's revisions. Demolition finished, the new foundation stone was laid on 19 June.[21] The interior building was to be of Corsham Down stone, and considerable freedom was left for the embellishment of the capitals and corbels. Hardy's designs for the capitals are delicate traceries of birds, fruits, and flowers in the French Early Gothic style, which he had probably learnt from the work of William Burges. Even more striking, though less successful, are the bearded heads serving as corbels. Furthest west, there is a particularly pert and lifelike owl, which is almost certainly Hardy's individual design. It resembles the small, witty animal drawings, also based on the work of Burges, which appear in Hardy's own architectural notebook, and in which an owl is actually included.[22] This delightful interior shows that Hardy, in church architecture at least, had brought considerable skill from his experiences in Blomfield's office. This commission also added to his knowledge of the great houses of the district; he later took Turnworth House as the model for Hintock House in *The Woodlanders*.[23]

This work, and other church architectural designs prepared by Hardy for Crickmay in Hicks's old Dorchester office, proved so satisfactory that, later in June, Crickmay came forward with a further proposal. This was that Hardy should come and work in his main office at Weymouth, for a three months' summer spell in the first instance, with possible longer extension.[24] Hardy, on 8 June, had just written an anxious letter from his home at Bockhampton to Tinsley the publisher about the fate of *The Poor Man*. It seemed likely to repeat its failure with Macmillan and Chapman. In the circumstances—and especially if he were contemplating marriage in any practical way—Crickmay's offer seemed providential. Sometime in June, Hardy took lodgings at 3 Wooperton Street, Weymouth, which gave him rooms with an open view to the Ridgeway and the downs to the north.[25] His first stroll along the seafront, coming away from his interview with Crickmay, delighted him. Bands were playing, the sun was shining, little pleasure steamers were leaving for Lulworth Cove and other excursions. June, July, and August were beautifully fine that year, and in a holiday town everything seemed set fair for pleasure over the next three months at least. He bathed at seven every morning, rowed a boat on the bay every evening, and felt better in health than he had done for nearly ten years.

Also to the point was that Weymouth, not Dorchester, was the central town for Tryphena Sparks, working at Coryates in the Waddon Vale; Coryates news, in fact, when it occurred, was reported in Weymouth papers rather than in Dorchester.[26] The place was easy of access, with the more energetic walking habits of that age, within a short distance of Weymouth through the village of Chickerell. This raised the question whether the small but intense revival of poetry in Hardy at Weymouth was connected with this new attachment. He had apparently written hardly any poems for a year or more; and poetry, with the young Hardy, always reflected a new emotional phase in his life. The few poems definitely written at Weymouth,[27] *Her Father*, *The Singing Lovers*, *The Dawn after the Dance*, and *At Waking*, three of them specifically dated 1869, are of very uneven quality. They range from a somewhat formal exercise in a conventional idea, in the first-named, to a poem of great emotional charge, reflected in its shifts and explosions of rhythm, *At Waking*, which is the Weymouth counterpart of his London *Neutral Tones*. This poem, like *Neutral Tones*, is a revelation of the power as a poet that was to come to the mature Hardy. Its vision of disillusion with

the beloved one is most dramatically conveyed in the sudden broken
beat of the last verse:

O vision appalling
When the one believed-in thing
Is seen falling, falling,
With all to which hope can cling.
Off: it is not true;
For it cannot be
That the prize I drew
Is a blank to me!

Just over a year later, Hardy made a notebook entry about "lying just
after waking", and the sad but accurate disillusion that it can bring.[28]
In the poem, incidentally, it is a vision, and not the actual appearance
of his love in bed that he is seeing. It is something, as the poem says,
that he "seemed to behold", an "insight" and a "thought". A cancelled line—"Those words she had written awry"—even suggests that
the vision was of a disillusioning letter. Yet it also suggests the doubts
that always came to his nature in human relationships, the mood of
earlier works such as *Revulsion* among his London poems. The difference
here is that he does not now accept as easily the idea that failure in love
may be better than success and its attendant risk of later loss. Here the
tone is anxious, possessive, and even hysterical. It is the note of Shakespeare's Troilus—"For it *cannot* be".

What passed between Tryphena and Hardy during this summer at
Weymouth is difficult to say. His obvious enjoyment of life at this time,
the delights of the sunlit promenade, the changing colours of the distant
cliffs, the bands playing the Morgenblätter waltz, all suggest that
pleasure was heightened by a lively, attractive companion. Yet their
meetings must have been circumscribed by her work alone, and by her
concern for the future. Only an absolutely unblemished moral character
could insure her entry into a Nonconformist college, or, indeed, any
teaching employment afterwards. As late as the 1880s, a Nonconformist
teacher was dismissed for having once been seen entering a public
house, and although she tried hard to get a teaching post in another
part of the country, the stigma followed her everywhere.[29] Tryphena
had her school-manager and patron, Miss Samson, living at Upwey,
halfway between Waddon and Weymouth. Very little would escape her,
and she would judge Tryphena as she would a servant. Indeed, when
Tryphena, as a head-teacher, stayed with her half-a-dozen years later,
Miss Samson, taking her to Weymouth by train, paid for her fare
second-class, while she herself travelled first, an arrangement most
employers made with servants.[30]

At the same time, the cousins' attachment deepened to such an
extent that Hardy bought her a ring. Again, any sequence of dates is

hard to establish, but the fact is clear; the story that Hardy at this time bought a ring for a Dorset girl was handed down through most reliable channels.[31] Tryphena's own daughter later said that Hardy actually gave Tryphena the ring, a small inconspicuous one, and here again the fact should be accepted, though the witness is less reliable.[32] What the ring meant to both of them is again less easy to say, at a time when the lives and careers of both were in the melting pot. As cloudy autumn came after this idyllic summer, there may well have been elements of crisis for Hardy. In mid-September, his final resolve to abandon all hopes of publication for *The Poor Man* led him to re-engage himself to Crickmay, who accepted with alacrity, in spite of the fact that a new young assistant had just joined the office. With obstinate determination, Hardy reckoned this would give him time for a new novel. He did not go back to the rural tale he had sketched a year before, but, with Meredith's advice in mind, launched on an invention of melodramatic plot and arresting title, *Desperate Remedies*. He wrote fast; and as always when he was writing at such a pace, filled in many of the descriptive and incidental details from actual experiences and happenings. Most of these were near at hand, though, as has been said, the melodramatic incident of the heroine's father falling abruptly to his death off a scaffold, which begins the book, certainly harks back to his own youthful experience of seeing the sudden drop of the hanged man.[33] Otherwise, much of the background of the book was reproduced from sources close to him. The beautiful July weather, with which the main part of the story opens, shows almost photographically the bay at Weymouth, the deep and varied colours of the water, the rowing in small hired boats, the steamer excursions to Lulworth. One of the most successful descriptions in the book, a disastrous fire burning the inn and several cottages, caused by a smouldering heap of couch-grass, owes much to an actual happening at this time. On 28 October, the paper carried the story of a destructive fire in the property of Mrs. Wood of Athelhampton near Puddletown, where "some workmen had been engaged in drying a quantity of flax near" and it was conjectured that "the sparks were blown by the wind on to the roof of the barn, which, becoming ignited, led to the outbreak", just as Hardy makes it happen in the novel.[34] It is almost equally likely that Farmer Springrove's failure to insure the property, after having done so for many years, had its real-life parallel in the account of another extensive fire in Puddletown itself a year earlier. In this "Mr. William Brown, whose premises had been insured for the past 40 years, had unfortunately only a few months ago discontinued his policy".[35] Brown's loss amounted to between four and five hundred pounds; Springrove's, in the novel, to six hundred. The most fascinating use of actuality is perhaps where Hardy fills out his novel with a satirical description of the doctors attempting to treat the mysterious lameness of the heroine's brother. First diagnosing rheumatism, they use "hot bran, liniments . . . and also severe friction". This is followed by a treatment during which "they pricked the place with a long needle several times". In Hardy's heavily-annotated copy of *Modern Domestic Medicine* by Thomas J. Graham, heat (though not necessarily produced by bran), liniments, and severe friction are advised for rheumatism; but what makes the source certain is that Graham, unusually for the time, recommends "Acupuncturation", which "consists in making a small puncture in or near the part of the body affected, with a long needle".[36] After this treatment, specifically with "a long needle", the exact phrase used by Hardy, it is no surprise that when the doctors in the novel then diagnose erysipelas, they give the remedies also found in Graham's book, "Blisters, flour, and starch".

While Hardy was using local life and his own interests to colour and enlarge his melodramatic novel, real and dramatic events close at hand caught his own emotional life, coming to a head in November 1869. In that month, the mother of Martha and Tryphena Sparks, the two girls on whose careers their family fortunes now mainly depended, had been dead just a year. Her firm influence had waned; perhaps the freedom had been too much for Martha, who now found herself heading for disaster. In this month, she discovered herself to be pregnant by the butler at her place of work in Kensington, William Duffield, a handsome and virile-looking man. He was the son of a farm-bailiff, and he probably came from Yorkshire, where the name is a common one.

Marriage by licence took place at Kensington Parish Church on 30 November;[37] but Martha's career as a ladies' maid was ruined. Mrs. Molineux, her employer, dismissed them both. Duffield found a job as a coffee-house keeper in the Notting Hill district, at 61 Kensington Park Road.[38] He did not take kindly to the work. Nor did her family take kindly to him; Rebecca Sparks was full of lamentation for the fate of the brilliant and attractive Martha, "the flower of our flock".[39] Whether Hardy viewed the event in the same light, or indeed how he viewed it, one cannot tell; but Martha was a girl who, on good authority, he had once wanted to marry. The pregnancy of girls to other men had been a theme in his earlier poems. It may be that with his extremely volatile nature towards women, the attraction to Tryphena had driven out or lessened the feelings he had once had for Martha. Yet the date of 7 November 1869, which he put in the margin of his prayer book against verses 14–17 of the 35th Psalm,[40] is significant; the 15th verse reads

But in mine adversity they rejoiced, and gathered themselves together; yea, the very abjects came together against me unawares, making mouths at me, and ceased not.

Perhaps this refers to his working struggles; but it may not be accident that it coincides with news of Martha's ruin, perhaps hinted at in verse 17, "O deliver . . . my darling from the lions".

On the other hand, whether or not he was at all deeply affected by Martha's worldly failure, he must have been closely affected in this same month by Tryphena's success. In this month, she completed the three years as pupil-teacher that would qualify her for training college.[41] She could easily be recommended personally to any of the colleges of the British and Foreign School Society by the powerful local Congregationalist group. Miss Samson's friend, Mrs. George Wood, lady of the manor of Athelhampton, had the maiden name of Vaizey.[42] Her niece, Mrs. John R. Vaizey, was a Life Governor of the British and Foreign School Society,[43] and branch meetings of the British and Foreign Bible Society, attended by all of them, were held at Athelhampton Hall.[44] A reference from a minister of religion was generally needed, and this was probably provided by Mr. Miles of Athelhampton, since he, like Miss Samson, is found visiting Tryphena during her first job. The favour of this Athelhampton group insured Tryphena a place; entry was often by personal recommendation only, and an allowed ten per cent of the entry were not even pupil-teachers first. She seems to have been successful at Coryates, to judge by the happy tone of a letter written in the month's Harvest Holiday that summer. With the character she had retained, she could enter without even doing very well in the college examination. In point of fact, she passed in at second class, not first, but this was enough for her to be accepted by Stockwell Normal College in South London for the term beginning at the end of January 1870.[45]

The effect this was likely to have on her relationship with Hardy must be measured by the discipline of the colleges, and their attitude to these girls, largely escaping in this way from the only other employment open to them, domestic service, in which Tryphena's own sisters had been. Only a very few years later, the senior teacher at Stockwell College wrote these rules[46] on the first page of a student's autograph album:

1. Never go out alone.
2. Don't speak at dinner time.
3. Never speak after 10–10 p.m.
4. Always wear a bonnet on Sunday.
5. Never go upstairs without asking.
6. If you go for a walk with a young gentleman always leave at the corner.
7. Never leave a square inch of dinner on your plate.
8. Take a constitutional daily either between 12 and 1 o'clock or 6 and 7.

These, it must also be observed, were intended as friendly advice, rather than setting out the official regulations of the college, which were even more stringent.

So, while the improvident Sparks family were whipping round to

scrape together the money for her text books,[47] Hardy was faced with
the prospect of losing Tryphena for large portions of the year; for the
holidays, even in the summer, were particularly short at Stockwell, and
Tryphena, in her second year there, joined in signing a round robin
pleading for a longer break.[48] After the relative freedom of Weymouth,
a life where short walks with young gentlemen were barely coun-
tenanced was acute deprivation. Yet Tryphena's determination to do
well in her career, and rescue her family, was obviously strong, and
carried on after college into her first job. Reasonably, it was something
to encourage. Irrationally, it might be a total blow to their relationship.
What Hardy made of it, and what went on between them in this crisis,
is unknown, though poems now and later seem to speak of conflicts,
perhaps associated with this time, between duty and desire, and are
filled with a sense of sudden unforeseen, yet foreseeable deprivation. All
we know is that Hardy plunged this month into the winter dancing-
classes at Weymouth, to which, he says, he had been introduced by the
new recruit to Crickmay's office; he also wrote even more desperately at
Desperate Remedies.[49] There is, in fact, a slightly hysterical tone about
the half-dozen poems Hardy wrote at Weymouth. In the final verse of
At Waking, as we have seen, there is almost a note of panic—

> For it cannot be
> That the prize I drew
> Is a blank to me!

Other poems are artificial and strained. *The Dawn after the Dance*, with
its commonplace sentiments matched by its commonplace metre, is an
artificial "situation" poem, and seems to tell a contrived and fictional
story.

One poem, however, fused the authentic Hardy mixture of a place
and an emotion so that they stand for one another indissolubly. Originally
called *In the Crypted Way*, he ultimately printed it as *In the Vaulted
Way*, somewhat obscuring the picture of two lovers huddled under a low
archway, and making it sound as if their emotional parting took place
in some high-arched cathedral. With its original opening restored, it
catches, in simple, moving terms the feeling of an actual situation.

> In the crypted way, where the passage turned
> To the shadowy corner that none could see,
> You paused for our parting,—plaintively;
> Though overnight had come words that burned
> My fond frail happiness out of me.

> And then I kissed you,—despite my thought
> That our spell must end when reflection came
> On what you had deemed me, whose one long aim
> Had been to serve you; that what I sought
> Lay not in a heart that could breathe such blame.

But yet I kissed you; whereon you again
As of old kissed me. Why, why was it so?
Do you cleave to me after that light-tongued blow?
If you scorned me at eventide, how love then?
The thing is dark, Dear. I do not know.

If the poem, written in 1870, was composed in the January of that year, it may represent, with its account of an ambiguous parting, with fluctuating emotions, something of the situation between Hardy and Tryphena; its scene may be Sandsfoot Castle, Weymouth, also used in *The Well-Beloved* as the setting for an assignation and lovers' separation.

The most likely guide is again Hardy's Bible.[50] Tryphena entered Stockwell College at the week-end of 28/29 January 1870. In his Bible, Hardy wrote the words "Sunday night Jan. 29–70" at the head of the book of Joel. An inch further down, in this unlikely prophet, he underlined verse 5 of chapter 1:

That which the palmer-worm hath left hath the locust eaten; and that which the locust hath left hath the canker-worm eaten; and that which the canker-worm hath left hath the caterpillar eaten.

Associated with this date, which has no relevance in the Church calendar, this marking seems to show a triple deprivation such as Hardy had suffered in the strange repetitive history of his three cousins. Moreover, all his other underlinings in Joel speak of acute deprivation;[51] the fig-tree is stripped bare, the pasture has ceased, "the stars shall withdraw their shining". The full force of this history may have overwhelmed him at this week-end, and aroused his homing instinct; for within a few days of Tryphena's college incarceration, Hardy gave up his Weymouth lodgings and was back with his mother at Bockhampton.[52]

The long, low cottage-like house at Bockhampton, on the edge of the heath, was always his refuge in stress; and here, reassuringly, he found his family in full strength. His father, by now prospering, had set up a little office by the stairs, with a tiny window facing the heath, through which he paid his workmen, who filed past the outside of the house. One can see here Jemima Hardy's dislike of muddy boots in her neat rooms. With his father was now Hardy's brother Henry, aged eighteen, and officially known as "father's assistant",[53] especially in his family capacity as mason. He was a cheerful, outgoing youth, a complete contrast with his withdrawn elder brother. Identical with Hardy in quiet unassuming temperament was his sister Mary, now living permanently at home. She had left Minterne Magna and was now teaching in Piddlehinton,[54] the next village up the Piddle valley, and in easy

distance of Bockhampton. The renewal of this brother–sister relationship meant much to Hardy, and was reinforced by its frequent
appearance in his favourite poet, Shelley. Finally, there was Kate, aged
thirteen and still at school, but starting on a course that would lead her
to her sister's college, and a similar career as a school-teacher. Like
Henry, she was cheerful, forthright, and amusing. In this family
atmosphere of encouragement, Hardy pressed swiftly on with his
novel, and by the beginning of March, he had finished it, all but the last
three or four chapters.[55]

On 5 March, he sent the manuscript, as far as he had gone, to Macmillan, hoping that John Morley would find the same power he had
noted in *The Poor Man*, together with the greater care over plot that he
had demanded. The long friendly letter he had first received from
Alexander Macmillan, and his subsequent kindness, added to his hope.
There was one significant difference from his earlier application to
Macmillans. Hardy did not, this time, consult Horace Moule, nor
apparently get him to write a recommendation.[56] It is possible that
Moule did not altogether approve of a novel of sensation, written so
much with the advice of Morley and Meredith in mind, since Hardy in
his poem, *In the Seventies*, suggests that "my friend" looked askance at
the course he was taking. On the other hand, the main reason may
simply be that Moule had enough troubles of his own. Just over a year
before, at the end of 1868, he had gone into "unexpected retirement"
from his teaching job at Marlborough.[57] There is nothing official to show
that he left under a cloud, and in any case a fairly newly-fledged public
school would need to be reticent; but this was one more in the series of
mysterious failures that beset his career, and their cause was now
becoming a more or less open secret. Horace Moule had for some years
already devised his own way of dealing with the cycle of depression,
which he tried to relieve by drink, which in its turn prevented his work.
He had reached a stage in this cycle when the drinking was beginning to
show itself in prolonged bouts. Unwilling to give pain to his father, and
his family at Fordington, he would go off by himself to remote Dorset
villages, and disappear into solitary drinking. When these absences
became prolonged, his younger brother Frederick, who had for some
years assisted their father as curate in Fordington, would search through
the likely places until he could find Horace and bring him back.[58]
Unfortunately, perhaps on the assumption that Horace was settled in
his job, the sympathetic Frederick, who was married, had in 1868 got
himself a living at Yaxley near Peterborough. It is therefore possible
that Horace's troubles had become more obvious about now, with his
return to live at Fordington Rectory, unemployed, and self-styled as a
"classical scholar".[59] At all events, it is pretty clear that Hardy, who
knew Moule as well as anyone, had a close idea. Some years afterwards,

in his Literary Notebook, he broke off his philosophic quotations from George Eliot and Carlyle to enter the description from Trollope's *Orley Farm*:[60]

> But Mr. Moulder did not get drunk. His brandy-and-water went into his blood, & into his eyes, & into his feet, & into his hands—but not into his brain.

The irony of the similar name was part of a deeper irony. To see this collapse of his friend was enough to convince Hardy alone that the universe was ruled by a power indifferent to Man.

With his own manuscript off his hands, Hardy had to attend to a matter over which Crickmay had been pursuing him. This was one of Hicks's former commissions for church-restoration, which had come unexpectedly to light just when Hardy thought he had finished the whole batch.[61] It concerned the mouldering parish church of St. Juliot, near Boscastle, in North Cornwall, with its dropsical and dangerous tower, needing a massive restoration long-delayed by lack of money and an absentee patron who lived in Antigua. Hicks surveyed it and drew up a plan in April 1867;[62] but only two months later, the wife of the elderly rector, the Reverend Caddell Holder, died, and the plan was put into cold storage. However, the rector quickly married again, this time a woman half his age, who, like Hicks, came from a Bristol family, and she took up the cause of church restoration with energy. Then Hicks himself died, but his successor was pursued with summonses to St. Juliot, and wrote to Hardy on 11 February, asking him to go and make a fresh survey at this remote place, all expenses paid. Hardy, intent on getting the novel off to Macmillan, did not at once respond; but after another urgent appeal from Crickmay, he set off at four o'clock in the starlight from Bockhampton on Monday, 7 March. It took him twelve hours by various trains to reach Launceston, from which he had to hire a trap to go the final sixteen or seventeen miles. A poem he drafted shortly afterwards describes his thoughts of Tryphena Sparks in her college in London as he progressed toward a spot that seemed as far west from her as it could possibly be. Indeed, he was scribbling a poem on a piece of blue paper now. As the fine day darkened in the early March evening, his journey took on a weird strangeness, heightened by the approaching sound of the Atlantic breakers, and the swivelling flash of the coastal lighthouses. A small lane to the left led to the rectory, and he rang the bell in complete darkness, hastily thrusting the blue paper with the poem into his pocket. He was led into the drawing-room, and found there neither the rector, who had suddenly retired to bed with gout, nor his wife, who was nursing him. Instead, he was received by a young lady in a brown dress. She was a full-bosomed creature with a high colour, bright blue eyes and masses of blonde hair. Her open-air complexion and her energetic movements were dazzling to the tired traveller. In her extreme vitality, she seemed unlike any woman he had met before. She was the rector's sister-in-law, Emma Lavinia Gifford, Hardy's future wife.

12

Emma and the Giffords

EMMA LAVINIA GIFFORD, named after her mother and an aunt who died in infancy, was the youngest daughter of John Attersoll Gifford and Emma Farman. Though her father's family had originally come from Staines in Middlesex, he and his bride were both Bristolians, and at one time had been brought up in the same street in that city, Norfolk Street in the parish of St. Paul's.[1] Mr. Gifford was the son of a school-master, Richard Ireland Gifford, one of whose early eighteenth-century connections had kept a girls' school at Kingston. His own profession may have prompted his granddaughter's quaintly ingenuous remark that "the scholastic line was always taken at times of declining for-tunes";[2] he himself kept a small private school, described as "French and Commercial", at his home in Norfolk Street. Emma Farman, whom John Attersoll Gifford married at Raglan, Monmouthshire, on 24 April 1832, came from an old-established Bristol family. Her ancestors had been traders and merchants, and her father, William Farman, was an apparently well-to-do accountant.[3] John Attersoll Gifford had qualified as a solicitor, and had practised in Plymouth for a short time before his marriage. He returned to his native Bristol and practised there for the first five years of his married life, before going back again to Plymouth, where his mother, a Devonshire woman, had moved after her husband's death. Emma Lavinia Gifford, the youngest but one of a family of five, was born there on 24 November 1840; she was therefore a few months younger than Hardy himself.

She herself described her childhood home as "a most intellectual one and not only so but one of exquisite home-training and refinement". In her recollections in old age, there are idyllic pictures of family music and singing, of readings and discussions of books.[4] Yet there was a darker side, which even memory could not altogether disguise. Part of this came from a peculiar money situation. John Attersoll Gifford was his widowed mother's favourite son. When he rejoined her in Plymouth, she decided to live in the same house with him, contributing her own con-siderable private income. She not only used this to bring up his children, but, in his youngest daughter's words, "she considered it best that he should give up his profession which he disliked, and live a life of quiet cultivated leisure".[5] One gets the impression, incidentally, that his own wife, a simple character who read nothing except the Bible and *East*

Lynne, did not count for much in this household dominated by the older woman. The awakening came when the latter died in 1860. She had set up a trust, from which her favourite son and his wife were to receive all the interest. Unfortunately, she had so depleted the capital that there was hardly any left, her estate being sworn at under £1000.[6] Though still appearing in the Law lists as a solicitor, John Attersoll Gifford had evidently taken his mother's advice, and failed to build up a practice. Money was desperately short; the house had to be sold, and the family moved to the remote district of Bodmin in North Cornwall, where living was cheaper. Even then, Emma and her elder sister had to go out to work as governesses. The sister, Helen Catherine, then became an unpaid companion to an old lady, in whose home she met her husband, the Reverend Caddell Holder. Emma joined her in 1868, and was helping with the duties of the rectory two years later when Thomas Hardy arrived on the scene.

As well as poverty, there was an even darker shadow on the Gifford household. In times of crisis, John Attersoll Gifford drank heavily. As his daughter artlessly but frankly put it, "never a wedding, removal or death occurred in the family but he broke out again".[7] The origin of this pattern of outbursts is more than a little puzzling. Its so-called explanation came from his mother, who "sympathised with him in the great sorrow of his life". Her own father, William Davie, had had the reputation of never going to bed sober,[8] so that she may well have felt sympathetic. Her son's alleged sorrow was that he had originally been engaged to his wife's elder sister, a girl of eighteen with beautiful golden hair. She had died of scarlet fever; his drinking habits started then, and continued through his subsequent marriage. Emma was his only child with fair hair like her dead aunt; he used, she said, to stroke it, sighing at the memory. This romantic story, which Emma obviously felt gave her a special place in her father's affections, is perhaps not true. Neither in the St. Paul's parish registers, nor in the Bristol newspapers is there any trace of the death of an elder Farman girl.[9] Though there may be some other explanation, it is at least possible that the story was partly invented by his doting mother to excuse her favourite son's alcoholic outbreaks. Its probable basis is that a younger Farman girl did die, aged fifteen, three weeks before John Attersoll Gifford's marriage.[10]

Emma Lavinia Gifford certainly appears, in the light of all this, as the spoilt child of a spoilt father. There is no doubt at all that wilfulness and lack of restraint gave her a dash and charm that captivated Hardy from the moment they met. He did not consider, any more than most men would have done, that a childish impulsiveness and inconsequential manner, charming at thirty, might grate on him when carried into middle age. It is likely, too, that her spontaneous gaiety and high spirits lightened the somewhat heavy mouth and powerful jaw, which were to become so sadly grotesque in her fifties. Yet as disillusion later set in, there was one more sinister trait which Hardy came to think he should have observed.

Briefly, Hardy came to convince himself that there was a strain of insanity in his wife's family; moreover, he led himself or was led to believe that he could have observed its signs in Emma herself in the early days of their courtship. This is most clearly indicated in poems such as *The Interloper, At the Piano*, and possibly though not quite so certainly, *The Man with a Past*. The image he uses for this threat of insanity—"that is a better word than 'madness'", he himself remarked —is that of a spectrelike figure, gaunt, grim and menacing, which intrudes on even the most happy occasions. *The Interloper* in Hardy's manuscript was first entitled *One Who Ought Not To Be There*,[11] and in that poem the warning is present even in these first light-hearted days in Cornwall. When questioned about the poem eight years after his wife's death Hardy would say nothing more definite than to remark, "I knew the family". It was the second Mrs. Hardy, however, who firmly pinned the label of insanity on Emma Hardy's family, saying: "She came of tainted stock. More than one of her relatives had been in a lunatic asylum". In various remarks, she picked out which members of the Gifford family she meant. She specified Walter Edwin Gifford, Emma's younger brother, as having "died in an asylum", and his daughter, Ethel Lilian Attersoll Gifford, as having been in and out of asylums too.[12] Later, she actually said that Emma's father was "in an asylum" when Hardy first met Emma.[13]

The question seems to be exactly on what evidence Hardy came to accept his second wife's judgement—for all the poems containing this belief appear to have been written in the years after his remarriage. His only personal statement was, as has been said, "I knew the family". In point of fact, he seems to have known very few of them, and characteristically only troubled to get in touch with many of Emma's relatives after her death. When he did, he seems to have gone into it fairly closely and compiled a tentative family-tree of the Giffords, to match that of his own family and of the family of his second wife.[14] How much he found during these researches is uncertain, for none of these genealogies is entirely accurate; but it is likely that his enquiries into the Giffords did reveal something that he might take for a strain of insanity. In fact, one Gifford in each generation, Emma's own and the generation before and after her, could be said to have had mental trouble. There is, however, no indication, and much to the contrary, that these showed any familial strain; and the most remarkable fact that emerges is that, in all three generations, the sufferer was not the one named by Hardy's second wife. She was doubtless speaking at random, and certainly on hearsay only; yet a curious pattern can be seen in her accusations of mental instability. In every instance, she makes the relationship closer than it was to Emma. Even when the victim was a brother, it proves to be a brother whom Emma hardly even knew, and not the one with whom Emma was in constant touch, named by Florence Hardy. Florence Hardy herself became obsessed with the idea that Emma Hardy was mad, and there is a clear reason for this obsession. She was determined to pluck out of Hardy's mind the things said in the derogatory diary that Emma had kept about her husband, and which he destroyed after her death. She was terrified that he would end by believing it.[15] She therefore tried to prove it the work of a madwoman. To prove the diary insane, she consistently shifted insanity nearer to Emma, without the slightest regard for the truth, as can be seen.

To begin with Emma's father: though the second Mrs. Hardy said he was in a lunatic asylum at the time of Hardy's courtship, he was not. In the early 1870s he is found living at home, at Kirland near Bodmin.[16] He visited Emma at her home soon after her honeymoon,[17] and he continued to visit other members of his family until late in his life.[18] There is, moreover, quite specific medical evidence that he was in good mental health at the age of eighty.[19] In 1890, his death was given, at the age of eighty-two, as due to senile decay and a long-established prostate condition;[20] but this, though showing his health had failed in old age, is hardly insanity. The truth was, he had a brother who had died *non compos mentis* long before Emma was born. Most of Emma's uncles and aunts show the pattern familiar in large Victorian families by either dying young or living to a ripe and tough old age. Her uncle, the Reverend Canon Edwin Hamilton Gifford who officiated at her marriage, lived to be eighty-five, and to complete his magnum opus, an edition of Eusebius, two years before his death.[21] An aunt, Charlotte Eliza, was sufficiently *compos mentis* to make a codicil to her will at the age of seventy, two years before her death.[22] On the other hand, several died young, including John Attersoll Gifford's elder brother, William Davie Gifford, who succumbed to tuberculosis in his twenty-fifth year, and his youngest brother, Nathaniel Richard, who died aged sixteen of typhus. Among these younger deaths, Philip Henry Gifford, the third Gifford boy, is recorded as having died at the age of twenty "of a deep decline",[23] but family papers explain this vague non-medical phrase by adding the words *non compos mentis*.[24] In actual fact, the two terms, together with his brother's tuberculosis, almost certainly indicate that he died of tubercular meningitis,[25] a non-familial condition, and one that can hardly be characterized as insanity.

Emma's father, then, was not "in an asylum" or insane at the time of her marriage or any other time; nor was he, as the second Mrs. Hardy also said, a bankrupt.[26] Of Emma's own generation it will be remembered that the second Mrs. Hardy picked on Emma's younger brother Walter as having died "in an asylum". Walter, however, died in his own London home at the age of fifty-eight of a prostate condition like his father.[27] He was certainly a lifelong hypochondriac and grumbler, characterized by Hardy himself as "a tiresome brother whose children Emma largely helped to educate".[28] In fact, Walter, who worked all his life in London at the Post Office Savings Bank, had the habit of dumping his two elder children, Gordon and Lilian, on any of his out-of-town relatives, his excuse apparently being that it was so damp and unhealthy in his own house in Maida Vale. Not only Emma but Hardy himself virtually adopted this niece and nephew, the latter being sent to school in Dorchester and trained as an architect with Hardy's help.[29] Walter, therefore, far from being insane, showed a self-protective shrewdness, which included, as Hardy said, never doing anything in return for his helpful relatives. He certainly did not die in an asylum. On the other hand, Emma's eldest brother, whom she hardly ever saw, Richard Ireland Gifford, certainly did. His death is recorded in the Warneford Asylum at Oxford in 1904 at the age of sixty-nine.[30] It is worth noting, though, that the dementia, from which he had suffered for several years, was apparently not at all familial, but proceeded from chronic Bright's disease.

In the next generation, the second Mrs. Hardy singled out the niece, Ethel Lilian Attersoll Gifford, Walter's daughter, whom the Hardys virtually brought up, as having been "in and out of asylums". There is no evidence of this, and although, like Emma, she had rather a childish manner, this could be quite charming. When she first stayed at Max Gate as a small girl, Hardy drew her a number of comic sketches. On the anniversary of her aunt's death, when she was helping to keep house for the widowed Hardy at Max Gate, she wrote him a pathetically sentimental little note,[31] in which she reminded him that "It is more than a year ago that I renamed you 'Daddy-Uncle' and that is what you are to me, and God bless you". In his will, drawn up in 1922, he left her a legacy, in addition to the annuity he and Emma had already provided for her, and there is no doubt she was treated as mentally capable in every legal sense. She died, like her brother Gordon, in her seventies, of a long-standing heart condition. There is no hint of mental trouble in the medical history of either. Far from providing any hint of mental instability in his first wife's family, Lilian Gifford was a supporting factor in Hardy's life after Emma's death. On the other hand, though he may not have known this, there was one member of the younger Gifford generation who had some form of mental trouble. This was Emma's much-loved second cousin, Leonie Gifford. She was the daughter of Emma's cousin, Charles Edwin Gifford, who held the post of Paymaster-in-Chief in the Royal Navy, and was part-editor of a handbook of Naval Law. His own father, Emma's uncle, George

Mitchell Gifford, was a bank manager in Launceston, a profession that does not suggest insanity. Leonie Gifford, however, had a series of "nervous breakdowns" from her forties onward,[32] which might lend colour to the idea that some mental instability was present in the generation after Emma.

From this family pattern, it is apparent that the story of Emma's relatives having been insane was slanted by the second Mrs. Hardy to bring it closer to Emma herself. As to Emma's own mental health, it is true that Hardy twice wrote of her suffering from delusions in later life. Immediately after her death, he wrote of "certain painful delusions she suffered from at times",[33] and two years later, on 23 November 1914, he wrote to her cousin Kate Gifford of "In later years an unfortunate mental aberration for which she was not responsible". It is not true, however, that any of her Gifford relatives noticed anything wrong with her.[34] It must be noted also that the hospital report on her brother Richard said that none of his siblings showed any signs of insanity.[35] Perhaps the best judgement was given by the person best placed to judge, the second Mrs. Hardy's trustee, Irene Cooper Willis. She examined a large collection of letters to Emma, some of which still exist. Her verdict was, "These letters seem to me to dispose of the idea that Mrs. Hardy No. 1 was 'mad'—as Mrs. Hardy No. 2 so often declared". It seems absolutely certain that Emma was never insane in any medical sense, and that there was no familial strain of insanity in the very large Gifford family. If Hardy came to think afterwards that there was an inherited abnormality he should have observed when they first met, it is mainly because his second wife persuaded him this was so.

Whether her over-protective action sprang from jealousy or irritation —and the second Mrs. Hardy had good reason for both—it is a paradox that she persuaded Hardy into a belief which produced some of his most poignant poems. It is an even greater paradox that there was, in fact, an inherited tendency in Emma to account for this "aberration" of which her husband spoke. This again was pinpointed by Irene Cooper Willis after her study of Emma's letters. She concluded that Emma had an obsession about "Romish practices in the Church of England".[36] This has been shown, from Gifford family papers, to be inherent in Emma's family, especially on the female side. A letter from her grandmother Gifford warns one of Emma's uncles against the wrong type of clergyman, "a double minded man—who will lead the people half-way to Rome".[37] Emma's mother, with her belief in the literal truth of the Bible, seems to have been some sort of fundamentalist. It was perhaps Emma's tragedy that her erratic fifties coincided with the foundation in 1890 of the notorious Protestant Truth Society, whose members disrupted ritualistic services. Though Emma herself subscribed later to the more tolerant National Protestant Church Union, she is said to have written religious letters to the local Dorchester paper, and she did not stop at letters. To a relative, Leonie Gifford, she announced[38]

> I have been scattering beautiful little booklets about—which may, I hope, help to make the clear atmosphere of pure Protestantism in the land to revive us again in the *truth*—as I believe it to be—so I send you some of them. Do read & *pass them* on.

There was also, it appears, a Gifford family tradition that, presumably in the war scares of the early 1890s, Emma Hardy kept a suitcase packed with supplies; her fear was that the French would invade England to enforce their Romish practices, and she was prepared for herself (and perhaps her husband) to take to the fields.[39] This, though highly eccentric, was no stranger than some actions of the Protestant Truth followers of the well-known John Kensit; but one can imagine the effect on Hardy, never very tolerant of extreme forms of belief. Her action in sending the typescript of her apocalyptic vision *Spaces* to Horace Moule's brother, President of Corpus Christi College, Cambridge, must also have shaken Hardy badly.[40]

The truth seems to be that in her impulses, her foibles, her frequent angers and jealousies, but also in her enthusiasms, ideals, and gaieties, Emma remained all her life a perpetual adolescent. This was her charm. Her recklessness and wilfulness, though sometimes alarming, were equally fascinating for Hardy. In her own words,[41] we see her as he must first have seen her

> scampering up and down the hills on my beloved mare alone, wanting no protection, the rain going down my back often and my hair floating in the wind . . . The Villagers stopped to gaze when I rushed down the hills. A butterman laid down his basket once to exclaim loudly for no one dared except myself to ride in such wild fearless fashion.

This, for all its ludicrous and pathetic contrast, is the same woman who, thirty years later, and grossly overweight, wearing a green velveteen dress, freewheeled on her matching green bicycle down the steep Dorchester High West Street to distribute Protestant tracts, while the stubborn locals tapped their foreheads significantly.[42]

What, even more than religion, seems to have convinced some of Dorchester that Emma was "half-cracked", as one of her neighbours put it,[43] was the fact that she wrote bad poetry. She was said to keep wooden boxes full of her poems in an attic at Max Gate.[44] We may be more tolerant, since the modern flood of "vanity" publishers has revealed how many people of little or no talent think they are poets, and are ready to get into print at all costs. Emma Hardy's "poems" are certainly no worse than those which are now printed, at a price, by presses which feed on such innocent and pathetic impulses. What seems obvious is that her husband's *Wessex Poems*, published in 1898, with its verses so explicitly about other women in his life, was a wounding shock to her. Although a kind friend[45] tried to reassure her over these poems by Hardy "that all his reminiscences are little fancies evoked from the days of his youth & absolutely without bearing on the real happiness of his life", the message in them of his extreme susceptibility to women was plain to see. Her own poems, prolific from this date, are some form of self-justification. Another form was her estimate of her own power of composing tales and novels. Up to *Tess of the d'Urbervilles*, she had helped him by suggesting incidents;[46] after, she began to claim she could actually have written such novels as well as he. This again sprang from simple sexual jealousy. In 1893, Hardy met and was deeply attracted by Florence Henniker, novelist and short-story writer. He helped her with her work, partly portrayed her in his next novel, *Jude the Obscure*,[47] and actually collaborated with her.[48] To Emma, with her own literary aspirations, and not inconsiderable, though unorganized, gifts of expression, this was, once again, deeply wounding. Finding that Hardy had introduced his new lady-friend's short stories to be handled by the well-known literary agent, his friend A. P. Watt, Emma appointed the embarrassed Watt,[49] a few months later, to be agent for the stories she herself had written. It does not seem that he was able to place any; but her action is fully understandable as a symbol of hurt sexual and intellectual pride, and carried with it no hint of abnormality.

Ironically, too, there were elements of real and shared poetry in Hardy's first acquaintance with her. There is no doubt at all that Hardy and Emma Gifford found themselves caught up in a love situation from the moment they met; though some modern writers have expressed doubts, all the evidence points to the truth that they were genuinely in love from the start. The second Mrs. Hardy, as well as telling Irene Cooper Willis that Emma was "mad", told her that Emma's sister, Mrs. Holder, trapped Hardy into marrying her;[50] but this seems to have been yet another of her jealous inventions. If Mrs. Holder had engineered the match, Hardy and Emma would surely have been married by Mr. Holder at his church, not by Emma's uncle in London. Nor was the interval of four years between their meeting and their marriage a long one by the standard of the age, but, in fact, a comparatively short time; the famous Pre-Raphaelite picture, "The Long Engagement", presents a situation that was meant to be self-explanatory to its mid-Victorian viewers, and the idea that the four-year gap indicated something wrong[51] is quite unhistorical.

Certainly there were elements of illusion, or "magic" as Hardy later called it, about this first meeting; there are about the meeting of most lovers, and there was much to heighten this one. The "lovely Monday evening in March", as Emma remembered their first encounter,[52] was itself part of a weather-sequence that seemed to have something unnatural or magical about it. Ever since 22 January, the climate all over England had been fine and rainless,[53] and this abnormal drought was to continue, with its charged and dreamlike atmosphere, through this first year of Hardy's attraction to Emma, until the third week in August. As for the setting, its startling and wild nature has to be seen, as Emma said,[54] in the winter months to be truly appreciated—

> the wild Atlantic ocean rolling in with its magnificent waves and spray, its white gulls and black choughs and grey puffins, its cliffs and rocks and gorgeous sunsettings sparkling redness in a track widening from the horizon to the shore.

Nothing had prepared Hardy for the full force of this Atlantic seascape, with its dark cliffs against which the rollers broke in huge pillars of foam, shooting hundreds of feet up the perpendicular rock. Even the bulk of Portland Bill, the grinding undertow of West Bay, or the battery of windblown spume flying inland across the Chesil Bank, could not compare with this gigantic and ghostly atmosphere, haunting his mind for the rest of his life. The scene still held something unearthly for him, even when the magic had dismally faded from their love. In 1895, in the lowest depths of married estrangement, he could write of it as

> the region of dream and mystery. The ghostly birds, the pall-like sea, the eternal soliloquy of the waters, the bloom of dark purple cast, that seems to exhale from the shoreward precipices, in themselves lend to the scene an atmosphere like the twilight of a night vision.[55]

Quick to plunge into any new experience, Hardy absorbed in a few days both the unfamiliar landscape and a fresh relationship. His work of drawing and measuring for the church restoration seems to have kept him there only a day; he noted how the bells, taken down for safety from the cracked roof, were tolled for a funeral by a man lifting the clapper and letting it fall against the side, as it stood inverted in the transept. In the evening there was singing by the ladies at the rectory, where he had returned for his meals. Next day, partly for work, partly for pleasure, he drove with them in the family basket-carriage to the Penpethy slate quarries, to select some for the new church roof, and to Tintagel, where the castle ruins jutted into the ocean. The next day, still prolonging his visit, he spent the morning on Beeny Cliff, looking down its sheer drop to the seal-caves. He was alone with Emma; he walked and she rode her mare recklessly to the edge. "The run down to the edge. The coming home" are all he allowed to survive from his laconic journal, but the emotional tension that was growing between them is hinted by his quotation from the last lines of Tennyson's *Break, break, break*:

> Break, break, break,
>   At the foot of thy crags, O Sea!
> But the tender grace of a day that is dead
>   Will never come back to me.

By the afternoon, when Emma and her sister walked with him for three-quarters of the way down the Vallency valley to Boscastle, she had become "E". in his diary, after the more formal stages of "Miss Gifford" and "E.L.G.", and had begun to tease him flirtatiously—"E. provokingly reading as she walked". The fine March weather allowed them to stay late in the rectory garden that evening, and then again there was singing in the house. At dawn the next morning she saw him off on his journey home; a somewhat elliptical remark in his autobiography suggests that he snatched a kiss in parting.[56]

Emma afterwards wrote,[57] "Scarcely any author and his wife could have had a much more romantic meeting with its unusual circumstances", and there is no doubt that this strange coast, with its booming artillery of waves, its edge-of-the-world atmosphere, and the great sweeping lighthouse eyes of Hartland Point and Trevose Head, themselves like legendary Cornish giants, caught them up in a mood of poetic romance. Yet there were real sympathies and common interests as well, and poetry itself was one. Hardy's quotation from Tennyson was not fortuitous, suggested as it was by the crash of waves on Beeny Cliff. He and Emma read the Poet Laureate, and there is interesting proof in the poem Hardy himself wrote after their meeting. Its first stanza is unlike anything he had written till then.

> Beneath a knap where flown
>   Nestlings play,
> Within walls of weathered stone,
>   Far away
> From the files of formal houses,
> By the bough the firstling browses,
> Lives a Sweet: no merchants meet,
> No man barters, no man sells
>   Where she dwells.

This, avoiding the Laureate's glutinous syllables, yet with its own effective double rhymes, is closely related to Tennyson's popular early poem, *Claribel*.

> At eve the beetle boometh
>   Athwart the thicket lone;
> At noon the wild bee hummeth
>   About the moss'd headstone:

At midnight the moon cometh
And looketh down alone.
Her song the lintwhite swelleth,
The clear-voiced mavis dwelleth,
The callow throstle lispeth,
The slumbrous wave outwelleth,
The babbling runnel crispeth,
The hollow grot replieth
Where Claribel low-lieth.

There was another poet shared on this first meeting, even more appropriate to the wildness and grandeur of the surroundings. This was
Coleridge. One of Emma's favourite poems was his *Youth and Age*, learnt
by heart at school, and quoted by her more than once even in her own
old age.[58] Hardy, too, associated his experience in Cornwall with Coleridge, to judge by his famous poem recalling it many years later. In this,
he catches the tone of Coleridge's *Kubla Khan*—

And all should cry, Beware! Beware!
His flashing eyes, his floating hair!

almost exactly in his own poem's ending—

All marked with mute surmise
My radiance rare and fathomless,
When I came back from Lyonnesse
With magic in my eyes!

Yet, however much they were instantly drawn together by apparently
shared interests, there were grave elements of self-deception in the
sympathetic magic of their first association. Neither saw the other truly;
both had illusions, which were liable to become dangerous. To Emma,
isolated in remote provincialism, Hardy seemed part of a much larger
world of sophistication, a London-trained and qualified architect. She
did not see that he was, as he himself insisted,[59] simply an assistant, or
rather, as he was described in the following year, an architect's clerk,[60]
who had the good fortune to belong to a notable firm in London. She
herself was collecting Cornish folklore to make into stories, and it was a
romantic form of fellow-attraction that he had written many poems
and two novels; yet at that time all the poems had been rejected. So
had the first novel; the second was to suffer the same fate within a
month. His life in London had not been at all what she must have
imagined; she cannot have dreamt that he had walked out with a
ladies' maid and actually wanted to marry her. Nor had she any conception of the side of his life associated with Puddletown, the cobblers,
carpenters, labourers, and servants who were his relatives there. She
cannot have known, or perhaps, flattered, may have concealed the
thought from herself, of his extreme susceptibility to every fresh

woman: she had no inkling of the three successive sisters, dressmaker, ladies' maid, and pupil-teacher, to whom he had become attracted. In her dull life, among people "slow of speech and ideas", he seemed far more of an exotic than he actually was. His intellect, self-developed and concealing his immaturity in emotions and experience, dazzled her.

The same falsity may be seen in his view of her. To him, conditioned by his fantasy of poor man and lady, she was better connected and more intellectual than she was to prove. To a man who, only five years before, had considered going to Cambridge and entering the Church, it counted for much that her uncle was a former Fellow of St. John's, an honorary Canon of Worcester Cathedral, and Examining Chaplain to the Bishop of London,[61] while her brother-in-law had been to Oxford. Her gift of quotation from Shakespeare, learnt from her father who recited particularly well during his bouts of drinking,[62] and a school acquaintance with other poets, concealed a basic lack of education. While her talented uncle and her two elder brothers had been taught at the admirable Queen Elizabeth Grammar School, Plymouth, Emma was sent to a local school run by "dear refined single ladies of perfect manners . . . two daughters of a Colonel in the Army". The actual teaching at such schools had just been exposed, by the Schools Enquiry Commission of 1864–66, as scrappy, lifeless, and superficial.[63] Even without Horace Moule's further coaching, Hardy had received from Isaac Last in Dorchester a far better education than Emma with the Plymouth ladies. Moreover, her family background, though respectable, was excessively provincial; both her mother and grandmother interlarded their conversation with local terms.[64]

These are the illusions they had about one another. What each really found in the other was the cure for a lack in their own lives. Emma supplied for the two of them all the physical vitality and energy in which Hardy was so obviously wanting. It was her quality of "living", as he afterwards realized, that attracted him, and had always attracted him in women, the violent bodily gusto for life, of which he always seemed such a wistful spectator. For Emma, Hardy seemed the answer to her ten barren and barbarous years in Cornwall, cut off from what she remembered as the "most intellectual" home she had enjoyed in her girlhood in Plymouth. He could not possibly foresee that her very energy would lead her to bully and domineer in later years, and even to insult and belittle his own mental powers; nor could she imagine the huge intellectual gulf that would widen between them. For the moment, buoyed up by their separate illusions, they seemed miraculously at one.

13

Desperate Remedies

ON SATURDAY, 12 March, Thomas Hardy, returned from his Cornish trip, went to Crickmay's office in Weymouth for his expenses of £6 10s. 9d.[1] His mind was in a ferment, and although he took up again his Weymouth lodgings, and proceeded to elaborate the plans for St. Juliot in some detail,[2] his thought was elsewhere. He was caught in the type of ironic complex that he was to use so frequently in his own later stories and novels. He was swept off his feet by the energy, dash, and obvious attractions of Emma Gifford, all the more since it was the first time since his childhood that a woman of superior social class had shown interest in him. It was a boyhood fantasy come true. On the other hand, Tryphena Sparks in London had his ring. Though he might—and probably did—argue that in choosing a career first rather than him, and shutting herself away, she somehow justified his inconstancy, this would be impossible to explain to her, when, all too soon, she was in Puddletown to take her brief Easter break. In the background, but still present in his thought, there was her sister whom he had first wanted to marry, the small-bodied Martha, growing heavily pregnant by another more virile man. He hugged to himself the secret power he felt he possessed in his novel, *Desperate Remedies*: but on 5 April, he received a letter from Macmillans. They had refused to publish it.[3]

The novel was, in fact, a curious amalgam of composite elements, though that was not the reason for John Morley's horrified rejection. In his haste, Hardy had packed it with local incidents known to him, details from his surroundings, and even extracts, such as the medical information, from his daily reading.[4] On the other hand, to write a novel with a plot, which both Morley and Meredith demanded, he had delved into a former work which had held him fascinated since childhood. It is often said that the story is a mixture of the sensation-novel of the contemporary Wilkie Collins and the older form of Gothic romance; but the point is that they do not combine. Indeed, almost mathematically, the first half of the book is semi-Gothic romance, the second half is the realistic detective-type affair of clues and the unravelling of factual incidents that lead to the exposure of a murder. The murder itself takes place precisely halfway through the book, and dictates this change. This double plot necessitates a double ending to the book. The final chapter first clears up the circumstances of the murder, by the villainous steward's confession of how he killed and concealed his wife, and then reveals the original Gothic mystery, namely that his power over the Lady of the Manor derives from his being her illegitimate son. For this Gothic atmosphere, which dominates the first half of the book, Hardy borrowed a style and manner from an early favourite.

This was the fustian historical novel, *Old St. Paul's* by Harrison Ainsworth. Hardy himself said it "was the most powerful literary influence of his boyhood", and it was more than that. He immersed himself so deeply in this novel as a child that he never quite threw off its influence on his style. The first great romantic event of his life, his stay in London, at the age of nine, with his attractive mother on their way back from Hertfordshire, was linked with this romantic novel, which he had already read. The small boy got himself a map of the city of London, marked all the streets and alleys mentioned in *Old St. Paul's*, and then, imagining himself the hero, followed every one of them on foot.[5] His mother, looking in every closet of their lodging in case a man were hiding, was to him like the heroine, who is continually finding the villainous Earl of Rochester concealed in her father's city house, ready at any moment to carry her off. Not only plot, but the style of Ainsworth's novel made its lasting mark. This is the origin of both the grandiose and the flat prosaic that never ceased to haunt Hardy's writing. Ainsworth's characters "vociferate" rather than speak; they "traverse" rather than cross a street. On the prosaic side, nearly every paragraph begins with a resounding, dull cliché. These—"The foregoing description"—"Involuntarily drawing in his breath"—"Repeating his injunctions"—"At this juncture"—"thus ruminating" and thousands more, may make the book virtually unreadable today, but, deeply absorbed in childhood, they were the stuff of which Thomas Hardy's style was first made, when he tried to write what he thought would be an acceptable, readable novel. "Thus musing"—"Relieved from her apprehensions"—"At this announcement" invade the story from its beginnings, and the grandiose is equally pervasive. The love-affair of the heroine's father does not end: it "terminates"—and so on.

This stylistic habit never left Hardy. Even after his prose came to acquire the most subtle and often beautiful effects, this deep-laid influence perked out to disconcert the faithful readers of his major novels. So, too, did the Ainsworth villain. The features of the Earl of Rochester, "the almost feminine beauty by which they were characterized" which "gave place to a fierce and forbidding expression" are those of nearly all Hardy's villains; though he finally gave Alec d'Urberville a certain coarseness, he did so explicitly because Alec was not really an aristocrat. The smooth face hiding incredible evil-doing reached its height in the baby-faced and demonlike Dare in *A Laodicean*. In fact, Hardy himself, with his own childlike features, may have seen himself in fantasy as the Earl of Rochester, prototype of these ingenious miscreants. It is hard to see otherwise how he should have thought *A Laodicean* contained more of his own life than any other novel,[6] for the poetry, architecture, and arguments for infant baptism of the hero take up very small space in that book. If Dare-Rochester was his own fantasy self, Hardy's comment has some point.

The perverse ingenuity of a small boy in Hardy's plotting of the second half of the book, outdoing even Wilkie Collins in factual detail and attention to the smallest points of realism, drew from John Morley his reluctant praise, "the plot being complex and absolutely impossible, yet it is worked out with elaborate seriousness and consistency".[7] Literary influence is slighter here, though Collins and perhaps even more Dickens in his own later Wilkie Collins phase are present; both Hardy's detective and, particularly, his journalist have the touch of a Dickens sketch. Their laconic understatement is matched by a change in style. Nothing could be further from this quiet realism than the scenes in the first half when the villain fascinates the half-horrified heroine by playing the organ to her in an ancient building illuminated by flashes of lightning from a tremendous storm. Realism that owes nothing at all to literature is certainly dominant in the scenes of sordid London lodging-houses, in which the heroine's defenders seek for clues. Some of the social protest of lost passages in *The Poor Man and the Lady* had clearly been worked in here, notably in the *tour de force* "picture of married life among the very poor of a city".

> A few chairs and a table were the chief article of furniture in the third-floor back room which they occupied. A roll of baby-linen lay on the floor; beside it a pap-clogged spoon and an overturned tin pap-cup. Against the wall a Dutch clock was fixed out of level, and ticked wildly in longs and shorts, its entrails hanging down beneath its white face and wiry hands, like the faeces of a Harpy ('foedissima ventris proluvies, uncaeque manus, et pallida semper ora').

The spoon "pap-*clogged*" and the clock "fixed out of level" remind one what a social realist the early Hardy could be. On the other hand there is the extraordinary out-of-place "faeces of a Harpy" and the obtrusive Virgilian quotation. This type of learned allusion has been thought to be borrowed from Ainsworth, but it was natural to Hardy's own self-taught mind, and runs through all his work to the last, loading his novels with untoward digressive references to literature, painting, and architecture. In *Desperate Remedies*, the heroine becomes sexually and personally attractive to the mysterious Lady of the Manor by a chance look which "Those who remember Greuze's 'Head of a Girl'" are asked to appreciate.

There is, in fact, a constant tension throughout the book, not only between the Gothic and the factual, but, cutting across these, between real life observation and laboriously acquired taste. For instance, there are no less than three other quotations from Virgil in the book, one in the original and two in Dryden's translation, and all appear forced. The final one, when epic terms are applied to the villain chasing the heroine round a table, topples over into absurdity. On the other hand, Hardy's quotations and half-absorbed echoes from Shelley are beautifully adapted to the feeling of the book. They fit with the brother and sister relationship, which is at the heart of the novel, and they heighten the natural description. Hardy had marked his own Shelley specially for its passages about nature.[8] Here, the idyllic sea-pictures, though taken from Weymouth, are completely Shelleyan, with their glassy surfaces, purple and blue shades, and strange shapes of weeds on the sea-floor. Most directly, and half-quoting, is his landscape without hope, viewed by the heroine in depression, taken from Shelley's *The Sensitive Plant*. Hardy's garden, "purposeless, valueless . . . overgrown and choked with mandrakes" is the "leafless wrack . . . the mandrakes" of Shelley's poem.[9]

Hardy's own gift for natural description is, in fact, so strong that elsewhere it clashes with the more artificial parts of the novel. His harbour lights "seeming to send long tap-roots of fire quivering down deep into the sea", his cottage hearth-fire "giving to every grain and tumour in the paving a long shadow", show such loving care in their observation, that there is a shock when they are then associated with some piece of Gothic fustian. The overdrawn Gothic thunderstorm, when the villain fascinates the heroine by playing the organ in a mouldering mansion, begins with beautifully simple natural observation:

He pointed to a round wet spot as large as a nasturtium leaf, which had suddenly appeared on the white surface of the step.

The heroine's Gothic nightmare, during which, with extraordinary masochism, she "dreamt that she was being whipped with dry bones suspended on strings" while being tied to a wall, gives way to a wonderful naturalistic explanation, in its picture of a heavy night-frost weighing down and cracking the boughs of trees.

The chief tension in the novel, though, comes not from style and description, but from the disparate characters. The sinister outsize literary people simply do not fit with those observed from real life. The mysterious middle-aged Lady of the Manor, her evil illegitimate son, who has the habit of quoting the Bible in the midst of his villainy, even his "American actress" wife and his mistress, "an improper woman" from the haunts of "Paphos" (a word much on the lips of Ainsworth's Restoration gallants) are in a different world from the simple heroine, her brother, her architect lover, and his countryman father. These are real because they are close to Hardy's experience. The passive, patient, and modest heroine, with her occasional panic moments of spirit, seems in almost every respect a close portrait of his own sister Mary, with whom he had taken up their always fruitful quiet association while writing the novel. Equally, the brother and the lover, both architects, seem to be two sides of himself. The brother Owen, ineffective, withdrawn, until reluctantly spurred to action on his sister's behalf, is the shy, socially-uncertain Hardy in youth. Small incidents are even autobiographical. Owen is asked to come into an architect's office, where there is no vacancy, to fill in time doing drawings, just as Hardy had been when he first went to London. His first big job on his own is the superintendence of a church "which was to be nearly rebuilt" fifteen or sixteen miles from Weymouth, which has been identified convincingly as Turnworth.[10] On the other hand, the architect lover, Edward, though physically drawn from the fellow-worker in Crickmay's office, is in every other way the more ambitious Hardy, the country boy made good, the man who knows Shakespeare "to the dregs of the footnotes", and has written, though given up, poetry. His relationship, too, with his easy-going father is Hardy's. This close identity is increased by Hardy paraphrasing into prose some of his own unpublished poems. The heroine's long meditation on how future generations will regard her[11] is prosed direct from Hardy's 1866 sonnet beginning

> Perhaps, long hence, when I have passed away,

even more like in the original manuscript, where the "two small words" of the world's verdict were, as in the novel, "Poor girl!". Incidentally, since the meditation in the novel is addressed by the heroine to her brother, it increases the likelihood that the "She" of Hardy's "She to Him" sonnets is his own much-loved sister. Their whole relationship, their sympathies, and equally their irritations and differences, form perhaps the most convincing part of the novel, against the lurid backdrop of the more melodramatic characters.

It was not, however, these discrepancies that caused the novel to be rejected: but, in Morley's verdict,

> the story is ruined by the disgusting and absurd outrage which is the key to its mystery—The violation of a young lady at an evening party, and the subsequent birth of a child, is too abominable to be tolerated as a central incident from which the action of the story is to move.

"After reflection", he added ruefully, "I don't see how this could be modified in any way . . . Don't touch this—but beg the writer to discipline himself to keep away from such incidents as violation—and let us see his next story."[12] It is worth noticing that Miss Aldclyffe's early lapse *was* modified, at the request of another publisher, and its only description in the novel we now have is simply the words "a young girl of seventeen was cruelly betrayed by her cousin, a wild officer of six-and-twenty". There is no "evening party" and no described "violation". Obviously, Hardy had treated this clumsily and with the "certain rawness of absurdity" that Morley had already found "very displeasing" in *The Poor Man and the Lady*.

Morley also noted that there were "some scenes (e.g. between Miss Aldclyffe and her new maid in bed) wh: are highly extravagant". This we still have; and it raises the question of Hardy's portrayal of sex. What has been called the "sexual comment" of the novel has perhaps been exaggerated;[13] much of it seems to be of the pasteboard *Old St. Paul's* type, especially that of the Rochester-like Manston. If Hardy did later find in this early work of his "a similar plainness to *Tess*"— which is doubtful[14]—it is probably because what he described naïvely and almost unconsciously in this first published novel had by then become explicit to him. In later life, he also said that *The Poor Man and the Lady* had shown "a wonderful insight into female character", and added with what was perhaps a false simplicity, "I don't know how that came about!".[15] How it came about in *Desperate Remedies* is probably that Hardy was copying literally something he had been told personally, without perhaps understanding its full implications. After all, his cousin Martha Sparks had been for many years a ladies' maid. There are plenty of instances where the master of the Victorian household gets into bed with the ladies' maid, and there is no reason to believe that the mistress of the house did not do so too. The highly sexual lesbian scene is most probably a straight retelling of one of Martha's experiences, and its realism is not so much evidence of Hardy's maturity as of his still youthful immaturity. Similarly, the comic naïvety of Cytherea's remark to the villain, "I am not at all used to an organ", simply echoes the words of Mary Hardy in her first village job at Denchworth.[16]

One does not know how much of Morley's criticism, if any, was passed on to Hardy in Macmillan's letter of rejection. Very little, it would seem; for Hardy at once sent the unaltered manuscript, with a précis of the four missing final chapters, to William Tinsley. He afterwards pretended to believe that this was a mistake, and that Meredith, at Chapman and Hall, would have taken more interest in the book. Almost certainly, such a work would have only earned him another Meredithian lecture, whereas Tinsley, with a list of sensation-novels, was a much likelier house. Even he took time to consider, and it was exactly four weeks before he sent Hardy his reader's report. This indicated that the novel could not be published without some alteration—probably including the dropping of the "violation" scene—and Hardy wrote by return promising to comply in every way. This brought an offer from Tinsley, on 5 May 1870, to publish the novel when revised, if Hardy would pay in advance £75 of the expense. Again Hardy at once agreed, and Tinsley confirmed for an edition of 500 copies.[17]

A week later, on 16 May, Hardy dropped Crickmay's work, and left Dorset for London again.[18] His own evasive phrase, "possibly as a result of the correspondence", fails really to explain. It is true that a section of chapter 16 takes place in London, but that had almost certainly been written, since there are four chapters after it; nor, as he confessed later, did he do anything much toward the novel when he got there. Tryphena's daughter afterwards claimed that he was "tagging after" Tryphena at college; but her regulations gave him little encouragement, and the signs are that he was avoiding rather than pursuing her, for much of his time was taken in writing letters and sending books to Emma Gifford in Cornwall. In another evasive phase, he admitted "it is not clear what he was waiting for there".[19] The exact time, the second half of May, may be more significant; it was now that Martha was due to give birth. The event proved to share the tragi-comedy that seems to haunt so many of the actual events of Hardy's personal life. On 30 May, she gave birth to twins, James Sparks Duffield and Martha Mary Duffield.[20] At one stroke, the Duffields were set on a path of poverty that was to send them to Australia in half-a-dozen years. It may not be without deep personal meaning that Hardy entered in his notebook this month "A sweet face is a page of sadness to a man over 30"—he was within two days of his thirtieth birthday—"the raw material of a corpse".[21] The almost grotesque metamorphosis of the smart Martha, whom he had once hoped to marry, may have had much to do with his mood, quite apart from all the other complications he had now brought on himself. It is no wonder he found himself desultory, doing a little work in Blomfield's office, a little more for an interesting older architect in Clement's Inn, Raphael Brandon, and seeing a good deal of Horace Moule, who had come out of his retirement in Dorchester to take up his literary-journalist work in London. He was able to confide in Moule his new attachment to Emma Gifford, the "vague understanding" he already felt it to be.[22] It is unlikely that he told Moule anything about Tryphena Sparks.[23] To judge by dates, Hardy was playing an extraordinary and evasive game of Box-and-Cox with Tryphena, which may mirror his emotional dilemma. Late in June, midsummer brought her summer holiday, and it is likely she went down to Dorset, to help her sister Rebecca with dressmaking assignments, and look after their widowed father, as she had certainly done on her holiday from school in summer 1869. Hardy, however, stayed in London, working in an on-and-off way for Brandon. On the other hand, directly Tryphena returned to college, at the beginning of the second week in August,[24] Hardy hastily threw up his job with Brandon, and set off on 8 August for Cornwall.

This was, he afterwards emphasized, not a professional visit;[25] the demolition and rebuilding of St. Juliot church did not start till the following year. He had been invited by Emma's brother-in-law, presumably at Emma's prompting, though he himself seems to have been on good personal terms with Holder, an easy-going tolerant cleric, with the actor's gift of counting the number of people in the pews in the first few moments of the service.[26] It was for him an occasion of supreme adventure: would the first lightning attraction, fuelled by letters, prove permanent? The whole journey afterwards seemed to him to have elements of destiny. Even climatically, it was a strange year. There had been persistent drought since the last week in January. He travelled through a countryside where the foliage was crisped and almost charred by lack of water, crops and vegetation stunted on every hand.[27] On a larger scale, it was the summer of the Franco-Prussian war. The French nation was falling, "heart-rending" as Moule observed to him, continuing to send Hardy his own articles and leaders to read with Emma in Cornwall.[28] He and Emma had the sense that their own drama was being played against this mighty background, and he remembered their domestic incidents by the dates of the great battles. They were left alone to do more or less what they liked with the fine days. The few clouds that there were, dazzling white, hung almost motionless in still air. Emma, in the brilliant weather, wore a light blue summer dress. They walked, picnicked, and sketched each other, Emma's sketches showing a good deal more dash and freedom than his designs, still reminiscent of the drawing-board. They forgot the time in Tintagel Castle, and were nearly locked in for the night. They went to church at the neighbouring Lesnewth on Sunday 14 August,[29] for Hardy, under Emma's influence, had regained the habit of church-going. On 18 August, after a walk up the hill in the morning, they read Tennyson in the garden during the afternoon, and talked about the war. The sight of an old horse harrowing the dry earth in the valley below, symbol of peaceful habit in a time of destruction, made an indelible impression on Hardy, and he returned to it forty-five years later in one of his most famous lyrics. The next day they took a picnic down the winding fern-green Vallency valley, whose shaded banks were fresh even in the drought. The little picnic tumbler they lost in the stream, wedged for ever between two boulders, became for both a symbol of undying love. On 22 August the long drought broke, but they faced the rain that swept in over the beak of Beeny Cliff, and Hardy sketched Emma in a scene that was to reappear in much of his writing.

Indeed, writing was never far away, and as the bad weather set in, they had plenty of time to discuss it. She was taking pains to copy his reading, and he must have been pleased to find her reading his mother's favourite, Dante.[30] Before leaving London, he had rescued the manuscript of *Desperate Remedies* from Tinsley's office. He began the alterations, and she offered to make a fair copy, so that the publisher should be favourably impressed when he had the revised version. They were full of shared hopes for the future. All the same, past experience had made him cautious, and the advice of friends that he might never make money from writing had sunk in. On 25 September, he dated in his Bible the proverb: "in all labour there is profit; but the talk of the lips tendeth only to penury".[31] In the middle of the next month, he made a deeply-felt note about how a "noble nature" might unfit one for earning a living—"a high soul may bring a man to the workhouse".[32]

Even more than economic problems, emotional ones continued to press on him. He seems to have returned to his safe home at Bockhampton, and reassuring contact with his mother. Yet his dating on 16 October of the text "So I returned and considered all the oppressions that are done under the sun" may well show personal unease. In the last week in October, he had a letter from Emma, who was copying the novel with the new chapters which he was now writing and sending to her. She wrote that all around her seemed a dream, their love the reality. More than that: she gave him confidence that his shy, withdrawn nature, his uncertainties about himself, which he had confided to her, would be no drawback to their love. "I take him (the reserved man)" she wrote,[33] "as I do the Bible: find out what I can, compare one text with another, & believe the rest in a simple lump of faith." The time was far distant when he would be irritated by such simple-minded Protestantism. He felt full of gratitude at her sympathy. Moved by this, and by memories of their halycon August days, he put her initials and the date—28 October—against the first two and a half verses of the fourth chapter of the Song of Solomon,[34] beginning "Behold, thou art fair, my love" and ending "Thy lips are like a thread of scarlet, and thy speech is comely". Perhaps it was also at this time that he put her initials to a stanza of Spenser's *Epithalamion*. Yet he still had the unresolved problem of Tryphena, who was in a different class and world, with a good many less than comely associations. A feeling of fate overcame him, the maladjusted timing of events, and the frustration of over-optimistic hope. Two days later, he entered in his notebook[35]

> Mother's notion, & also mine: that a figure stands in our van with arm uplifted, to knock us back from any pleasant prospect we indulge in as probable.

It was not so much that fate was malignant, but that one's own indulgence in any form of hope could lay one open to disaster. In such a dilemma, he felt he could do nothing; or at least, he did nothing, in this emotional double path that seemed inevitably to lead to some clash.

Earlier that summer, he had made an aphoristic note[36] on how to conduct one's public life,

> It is not by rushing straight towards fame that men come up with her, but by so adapting the direction of their path to hers that in some point ahead the two must inevitably intersect.

In his private life, the intersection seemed to be growing more and more dangerous, and he did not see how any adaptation could prevent it, or resolve it happily.

At all events, *Desperate Remedies*, revised, finished, and copied by Emma, was finally "packed off" to Tinsley early in December[37] and acknowledged by the publisher on 9 December. On 15 December, Tryphena finished her first year at Stockwell College triumphantly. By hard, concentrated work, she had improved the second class, with which she had entered, to a first class.[38] Yet the date, for Hardy, meant her return to Dorset where he was deeply involved in correspondence with quite another lady. He was also on tenterhooks about his novel; but it was almost certainly for emotional reasons that he wrote[39] this exact date, 15 December, in the margin of his copy of *Hamlet* against the words

> Thou wouldst not think how ill all's here about my heart: but it is no matter.

On the exact date of Tryphena's college entrance, he had noted his sense of complete deprivation in his Bible; now, with the advent of Emma in the meantime, he marked the exact date of Tryphena's breaking-up day with a far different sense.

On 20 December, his professional life at least took an upward lift. Tinsley had written that his reader now approved of *Desperate Remedies*, and thought that, with the alterations Hardy had made, the book ought to sell. He would publish it on the terms he had offered before, a down payment of £75 by Hardy. The only further suggestion was another small alteration "that the woman who is Mrs. Manston's *substitute* need not be put forward quite so prominently as his *mistress*".[40] Hardy willingly agreed. He also snatched at the chance of escaping from embarrassment during the holidays in Dorset by going to London on the pretext that he wanted to hand over the £75 personally in Bank notes, "rather, as it seemed, to Tinsley's astonishment", as he himself remarked.[41] No wonder, since the publisher could hardly know the complications of his author's private life. He then returned to Dorset, as Tryphena went up for her second year. What she made of all this is unknown; but she was a young woman with a good deal of shrewdness and knowledge of human nature, which emerges in her own letters. A few years later, as a respectable headmistress, she still made broad jokes about "baiting her hook" for young men.[42] She doubtless had her thoughts.

In fact, with Hardy in this position, there were plenty of occasions for embarrassment in his life. The next came on St. Valentine's Day, 1871. Hardy had very special feelings about home-made valentines. In his middle-age, he wrote[43] to a young woman that her valentine had made him feel young again,

> very young . . . for I can just remember the time when written Valentines were customary—before people became so idle as to get everything, even their love-making, done by machinery . . .

He was in the habit of sending them. Now he had to send to two young women. It is no wonder that he put the date, 14 February 1871, against a marked sentence in the Book of Isaiah, "They that see thee shall narrowly look upon thee".[44] What he was doing would hardly bear looking into. The fatal effects of a personal valentine were to be recalled in *Far From the Madding Crowd*. It was about now that he recorded the long note about lying at dawn just after waking—"The sad possibilities of the future are more vivid than at any other time".[45] He was marking time, doing little with it except copying down from old people the words of the country ballads[46] that the improvements of Squire Brymer were beginning to banish from Puddletown. Yet if he was at a standstill, his book was not. Advertised as ready by 11 March, it was in his hands on the 25th. Long after, he recalled[47] that no sensation could match the feelings of an author on first publication. "Never will I forget the thrill that ran through me from head to foot when I held my first copy of *Desperate Remedies* in my hand."

14

Under the Greenwood Tree

HARDY went back to Weymouth, to work for Crickmay while he waited for the reviews. It was a necessary move. In all his years as assistant architect, he had managed to save £123. Now £75 of that was invested in the book. If the gamble failed, he would have to earn again, for marriage or for another book. He was not only unknown, but anonymous, and had nothing to recommend the book to the reading public. This public, for a three-volume novel on the usual pattern, was largely a family and circulating library readership. If the reviews approved of the book for general and family reading, he was started on his way financially. If they did not, however they might praise it as a book, he might never have written it for any money that it would bring.

He did not have long to wait. The *Athenaeum* had a regular section for novels of the week, which it kept admirably up to date. On 1 April, *Desperate Remedies* was one of the books reviewed. It was a mixed notice. The story was "unpleasant", dealing as it did with crime, but it was certainly powerful and well-told. The country scenes were praised, specially that of Farmer Springrove's cider-making, and Hardy must have smiled to be congratulated on his authentic west-country dialect. What partly bothered the reviewer was the exact sex of the anonymous author. A woman, he first thought, since the book showed such "close acquaintance with the mysteries of the female toilette", which, the reviewer permitted himself to say, seemed entirely accurate. On the other hand, it contained some expressions "so remarkably coarse" that he could not believe a lady could have written it. The mystery would have easily been solved if the reviewer had known anything of Hardy's private life. An author who had walked out with a ladies' maid, and heard from Martha Sparks about her work and her employers, could hardly fail to be accurate about the "toilette". As for the coarseness, he had heard plenty of that, and from women of his own class. Basically, what the reviewer did not realize was that here was a novel about middle-class people written by someone of working-class experience. He returned in a puzzled way, to this "occasional coarseness, startling as it once or twice is". Almost certainly, he was thinking of Miss Aldclyffe's sexual and explicit use of the word "had"; it was a use that the mature Hardy was to repeat with tremendous and dramatic effect in a later novel *The Woodlanders*. He concluded, in an encouraging way,

> if the author will purge himself of this, though even this is better than the prurient sentimentality with which we are too often nauseated, we see no reason why he[1] should not write novels only a little, if at all, inferior to the best of the present generation.

This, though encouraging and gratifying, was not wholly the selling review that the author wanted. An imputation of coarseness, however occasional, might frighten off the circulating libraries and the watchful paterfamilias. It was all the more welcome then that on 13 April, the *Morning Post* gave it a short but unreservedly favourable notice. Though it noticed passages that seemed to imitate Wilkie Collins, it judged the book "eminently a success" of its kind.

On 22 April, however, the *Spectator* reviewed *Desperate Remedies*. It was, he saw as he bought the copy in Dorchester, immensely long, and he carried the magazine with him to the stile into Kingston Maurward ewelease on his way home. As he read the first sentences, as he afterwards said, "The bitterness of that moment was never forgotten; at the time he wished he were dead".[2] It expressed the kind of horror that John Morley had anticipated, and fixed the blame firmly on the anonymous author, adding that it was hardly just that the publishers had to reveal their names in association with such a work, which contained "no display except of the brute kind", and was devoid of any hint of Christian virtue. As a parting shot in this introductory onslaught, the reviewer said he had set this down in the hope of stirring the author "to better things in the future than these 'desperate remedies' which he has adopted for ennui or an emaciated purse".

One wonders if Hardy read any further than this ill-timed joke, which, as has been pointed out,[3] he quoted in old age inaccurately, making it sound even more damning than it was. For the major part of the review, which then followed, was something that many authors would have welcomed. As if feeling he had perhaps gone too far, the reviewer proceeded to quote, at very great length, what he called the redeeming features of the book, as examples of "powers that might and ought to be extended largely in this direction". Like the *Athenaeum* critic, he enjoyed the cider-making scene, and reproduced several paragraphs. To these he added the dialogue between the bell-ringers at the wedding from the end of the book, also at length. Then he praised the passages of natural description, and chose, with some acuteness, two from early in the book, the scene in the cool of the Town Hall, where the heroine sees, framed in her view from the window, her father on the building-scaffold outside, and the detailed effects of a hot summer on the landscape, as the heroine journeys down to Weymouth, drawn closely from Hardy's real-life experience there. "We wish", he added, "we had space for the description of the village fire, and its silent and stealthy growth in the autumn night", a phrase which showed how much he appreciated the good things of the book, and Hardy's power to create authentic atmosphere.

Yet all this literary appreciation, which might have led a less one-track mind to accept the moral strictures, was useless comfort in face of Hardy's immediate obsession that the book must be a financial success. The verdict that the villain was moved throughout by "the merest sensuality", and that Miss Aldclyffe, his key-figure in the plot, was "uninteresting, unnatural, and nasty"—the reviewer could not bring himself actually to mention her scene in bed with the ladies' maid—would totally ban the book from family reading. No library and very few private purchasers would risk it. He had lost his money. He plunged into the depths; his habitual lack of confidence as always threatened to erode his compensating conviction, expressed in his prophetic Bible entries, that he was somehow destined for greatness. When he completed the book, in the middle of the previous November, he had dated the passage in Revelation, "Thou must prophesy again before many peoples, and nations, and tongues, and kings".[4] Now, utterly chastened, he wrote a note, "Strictly, we should resent wrongs, be placid at justice, and grateful for favours. But I know one who is placid at a wrong, and would be grateful for simple justice; while a favour, if he ever gained one, would turn his brain".[5] All his life, he remained quietly, bitterly sensitive. His friend, Horace Moule, now becoming even more horribly involved in his own depressions, realized the effect this review would have on Hardy. He wrote a brief note, telling him not to mind the article, and got the book, over which he had not been consulted, to review himself for the *Saturday Review*. Here again, there was an ironic turn to Hardy's fortune. If Moule had placed a notice quickly, some of the damage might have been repaired. Yet, one must suspect because of the increasing frequency of his own drinking bouts, this did not appear for another six months, far too late to do any good.

The one remedy, for pride and for purse, was Crickmay. Also, the St. Juliot commission provided an excuse for Hardy to take his hurt feelings to Emma. She, at least, copying the book in her admiration for Hardy, had seen nothing wrong with it. The St. Juliot restoration, having hung fire for a year, was set in motion, perhaps by Hardy's contriving, and in May he was off for a long visit to Cornwall, for professional reasons this time, as he carefully noted.[6] Crickmay's designs of the previous May were put into operation, under Hardy's supervision. One intention was frustrated by the local builder. Hardy had drawn a careful restoration of the medieval screen, using as much as possible the old framing.[7] Going into the church one day, he found his design executed throughout in glaring modern yellow pitch-pine, and heard the builder's well-meaning explanation: "Well, Mr. Hardy, I said to myself, I won't stand on a pound or two while I'm about it, and I'll give 'em a new screen instead of that patched-up old thing".[8] Possibly, for various reasons, he did not supervise the job as closely as he might have done. Emma, energetic, forceful, and anxious as he for their future, seems to have helped him to collect a number of favourable extracts from the three reviews, to use as publicity and offset the *Spectator* notice. It was too late, though he sent these to Tinsley on his return to Weymouth on 7 June. On his way back to Dorset on 3 June, he had seen the fatal sign of lack of sales. His three-volume book was already remaindered by W. H. Smith on Exeter station at 2s. 6d.

Yet Emma, it may be suspected, had restored his confidence, and given him the next move. Ever since, Morley's first report on *The Poor Man and the Lady* in the summer of 1868 he had played with the idea of a novel with an entirely rural setting. Now, the tone of the reviews, good and bad, the popularity of the cider-making scene, and Emma's faith in him spurred him on. His personal life was still in chaos, and Tryphena's return to Dorset at midsummer, as much as his failure as a novel-writer, may have prompted his marking of *Macbeth*.[9]

> Things at their worst will cease, or else climb upward
> To what they were before.

Yet for all ills, writing now seemed to be the obvious cure. This was not to say, though, that Hardy could ignore the immediate advantages of work for Crickmay; so he put himself this summer into double harness, to write a novel—necessarily a short one—and to carry out Crickmay's local designs. Two jobs to hand were the new schools at Radipole and Broadwey, both just north of Weymouth. This was part of the urgent drive by the voluntary school societies to provide adequate schools to fulfil the recent Education Act of 1870; if they did not, a secular school board would take over. The number of Church schools built in the six months after 1870 was enormous, and these two both opened in 1871. Drawings of details for both exist, in Hardy's hand,[10] and for a few months they were his main task. As general work, there was the Green Hill housing estate, which can be seen today. Green Hill, a gentle slope, starts just where Weymouth Bay begins to curve to the east. The spiky pale-grey Gothic of St. John's church, vicarage, and schools had already been built; but behind it there was a residential area to fill. Following Crickmay's plans, and under Hardy's direction, imposing stone-built villas of multiple bow-windows and slightly crazy turrets began to appear nearest the sea, and, behind them, more modest pairs of brick villas on a smaller scale. As to materials, yellow brick alternated with polychrome red and blue; Hardy was putting his R.I.B.A. prize essay into practice. Not that he was showing any originality; this was, by every neighbouring sign, the standard Crickmay style for domestic buildings. When Hardy later built his own house at Max Gate, he took up the Crickmay manner, and gave it the Crickmay trade-mark of a useless turret. Domestic building was something of a routine chore to him, and though he paid careful attention to detail,[11] there is no evidence that his heart was much in the houses, which were probably as uncomfortable as Max Gate proved to be.

The new book, of course, was a major concern. He wrote fast, helped by incorporating scenes that had been praised in *The Poor Man and the Lady*. The party at the tranter's, which Macmillan had liked, probably went in more or less wholesale. A bee-keeping scene took the place of the popular cider-making from *Desperate Remedies*. Its original title, *The Mellstock Quire*, embodies the theme, an evocation of the doings of Stinsford church choir in the days of his own father and grandfather, slightly updated to bring the choir into conflict with the new church music, approved by the new vicar, and played on the organ by the new-style college-trained school-mistress, Fancy Day. Music, as has been said,[12] runs throughout the slight story, dance, song, and church voices all playing their parts. Fancy's unsuitable suitor, the rich farmer, a character adapted from an innkeeper in *The Poor Man*,[13] bellows the unseemly pothouse ballad about "three sons of whores" that Hardy had heard from his Hand uncles. Not that there is an unsuitable word in the whole of the writing. The *Spectator* review had taught its lesson, and it was not until 1896 that Hardy, writing a new preface for the work, dared to mention "that ancient and broad humour which our grandfathers, and possibly grandmothers, took delight in, and is in these days unquotable"—the "possibly", even at that late date, a concession to the horror at the coarseness found in his first work by middle-class reviewers.

The book seems to have started, indeed, as a set of pictures, designed to carry out the *Spectator*'s approval of scenes in *Desperate Remedies* which reminded the reviewer of the genre paintings of Teniers and Wilkie. In fact, changing the main title to *Under the Greenwood Tree*, Hardy put as sub-title "A Rural Painting of the Dutch School". This might suggest his habit of dragged-out artistic analogy. Yet, refreshingly, there is hardly any of this in the book itself. A suggestion that the silhouetted choir look like figures on a Greek vase, and a reference to the paintings of Moroni, are all that obtrude. Even more welcome, the simple characters and plot, or lack of plot, absolved Hardy from feeling he must write in the grand Harrison Ainsworth manner. His style is miraculously, and for the only time in all his output, purged of these

pomposities. The lapses can be counted on the fingers of the hand—
"adhering thereto", "consequent upon", "subjoined words", "just
subsequent", and hardly any others. The purity and unity of the style
is miraculous. Partly, this is due to a very simple and unsensational plot.
It would have been even more simple; but Hardy, perhaps realizing
that it was too much like his very earliest "Story with no Plot", added
at a late stage a third rival for the hand of Fancy Day. As well as the
tranter's son, Dick, and the rich farmer, Shiner, he gave an interesting
sociological twist to the story by making the new young vicar fall in
love with the coquettish Fancy, incidentally but unconsciously also
giving him the Christian name of his own Stinsford vicar.

It seems likely that Fancy herself, the girl who has bettered herself
by becoming a certificated teacher, has a good deal to do with Tryphena
Sparks. Her brunette beauty certainly corresponds in general with
photographs of Tryphena, and her lively character is much the same as
Tryphena's letters, though purged, like the whole novel, of any coarseness. She has plenty of faults, and the last words of the book underline
both them and her native shrewdness, such a feature of Tryphena, when
she decides not to tell her newly-wedded Dick ever of the young vicar's
proposal to her. In later years, Hardy was asked the sort of stupid
question inflicted on novelists about their creations, "what kind of a
wife he imagined Fancy Day . . . would turn out in the future".[14]

> He replied, "I don't quite know. We had better draw a veil over her;
> and yet I have known women of her type turn out all right, some of those
> early examples of independent schoolmistresses included."

The personal tone of his reply suggests a personal application. The
other "early" schoolmistress he seems to have known was his own
mouse-like sister Mary. Triffy Sparks seems indicated—perhaps even
by her name—as Fancy Day.[15]

The speed of writing, and the brevity of the book, meant that by
7 August Hardy was able to send it, with carefully selected extracts
from the *Desperate Remedies* reviews, to Alexander Macmillan, who had,
of course, heard rumours of such a work for the past three years. The
publisher had just lost his wife, and on 17 September his son Malcolm
replied, enclosing John Morley's report.[16] Morley found the book
praiseworthy but slight. He made the curious criticism that it was not
as good as George Sand, and that Hardy should study that author.
Horace Moule's belated review of *Desperate Remedies* in the *Saturday
Review* of 30 September was evidently written after Hardy, in puzzle-
ment, had sent him this comment, for in it he claims that Hardy is *like*
Sand. Moule liked the characters in a way neglected by earlier reviewers
—"the essence of the book is . . . the evolution of characters". He even

approved of the study of Miss Aldclyffe, and found her lesbian scene showed "an effective and analytical power that recalls the manner of George Sand". Following the *Spectator*, he developed the slow progress of the fire as an example of Hardy's mastery of narrative. He criticized Hardy acutely for seeming to delight too much in what he called *sententiae*, or moral reflections and aphorisms. This ingrained habit hardly ever left Hardy, though again fruitfully dormant in *Under the Greenwood Tree*. It was not, as Moule seemed to suggest, a borrowing from George Eliot. It was a legacy from his reading in eighteenth-century authors. As early as his first days in London, he had read Henry Fielding's *Joseph Andrews* and carefully marked the "Moral Reflections" on page 166 and the "Philosophical Reflections" on pages 219 to 220;[17] but the chief influence in this direction was his habitual reading in the six-volume *Letters to Sir Horace Mann* by Horace Walpole.[18] The Walpole type of aphorism in his work should be perhaps distinguished from the less obtrusive type of observation which comes from Hardy's own experience. One at least, in *Desperate Remedies*, seems to point to his grandmother Elizabeth Swetman, her library of books, and her marriage beneath her:

> In looking back upon our line of descent it is an instinct with us to feel all our vitality was drawn from the richer party to any unequal marriage in the chain.

Moule's review, anyhow, led to a new chain of activity by Hardy, both about *Desperate Remedies* itself and about the new work. Though in a gloomy poem, *The Moment Before Meeting*, he categorized any meeting as only leading to further separation, he set off, as if unable to help himself, on another architectural expedition, early in October, to St. Juliot. There, probably at the urgings of Emma, Hardy wrote to Tinsley that he had done "a little rural story"—which, of course, though he did not say so, he had submitted to Macmillan—but "the representation of critic-friends"—in fact, one friend, Moule—had now made him start on yet another novel with more plot, "*without crime*—but on the plan of D.R.".[19] This letter on 20 October followed a disappointing letter he had just received from Macmillan about *Under the Greenwood Tree*. He liked the novel but found it slight, and wanted to postpone doing anything about it till the following spring, when he might publish it if it were still free. Involved still with two women in his private life, Hardy anticipated no difficulty in keeping two publishers in play; but the publishers were less easy to hoodwink. Tinsley, who had already remarked that Moule's review had come too late for sales, wrote on 23 October to point out just how small these sales were, and how much money Hardy was liable to lose on *Desperate Remedies*. He did not rise to the bait of the new plot-novel without crime, which seems to be the first mention of *A Pair of Blue Eyes*, sketched with its Cornish setting at this time, and with a heroine based, at least physically, on Emma. Hardy now had two novels on hand, one more or less complete, one half-started, both unwanted at this stage. He also had two women on hand, each corresponding to the heroine of a novel.

In these dilemmas, he left St. Juliot, his work there finished, on 30 October, to plunge into the Green Hill work at Weymouth. He was disillusioned, tired of critics, about whom his covering note to Macmillan had contained some foolish remarks.[20] He wrote to Emma renouncing novel-writing, and was urged by her not to despair. All the same, in his own words, "he applied himself to architectural work . . . more steadily than he had ever done in his life before", and the polychrome brick of Green Hill continued to spread. Meanwhile, one of his heroines had reached a point of decision. On 15 December, Tryphena Sparks completed her course at Stockwell. She maintained the first class she had achieved in the first year, and added to it a certificate for drawing. Her next move was dramatic. She applied for and obtained the headship of the Plymouth Day (Girls) School. This was a startling achievement for a girl just out of college. Her own brother said that it was the second largest school in the provinces.[21] It shows how her record impressed the managers, in spite of her youth. What her feelings toward Hardy were by this time, it is impossible to say. She may well have grown tired already of his vacillating and wavering behaviour, his lack of decision, and his mysterious movements. It is not certain she still had his ring, though it seems likely she at least took it with her to Plymouth.[22] On the other hand, there is a family tradition that she applied for the Plymouth job partly because Plymouth was on the normal route from London, where Hardy was now intending to work again, and Cornwall, where he always seemed to be going.[23] Either by express from Paddington, or by coastal packet from the Port of London it would be the obvious way; Hardy used both these methods in the next year, both in real life and in the story of *A Pair of Blue Eyes*. What is absolutely certain is that with great strength of mind, Tryphena had done all she had set out to do. Her salary was just under £100, just over with private pupils. She was the only one of the Sparks family to earn anything like that, and the only one with the sense to save. In her half-dozen years as head teacher, she saved £400,[24] an unheard-of sum for a girl whose labouring relatives earned at most £25 a year. It is an ironic thought that financially she was far better off than Emma, with her small portion of her grandmother's depleted New River Company shares: but for her class, Tryphena was a better match. Whether by choosing her career so wholeheartedly, she sacrificed Thomas Hardy on the way may possibly never be known.

Hardy did not stay long in his new lodgings at 1 West Parade, Weymouth. By 19 March 1872, he was in his new London lodgings, situated, for cheapness, in a less fashionable area and above a tailor's shop, back in Paddington, but this time at 4 Celbridge Place, Westbourne Park. Here he received a cheque for just under £60 as the final account for *Desperate Remedies*—£15 less than he had invested in it. Tinsley sent with his statement a well-meant remark, "I hardly think you *should* be disheartened because the first book has not done well, but this you know best about".[25] What Hardy knew was that he must make some money soon. His method of doing this showed the same self-protective shrewdness that his cousin Tryphena had followed in choosing a career. He attached himself to Thomas Roger Smith, Professor at the R.I.B.A. and twice President of the Architectural Association. Hardy, incidentally, lost his membership of the latter body just at this time for not paying his fees, some indication of his poverty.[26] The connection with Smith was particularly valuable at this moment. He was concerned with designing schools for the London School Board. The Education Act of 1870 had just given wide powers to school boards to create schools where needed. The need was urgent; there were vast areas of London, where, with the increase in population, no school existed at all. It was a key job in the society of the day; like his cousin, Hardy was to benefit by the boom in education. Hardy's intense concentration on this essential work, though, led to yet another complication in his life, which threatened once more his peace of mind.

He had not seen Horace Moule for some time; Moule's habits, as depression and drink increased, seem to have been getting less and less accountable. Meeting him quite by chance in Trafalgar Square, Hardy told him of his concentration on architecture as a career. Moule warned him that the intense work might lead to eyestrain, and advised him, even if only on these grounds, not to give up writing as a career. Whether Moule had seen actual signs of strain, or Hardy, in his agitated state, was ultra-suggestible, within a few days floating spots began to appear before his eyes. Would the temporary blindness he designed for his hero in *The Poor Man and the Lady* afflict its author in real life? He wrote to Moule, who had gone back to Dorset. Moule consulted his mother, and, in London again, wrote to Hardy from his lodgings in Garrick Chambers to say that Mrs. Moule strongly recommended one of the leading ophthalmic surgeons of the day, William Bowman of 5 Clifford Street.[27] Whether or not Hardy took her advice, he may have noted the coincidence that the specialist's surname was already one which he had introduced, presumably at random, among those of his rural choir in *Under the Greenwood Tree*. For the fortunes of that novel had revived. Another chance meeting, this time in the Strand, brought Hardy face to face with Tinsley; that is, if we are to believe his own account in old age, which has many marks of fiction—Tinsley, for instance, is made to talk a kind of stage-cockney throughout their interview. Whatever the truth, Tinsley read the short novel, and on 22 April he offered Hardy £30 for the copyright.[28]

This was not specially generous, but Hardy was in no position to bargain. He agreed, and Tinsley, in fact, paid him £10 extra for the Continental copyright. Faith in himself as a novelist revived. Moule promised that he would review the book for the *Saturday Review*, "Before another member of the staff gets it". In point of fact, though the book came out early in June, Moule, who was more than usually occupied at this time with his own problems, did not get his review in until late that September. Luckily, however, the book did not need his help. *The Athenaeum*, in its books of the week for June 15, gave it generous attention. Hardy was praised for following up all the good qualities the reviewer had noted in *Desperate Remedies*, and developing them with great skill. The love story was thoroughly approved. The only criticism was that his villagers spoke rather too grandly. It was a good selling review and so was that of the *Pall Mall Gazette* on 5 July. Here again it was objected that "the humble heroes and heroines of the tale are much too shrewd, and say too many good things to be truthful representatives of their prototypes in real life"; but the freshness and originality of the book were soundly praised, though the reviewer did not like the late introduction of the vicar's romance into the story, and thought it spoiled the simplicity of the plot.

At all events, it was a good enough start to attract the publisher to further things, and three days later, on 8 July, Tinsley wrote to Hardy with an electrifying suggestion.[29] Tinsley ran a monthly popular publication, *Tinsley's Magazine*, which even contained scurrilous articles about the Queen and her gillie, John Brown. On the more serious side, he was looking for a serial story to start in the September number, which would appear in the middle of August, and asked if Hardy's "new story"—*A Pair of Blue Eyes*, known tentatively at this time as *A Winning Tongue Had He*—was far enough advanced to fill the bill. Hardy had put out feelers for his novel before, but he had not dreamt such an offer would come, or so soon. His account of the negotiations that then ensued, written up in his old age, is once more almost entirely fictional. For one thing, he represents his encounters with Tinsley as taking place in the street on his way to Roger Smith's office in Bedford Street, near the publisher's own office in the Strand, and purely by chance. In actual fact, the whole proposal, and the discussion over financial terms, seems to have been conducted quite normally through letters, which still exist.[30] Hardy's written-up account, in which Tinsley once more appears as a heavy-handed comic cockney,[31] is therefore very much to be doubted. For example, Hardy's copy of *The Law of*

Copyright in Works of Literature and Art by A. W. Copinger, which he said he bought to help him in negotiating with the wily publisher, was not, in fact, purchased until the following year.[32] There was no doubt, however, about the result. On 27 July, Hardy agreed for publication as a serial and in a three-volume edition for the sum of £200.

15

A Pair of Blue Eyes

BY ONE of those coincidences whose truth Hardy was often to defend in his novels, the month of August 1872 marked a time of similar personal crisis both for Hardy and his friend Horace Moule. Moule had been unemployed for nearly three years. Though he continued his reviewing work, this was not well-paid. Now something made him seek work with a permanent salary. Though there is an absence of dates, the most likely reason is that this was the time of his engagement to that "highly cultivated governess of sterling character", which his family so well remembered,[1] and which, they hoped, would defeat the depression and the drinking that threatened to destroy his life. Yet even to think of marriage, he would need money. He had hardly any. Thirteen months later, after drawing a year's regular salary, his assets were under £200.[2] As an attempt to earn, he obtained this August a post as Assistant Inspector to the Local Government Board for the district of East Anglia. It was dull and routine work, involving the administration of workhouses and other local institutions, but there were certain advantages in the area chosen. He could make his centre Cambridge, where one of his brothers, Charles Walter Moule, was a Fellow of Corpus Christi College. He would also be within thirty miles of Yaxley Vicarage and the sympathetic Frederick Moule, who had so often before rescued him when stranded on his drinking bouts. Both would be able to keep an eye on him. As a further precaution, a local doctor, James Hough of Trumpington Street, was entrusted with his care. He was to inform Charles Moule of any onset of depression and, when necessary, provide a nurse, so that Horace Moule should not be alone in his lodgings.

Thomas Hardy's crisis this August was of a slightly different nature, but it also concerned work and marriage. Tinsley's advance of £200 for *A Pair of Blue Eyes* gave him for the first time a reasonable financial footing. This, with his architectural earnings over the last intensive year, put him at least in a better position than Moule to offer marriage. On the other hand, unlike Moule, it is doubtful whether he had the approval or even the knowledge of his own family, and he had not approached Emma's father. His absence from the dedication of the newly-restored St. Juliot church earlier that year[3] may have been a politic one. Mr. Gifford, attending a ceremony taken by his son-in-law, might not have been in a mood to meet another prospective one. His own outbursts were apt to coincide with the idea of marriage in his family.[4] It was therefore essential that Hardy should make a good impression and appear to have money in his pocket. It was perhaps to heighten such an impression, as well as for convenience, that Hardy instructed Tinsley to send the proofs of the September instalment (five opening chapters) to him, care of Mr. Gifford at Kirland House, near Bodmin. He himself left London for the west country on 7 August, taking the steam packet-boat from London Bridge to Plymouth. It is highly probable he saw Tryphena Sparks in her new job at Plymouth. One does not know exactly what state their relationship had now reached; but it is also possible that this marked the end of their relationship, and the return of his ring.

At all events, he went straight away to Mr. Gifford's house near Bodmin, for the proofs of *A Pair of Blue Eyes* had to be dealt with at once for publication on the 15th. At this point, Hardy's own reminiscences show all the irrelevance and evasion he reserves for something deeply personal and sometimes unpleasant. He dismisses the whole visit to Cornwall in a short paragraph.[5] He does not mention Mr. Gifford, nor even Emma. He does not say where he was staying, speaking vaguely of driving to St. Juliot, walking to Tintagel, and calling on some friends[6] of Emma at Lanivet, Captain and Mrs. Serjeant. A large part of the paragraph is taken up with a pointless anecdote about another elderly friend of Emma, Miss d'Arville, and her canary, which fainted whenever a cat came into the room, or even when it was shown a picture of a cat. There is absolutely no mention of Mr. Gifford nor Kirland House. Hardy's complete silence at this point has led some biographers to invent an exciting and dramatic scene, in which Mr. Gifford abused him for being of low origins. There may well have been some scene, since the unwelcome thought of a daughter's marriage inclined Mr. Gifford to drink, but it is not certain that it took this form. Admittedly, Irene Cooper Willis annotated her copy of Hardy's reminiscences with the remark that Mr. Gifford "was very contemptuous of Hardy's social position";[7] but she had the information from the second Mrs. Hardy, a suspect source, and even she did not speak of any angry confrontation. She described Mr. Gifford as "that amiable gentleman who wrote to him [Hardy] as a 'low-born churl who has presumed to marry into my family.'"[8] The imputation of low birth was, then, by letter, and even sounds as if it were made after marriage; for it is difficult to see how Mr. Gifford could have visited the Hardys, as he did, after their marriage, if he had made such a remark before.

On the other hand, some deep emotional conflict certainly happened. It is hinted by the curious companion poem Hardy wrote to balance his famous *When I set out for Lyonnesse*. This is the poem, almost identical in metre, *I Rose and Went to Rou'tor Town*. The place of the poem is

Bodmin, from the prominent height Rough Tor, just under ten miles away.[9] The poem mentions "The evil wrought at Rou'tor Town". When Hardy, in his old age, was asked point-blank what this "evil" was, he answered gruffly and cautiously, "Slander, or something of that sort".[10] This hardly sounds like an accusation of low birth only, but of something to do with his personal character.

Two other poems by Hardy, one almost certainly drafted at this time, may, when taken together, and their connection shown, indicate what this "slander" was. They sound as if Emma learnt that Hardy had been involved with other girls before her. Whether this was simply a lucky shot by Mr. Gifford, the natural and usual gambit of the Victorian father to point out his daughter knew little of Hardy's past, or whether he had heard something, is unsure; but the Giffords still had many friends and relatives in Plymouth, and it is conceivable that, with Tryphena now there, something about her and Hardy had leaked out. The two poems, which seem to indicate this kind of emotional crisis, are *Near Lanivet, 1872* and *The Chosen*. Curious and mysterious when apart, they may help to explain one another. The first at least was drafted early in Hardy's life, and probably, as its dated title shows, at about this time. Hardy referred to it frequently after he published its final version in 1917. He told Edmund Gosse it described a scene between him and Emma before their marriage; to Mrs. Henniker, he wrote that it was "literally true". He was disappointed that critics did not select it for comment, expecting them to do so, as he said, because it described "a strange incident, which . . . really happened". He took pains to identify the setting of the poem precisely as "Handpost on the St. Austell Road". This was Reperry Cross, under a mile from Lanivet, where there is an ancient monument consisting of a pillar two feet high, surmounted by an eighteen-inch circle with a cross carved on it, a typical Celtic, early Christian relic.[11] He describes how Emma, weary and depressed, leant against this, and laid her arms along the arms of the cross. He feels a touch of horror at her attitude; she too says "I wish I had not leant so!"

> And wordless we moved onward down from the hill
>   In the west cloud's murked obscure,
> And looking back we could see the handpost still
>   In the solitude of the moor.

Yet the poem does not end there, as a less deeply-felt poem might. Both he and Emma are haunted by the accidental vision of her crucifixion, if not bodily at least possibly "In spirit".

> And we dragged on and on, while we seemed to see
>   In the running of Time's far glass
> Her crucified, as she had wondered if she might be
>   Some day.—Alas, alas!

The poem is mysterious, as so many of Hardy's more personal poems are, because its terms are not completely stated; one is left in doubt about the exact nature of Emma's ultimate "crucifixion".[12]

It may have more meaning, though, if it is taken in association with another mysterious poem, *The Chosen*. One must be warned that there is much that is in doubt about this second poem. No one knows when Hardy composed it; he himself announced it in a sub-title as an allegory; and it has already been subjected to highly imaginative interpretation.[13] What strikes anyone reading it without preconception, however, is the likeness to the landscape and setting of *Near Lanivet, 1872*. In the same dark twilight, the woman breaks away from the man,

> And wanly she swerved, and went away.
> I followed sick: night numbed the air.
> And dark the mournful moorland lay . . .
>
> At length I came to a Christ-cross stone
> Which she had passed without discern;
> And I knelt upon the leaves there strown,
> And prayed aloud that she might turn.

The reason for the woman's horror and flight may help to explain both poems; for *The Chosen* begins,

> "A woman for whom great gods might strive"
> I said, and kissed her there:
> And then I thought of the other five,
> And of how charms outwear.

Hardy then recalls the features and ways of five women loved previously, and admits these to "the woman desired—at last!" She, on the other hand, greets the news with utter dismay:

> "—I feel a strange benumbing spell,
> As one ill-wished!" said she.
> And soon it seemed that something fell
> Was starving her love for me.
>
> "I feel some curse. O, *five* were there?" . . .

She turns back, however, to the "Christ-cross stone", though drooping and weary, as Emma had done in the other poem. Hardy then perceives, in allegory, that she has become in herself all the other five women. He takes her "composite form", and cares for it tenderly,

> Not passion-moved, but even because
> In one I could atone to all.

This highly-complex and curious poem, with its incantatory ballad-metre, its hardly-concealed sexual guilt, and its Christian echoes of the doctrine of atonement, is perhaps most interesting for the light it throws on the far more finished and profound poetry and meaning of *Near Lanivet*. It may give some hint of the stress of the occasion in Cornwall, if Hardy had admitted, or been forced to admit to Emma, that there had been a number of girls in his affections before her—and five seems roughly the number, though identification is perhaps misleading. However lightly he may have glossed this at the time, Emma's "crucifixion" may be said to have come in her fifties, when his *Wessex Poems* produced publicly his poems to all these loves; even the assurance of her own friends could not prevent her from feeling exposed and humiliated. Quite literally, at that time, she mourned to a friend, "alas . . . The *thorn* is in my side still",[14] actually using some sort of muddled crucifixion image of her own to express her wounded, martyred feelings.

This month of stress is perhaps reflected in Hardy's movements in Cornwall. He briefly visited St. Juliot, and made a long note about the look of Beeny Cliff, "green toward to the land, blue-black towards the sea. Every ledge has a little, starved, green grass upon it; all vertical parts bare."[15] This was to be expanded to startling effect later in the serial. Towards the end of the month, he was just over the Devon border, at Brent Tor, on the edge of Dartmoor, a few miles east of Launceston;[16] this was probably on some visit to Emma's favourite uncle, George Mitchell Gifford, bank manager at Launceston. Meanwhile, he had to provide another instalment of three chapters. He settled at St. Juliot once more, and on 30 August wrote to the publishers promising copy in a week's time, only to receive, on 4 September, a peremptory demand for it. He got it off, with apologies, on 7 September, assuring them that in future the instalments would arrive on the first of each month.[17] Whatever may have happened with Emma's father, he was well received by her brother-in-law, who on Sunday, 8 September, allowed Hardy to read the first lesson at evening service, Jeremiah chapter 36, in the new St. Juliot Church.[18] His attachment to Emma had survived whatever had passed between them; but the strain of an emotional crisis and the writing of a regular serial-story was considerable.

This is reflected in the first eight chapters of *A Pair of Blue Eyes*, though some of the uneasy construction of the early parts of the novel must come from the fact that this was Hardy's first commissioned serial, written to order. For the first instalment, corrected in proof when he was at Mr. Gifford's, he had frankly fallen back on previous experience and previous work. Once more, he cannibalized *The Poor Man and the Lady*. Even the heroine's family name, Swancourt, is only a few letters off Allancourt, the squire's name in *The Poor Man*, and her father's insistence on blue blood is very much the squire's too; biographers who see Mr. Gifford in this snobbery have failed to notice that these chapters were written before Hardy met him. The Swancourts' London address

9   (*a*)   Emma as Hardy first knew her

(*b*) Emma in middle age

11 Emma and Hardy during their courtship, August 1870

Searching for the glass (watercolour sketching in Valenc valley)

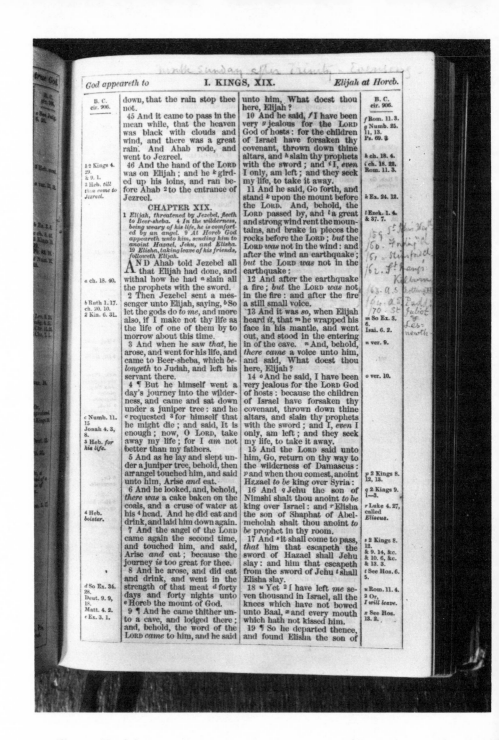

[handwritten: ninth Sunday after Trinity. Evensong]

down, that the rain stop thee not.

45 And it came to pass in the mean while, that the heaven was black with clouds and wind, and there was a great rain. And Ahab rode, and went to Jezreel.

46 And the hand of the LORD was on Elijah; and he *k* girded up his loins, and ran before Ahab 2 to the entrance of Jezreel.

CHAPTER XIX.

1 *Elijah, threatened by Jezebel, fleeth to Beer-sheba.* 4 *In the wilderness, being weary of his life, he is comforted by an angel.* 9 *At Horeb God appeareth unto him, sending him to anoint Hazael, Jehu, and Elisha.* 19 *Elisha, taking leave of his friends, followeth Elijah.*

AND Ahab told Jezebel all that Elijah had done, and withal how he had *a* slain all the prophets with the sword.

2 Then Jezebel sent a messenger unto Elijah, saying, *b* So let the gods do *to me*, and more also, if I make not thy life as the life of one of them by to morrow about this time.

3 And when he saw *that*, he arose, and went for his life, and came to Beer-sheba, which *belongeth* to Judah, and left his servant there.

4 ¶ But he himself went a day's journey into the wilderness, and came and sat down under a juniper tree: and he *c* requested 3 for himself that he might die; and said, It is enough; now, O LORD, take away my life; for I *am* not better than my fathers.

5 And as he lay and slept under a juniper tree, behold, then an angel touched him, and said unto him, Arise *and* eat.

6 And he looked, and, behold, *there was* a cake baken on the coals, and a cruse of water at his 4 head. And he did eat and drink, and laid him down again.

7 And the angel of the LORD came again the second time, and touched him, and said, Arise *and* eat; because the journey *is* too great for thee.

8 And he arose, and did eat and drink, and went in the strength of that meat *d* forty days and forty nights unto *e* Horeb the mount of God.

9 ¶ And he came thither unto a cave, and lodged there; and, behold, the word of the LORD *came* to him, and he said

unto him, What doest thou here, Elijah?

10 And he said, *f* I have been very *g* jealous for the LORD God of hosts: for the children of Israel have forsaken thy covenant, thrown down thine altars, and *h* slain thy prophets with the sword; and *i* I, *even* I only, am left; and they seek my life, to take it away.

11 And he said, Go forth, and stand *k* upon the mount before the LORD. And, behold, the LORD passed by, and *l* a great and strong wind rent the mountains, and brake in pieces the rocks before the LORD; *but* the LORD *was* not in the wind: and after the wind an earthquake; *but* the LORD *was* not in the earthquake:

12 And after the earthquake a fire; *but* the LORD *was* not in the fire: and after the fire a still small voice.

13 And it was *so*, when Elijah heard *it*, that *m* he wrapped his face in his mantle, and went out, and stood in the entering in of the cave. *n* And, behold, *there came* a voice unto him, and said, What doest thou here, Elijah?

14 *o* And he said, I have been very jealous for the LORD God of hosts: because the children of Israel have forsaken thy covenant, thrown down thine altars, and slain thy prophets with the sword; and I, *even* I only, am left; and they seek my life, to take it away.

15 And the LORD said unto him, Go, return on thy way to the wilderness of Damascus: *p* and when thou comest, anoint Hazael *to be* king over Syria:

16 And *q* Jehu the son of Nimshi shalt thou anoint *to be* king over Israel: and *r* Elisha the son of Shaphat of Abelmeholah shalt thou anoint *to* be prophet in thy room.

17 And *s* it shall come to pass, *that* him that escapeth the sword of Hazael shall Jehu slay: and him that escapeth from the sword of Jehu *t* shall Elisha slay.

18 *u* Yet 2 I have left *me* seven thousand in Israel, all the knees which have not bowed unto Baal, *x* and every mouth which hath not kissed him.

19 ¶ So he departed thence, and found Elisha the son of

Margin left column:
B. C. cir. 906.

2 Kings 4. 29. & 9. 1.
2 Heb. *till thou come to Jezreel.*

a ch. 18. 40.

b Ruth 1. 17. ch. 20. 10. 2 Kin. 6. 31.

c Numb. 11. 15 Jonah 4. 3, 8.
3 Heb. *for his life.*

4 Heb. *bolster.*

d So Ex. 34. 28. Deut. 9. 9, 18. Matt. 4. 2.
e Ex. 3. 1.

Margin right column:
B. C. cir. 906.

f Rom. 11. 3.
g Numb. 25. 11, 13. Ps. 69. 9.

h ch. 18. 4.
i ch. 18. 22. Rom. 11. 3.

k Ex. 24. 12.

l Ezek. 1. 4. & 37. 7.

[handwritten: 159 St. Abbr's Hill; 160. Ending of; 161. Sturbridge; 162. St Maur's Kilburn; 163. a.s. Tollington?; 164. a.s. Paddington; 170. St Fulbot? of; Lesnewth]

m So Ex. 3. 6.
Isai. 6. 2.

n ver. 9.

o ver. 10.

p 2 Kings 8. 12, 13.

q 2 Kings 9. 1—3.

r Luke 4. 27, called *Eliseus.*

s 2 Kings 8. 12. & 9. 14, &c. & 10. 6, &c. & 13. 3.
t See Hos. 6. 5.

u Rom. 11. 4.
2 Or, *I will leave.*
x See Hos. 13. 2.

---

12   Thomas Hardy's annotations to his favourite passage, I Kings, xix, 11 and 12, in his Bible, 1859–1870

13　Thomas Hardy in 1875, sketched by Emma in her "honeymoon" diary

14 (*a*) Death-bed sketch by John Antell junior of Hardy's uncle by marriage, John Antell, partly the original of Jude Fawley in *Jude The Obscure*

IN · MEMORY · OF
JOHN ANTELL
Who was Born

_____ _____ 18...
Died ... - - - - - - 1878

HE WAS A MAN OF CONSIDERABLE
LOCAL REPUTATION AS A SELF-MADE
SCHOLAR, HAVING ACQUIRED A VARIED
KNOWLEDGE OF LANGUAGES, LITERATURE
AND SCIENCE BY UNAIDED STUDY, &
IN THE FACE OF MANY UNTOWARD
CIRCUMSTANCES.

(*b*) Sketch by Hardy for John Antell's tombstone

15 Hardy's relatives (foreground) in the High Street, Puddletown (identified by Gertrude S. Antell)

16 Thomas Hardy in his old age, sketch by Augustus John

turns out to be the same as the Allancourts'. Even more strikingly, the style reverted in haste to old faults. The *sententiae* Horace Moule had criticized pervaded it from the first; the serial began with two paragraphs of sententious moralizings, though these were cut in the published book.[19] Still worse, the notebook-style references to painters and literature invaded the writing again; the second page of the final book introduces Rubens, Correggio, and the Madonna della Sedia, while it is not long before a Cornish servant has "a double chin and thick neck, like Queen Anne by Dahl"; Elfride, just as Cytherea had done, strikes a Greuze attitude.

Even more remarkable is Hardy's use of scenes from real life. The opening chapters are a word-for-word reconstruction of his own first experience of the St. Juliot Rectory, though the architect is made much younger, and Emma's elderly brother-in-law is made the heroine, Elfride's, clergyman father, as the real Mr. Holder was old enough to be. One wonders, in fact, what Hardy's host made of all this; for though his sense of humour is portrayed in quite a kindly way, he is, from the first, a terrible snob, as the plot, or that part of it borrowed from *The Poor Man*, compels him to be. He is also somewhat of a fool, not to have realized that the young architect, Smith, is, like Strong in the lost novel, the son of a local workman. Yet he is introduced with every sort of circumstantial detail, such as his attack of gout on the night the architect arrives, which pinpoints his resemblance to Mr. Holder. The latter must have needed all his sense of humour as he read his fictional likeness in the printed pages.

Elfride, the heroine, was as Hardy confessed, based in character and physical detail on Emma,[20] though not, he hastened to add, in the story of love-affairs and adventures that Elfride experienced. Yet it is clear that much of her actual dialogue is also based on things Emma had said or written; if more of Emma's letters and diaries survived, it is likely that the resemblance would be startling. For instance, one of the few fragments from an Emma letter to Hardy is her comforting comment on her attitude toward such a reserved and withdrawn character as Hardy was:

> I take him (the reserved man) as I do the Bible: find out what I can, compare one text with another, & believe the rest in a simple lump of faith.

In the middle of the novel, when Elfride is talking to the reserved and withdrawn literary man, Knight, who becomes unknowingly the younger architect's rival, she says,

> I suppose I must take you as I do the Bible—find out and understand all I can; and on the strength of that, swallow the rest in a lump, by simple faith.

Since this is copied into the novel with only minor transpositions of words, we probably have a great deal of Emma's actual sayings in Elfride's dialogue, if we could recover them; while Smith, visiting Emma's former home, Plymouth, echoes her letter, in which all going on around her seemed a dream.[21]

If the major characters all borrow from real life, so much more do the minor persons and incidents in the book. The satirical and elaborate description of the rings worn by the heroine's stepmother must come, possibly by way of *The Poor Man*, from one of Martha Sparks's accounts of her employer's dressing-table, another verbatim picture of "the female toilette" for reviewers to ponder. The long padding chapter when the chief characters, for no reason, decide to travel from London to Cornwall by boat, reproduces Hardy's own journey that August. As for minor figures, although Hardy once said that Voss, the chorister in *Under the Greenwood Tree*, was the only real person in the novels to be introduced under his own name, he had forgotten the pig-killer's anecdote in *A Pair of Blue Eyes* about the pig that was deaf:

> Ye could play tricks upon en behind his back, and a' wouldn't find it out no quicker than poor deaf Grammer Cates.

This was Rachel Keats, who lived next door to the Hardys at Higher Bockhampton, and who was stone deaf.[22] She had already appeared casually, in *Under the Greenwood Tree*, as "Grammer Kaytes", from whom candles are borrowed by the tranter's wife. Her son, who was a tranter or carrier, William Keats, lived exactly opposite the Hardys, and he and his family were the Dewys in that novel. Hardy's two spellings of her name were typically East Dorset, representing local pronunciation. In Cornwall, where she appears in the later novel, she would probably have been Keat or Keate.

Such resemblances, though some, like the last, have remained unobserved till now, tempt biographers and critics to see the two rivals in *A Pair of Blue Eyes* as Hardy and Horace Moule, the humble young architect and the man of letters who has befriended and tutored him.[23] Superficially, the relationship is certainly suggested. Knight writes for London reviews, and is very slightly patronizing to Smith, his former pupil. Hardy, however, maintained that Knight, aged thirty-two, his own age when writing the novel, had much more in common with himself; and a closer examination seems to bear this out. Not only does Knight write for a radical paper, while Moule wrote for the High Tory *Saturday Review*, but in every way Knight is intellectually most unlike Moule. All accounts of Moule stress his easy manners, his direct way of expressing himself, his simple methods of teaching, his personal charm;[24] his family, his sister-in-law,[25] his friends, all witness this. Knight is pedantic, comparatively charmless, and even something of a prig. Moreover, he uses in criticizing poor Elfride's romantic novel just those heavy-handed *sententiae* or moralizings that Moule had advised Hardy to avoid, and from which Moule's own reviews were refreshingly free. Knight is made to utter remarks that seem to come straight out of Hardy's own quotations in his Literary Notebook. When he produces a damning letter, signed with Elfride's name, he pontificates, incredibly at such a moment of emotional stress,

> In the time of the French Revolution, Pariseau, a ballet-master, was be-headed by mistake for Parisot, a captain of the King's Guard. I wish there was another "E. Swancourt"...

Quite apart from difficulties in making the distinction clear in pronunciation, this,[26] and similar oracular and literary utterances, are precisely what Moule avoided. His great gift was to simplify. It was the self-improving Hardy who could not resist the learned allusion. Some critics have seen Knight as a failed intellectual with morbid uncertainties, and drawn a parallel between these and the history of Horace Moule.[27] Yet the occasional references to *Hamlet*, a play which anyway pervades many scenes in the book, are hardly enough for that. Knight's weaknesses are nothing like the grim reality of Moule's dilemma, caught between constitutional cyclic depression and the drink that made him incapable. Above all, Knight is never humiliated academically; he achieves the college fellowship which poor Moule never attained.

What Hardy seems to have done, urged by the effort of serial-writing, was to repeat with more care and maturity a part of his technique in *Desperate Remedies*. In that novel he had represented two sides of his own nature by the two architects, one nervous and ineffective, the other intellectually accomplished even though self-taught. Now, merely taking the pupil and teacher pattern as a framework, he demonstrated in the two characters two deeper aspects of himself. There is the emotional immaturity, which is part of the boyish charm of Smith. There is the advanced intellectual stature, which nevertheless sits uneasily on Knight, because he too is emotionally unsure. "His lateness of development in virility, while mentally precocious",[28] Hardy's description of the key to himself, might apply exactly to Knight, like Hardy always uncertain when put to the test of a real human relationship. These two sides, underlined physically by the boyish Smith, spring from Hardy's inner self, and are the making of the two men in the novel. He himself was at pains to say[29] that he had made Smith look like a nephew of Hicks the architect, but he is essentially the young Hardy.

Yet when all this is said, and however much the novel in its haste became "a kind of rag-bag of information, ideas, descriptive vignettes, personal experiences, fragments of the author's brief literary past",[30] there is an impressive and professional side to the writing, which explains why it was so much admired by readers as different as Tenny-son, Coventry Patmore and Proust. The inconsistent, shifting, and even stagey manner of the work in the early chapters gradually settles to be a more controlled style and a study of character in far greater depth. This was preceded and eventually helped by a change in the place and circumstance of Hardy's own life. Back in London on 11 September, he found he could not write there. Nor could he do his architectural work for Roger Smith, whose surname and experiences in India he had given to his young hero. Smith was anxious to give Hardy a better contract and wider employment, since the Board School plans had been success-ful, and this was an expanding market. Hardy realized he must decide once and for all to give his time to writing, and Smith let him go. He was encouraged by the delayed but excellent review of *Under the Greenwood Tree* by Horace Moule in the *Saturday Review* of 28 Septem-ber, as "the best prose idyl we have seen for a long while past". Moule had also the intelligence to praise the social aspects of the book, and to see that, like all Hardy's early novels, it commented on society. Hardy's countryfolk were not to be regarded as quaint literary characters, recorded in patronizing pages, but

> It is a book that might well lie on the table of any well-ordered country-house, and that might also be borne in mind by the readers during kindly rounds undertaken among the cottages.

Pursuing this theme, and in a gentle vein of criticism that distinguishes Moule once more from any likeness to Knight, he added that it was a weakness in the author occasionally to make these genuine countryfolk "express themselves in the language of the author's manner of thought rather than in their own". His review came as timely and welcome encouragement; on the same day that it appeared, Hardy left for Bockhampton. He was to stay there, with no distractions, no other job nor personal problem, until he had finished the serial, ahead of time as it proved. The healing power of a settled and familiar background begins to make itself felt in the greater assurance of touch, which he shows from the middle of the book onward.

The far more serious nature of the love-affair between Elfride and Knight brings a more mature tone to the second half of the book. How-ever much of a bookish figure Knight may seem, we accept that Elfride preferred his "instructive and piquant snubbings" to the diffident expressions of the youthful Smith, just as Emma, in spite of her different class, was impressed by Hardy's own intellect. The rather tiresome and often-pouting young lady of the first half, Miss Capricious as Hardy was unfortunately led to call her, gives way to a real character of a woman, with overtones that verge on tragedy, and excite our interest and sympathy. This was once more acutely noticed by Horace Moule, when he received the published book in the following May. He at once commented how much better Hardy drew the woman than the lady.[31] Elfride, the superficially described lady of the first half, becomes a woman in the second.

As so often in a Hardy novel, a striking natural event serves as a fulcrum in the middle part of the book, to tip the balance of the writing into a higher seriousness and maturity. Such had been the fire at the inn in *Desperate Remedies*, ushering in at least more reliance on real life and less on Gothic melodrama. In Hardy's coming novel, *Far From the Madding Crowd*, the enormous thunderstorm, during which Bathsheba helps Gabriel Oak to cover the ricks in her farm, draws together their characters into a deeper relationship that pervades the second half of that book. In *A Pair of Blue Eyes*, the point is reached in the chapters where Knight slips over the cliff, and is rescued, after his agonizing ordeal, by Elfride's improvised rope of underwear. For the first time, Hardy exploits in prose what he had already achieved in some of his poems, the union of a scene from nature and an emotional relationship of his people. The cliff, minutely described from Beeny and its coastline companions,[32] becomes a part of the emotional life of Knight and Elfride; their instinctive embrace when she pulls him back to safety is the beginning of their love and their tragedy. The end of their drama, though not so often noticed, shows the same power to make a natural scene draw out the living state of the people in it. When Knight, by relentless and jealous cross-examination, produces from Elfride the final confession of her former love-affair with Smith, the two of them restlessly wander in an autumn stubble field that surrounds them with half-seen decay, as their love itself disintegrates around them, until the scene itself is made explicitly a symbol of their tragic desolation.

> The scene was engraved for years on the retina of Knight's eye: the dead and brown stubble, the weeds among it, the distant belt of beeches shutting out the view of the house, the leaves of which were now red and sick to death.

This is the type of unity that Hardy had till then only effected in poems such as *Neutral Tones*, where the frozen pond and fallen leaves are totally at one with the lovers' disillusion and icy parting.

Not all this second half is equally realized, though Elfride's hasty, instinctive, even sometimes absurd, prevarications under Knight's obsessive harrying, have a reality that derives perhaps from Hardy's own manoeuvres in trying to keep a former and a later love, Tryphena and Emma, separate and secret from one another. It must also be said that the stagey conventions of the earlier chapters take over the final episodes of the novel. Elfride's tragedy suffers from Hardy's falling-back on the novelettish convention that a Victorian heroine should tell enough of the truth to make her seem guilty, and remain unnaturally silent on the final facts which would exonerate her. Elfride's confessions end with the admission that she had spent a night alone with Smith. Her author, anxious to leave the implication of sexual misconduct in Knight's mind, does not allow her to add *how* she had spent it; that is, in a journey by express train from Plymouth to Paddington, a mad rush, when doubts assail them, by the two young people from platform to platform at Paddington to catch the down train back, and a journey home via Bristol, during which it is carefully and explicitly planted that there were two or three other persons in their compartment. Theatrical convention, too, takes over in the final stages when, in yet another train journey—Hardy was not immune from the typically Victorian pride and wonder at the steam-engine—the two rivals, now self-confessed, find that the special compartment coupled on to their train contains the body of Elfride in her coffin, thus providing a curtain scene of frank melodrama.

Yet if the ultimate effect of *A Pair of Blue Eyes* is still one of confused abilities and uneven performance, it had enough mastery over its materials to add to Hardy's confidence. He had overcome the haunting demands of serial-writing, and even turned them to advantage; he had learnt not to let the standard of a novel drop, but increase in power as it progressed. Indeed, the falling-off at the very end, and the perfunctory finish, may not be so much that Hardy had run out of ideas, as that a new and dominant idea for further writing had already occupied his attention, and a chance to present it had been offered to him in a quarter more important than any which had so far come his way.

16

Far From the Madding Crowd

HORACE MOULE's belated review of *Under the Greenwood Tree* was too delayed, thought Tinsley the publisher, to rescue the sales of that book; for although the other reviews were also universally good, the public had not responded. Yet on 4 October Tinsley at least promised to try more advertisement, quoting Moule's praises from the *Saturday Review*.[1] The public, however, continued to find the story, just as Alexander Macmillan had prophesied they would, "very slight and rather unexciting".[2] Tinsley softened the blow by promising a massive advertising campaign for *A Pair of Blue Eyes*, and encouraging the author to press on with the next instalment. "I *shall* lose my reputation as a judge of good fiction if you don't do great things", he wrote, although he had so far seen only two rather scrappy instalments of Hardy's serial, and afterwards confessed that he thought it "by far the weakest of the three books I published of his".[3] Moule's review, though, even if useless for general publicity, probably, by its very isolation, brought the book more attention in intellectual circles. Then, at the beginning of November, it was seconded by an even more delayed notice in the dreaded *Spectator*, which, far from its previous satirical style, seemed to be almost a copy of Moule's own review, praising the same points, and having the same minor reservations about the unnaturally literate rustic conversation.

Yet though these reviews failed to make the public clamour for the book at the circulating libraries, they were perhaps the most important literary assistance in all Thomas Hardy's early writing life. For they drew the still-anonymous author to the attention of one of the country's leading literary figures. In November 1872, Leslie Stephen read *Under the Greenwood Tree*. Stephen was the dominant English man of letters of the second half of the nineteenth century. Just forty, he was at the very height of his powers, which included top-class athletics and mountaineering as well as literature, and a college tutorship, which he had resigned in 1862 when fashionably losing his faith although still in Holy Orders. In 1882, having started the "English Men of Letters" series, he went on to initiate the *Dictionary of National Biography*, and become the father of Virginia Woolf. In the present year, 1872, he had been for the past twelve months editor of the *Cornhill Magazine*, which had been started in 1860 under the editorship of Thackeray. It had acquired a reputation for serialized fiction and essays of the highest quality, and

Stephen was looking for new young talent. Reading *Under the Greenwood Tree*, he found it pleased him as much as Moule said it would. It was not, he saw, a magazine story in itself, and he had evidently not yet identified the current serial by the same author now appearing for Tinsley; but the style of the rural "prose idyl" made him read it with great pleasure. It was well known that Horace Moule had written the notice. Stephen obtained from him the author's name, and wrote to Hardy himself with a proposal that would have delighted any new author: "If you are, as I hope, writing anything more, I should be very glad to have the offer of it for our pages".[4] He hinted that if Hardy agreed, the financial terms would be generous.

Stephen's letter reached Hardy at Bockhampton early in December, just when he was despatching the instalment of *A Pair of Blue Eyes* for January, nearly halfway through the book. The inspiration of feeling wanted in such distinguished company may have helped to give Hardy the greater confidence of the later instalments. The problem was, how to reply promptly, and keep this glittering proposal in play. He must say something concrete and practical, knowing how soon editors and publishers cool off. Stephen's letter had already been delayed by the rural post, picked up from being dropped in the muddy lane.[5] Eventually Hardy answered, with a mixture of frankness and shrewdness. He could not start at once on a fresh work, since he was already committed to his present serial. If Stephen could wait, the next novel should be at his disposal. It was necessary not merely to leave it at that, but to say something about what this might be. It was to be, he said, a pastoral tale with a pastoral title—*Far From the Madding Crowd*; both were calculated to attract Stephen, who had already found Hardy's "descriptions of country life admirable". More than this was needed, though, and Hardy added that the chief characters would probably be a young woman-farmer, a shepherd, and a sergeant of cavalry.

Whether Hardy made this up on the spur of the moment, or whether he had genuinely planned such a book, may never be known; but all the signs are that the main idea came into his mind this December. They were the peaceful first-fruits of his return to the home surroundings that had first nourished him. Gradually, from October through the autumn and winter, calm and certainty returned to his life, the familiar healing of all he saw and met. In misty October, walking back from Dorchester, or travelling in Burden the carrier's one-horse van with village food, saltfish and sides of bacon, dangling around the passengers,[6] Hardy could look back on Dorchester from Stinsford Hill,[7] and see, in the gleaming wet dusk, the town encircled by a halo like an aurora, a place of fearful yet familiar mystery, as it had appeared to him as a child. Next month, out early in the tranced November dawn, everything he saw seemed as still and remote as if it were at the bottom of a pond.

When the first frost came in the middle of the month, he noticed the miniature ruin of the cottage vegetable gardens, scarlet runners and cucumber leaves collapsing at a blow. Frost and December drove the family indoors, to long evenings of talk and memory round the glowing kitchen hearth. Here, as always, Hardy was in the spell of the most powerful presence in his life, his mother. His summer manoeuvres with other women, the awkward break with an old love, and the perils and uncertainty of a new one, were nothing to the assured care and special understanding she gave him as a matter of course. Though Mary, his second self, might add to the calm and pleasure, coming home each day from school-teaching, even she was only a shadow to Jemima in Hardy's life; she could add to their mother's memory of old children's rhymes, the special local verses used by her own school-children at Piddlehinton,[8] but hers, as always, was the supplementary role in the firelit evening kingdom of which their mother was the centre.

The long strange history of his mother's own childhood was the chief theme of their nights of talk: how her own mother, the dispossessed daughter, had lived in a mean cottage at one end of Melbury Osmond, while her father, wealthy farmer, lived at the other: how, penniless for life through her improvident marriage, she had brought up seven children, after her husband's death, on parish relief; how even before his death, her husband, farm servant, out of work for the most part by family tradition, got occasional jobs as a shepherd. She talked of the superstitions and weird apparitions of an isolated childhood. In one long evening this December, she talked to Hardy about his aunt Martha, and the strange figure of the fortune teller, who used to pass through Melbury Osmond every month. Martha gave him the day and hour she was born, from which he prophesied her large family and her emigration[9] with her ex-cavalry husband, to die in Canada. Mother and son were reminded of their three weeks' visit to Martha in Hertfordshire, when Hardy was only nine. That journey in his mother's company, to break the spell of Mrs. Martin, held many memories for Hardy as the great emotional adventure of his childhood, touched with magic and tragedy. Did his dashing uncle, a riding master, Hardy thought, in crack regiments, dazzle the small nephew one evening in his scarlet regimentals? At any rate, he and the daring, impulsive aunt,[10] now unhappily dead, were brought as vividly back to Hardy as was his grandmother, the farmer's daughter, married beneath her to a poverty-stricken shepherd.

So, by some such process, and by the folk-ballad atmosphere always evoked by his mother, perhaps even by her singing of *On the Banks of Allan Water*—

> For his bride a soldier sought her,
> And a winning tongue had he—

he could well believe that he had in his head for Stephen a tale about a woman, a shepherd, and a sergeant of cavalry. How then did he arrive at the bold stroke of the woman-farmer? As we have already seen, this almost unheard-of fancy was, again, something he had literally heard, and from yet another member of his mother's family. Bathsheba came to Hardy through Tryphena, when she was teaching at Coryates, from her stories at Weymouth about the landowner of Waddon, half a mile from her school, Catherine Hawkins. Widowed early in her thirties, Mrs. Hawkins had disregarded the advice of her relative and trustee, Granvile Hill, to sell the 525-acre farm and another property, with all their stock, combine the proceeds with her marriage settlement, and live on the income.[11] She refused and, though with little experience, determined to run the farm for her seven-year-old son Charles, to keep it in the family until he came of age. The first test of her resolve had been the terrible winter of 1865–66. Thanks to a shepherd with thirty years' knowledge behind him, William Slade, she had lost only four ewes and a few lambs; but, a worse disaster than any other, she had lost the shepherd, who died suddenly, and left her looking for another, though she felt it would be "a long time before his place will be so well supplied".[12] The fruit of Hardy's attachment to Tryphena was her story of the lady at Waddon, who ran the farm and needed a shepherd; Catherine Hawkins's venture combined with the bold character of Hardy's aunt to make Bathsheba Everdene, whose farm, otherwise so well equipped, is unaccountably in need of a shepherd, among all the Puddletown rustics of *Far From the Madding Crowd*, just when the first snows of winter fall.

Indeed, Tryphena herself may have recalled this offshoot of their 1869 attachment by her presence in Puddletown this same December. She had come to visit her ailing father, and to be involved, as it proved, in an odd family affair. Her sister Rebecca had decided, at the age of over forty, to marry a man she had been keeping company with, Frederick Pain, a Puddletown saddler. Three months after their marriage on Christmas Day, with Tryphena and her father as witnesses, she left him, and went to live with Tryphena at Plymouth. None of the Sparks family knew why she did this,[13] though a sensational and totally undocumented theory has been evolved that she was not Tryphena's sister but her mother, something which, if true, would certainly have appeared in the family papers. The probable cause, as of most actions in the Sparks family, was money, or lack of it. It may be conjectured that Pain had none, since he almost immediately emigrated to America.[14] Rebecca, more than the rest, was obsessive about money; she made a bee-line for the only member of the family who had any, possibly on the rebound of disappointment with Pain, and settled down at Plymouth as her sister's housekeeper. This Christmas visit may have been the last time that Hardy ever saw Tryphena, if indeed his own mother let him.

For Hardy had returned, just like some man in a D. H. Lawrence story, to the world of his mother, a fortress against the vagaries of other women. Although he seemed in old age to remember a flying visit to Cornwall in the New Year of 1873, other evidence suggests his memory misplaced this, and that winter and spring were spent entirely in his mother's home.[15] From this time there began to appear in his books the sharp aphorisms about the wiles of marriageable women that have disturbed some critics, who rightly find them obsessive in their frequency,[16] and even surprising in a man working toward marriage. They are not so surprising when one hears in them the voice of Jemima Hardy, providing, from the depths of folk-wisdom, a sexual philosophy for her favourite son. "Well, mind what th'rt about. She can use the corners of her eyes as well as we can use the middle"—Hardy, noting this saying, merely added the words, "Heard in Dorset";[17] but if he did not actually hear it at his mother's fireside, he certainly heard many similar warnings. As winter deepened, the hearth grew increasingly a place for folk-lore, and the legends of Melbury Osmond flowered in full superstition. His mother told him of the haunted barn there, where a lady in a white riding habit could be seen riding a buck at midnight, only to vanish at the sound of a chance spectator's sneeze.[18] The rationalist Hardy, sceptic and anti-clerical, retained to his end a belief and a relish in the supernatural that surprised his contemporaries.

In these surroundings, protected, without even the need to lift a finger for meals or mending, Hardy raced ahead with the instalments of *A Pair of Blue Eyes*, so fast that Tinsley was able to bring out the revised and completed book at the end of May 1873, before the last instalment had actually appeared in magazine form. The postponed discussion with Stephen about the new novel was, of course, partly behind such speed, and the perfunctory ending of the Tinsley serial has been noticed. On 9 June, Hardy, in his first break from home since the previous September, left for London to pick up threads, including the most important one of his interview with Stephen. In actual fact, he avoided seeing Stephen, perhaps becoming nervous at the last minute that the great man might treat him as Meredith had done. On the wave of undisturbed writing, however, Hardy managed to send him instead a few loosely-sketched chapters of the new book, and a few others in outline. Stephen approved, though he did not officially accept the novel until the autumn. Meanwhile, the publication of *A Pair of Blue Eyes* had for the first time revealed Hardy's name to the public. The response in the June reviews was a good one. The *Spectator*, perhaps taking to itself some credit for the lesson taught over *Desperate Remedies*, was officiously complimentary about the author's "rapid strides". It praised the humour, the artistic observation, the analysis of character, as well as Hardy's usual power in narrative. It even commended him for having an unhappy ending instead of a more conventional one, and so maintaining truth and artistic integrity though the reviewer, John Hutton, wrote to Hardy personally regretting this as a member of the reading public. Hutton had been the reviewer of *Desperate Remedies*, and his correspondence[19] this spring and summer shows him in a better light than the still-touchy author. He did not apologize for his previous review,[20] though regretting that he had tactlessly brought it again to Hardy's notice; indeed, he exclaimed, "I should much like to know why you wrote that sensation novel",[21] since he now recognized Hardy had such high potential abilities. Also, in both letters and review, he sounded a warning note. In the review he hoped to "hear of Hardy soon but not too soon again".

For Hardy this was a brief break from home and writing, diversified for a few days by showing London to his country-bred brother Henry. The first personal tie to be renewed was his old friendship with Horace Moule, a theme of impending crisis. At the New Year, Moule had obtained rooms in his old College of Queens', Cambridge, a privilege possibly linked with taking his M.A. that year. He was at any rate to have the company of dining in Hall,[22] and was not in lonely lodgings, but the signs are that once more all was not well with him. He was not only finding his work for the Local Government Board increasingly arduous and exacting; but it was almost certainly now that something went wrong with his engagement to the governess which, his family hoped, might save him from himself. She broke it off, under circumstances which will never be known. A sensational story that she was alienated by an exhibition of drunkenness may probably be discounted,[23] for, as will be seen, there was another even more sensational factor in his story. His watchful physician, James Hough, kept an eye on his increasing depressions, and provided a nurse when necessary. Moule confided to him his fears that he would be unable to carry on his Local Government work, though the district inspector was so far satisfied with it. When it was term-time, and Cambridge was full of young people, he found relief in his habitual though unofficial care for them. Late in May, he wrote to Hardy[24] on office notepaper to ask advice for a young B.A. of Trinity, who wanted to be an architect. He also gently chided Hardy for getting his designation of Lord Luxellian wrong in the recently-published *A Pair of Blue Eyes*, a solecism which Hardy corrected in later editions. In the most affectionate terms he proposed a meeting. This took place on 15 June in London, and was followed on 20 June by Hardy's first visit to Cambridge, where he stayed in college with Moule. After dinner, they strolled about the Backs in a magnificent sunset. Next day, Moule took him on the classic site for a visitor, the roof of King's College Chapel, where in the morning sunshine they had an unforgettable view over the flat East Anglian levels, all the way to Ely Cathedral. He also opened the west door of the chapel, for Hardy to have a view of the rich, dramatic interior, with the fan-vaulting, on which they had walked, like a huge stone flower. He saw Hardy off for London, in an affectionate parting.[25]

The next journey was also a visit of affection. Emma Gifford was staying at Bath with her friend the old lady, Miss d'Arville, owner of the sensitive canary. Hardy travelled down there that same night, and spent a happy ten days with Emma, discreetly chaperoned, in expeditions about Bath and Bristol. On 1 July they got away on their own to Chepstow, the Wye Valley, and Tintern Abbey, where they repeated Wordsworth's lines to one another in the sky-roofed tracery by the river. Looking through the empty windows at the green steep hills around, Hardy characteristically compared the age of these to the stonework of ephemeral man which they guarded, a parallel to the reflections of Knight as he clings to the age-old cliff-face.[26] One does not know what was settled between them on the emotional side, but Emma, in old age, wrote of Hardy being at that time her "chosen",[27] and Hardy remembered their love in a tender poem.[28] Stephen's offer must have made the prospect of an early marriage more practical, and Hardy confidently pressed on with more specimen chapters for the editor.

For, having once found the background for successful work, he did not stay long away, even with Emma. By the next day, 2 July, he was back at Bockhampton, getting ahead with the new novel, *Far From the Madding Crowd*, in a setting that lived up to its title, based closely on the old, unreformed Puddletown, before it was improved by the Gothic building and public institution of a respectable façade by Squire Brymer. It was, as Hardy said in a later preface to the book, a place "notoriously prone" to "that love of fuddling", which he knew very well from his Hand uncles, with their drinking and wife-beating. In fact, he eventually made one of the key turns of the plot depend on an inhabitant getting drunk, the incident of Joseph Poorgrass, drawn from an actual Puddletown man, and his "multiplying eye" after drink. He brought everything into close contact with his own immediate surroundings. The woman-farmer, borrowed from the example of Mrs. Hawkins of Waddon, acquired a Puddletown setting, and the farmhouse he had chosen for his heroine, Waterston House on the way up the valley to Piddlehinton, took its fine Caroline gables on what Hardy afterwards called "a witch's ride of a mile or more" closer to Puddletown itself. The picture of an unreformed, partly unenclosed rural community of the old sort was deepened by the exact painting of an area only a very few miles in size, and known to Hardy all through his impressionable youth.

The foreground figures to this background were still the three he had promised Stephen, and probably remained so for the first dozen chapters, which, it has been plausibly conjectured, were what he had completed by the end of September.[29] These, the woman-farmer, the shepherd, and the cavalry sergeant, are already there, though the shepherd has been given a more respectable pedigree, being formerly a small independent farmer who has lost his stock by natural disaster, and the sergeant, though present, is still more or less waiting in the wings of the action. The fact that a fourth and deeply tragic figure was eventually added to this dancelike quadrille of folk-ballad characters may have been due partly to the stunning real-life tragedy which now invaded Hardy's peaceful and settled world of deep-laid affection. On 2 August, Horace Moule made what proved to be his last gesture for his former pupil's career in literature. Though he had sworn never again to review a friend's book, he broke the rule in the *Saturday Review* of that date. It was the best of all his reviews of Hardy's work. He found that though Hardy had produced rapidly, this was a work of mature thoroughness, and genuine depth. "Out of simple materials there has been evolved a work of really tragic power." Once more recognizing the social nature of Hardy's mind, he showed that this was a real portrayal of some of the more destructive social barriers of their time. He admitted that Hardy still had "much to learn and many faults still to avoid", and was uneasy at the priggishness of Knight. This criticism was, again, an additional sign that the portrait of the reviewer in the novel was not in any way meant for his own generous self, and that the relationship between Smith and Knight had very little to do with the friendship Moule enjoyed with Hardy. In details, he picked on the obvious and literal cliff-hanger of Knight's two chapters of peril on the rock-face: "worked out with extraordinary force . . . they recall the intense minuteness and vivid concentration of the most powerful among French writers of fiction." None of this friendly criticism could have prepared Hardy for the coming event, which caused him later to double-mark the two lines from *In Memoriam*,

> Diffused the shock thro' all my life,
> But in the present broke the blow.

17

Moule

MOULE's words were the last message he was to direct towards Hardy. On Friday, 19 September, he came back from a summer holiday to his rooms in Queens'. Cambridge was empty, a fortnight before Michaelmas Term, and even his brother Charles was not yet in his rooms at Corpus. The onset of autumn is a melancholy time in Cambridge, with the mists rising from Coe Fen over the causeway, and the drenched Michaelmas daisies drooping their heads in the college gardens. A wave of melancholy and restless agony about life and work seized him in a way that at once alarmed his doctor. It was the worst bout he had seen, and he felt it urgent to provide a nurse, who came on the Saturday morning, and to send a telegram to Charles Moule that night. His brother arrived on the Sunday, and had a distressing and all-too-familiar talk with him. The drink he took to try and combat his depression seemed to him to threaten his work. The possibility of losing his position was very much on his mind, and he became at first excited and then deeply depressed. After a three-hour discussion, he said he felt so ill that he was going to bed. Charles remained writing in the outer room. After a few minutes he heard a sound, which at first he could not place, a kind of trickling. He went into the bedroom, and found Horace Moule lying on the bed covered in blood. Thinking at first he had broken a blood vessel, Charles Moule ran to the Porter's Lodge, and sent a messenger for Dr. Hough. Hastening back, he found his brother lying there, bleeding but still just able to speak. He said, "Easy to die" and "Love to my mother". Only then, perhaps, did Charles realize that Horace had done what he long ago threatened to do, and taken his own life. The surgeon, when he arrived, confirmed that he had cut his throat. The nurse, also summoned, found an open razor. Horace Moule never spoke again. At the inquest, held the next day, the jury returned a verdict of "suicide whilst in a state of temporary insanity".[1]

On the Sunday his friend died, Hardy had spent the day walking to and from the great autumn fair at Woodbury Hill, east of Bere Regis, which was to appear in *Far From the Madding Crowd*. On Wednesday, 24 September he heard the news. Next day, Horace Moule's body was brought to Fordington, for burial on the Friday in consecrated ground, which the form of words of the jury's verdict had allowed. On the previous evening, 25 September, Hardy, according to a later poem, went to Fordington churchyard, and contemplated the mound of chalk dug from the newly-prepared grave. It was this day, rather than the day of death, or that of the funeral, which he attended, that he always remembered.

Hardy reserves for this cataclysmic event in his life the almost total reticence he displays when anything has moved him most deeply. Any notations of it, when they occur, have therefore all the more meaning. In the poem, *Before My Friend Arrived*, he says he sketched the mound of chalk in the churchyard that Thursday evening. In his copy of *The Golden Treasury*, given to him by Moule, he sought out Shakespeare's Sonnet 32, ironically finding it under Palgrave's title of *Post Mortem*, and put the Thursday's date against these bracketed lines:[2]

> "Had my friend's Muse grown with this growing age,
> A dearer birth than this his love had brought,
> To march in ranks of better equipage:
>
> But since he died, and poets better prove,
> Theirs for their style I'll read, his for his love."

His journey to Cambridge that June now moved him so much that he added to his account of it, retrospectively, the words, "His last smile". Reading *In Memoriam* later in the 1870s, he came across the section where Tennyson revisits the university, with its memories of Arthur Hallam, and against the opening lines,[3]

> I past beside the reverend walls
> In which of old I wore the gown;

he noted "(Cambridge) H.M.M.", also pencilling the line

> Another name was on the door:

Otherwise, there is barely a mention of his tragic friend. Though it has been said[4] that Hardy left instructions to his second wife and executors to destroy anything about "M—", this is not in fact true. Quite apart from the Hardy notation for Moule always being, as we have seen, "H.M.M.",[5] which was Moule's own way of signing his letters to Hardy, the abbreviated instructions are to delete "M——ls",[6] that is Memorials, meaning useless memoranda.

We have little evidence, either, of what Hardy thought of the whole question of suicide, though his later notebooks deal extensively with quotations about this topic, as they tend to do about all morbid states of mind. It may be significant that in his Milton, which he had been reading since the middle 1860s, he heavily lined the margin of Eve's long plea for suicide in *Paradise Lost*, Book X, and that in *Samson Agonistes*, where Samson's death is described as "self-kill'd Not willingly", he underlined the words and put an exceptionally large question-mark against them, thus perhaps tacitly opposing the verdict of the Cambridge jury.

With so little direct evidence, and in the absence of some vital dates in Moule's life, much must necessarily be speculation. There is, though, one hitherto unknown factor, which is perhaps the most important of all. It may even be that it was first revealed to Hardy on that memorable last visit to Cambridge, for it remained vividly in his mind in his old age, when he confided it in detail to the second Mrs. Hardy.[7] On that evening of 20 June, as they talked in Moule's rooms in Queens', the conversation between the two men went on deep into the summer night. Moule stood by the mantelpiece of his keeping-room, with the candles guttering behind him. As he spoke on and on excitedly, he seemed to Hardy to be pointing unconsciously at the long trailing overflow of wax that was gathering on the candle. This, in country-superstition terms, was known as the "shroud", and it was held to foretell the death of the person to whom it applied. This is the factual basis for Hardy's later poem *Standing by the Mantelpiece*.[8] There was another fact, though, far more significant than a mere legend, that must have entered into the long discussion. This was the fatal secret of Moule's personal life; whether it caused or followed the open secret of his drunken bouts, will probably never be known, though the fact itself, concealed by his own family, is fully attested. At some unspecified time, Moule had had, or had been persuaded he had, a bastard child by a low girl in his father's parish at Fordington. This was, according to Florence Hardy, the "tragedy of his life". There were other even more lurid details. At all events, and whenever in fact Hardy first knew it, it certainly bears on the one poem by Hardy, to which he gave the date of composition in this year, 1873,[9] the brief verse Hardy called *She At his Funeral*.

> They bear him to his resting-place—
> In slow procession sweeping by;
> I follow at a stranger's space;
> His kindred they, his sweetheart I.
> Unchanged my gown of garish dye,
> Though sable-sad is their attire;
> But they stand round with griefless eye,
> While my regret consumes like fire.

There have been many guesses about the background to this poem (including the fantasy[10] that the girl is Tryphena Sparks, who on this very day[11] was nervously preparing her staff for a school inspection), but the "character of the girl", to quote Florence Hardy on Moule, gives sense for the first time to Hardy's words, "gown of garish dye". If this is indeed a literal picture, it is unjust to the Moule family, who were totally devastated by Horace's death, both at this time and for long after. Their grief was deep and genuine. Charles Moule himself wrote a poem in that year,[12] both depicting Horace's character, and trying to find acceptable terms for the suicide.

> O kindly heart, & tongue, & pen,
> To advise, to do unlooked-for good! . . .
> A strange disquiet wore his brain,
> Till restlessly he seized on rest.

Members of the Moule family regretted for years afterwards that they had been able to do so little for him. The heaviest burden of regret and horror at the event naturally fell on Charles, who had been a few yards from the suicide. The anniversary, mourned by the whole family, was always a time of particularly deep personal trial to him. Handley Moule, noting the day in his diaries[13] for the rest of his life, recorded five years after, "Our beloved H.'s day . . . Dear C. better than our fears", and, a few years later, "A fine day. Oh how solemn in its recollections of 1873. The Lord be with dearest Charlie". If Hardy shared in any way the feelings of the girl, and felt excluded from the grief of the Moule family, it was the exclusion of his own peculiar kind of grief. Modern thought is apt to deal heavy-handedly with the topic of Victorian male affection. Hardy has left the evidence we have seen that he felt for Moule in some way as Shakespeare did for his friend, and as Tennyson did for Hallam. There is no other point of definition.

What seems more sure, though not precisely definable, is the effect on his work. It does seem likely that, until this moment in time, *Far From the Madding Crowd,* for all its deeper assurance of style, was something of the mixture as before which Stephen had seemed to suggest he wanted. Bathsheba and Oak, in their early wooing scenes, are simply a more mature version of Fancy Day and Dick Dewy in *Under the Greenwood Tree* and even to some extent Elfride and Stephen Smith in *A Pair of Blue Eyes.* It is a conventional comedy treatment of the blunt and over-simple wooer and the capricious lady, who blows hot and cold in her moods. Even the figure of Sergeant Troy is so far only a worldly voice speaking through a barrack window, the sexually-accomplished male person whom Hardy never seemed to draw with much conviction or inside knowledge. Yet with Farmer Boldwood, at this point only a character who knocks at the door with an enquiry and goes away, an entirely new note of introspective tragedy is struck. It is probably right to regard Boldwood as a minor character developed into a major one, rather than a new character introduced,[14] but once developed, he takes on unforgettable stature. Not only does he play a decisive part in the chief action of the story; he is, as a man, more fully analysed than any Hardy character before him. It is a study in morbid psychology, which was very close to Hardy's inner life, but which, until this time, he had hardly allowed to be explicit in his work. Now he could write with frank power:

> The phases of Boldwood's life were ordinary enough, but his was not an ordinary nature. That stillness, which struck casual observers more than anything else in his character and habit, and seemed so precisely like the rest of inanition, may have been the perfect balance of enormous antagonistic forces—positives and negatives in fine adjustment. His equilibrium disturbed, he was in extremity at once. If an emotion possessed him at all, it ruled him; a feeling not mastering him was entirely latent. Stagnant or rapid, it was never slow. He was always hit mortally, or he was missed . . . Bathsheba was far from dreaming that the dark and silent shape upon which she had so carelessly thrown a seed was a hotbed of tropic intensity.

Such analysis of character in depth makes the conception in the previous novel of Knight, the man who cannot like a girl who has already been kissed, as trivial and superficial as it indeed is. This is not to say that Boldwood *is*, in any way, Horace Moule any more than Bathsheba owes anything more than the factual matter of farm-ownership to Mrs. Hawkins, though there are odd reminders. Hardy cannot bring himself to let Boldwood actually commit suicide after shooting Troy; he lets a servant knock the gun he turns on himself out of his hand; yet he brings him in, like Moule's jury, a verdict of insanity, even at the cost of denying himself the hanging he had meted out to the melodramatic Manston in *Desperate Remedies*. What Hardy is doing, almost for the first time, is to explore the morbid recesses he knew were concealed behind the appearances of human nature, and to face them unflinchingly. Moule's death taught his old pupil a more profound lesson than any they had shared in his lifetime.

For the influence of this personal disaster in Hardy's life went far beyond the novel he was writing at the time. Though it deepened the tragic sense of life in *Far From the Madding Crowd*, still that novel could end happily as its central hero, Gabriel Oak, overcomes the troubles and vicissitudes of his early wooing, and marries Bathsheba with some hope of their future stability. In the end, we are told of their love that

> the compounded feeling proves itself to be the only love which is strong as death—that love which many waters cannot quench, nor the floods drown, beside which the passion usually called by the name is evanescent as steam.

No Hardy hero from that time onward ever comes to such a settled and assured ending. From this moment, the tragic and defeated hero arrives for good in all Hardy's works. In the earlier novels, his heroes had indeed suffered, often quite severely, and often through their own faults, but the way had been made relatively clear for them at the end. Edward Springrove rescues and marries Cytherea, Dick weds Fancy Day, and never even knows of her love-passage with the parson. The joint heroes of *A Pair of Blue Eyes* are indeed cheated by death, but the tragedy is that of Elfride herself, and the novel ends with the two men recognizing the rightful grief of her mourning husband is greater than theirs. Even the most put-upon—and most Hardy-like—of all Hardy's heroes, Christopher in *The Hand of Ethelberta*, is eventually given the consolation prize of marriage with Ethelberta's younger sister Picotee.

Yet, from the time of Horace Moule's suicide, no hero of a Hardy novel ever receives anything like the optimistic comment which he even allows to Boldwood's reprieve in *Far From the Madding Crowd*, "Hurrah! . . . God's above the devil yet!" Such a remark would be unthinkable if applied to the tragic destinies of Clym Yeobright, Michael Henchard, Giles Winterborne, Angel Clare (even though the greater tragedy is that of Tess) or, most of all, Jude Fawley. Jude dies quoting the bitter reproaches of Job to God for bringing him into the world at all. The tragedy of these men is that not only do they suffer humiliation and various forms of defeat during life; nothing alleviates in any way that suffering at the end. Rather, turn after turn of ironic circumstance seems to conspire to make their agonies worse. Whether they have brought tragedy on themselves by fatal weakness, or whether it seems to attack them gratuitously, does not matter. Their plight is always accentuated and underlined by whole sequences of horrors that need not have been, and yet are. Life batters at them until they hardly think it worthwhile to live. Several of them, in fact, notably Henchard, Winterborne, and Jude, commit what is virtual suicide; though not of such an immediate and dramatic kind as Moule's own, in one way or another, their end is meant as self-destruction.

Even in the minor novels, where the deeper tragedy of self-slaughter would outweigh the lighter plot, arbitrary disaster is evoked to prevent a happy ending. Swithin is reunited with Viviette, in *Two on a Tower*, only to clasp her dead body, while in *The Trumpet Major*, John Loveday, in the last paragraph, is sent, by what seems a casual dismissal on the novelist's part, to a lonely grave in the Peninsular campaign. In all his later novels, Hardy never seems to tire of inventing twists of fate that will frustrate even the faintest hopes of his heroes. They no sooner have a respite than another damning circumstance is unravelled for their discomfiture. Hardy has been criticized for the coincidences by which he brings this about. The furmity-woman turns up at the critical moment to reveal the secret of Henchard's wife-selling twenty years before. In *Jude the Obscure*, the number of times that the ill-fated quartet of Jude, Arabella, Sue, and Phillotson accidentally cross each other's paths is almost beyond belief, and even totally minor characters such as Conjuror Vilbert reappear pat to the minute to add some further twist of irony.

Hardy rebuffed the idea that he was not playing fair in these coincidences, and always hinted darkly that real life could show instances even more strange, yet wholly true. This is borne out by yet another horror from Moule's tragic real-life story. Whether or not Hardy knew this at the time of Moule's suicide, he must certainly have known it by the time he came to write *Jude the Obscure* in the 1890s. For the bastard child of Horace Moule and the Dorchester girl was, according to Florence Hardy,[15] brought up in Australia, and, to add a final touch to the whole macabre story, was hanged there. When and why this happened is not specified; but the story obviously is closely connected with what has seemed to many critics the height of improbability in *Jude*, that part of the novel which has to do with Jude's son by Arabella. The child in the novel is brought up in Australia, and is then sent to Jude in England. In a sequence of events whose brutality seems out of key with even the worst of the rest of the novel, the boy eventually hangs himself, together with the two small children of Sue and Jude.

Once more, the timing of the real-life tragedy in Moule's life is uncertain. What is certain, because of all the circumstantial likeness, is that Hardy used this part of his friend's actual story to create the weird child, little Father Time, in *Jude*. Just as the real hanging of Martha Brown contributed to what seems the inevitable hanging of Tess, so the manner of life and death of Moule's bastard boy must have some bearing on the most terrible part of *Jude*. The alternations in Jude's character between the sensual—women and drink—and the spiritual—learning and religion—may not come entirely from the character of Moule. Hardy, in writing the novel, gave them some flavour of the other real-life character in his own class, who had started the idea of the novel, his own uncle by marriage, John Antell.[16] Yet the whole incident of the child, which gives such a gratuitous and fatal turning-point to the novel, by completely altering the former relationship between Jude and Sue, can only come from Horace Moule's disastrous history.

One wonders if it also throws light on one of the most debated symbols in all Hardy's poetry and prose. In *Jude*, the boy arrives by rail in a third-class carriage. He has the key of his box tied round his neck by a string, and his ticket is stuck in his hat. As everyone has pointed out, this is the same picture that Hardy paints in his poem, *Midnight on the Great Western*, the unforgettable appearance of the journeying boy.

> In the third-class seat sat the journeying boy,
>   And the roof-lamp's oily flame
> Played down on his listless form and face,
> Bewrapt past knowing to what he was going,
>   Or whence he came.

In the band of his hat the journeying boy
Had a ticket stuck; and a string
Around his neck bore the key of his box,
That twinkled gleams of the lamp's sad beams
Like a living thing. . . .

The current of barely-suppressed emotion both in this poem and in its prose counterpart is so strong that all critics agree it must be based on personal experience; and this would seem to be confirmed by the exact details of description precisely repeated in both. This has led to speculation, of which the most extreme example is that the child might be a bastard son of Hardy himself.[17] Even the reference in another very personal poem, *Wessex Heights*, to "a ghost . . . in a railway train" has been thought[18] to refer to this suppositious bastard, although an early manuscript version of that poem distinctly names the figure as "her".[19] With Moule's actual bastard fully vouched for, sharing at least some of the circumstances of the child in *Jude the Obscure*, it does not seem necessary to saddle Hardy with the fatherhood of a child who never existed.[20] The picture, for all that, may be a real one; it is even possible Hardy saw it, or at the least had it described to him in conditions of emotion, such as his last meeting with Moule, which burnt it into his visual memory. No one knows if the son of Moule by the Dorchester girl came back at any time to England; but if he did, as described with so much circumstantial detail in *Jude the Obscure*, it is not impossible that he might be sent to his father, Moule, in such a way. The Great Western Railway served both Dorchester and Marlborough, the two places where Moule lived.

This, however, must be conjecture. The certainty is that, from the time of the death of Moule, Hardy never portrayed a man who was not, in some way, maimed by fate. He did not hesitate to load the dice at every point against his tragic heroes. Even if a case can be made that their own weakness or foolishness or rashness of choice caused their downfall, Hardy also made sure that the results would be as dire as possible by introducing other elements of coincidence, irony, and what seems like divine indifference or even malevolence. He does this with absolute conviction, because, he is now fully persuaded, such things do occur, in all their extremes, in real life. However much his naturally sombre mind inclined that way before, however much his own identification with Job and the prophets of destruction may have coloured his expression, we can date the emergence of Hardy as a fully tragic artist, an expounder of man's true miseries, from the suicide of his friend, and the appalling revealed ironies of that personal history.

Success and Marriage

MANY other incidents in Hardy's personal life certainly seem to prefigure his later conception, in *The Dynasts*, of an overworld where spirits, ironic, sinister or pitying, play cat and mouse with human fate. One of these moments had now arrived with the death of Moule. For, within a few days of the funeral of his friend, Hardy received another letter from the man whose philosophy was to influence his own more than any contemporary,[1] and who was to have more effect on his actual progress as a writer than any other person. This was Leslie Stephen. By an extraordinary mixture of luck and irony, Stephen was exactly the same age as Moule, and everything that Moule had attempted and failed to be. It was not only his sound mathematical degree at Cambridge, nor his college fellowship, which he had been obliged to resign on his marriage in 1867.[2] Stephen had at once become one of the senior *Saturday Review* writers, discoursing, it was said, on every topic from the University boat-race—he himself was a bad oarsman but a marvellous coach—to modern metaphysics. Everything he touched turned to success. He had had his pick of magazines before Smith, Elder had given him the *Cornhill*, and he was married to the elder daughter of the first editor, Thackeray himself. He was the acknowledged leader of advanced thought in London; beside his brilliant light, Moule was a flickering candle, and now snuffed out.

Hardy had not yet met Stephen, but he was already attracted by him and his thought. Since the *Saturday Review* was High Church and Tory, he did not find Stephen's agnostic articles there. Stephen kept these for another periodical, *Frazer's Magazine*, edited by J. A. Froude, to which he had contributed since 1867. It is pretty sure that some of the realistic detail, in which Hardy described Knight hanging on the cliff-face in *A Pair of Blue Eyes*, was based on Stephen's essay, "A Bad Five Minutes in the Alps". This first appeared in *Frazer's*, and in it Stephen imagines himself in just such a situation on one of his mountaineering expeditions. When Hardy wrote a later sonnet on Stephen, he compared his personality to that of one of the famous mountains he had climbed, gaunt, craggy, and outwardly unprepossessing, "In its quaint glooms, keen lights and rugged trim". Stephen's daughter, Virginia Woolf, wrote that this poem was incomparably the truest and most imaginative portrait of her father.

In all this many-sided, and often contradictory, person, it was Stephen as a literary editor who affected Hardy most. For Stephen had a different view of editorial duties than any Hardy had yet encountered. Tinsley, for instance, after voicing a few of his reader's opinions, had put Hardy on the market more or less as he stood, with hardly any alteration of manuscript. This was not all Stephen's way as an editor. Muttering to himself in the manner pilloried by his talented daughter in *To The Lighthouse*, he would go through the manuscript scribbling in its margins and sometimes all over it.[3] He was an adept in seeing where an expression should be changed, and particularly where the proportion of the whole book demanded that a passage should be shortened or cut out altogether. He was also prompt and businesslike in his dealing with authors, leaving them in no doubt of his intentions, unlike all the other publishers Hardy had known. When he received the first dozen chapters of *Far From the Madding Crowd* from Hardy on 1 October, he wrote straight back, confirming the contract for the whole serial. Hardy was therefore able to press on with confidence, and was not caught out when Stephen wrote to him, at the end of the month, suggesting that *Cornhill* might start printing it in January 1874. Such instant occupation, and the pressure of such an influential mind, probably did much to keep Hardy from brooding on Moule's suicide. He was at once in a relationship with a powerful intellect, beside which Moule's, though remembered with personal affection, must have seemed slight. Hardy had, in fact, the best conditions for successful work, a much stronger guide and mentor than he had had before, and the inspiration of his home and family and neighbourhood, on which to draw for the deepening of his original story and its people.

The effect of these surroundings is evident in almost every sentence in the novel, and can even be traced to special words and phrases. Hardy gives some hint of it, when he speaks himself of helping his father with the cider-making while writing the novel, and of wandering in the countryside, finding he had no notebook, and scribbling ideas and phrases on large dead leaves, white chips of wood, pieces of stone or slate, whatever came to hand.[4] Every personal experience was pressed into service. On 3 November, Hardy put in his notebook the peculiar effect of the late autumn sunset:[5] "a brazen sun, bristling with a thousand spines which struck into and tormented my eyes." This strange sunset description, pointed by the unusual word "bristling", is reproduced in the beginning of the famous chapter 28 of the novel, *The Hollow Amid the Ferns*, which paints the scene as "evening, whilst the bristling ball of gold in the west still swept the tips of the ferns". On the next day, 4 November, he recorded a note on a thunderstorm at the Bockhampton cottage: "The light is greenish and unnatural . . . A silver fringe hangs from the eaves of the house to the ground."[6] In the equally celebrated passage in the novel, when Oak covers Bathsheba's ricks from the thunderstorm, the lightning is described as "emerald", and the rain, when it comes, is "in liquid spines, unbroken in continuity".

One of the most remarkable features of this book is, in fact, the large number of scenes of natural observation, each one more striking than the last. In earlier books, as has been noticed, a spectacular event concerned with man and nature has almost always formed the fulcrum of the book's balance, tipping the human characters in one direction or another. Such was the insidious spread of fire in *Desperate Remedies*, and, even more sensationally, Knight's ordeal on the cliff in *A Pair of Blue Eyes*. Now, the decisive and highly suggestive scene where Troy, in the fern hollow, woos Bathsheba by the wizardry of his sword drill, —a scene from real life, as Hardy once told a friend[7]—is followed, not many chapters later, by the even greater scene where the shared peril of the terrible thunderstorm and the saving of the ricks brings Oak and Bathsheba closer together. Just as the characters are not only deeper, but more deeply related, so the scenes from nature that form symbols of their emotional development become infinitely more varied. There are no less than three major scenes which involve, in a highly dramatic way, the vicissitudes of a flock of sheep, expertly described, and each one forming a background to some stage in Gabriel Oak's character—his stoicism as his own flock plunges to ruin on the precipice, his independence in the saving of Bathsheba's sick flock, and the shearing scene where his faithful wooing of Bathsheba is symbolized by his tender care for the shorn ewes. There might even have been a fourth sheep-flock scene, relating Oak and Troy, had it not been for Leslie Stephen.

For the corollary to such richness as Hardy was now achieving, while the people and places familiar from childhood took life from his pen, was that a firm editorial hand should be laid on any sign of over-writing. This is what Stephen provided, He had a genius for seeing not only where but how compression should be applied, just how far pruning was healthy to the progress of a whole book, what parts, though attractive in themselves, were out of proportion. It is not quite sure that the fourth sheep-flock scene[8] was actually omitted at his insistence, but almost certainly his general attitude persuaded Hardy to cut it, and this forms a case in point of a passage, highly interesting in itself, which would have held up the book at a critical stage, Hardy clearly wished to show in it that Troy, after his marriage to Bathsheba, tried to run her farm by "trickster" means, a tactic successful in his dealings with Boldwood, but foiled on this occasion by Oak's knowledge and honesty. The passage, of at least nine pages, requires a long, technical explanation to the reader of the effects of the disease of sheep-rot. If sheep are infected by this deliberately, by letting them graze in damp pastures, they will apparently fatten early—a result of the first stages of the disease—and be sold profitably to unsuspecting buyers. Hardy has Troy attempt this trick by artificially flooding the pasture, and be caught out by Oak, who had conveniently been absent long enough for Troy's strategem. Oak, outraged both as a shepherd and as Bathsheba's secret admirer, confronts Troy with proof of his wrong-doing, and forces him by physical violence to give up the practice. This passage, though intriguing, makes such demands on the reader's time and understanding, is so digressive, and, above all, out of character, that Hardy, almost surely at Stephen's suggestion, removed it bodily.

Often too, Stephen made exact and precise suggestions to Hardy about how to improve the novel. Another heavily-cut extract[9] shows how Hardy followed Stephen's advice about the chapters of the sheep-shearing and the shearing supper. These two, chapters 22 and 23, were originally three. Stephen, in a letter of 17 February 1874,[10] pointed out that it was one chapter too long, and asked whether the story told by the dismissed bailiff was relevant to the progress of the whole book, as indeed it was not. Hardy obediently, and to the good, removed seven pages of heavy-handed rustic humour, including a long pointless story by a minor character, Coggan, and an endless discussion about eating salad. As a result, not only is the action swifter, but the relation of the main characters, Bathsheba, Boldwood, Oak, to be joined in the following chapter by Troy, is kept in the forefront of the reader's attention, undistracted by picturesque but long-winded local colour. Another later example of Stephen's creative editorial intervention was the curtailment, presumably at his request, of the rather artificial scene where Troy goes for a swim and is thought to be drowned, which involved a cut of three and a half pages.[11] Even near the beginning, Stephen had apparently made firm and practical suggestions that the scene of Bathsheba paying her workmen was too long.[12] The malthouse conversations in chapters 8 and 15 also show heavy and beneficial cutting and revision.[13]

It does seem, then, that some of the mature quality of the book, astonishing when compared with much that Hardy had written before, its firmness of construction, its steady and adult development of character, was due to Stephen as a critic, shaping the luxuriant and often poetic material that Hardy presented to him, without losing its fullness and strength. Edward Garnett was to adopt the same method with D. H. Lawrence over *Sons and Lovers*, persuading Lawrence to revise, rewrite, and compress the whole book, with artistic judgement that Lawrence would have done well to heed in his own later work. It is most noticeable too, whether Stephen was responsible or not, that many of the pedantic and "self-improving" digressions seem also to have gone from Hardy's style, though only to return in later novels which did not have the benefit of Stephen's quick ear and eye. There is little recourse to the minor painters, though Bathsheba blushes like the painting "Sunset at Sea after a Storm" by Francis Danby, and the more homely features of her maid, Liddy Smallbury, take on the Flemish character of pictures by Terburg and Gerard Douw: Ruysdael and Hobbema are also invoked for the watery sunrise that shines over Fanny Robin's storm-ruined grave, and a farm woman in a brown work-dress has the mellow hue of a sketch by Poussin. Yet such educational nudgings are mercifully infrequent. Nor is there anything to match in inappropriateness the historical information that Knight, in *A Pair of Blue Eyes*, had provided about Parisot and Pariseau, though there is one curiously dragged-in reference to the quack doctor, John St. John Long.

The writing of *Far From the Madding Crowd* seems to show that Hardy wrote at his best under the guidance of a trained but sympathetic mind. He had always needed this, in a pathetic and almost Coleridgean want to supplement his own self-taught judgement. In addition, he needed, as he said to Stephen in the later stages of the book,[14] to be living on or near the spot that he was writing about, in this case Puddletown with its rich, varied and, for him, highly personal history, the home of his cousins, the Sparks and the Antells, of his uncles, the Hands, and farther back of the somewhat mysterious origins of the Hardy family itself. Most of all, he needed, in the marrow of his being, the reassurance of the familiar, the scenes and the people of his boyhood home, mother, father, brother, sisters, and the Hardy cousins down the road. It is highly significant that after his deep and convincing analysis of the character of Boldwood,[15] he adds, as if instinctively, a warning that such a character might become unbalanced because of its lack of just these family ties. "No mother existed to absorb his devotion, no sister for his tenderness, no idle ties for sense".

Being so close to his originals in real life, Hardy had no need of literary models. There is an almost total absence of the second-hand, the novelistic, the Harrison Ainsworth clichés that disfigure earlier novels. In fact, an attempt by one critic[16] to suggest that Hardy drew his thunderstorm from one in Ainsworth's *Rookwood* disproves the case it sets out to make, and can hardly produce more than two words, "lurid" and "metallic", that these accounts have in common. The artificial thunderstorm in *Desperate Remedies* had indeed borrowed Ainsworth's stage-properties. The storm in *Far From the Madding Crowd* is real life. Unlike Ainsworth and his generalities, it is so close to nature that the smallest details convince us. Oak, quick to observe weather signs, stumbles over a toad that is trying to squeeze under his door, "soft, leathery and distended, like a boxing glove", the description aided by Hardy and his brother Henry recently practising the "manly exercise" of boxing.[17] On his kitchen table he finds a large slug, and two big black spiders drop from the ceiling. He realizes that these creeping creatures, seeking shelter indoors, presage abnormal rainfall. He then observes the flock of sheep, huddled in a tight knot, their tails to the storm quarter. This means some abnormal storm. One prophesies a heavy soaking, the other dangerous lightning; both kinds of weather threaten Bathsheba's unprotected ricks. These precise details add an invincible air of truth, so that we then seem to go as readers with Oak through every phase of the storm, to be singed by the lightning, drenched by the downpour, equally with him.

That is the virtue of Hardy's life-study method. On the other hand, it leads him, as intelligent critics were to see, sometimes to be too particular and quaint. One cannot help feeling that Oak's defective old watch, and his "constant comparisons with and observations of the sun and stars" to tell the time are copied too literally from that habit in his own brother Henry, with whom Hardy was now sharing a good deal of his life at home. It also seems that the rustics, some of whom, Hardy said, were actual men from Stinsford and Puddletown.[18] were allowed too many proverbial quirks of expression and oddities of personal habit, as reviewers again pointed out. Henery Fray's insistence that the central "e" in his name should be sounded is like Hardy's actual uncle, Henery Hand, who carved this spelling of his name in Puddletown church. Above all, there is the pervasive influence of Hardy's mother, in the acid remarks about women and marriage, which critics of our own time have found obsessive and odd; there are gratuitous remarks on women enjoying a sense of power at the end of the shearing feast, and cynical sentences about woman's ability to deceive herself after Troy has first kissed Bathsheba.

In fact, one of the most remarkable things about this deeply home-centred production is that Emma Gifford was not allowed to see any of it, in draft. It is one of the few among Hardy's novels that do not have any pages fair-copied in her hand. In his memoirs, he claimed that he did this to give her a "pleasant surprise" when she should eventually see the printed serial.[19] Such a schoolboy excuse seems incredible, in a grown man who had discussed all his previous novels with her, used her as an amanuensis for them, and been inspired by her not to give up writing. The much more plausible explanation is a double one. With such a watchful and possessive mother, Hardy, even though in his thirties, may well have felt awkward about a to-and-fro constant exchange of letters and packages with his fiancée. Mrs. Hardy's disapproval of designing mates for her children was powerful and it is notable that Hardy was the only one eventually to marry. Secondly, this was a novel entirely populated by the working-people from whom Hardy himself was sprung. How much of this he had by now revealed to Emma is doubtful; but it is even more doubtful that he had told her anything like the whole truth—that his mother, for instance, had been brought up by Poor Law charity, and that all his relatives in Puddle-town and Stinsford had been, at one time or another, servants and labourers. This was a book deeply entwined with Hardy's personal background. Emma's bewildered remark when she read it in serial form, was "Your novel sometimes seems like a child, all your own and none of me".[20] It seems likely that this secretive man did not want to give away too much too soon to his middle-class fiancée.

He may also by Christmas have become aware that her superficial young-lady attainments were not quite so striking as they had seemed in the provincial isolation of remote Cornwall, where the occasional visiting clergyman, school inspector, school lecturer, or the dentist from Camelford provided the only intellectual stimulus.[21] For some time in December, Hardy at last had his meeting with Leslie Stephen, and was introduced to an intellectual world, which, if sometimes daunting, was unlike anything he had met before. His introduction was, in fact, invested with all the eccentricity of a former University don. A few days before Christmas,[22] Hardy called at his newly-built house in South Kensington, to be greeted at the gate by Stephen hauling back a huge barking dog. The apparition, which startled many first acquaintances, of this tall gangling figure, with strange flat-topped head and bright red hair, was accentuated for Hardy when Stephen's shouts of command revealed the dog's name as Troy. To Hardy's surprised remark, "That is the name of my wicked soldier-hero", his host replied, "I don't think my Troy will feel hurt at the coincidence!" When Hardy, typically methodical, revealed that he had looked up the street directory for this new area, and found there was another Leslie Stephen nearby, Stephen retorted in his brusquest Cambridge manner, "Yes, he's the spurious one."[23]

Stephen, however, touched Hardy's human heart at this first encounter by confessing that he lived in a street so brashly new that the paving and the road were not yet made up, because he had played in the fields nearby when he was a child. Hardy does not seem to have responded with the confidence that he had himself wooed Martha Sparks in the basement of another new house close to Stephen's own. Yet a shared reticence was obviously one factor that drew the two men together. Stephen, who could withdraw into gloomy silence with anyone over-forthcoming, did not treat Hardy to this alarming experience when he came to lunch the next day, in a thick yellow fog, to meet Mrs. Stephen and her sister Anne Thackeray. The ordeal of two other young writers, Edmund Gosse and Robert Louis Stevenson, on a recent similar occasion was not repeated. Then Stephen and his wife had sat in frigid wordlessness all evening, while his voluble sister-in-law had chattered, provoking occasional groans from Stephen, and imminent giggles from his young guests. Stephen was comparatively genial with

Hardy, even going so far as to treat him to an imitation of the extra-ordinary antics that Carlyle went through to light his pipe. True, he returned to form in a discussion by the ladies about the story of David and Saul, in which Hardy naturally extolled the Bible version of his up-bringing. Stephen sardonically recommended them all to read Voltaire's cynical account. Otherwise, he left Hardy with a friendly feeling that quite cancelled his first impression, and, added Hardy, "never changed".

This was the well-educated and distinguished intellectual atmosphere that Hardy enjoyed before going for a brief and parochial Christmas holiday to Emma at St. Juliot. He would not have been human if he had not felt the contrast. In one home, advanced women held an equal place with the men; though Stephen gave his deepest groans at his sister-in-law's extravagant housekeeping, he published her articles in the *Cornhill* and they were highly commended. This is not to support the theory, put forward by Siegfried Sassoon, that Hardy should have married Anne Thackeray.[24] A wild, amusing, creative, and muddle-headed creature of impulse, she shattered her freethinking but sexually puritanical brother-in-law by flirting with, and eventually marrying, her own godson and cousin, who was seventeen years younger than her-self. Her inconsequent chatter would surely have irritated the reserved and studious Hardy as much as Emma's eventually did, and in Emma he at least had a frugal housekeeper, brought up to make the most of genteel middle-class poverty. Yet Hardy noticed in Anne with ad-miration "some of her father's humour", and his later memoirs show how attractive he found it to be only one remove, so to speak, from one of his great heroes of literature.[25] Emma's breathless attempts at scribbling, perhaps not unfairly portrayed in *A Pair of Blue Eyes*, were in a different world from those envied names of English letters. It was a circle into which he himself was to be fully accepted in the following spring.

Even at the present time, everything connected with the new book seemed a startling step forward into another world. Coming back from Cornwall on the last day of 1873, Hardy bought the *Cornhill* at Ply-mouth station, and there was the first instalment of *Far From the Madding Crowd* in the chief place at the beginning of the magazine. Even more, it was brilliantly illustrated. Hardy had written more than one letter to Stephen, hoping that the illustrator would not make his rustics boorish and quaint, and saying that he could send authentic details of peasant clothes and farm implements. He added, though, that perhaps the illustrator might be "a sensitive man and . . . would rather not be interfered with".[26] To Hardy, brought up in a rural background, where only lucky girls like his cousin Tryphena could escape from a life of brute drudgery, it was inconceivable that an artist for a London paper

could be other than a man. It was one of the biggest surprises of his life
to find a woman illustrating his serial, and in the most expert fashion,
with authentic research and feeling for local colour. His own sister's
naïve little water-colours, and even the slightly more skilled sketches of
Emma had never prepared him for anything of the sort. A society where
women were competing on equal terms was, indeed, a new thing. The
first woman doctor had qualified in 1865, the first suffrage petition been
presented by J. S. Mill in 1866, and the Cambridge College for Women,
afterwards Girton, had opened in 1869. Hardy had seen the rigid
Saturday Review mount virulent attacks on the Girl of the Period and
her unpleasant manifestations. Yet here was one of them, Helen
Paterson, chosen by a leading editor to illustrate his story, and doing it
to perfection. Once again, his ideas of what constituted an educated
woman received a jolt.

Only a few days later Hardy received a curious shock of the same
nature, by having his own work mistaken for that of the most intellectual woman of the age. The *Spectator* of 3 January 1874, in its review of
current magazines, came out firmly with the idea that *Far From the
Madding Crowd*, which the *Cornhill* was printing without Hardy's name,
must be by George Eliot. "There is a passage descriptive of the companionship of the stars, so learned and so poetical that it seems to be
irrefutable evidence of authorship." This, to Hardy's ultra-sensitive
mind, was both flattering and irritating. Shepherd Oak's vigil under the
stars was such a personal part of Hardy's country-bred world that he
could not admit it might have been the work of a woman, country-born,
indeed, but for a quarter of a century town-based. He continued to
grumble at this otherwise complimentary guess all his life, though
Stephen at once wrote advising him to take the praise as praise, however
wrong-headed.[27] It must also have given Hardy food for thought to find
a critical article by Anne Thackeray highly praised in the same paragraph.

Yet even in this apparently brave new world, there were pitfalls for
the unsophisticated author, of a most unexpected and contradictory
kind. Stephen, though agnostic and progressive, was deeply imbued
with his Evangelical upbringing in one direction. This was sex. He had a
puritan obsession, which he attempted as an editor to disguise by
blaming it on the prejudices of the reading public. In March, Hardy had
an ominous little note suggesting that Troy's seduction of Fanny Robin
would have to be treated "gingerly". Stephen added, "Excuse this
wretched shred of concession to popular stupidity; but I am a slave." In
fact, the very independent editor was a slave to his own complex
emotions. On 13 April, he was deeply worried that Fanny had died in
childbed and wondered "whether the baby is necessary at all". When
Hardy dined with him on 24 April, Stephen tried to reinforce his own

prejudices by saying that some lady subscribers had been shocked by the humorous story in the very first instalment, where Bathsheba's father only keeps faithful to his wife by taking the ring off her finger and pretending "he was doing wrong and committing the seventh" in adultery with her.[28] With the usual display of groaning, Stephen blamed himself for passing the passage, but the whole exhibition was clearly designed to warn Hardy against any dangerous frankness in the ticklish later stages of the book. Hardy countered by a similar display of hypocrisy on his own part. He wrote

> The truth is that I am willing, and indeed anxious, to give up any points which may be desirable in a story when read as a whole, for the sake of others which shall please those who read it in numbers. Perhaps I may have higher aims some day, and be a great stickler for the proper artistic balance of the completed work, but for the present circumstances lead me to wish merely to be considered a good hand at a serial.

Nothing in Hardy's life has been more misinterpreted than this last sentence. Book after book repeats this as a guiding principle in his writing life, and patronizes him for having such low and utilitarian aims. The fact is, it should simply be taken as a gambit in his temporary manoeuvres with Stephen, to allay the editor's alarms, and to insure a profitable sale for his novel elsewhere; for this was Hardy's first big success in America, carefully prepared by skilful advertising. He needed the money; for now he was taking the plunge and intended soon to marry.

It is once more an irony that he took this decision when all the evidences are that he was moving among women very different from Emma. Just as Emma herself had seemed educated and "a lady" beside Tryphena Sparks, so the women he met with Stephen and with George Smith, the publisher, were in another class, of both intellect and manners, from the provincial Emma. He had in May met his woman illustrator, Helen Paterson; she too was about to be married, to William Allingham, the poet. In old age, Hardy had extraordinary day-dreams about what would have happened if he had married her instead of Emma, and wrote one of his most inept poems on this fancy.[29]

When Emma came up to London that August to stay with her brother Walter Gifford at 54 Chippenham Road, Westbourne Park,[30] she was very much of a country cousin, bewildered by the size of Town, the distances between places, and, in her own words, "very much embarrassed at going in an omnibus".[31] Hardy, putting in his own residence qualification for marriage at his old lodgings in the nearby Celbridge Place, cannot have helped noticing the difference between this and women such as Anne Thackeray, Helen Paterson, and the almost legendary literary lady, Mrs. Procter, whom he had just met.

Yet on 17 September 1874, the marriage took place at St. Peter's Church, Paddington. Though it is always said it was against the wishes of Emma's family, the fact remains that two of her relatives were there, and none of Hardy's. Her brother, Walter, gave her away and signed the register, while the ceremony was performed by her uncle, Edwin Hamilton Gifford, Canon of Worcester. The most remarkable absences are those of Hardy's own family. His mother and father, though the latter was beginning to suffer from rheumatism, could have had an easier journey to Town than Mr. Gifford from remote Bodmin. Perhaps the strangest and yet most understandable absence is that of Hardy's virtual other self, his sister Mary. She had shared nearly every decisive move in his life, except this one. Their relationship had been something like that of Wordsworth and his sister Dorothy. Perhaps, like Dorothy Wordsworth, she felt she could not bring herself actually to witness the ceremony. Nor was it to her that Hardy wrote home announcing that the wedding had taken place, but to his brother Henry,[32] now adult enough to be more of a confidant on a man-to-man basis. At all events, and whatever the attitude of either family may have been, the marriage took place in a mellow September sunshine, almost fifty-five years to the day after Keats had written Hardy's favourite *To Autumn*. The couple spent their wedding night at the Palace Hotel, Queensway,[33] and travelled next day to begin their honeymoon at Brighton on the way to Rouen and to Paris.

Ethelberta

BY THE time the newly-married couple reached Martin's Hotel in Queen's Road, Brighton, the Keatsian calm of their autumnal wedding-day had reverted to a stormy week-end, with rough seas and a gale. It was hardly a good augury for the channel-crossing they were to make early the next week, but Brighton provided plenty of bad weather distractions. Emma was fascinated by the aquarium, and noted closely the habits of the turtles, seals, and various fish. There were also concerts on both the Saturday and Sunday evenings, and a Brighton Sunday, she found, was like the type of Sunday she expected to see in Paris, "all enjoyment & gaiety & bands of music & excursionists". On Monday, Hardy braved the still-rough seas and bathed. Emma sketched in her tiny pocket-diary, and noticed with delight the exotic architecture of the Pavilion and the Dome. The night crossing to Dieppe, with the waves still white-capped, was an unmixed ordeal, with all the ladies, "low-lying", but she recovered enough on the train to Rouen to enjoy dinner at the Hotel D'Albion there,[1] in the Quai de la Bourse on the banks of the Seine.

Hardy himself left no account anywhere of this honeymoon. He had made to his brother the somewhat strange announcement, "I am going to Paris for materials for my next story". It may be conjectured that the stay at Rouen, on the way, was for him to see the French Gothic architecture he had so often studied in books. Like some of his later journeys with Emma, this was to be in one way or another a working trip. He says nothing of her. She would understand, however, a honeymoon on which one of the considerations was authorship, since she regarded herself as an author too, and her diary notes, often very vividly phrased, slowly develop into plans for stories. When the lively chambermaid at the hotel burst into their room unannounced, she found them both writing at the desk.[2]

Hardy's plans for future writing are obscured by various more or less vague statements he made much later in life. The idea that anyone writing about rustics might be mistaken for George Eliot seems to have weighed oddly heavily with him. So does a piece of newspaper gossip that he was a house-painter. He afterwards said it was events like these that made him give up a story also set in Dorset, and try one with an exotic background. The cancelled story was, he later said, one on the idea that became *The Woodlanders*. If so, it is a good thing he waited for that conception to mature, for he was clearly in no state for a considered work at this time. He felt a forced uprooting from the settled home atmosphere that had produced the unity and solidity of *Far From the Madding Crowd*, and did not apparently try to write another novel until the following March. A few days before marriage, he had posted off a pot-boiling short story to the *New York Times*. The main value of this feeble effort, called "Destiny in a Blue Cloak", was that it won him a contract for the American serializing of his next published novel. What, though, should the next novel be? In spite of his remark to his brother, Paris was not used as the setting of any subsequent story. Apparently the gossip about the house-painter, which otherwise he would hardly have remembered, made him feel that he must somehow conceal his own humble origins. Possibly he had not even yet revealed these fully to Emma, still less, in his abnormal reticence, to Leslie Stephen and his set. Already he foresaw problems raised by his own past. What would newspapers and column-writers make of an author whose mother had been a charity-child and a cook, and whose closest relatives, some of whom he had wished to marry, were in the servant class? What, for that matter, would provincial middle-class Emma make of the full story of his past life?

So Hardy seems temporarily to have given himself up to energetic sight-seeing, and shelved the future, while at home *Far From the Madding Crowd* ran through its final and much-praised instalments. With Emma he climbed the hundreds of steps of the central tower of Rouen Cathedral, up the incongruous iron spire surmounting it, the Fleche, and was rewarded with the view of the townscape breaking through dissolving September mists. After a few days, they moved to Paris on Thursday, 24 September, staying at the good, moderately-priced hotel recommended by Baedeker for English and American visitors. This was the Hotel St. Petersbourg in the Rue Caumartin, adjoining the Madeleine and the Opera, near all the sights.[3] These they did for a solid week, more or less in the order laid down by Baedeker, the Place de la Concorde by moonlight, the Louvre, the Tuileries, Versailles, Notre-Dame, the Hôtel Cluny, and the Morgue, which Emma found "*not offensive* but repulsive". Les Invalides and Napoleon's tomb were a point of pilgrimage for Hardy, with his family legends of the 1804 and 1805 invasion scares, in which his grandfather had been one of the local militia. Emma noted that, like many Englishwomen with a rather eccentric idea of fashion, she was subjected to a good deal of staring from men, women, and children. "Am I a strange-looking person—or merely picturesque in this hat?", she questioned herself, somewhat uneasily and a little pathetically, for she always tended to dress younger than she was, and she may have had secret doubts about the hat itself. She was, however, clearly reassured when Hardy, suffering from a cold since his bathe at Brighton, felt chilly and left her for twenty minutes alone, while he fetched his coat from the hotel. In that short space, there were attempts to pick her up by no less than "three hommes", as she confided to her diary in tiny writing.[4]

On the last day of September, the short honeymoon was over. "Adieu", wrote Emma, in the pigeon English-French of her Plymouth school. Everything had been "charmante", particularly the people, and even including the cats, which were "superbes" and "magnifiques".[5] It had been a schoolgirl dream come true, and though she hardly mentions her husband, clearly a time of great excitement for her. Some of Eustacia's obsessive longing for Paris in *The Return of the Native* may derive from this. London on the first day of October seemed "dirty London", and the week-end spent looking for houses in the Wimbledon and Surbiton area was a trial. Emma consoled herself by playing with an idea for a story derived from the conversation and appearance of ladies on the homebound cross-Channel steamer, while Hardy busied himself with his first task as a married man, rents and rooms. By Tuesday, 6 October, they were settled in St. David's Villa, Hook Road, Surbiton, and on that day they had a visitor for tea. This was Emma's father.[6] He brought with him the little daughter of Emma's eldest cousin, Robert Gifford Watson, whose father was abroad. One does not know how Mr. Gifford viewed his own daughter's beginnings of married life with her author husband; though the Surbiton district was a respectable enough address, no Victorian middle-class father would feel happy about furnished lodgings as a first home. It was possibly after this visit that he wrote the wounding letter about Hardy having "presumed" to marry into the Gifford family. At all events, it is the sole entry in Emma's diary for the Surbiton house, where they were to stay for the first five and a half months of their married life.

In the meantime, publication of *Far From the Madding Crowd* in two volumes took place on 23 November 1874. Hardy inscribed a copy to Canon Gifford, who had married them, and later signs show that he was far from being cut off from his wife's family. There is no mention, however, of his usual return to his own home this Christmas. He may have felt that it was not yet time for his family and Emma to be fully revealed to one another. Also, this December, Tryphena's poverty-stricken father, James Sparks, died at Puddletown, and the district was full of Hardy's Sparks cousins, dividing their father's few poor sticks of furniture, and making arrangements for a headstone in the church. It was not a time to bring home his new bride. So Hardy sat back at Surbiton, and read the reviews of his novel. By and large, they were very good, though by no means uncritical. The only bad one, which Hardy perhaps did not see, was a vicious attack by Henry James in the

New York *Nation*. James foreshadowed his later insufferably patronizing attitude towards Hardy's work by saying in this notice that "the only things we believe in are the sheep and the dogs", a remark which had the distinction of providing a model for a reviewer, nearly twenty years after, who could find nothing good in *Tess* except "the few hours spent with cows".[7] James, whose own novels seldom admitted any signs of his characters having to work for a living, was doubtless repelled by just what *The Times* of 25 January 1875 praised so discerningly.

> There is not a lady or gentleman in the book in the ordinary sense of the words. They are all working people, and ever so much more interesting than the idle lords and ladies, with the story of whose loves and sorrows Mr. Mudie's shelves are always crammed.

This review saw for the first time that Hardy was an essentially working-class author, of exceptional talent, best employed with settings and people he understood at first hand. He would have agreed with those modern critics who find the ultimate union of Oak and Bathsheba so satisfactory because it is a genuine working one.[8]

All reviews agreed on the book's power. The chief complaint was centred on the likeness, real or imagined, to George Eliot, and the over-written dialogues of the rustics, which even Stephen had questioned in the final instalments.[9] The *Examiner*, *Athenaeum*, *Spectator*, *Academy* (by Andrew Lang), *Westminster*, and *Saturday Review* all brought in George Eliot, some finding too much likeness, others finding that she excelled him in the same medium. It was an undertow of critical opinion which might well disturb the settled praise of the general verdict. Only the *Manchester Guardian* in February 1875 came out unequivocally for the "perfect, solid, and substantial" character-drawing, with no qualification. There were signs of individual prejudice too. The *Athenaeum*, which had long ago been bothered by the "coarseness" of *Desperate Remedies*, found it present again. More constructively, it advised Hardy to write more slowly and carefully. This was a note struck in a private letter[10] by John Hutton, who had not this time reviewed Hardy in the *Spectator*, his brother the editor, R. H. Hutton, having taken the book. R. H. Hutton had been among those who found the rustic dialogue far-flown. John Hutton's private letter recognized that Hardy knew more about rural talk and its semi-Biblical overtones than his brother did. Yet even he suggested that Hardy had "multiplied or rather drawn together into one society instances of this remarkable union of humour and satirical philosophy". He added a note that repeated the pointed warning of the *Athenaeum* in his own more tactful style.

> Will you pardon me if I beg you not to be prodigal of your power but to make *every* book better than the last, with the thoughtful conscientiousness of *true* genius & greatness.

This was only to underline what the publisher Tinsley was to say bluntly a few weeks later. Annoyed, admittedly, that Hardy had, as he thought, broken faith, by giving the serial and book without warning to the *Cornhill* and Smith, Elder, Hardy's former publisher wrote,

> I hope you will not think me impertinent but how you could have made such mistakes *in art* in a work so brim full of genius as "*The Madding Crowd*" is one of the things I cannot understand.

Prophesying all the same future greatness for Hardy, he naturally refused to part with the rights and stock of *Under the Greenwood Tree*, except for an exorbitant sum. Even with American publication of *Far From the Madding Crowd*, Hardy, with a wife now to support, could not throw money away.[11]

The winter of 1874–75, when she observed copies of the novel regularly carried by ladies in the trains between Surbiton and London, must have been one of triumph for Emma. She clearly had the Victorian, romantic view of the great man of letters as a popular hero. In this naïve but touching belief, she had brought back from Paris an ivy leaf from the grave of Balzac in Père-Lachaise.[12] It was glory that her husband was on a way to become one of that company, and perhaps a justification in the face of her own family. Sympathetic John Hutton divined this when he wrote,[13] "How your wife must glory and triumph in your genius—Tell her we sympathize in her glory". Yet bills had to be paid. Furnished lodgings in a middle-class suburb were a different matter from living at home with Mother, in a country cottage where meals came cheap and there was no responsibility. The hours writing in the little room with its view westward to Blackdown and the Hardy Monument, with no interruption except a call upstairs to say that supper was ready, must have seemed far away. Consulting Anne Thackeray, Hardy found her surprised that he should not like society, and positive that it was necessary for a novelist. He felt still that the settled life of his upbringing was the most productive, but he had got himself into an awkward position by marriage. One does not know the reaction at this point of the Hardy family to Emma, but to them as to all his cousins she was "a lady", just as Hardy's associates in London were those dubious things, ladies and gentlemen. One of these was even Jemima Hardy's old rival, Julia Augusta Martin, who, hearing of her former child-pupil's triumph, had written to him about it,[14] though, remembering the fiasco a dozen years before at Bruton Street, he did not try to see her.

Something of what the Hardy family felt about their relative moving in such incomprehensible worlds may be gathered by the attitude of the surviving members at his death. Even so many years later, when Thomas Hardy was a national and even international figure, his brother

Henry, his sister Kate, and his first cousin Theresa (his uncle James's surviving daughter) were bitterly and locally possessive. They felt that ladies such as Hardy's second wife, and gentlemen such as Sydney Cockerell and Sir James Barrie, had taken all the arrangements about their famous relative out of the hands of the people to whom he had belonged. To Kate, the official dispositions made by the society in which Hardy had moved were all "staggering blows" to what she felt was due to his nearest.[15] To find Florence Hardy and Cockerell had arranged the funeral in Westminster Abbey, cremation and not burial, and the removal of the heart only to the family grave in Stinsford churchyard, were virtual insults to those who shared blood-relationship.[16] His cousin Theresa, still living eccentric and witch-like in the lane in Higher Bockhampton, had a short way with enquiring ladies and gentlemen from London, since she always told them that Hardy should have led a useful life like his brother Henry the builder, and not bothered with writing.[17] If these were the reactions of Hardy's relatives after fifty years of his fame, one can understand how marriage to a "lady" and his mixing with London society must have seemed now, and his reluctance to risk confrontation yet.

The pressures of this situation were obviously great, and increased proportionately as the success of the book with the public aroused curiosity about its author. *Far From the Madding Crowd* had a sale whose speed and extent even surprised the publisher. By the third week in January 1875, after only two months, nearly the whole first edition of 1000 copies was gone, and Hardy was able to make some alterations for a second edition. These show, as usual, some influence of Stephen. Pompous or over-literary words, such as "circumambient" and "rotundity", had more simple substitutes in the passages of natural description they had previously disfigured, and a piece of abstract philosophy about Boldwood was removed bodily.[18] Another removal, this time bowing to Stephen's prudish side, was a cut in the description of Bathsheba's father as standing godfather to illegitimate children in the parish. In the early months of 1875, relations between Hardy and his editor deepened to a mutual sympathy and understanding. Both were abnormally reticent, and Stephen had no answer to Hardy's problems, even if he had been told them. It is all the more remarkable then that Hardy was witness to a phase of Stephen's own intimate life.

Reluctantly taking the advice of Stephen's sister-in-law, Hardy had moved with Emma on 19 March back to his familiar Westbourne Park area, a compromise that brought him nearer the fashionable West End, though not quite of it. Next day, Hardy went to the University Boat Race, presumably taken by the enthusiastic Stephen, though the latter must have groaned mightily at an Oxford win by nearly ten lengths. It was only a short step, for a country walker, across Hyde Park to

Stephen's home in South Kensington. Here, only a few days later, Hardy found himself urgently summoned, to call in the evening as late as he liked. Stephen was pacing his library in carpet slippers, his lean body encased in a heather-coloured dressing-gown. He briefly indicated that he could do with another serial for the *Cornhill*, but a more personal matter was occupying his mind. He produced a document, which Hardy at first took to be his will, but it was an even more intimate screed which he wished Hardy to witness. Stephen had never renounced Holy Orders. In 1870, the Clerical Disabilities Act debarred clergy from standing for Parliament. Stephen never entered politics, but thought it was time now to end a false position, which he had only partly removed by resigning from the college tutorship in 1862. It is notable that of all people in London, he thought Hardy the most appropriate to witness this symbolic act. The conversation that followed the witnessing is also revealing. Stephen, according to Hardy, spoke of having wasted his time on religion and metaphysics, and to be now fascinated by "the new theory of vortex rings".[19] This shows Stephen as a follower, at least at this time, of the Positive Philosophy of Auguste Comte. Comte, whom Hardy had also been reading for at least the past five years,[20] believed that mankind had passed through the stages of religion and metaphysics, and was now ripe for a more scientific or "positive" way of thought and worship. Though both Hardy and Stephen seem to have stopped short of Comte's ultimate Religion of Humanity, that curious hybrid with its pantheon of philosophers and scientists taking the place of saints, and a chapel of devotees off Lamb's Conduit Street, they evidently subscribed to Comte's idea of man's progress being in what Hardy called "a looped orbit".[21] This was a kind of evolution, it seemed to them, which allowed for apparent regression, but always curved round to a point of progress again, so that a temporary decay could be followed by an advance. Hardy even persuaded himself that similarity of ideas caused his writing to be mistaken for that of George Eliot, though she, in fact, was only marginally a Positivist;[22] he himself was sufficiently attracted by "the new religion" to believe that if Comte had retained Christ in its pantheon, it would have gained wide acceptance.[23]

At all events, here was an intellectual sympathy which made it all the more difficult for Hardy to deny Stephen's request for a new *Cornhill* serial. Stephen knew that Hardy had partly planned a new book; he did not yet know what form the book was to take, and Hardy himself had inklings that Stephen might be surprised. For Hardy had arrived at a decision, which was itself surprising, and must be suspected to be very personal indeed. It had to do, not perhaps at first consciously, with the situation in which he found his own life, as a writer of humble origins acclaimed by a society which might, if knowing, have found them contemptible. The general dilemma was perhaps made even more acute by his wife, still in half-ignorance of his true background. For Emma, like many middle-class housewives, regarded servants generally as "problems", and continued all her life to speak of them in those terms.[24] A family of servants was the last thing she would normally think of marrying into, or consider a fitting background for a famous author. As for their morals, she would have been horrified to learn that Hardy's cousin, Ellen Hand, had just had a bastard daughter.[25]

So, perhaps from an inborn necessity to write the teasing problem somehow out of his system, was evolved the most uneven and contradictory of all Hardy's novels, *The Hand of Ethelberta*. Its theme was to be that of a person moving in high, intellectual society, a writer, poet and story-teller, who, in fact, came from a family all of whom were servants and workmen. More than that: this family were to be shown sharing the principal character's life, a secret always to be kept and always on the verge of being discovered, to everyone's general shame and discomfort. The threat is made plain in one speech:

> People will find you out as one of a family of servants, and their pride will be stung at having gone to hear your romancing . . .

It would be too near home, however, in all sorts of senses, to make this chief character a male author; so Hardy, in his typically devious way, chose, as he had done in poems and tales before, to project his own dilemma into that of a woman.

So, or by some such process, was born his new heroine, Ethelberta Chickerel, who, by a rather improbable marriage with a rich young man who almost immediately dies, appears in society as Ethelberta Petherwin, a mysterious widow. Almost the first thing we know of her is that, like Hardy, she has written a large number of sonnets putting woman's point of view, a natural echo of the mass of "She to Him" sonnets written by the young Hardy. Unlike Hardy, but like him in intention, she has these published in a book; it will be remembered that Hardy had intended to print his own sonnets in *The Poor Man and the Lady*, and had even "prosed" one of them in *Desperate Remedies*. In the *Cornhill* serialization, which started in July 1875, Hardy called this book of verse by the really childishly improbable title of "Metres by Me". If it seems strange that he should employ such a schoolboy device to indicate his own part in the character of his heroine, it may be considered even more strange that he should use the title at all. At all events, he altered it in the volume version to "Metres by E."—i.e. Ethelberta—even though this entailed the rewriting of an incredibly laboured pun about Me and U. The whole novel, in fact, seems like an exercise in what Morley had called "a clever lad's dream", full of such schoolboy and private asides. The word "Hand" in the title has a double meaning: both the heroine's hand in marriage and her playing of her "hand", as in a game of skill, are indicated. There is surely a third and private meaning, personal to the novelist himself. "Hand" was the maiden name of Hardy's own mother, and Ethelberta's family, when they emerge, are other related members of the Hand family of Puddletown.

For Ethelberta, after her book of poems, goes on like Hardy to be a story-writer. Here again, though this thin disguise for Hardy's own career may seem far-fetched, it was obviously suggested by certain aspects of his own recent success in this form of writing. Quite apart from the George Eliot fable of the reviewers, it was consistently thought that the author of *Far From the Madding Crowd* might be a woman. Though the *Spectator* had corrected its first mistaken guess as early as February 1874, the legend still persisted. The basic idea for the Hardy-into-Ethelberta sex-change may have been started by a remark of Anne Thackeray. Besieged by enquiries about the sex of the author of *Far From the Madding Crowd*, and pestered by requests for an introduction to him or her—a situation parallel to Ethelberta's—she would reply, "*It* lives in the country, and I could not very well introduce you to *it* in Town".[26] Ethelberta, of course, tells her stories publicly by word of mouth; but there is some corresponding idea to that of Hardy serializing his stories in the *Cornhill*. Serial and first edition were extensively revised for the edition of 1892, and we can see that the earliest version, in fact, gives most clues to Hardy's secret intention in the novel. In this, the likenesses to himself and to his own nearest relatives, significant through their omission in later versions, are most obvious. The hero, Christopher, the name of Hardy's uncle, passive and ineffective, is the diffident side of Hardy himself, mutely accompanied by his pallid sister Mary, in the novel named Faith. Their scenes are much extended in the serial and first edition, and Faith, noted there and there only as "the youngest of old maids", is a speaking or more often unspeaking likeness of Hardy's unobtrusive sister. Hardy's mother does not appear, but a hint of her survives in most significant form. One of Ethelberta's upper-class suitors is a person called Alfred Neigh, most improbably surnamed as the caustic *Saturday Review* was to point out, though missing yet another juvenile joke in that the man's father had been a horse-knacker. Neigh is portrayed as hating servant-class women, because of the "goings-on" of his own father. These are revealed, again in the serial and first edition only, as the fact that the elder Neigh had actually married his cook. Hardy, the son of a cook, had already discovered, in his short experience of intellectual middle-class society, that this was the unforgivable Victorian crime. Mark Pattison, the distinguished Oxford scholar, became almost insanely furious at the idea—quite false

—that his sister Dorothy was friendly with a man who was alleged to have performed this socially unspeakable action.[27]

When Ethelberta's socially unmentionable relatives appear, they turn out to be a fascinating amalgam of Hardy's own. Her father, Mr. Chickerel, named after the village between Weymouth and Coryates where Hardy had walked with Tryphena Sparks, is a butler, an older version of William Duffield, whom Martha Sparks had married. Ethelberta's brother Sol Chickerel is, like Martha's brother James Sparks, a carpenter of radical tendencies, and has a fine speech of independence in his disgust at his sister's eventual marriage to a viscount. The other workman brother's name, Daniel, suggests Nathaniel Sparks. The backstairs and below-stairs scenes in London houses are sketched with the accuracy of a man who had visited and indeed courted his Sparks cousin in such circumstances. Even the most improbable incident in the novel, the infatuation of the juvenile Joey Chickerel for a ladies' maid twice his age, may refer to Hardy's own teenage excitement over his much-older dressmaker cousin, Rebecca Sparks. The winding-up chapter, where two of Ethelberta's maidservant sisters marry and emigrate to Queensland, coincides exactly in time with the emigration in May 1876, the month this chapter appeared, of Martha Duffield to Queensland, her ex-butler husband having failed to make a living in England.[28] Hardy was so involved with secret family history that he even wrote into his novel this otherwise unnecessary detail of his former love, whom he himself had wanted to marry.

The theme of class concealment is indeed such an obsession that it throws the novel out of balance in a way which puzzled all reviewers. As the *Saturday*, trying to be fair, said "An author prepares many difficulties for himself when he invents such a character", not knowing of course, that the character was in the author's own situation. The reviewer indeed felt that Ethelberta as a woman was difficult of belief. He might have noticed, had he known Hardy's emotional history, that she starts physically as Emma, powerful with white columnar neck "firm as a fort", and "squirrel-coloured hair", and only in a much later rewriting of the book borrows the dark eyebrows, arched "like two slurs in music" of Tryphena Sparks, via the portrait of the latter in *Under the Greenwood Tree*, when Fancy Day has just these "two slurs" above her dark eyes. This synthetic character and her dilemmas were meant to express, in secret guise, Hardy's own. They were also useful for a hard-pressed serial-writer, since he could import chunks of his own and his family's experiences to fill up a chapter. Hardy's boyhood experiences as a musician at dances accounts for at least two early chapters. Later chapters utilize Rouen—though not Paris—and even phrases from Emma's honeymoon diary. The French servants "spin" about, just as she described, the houses seen from the Fleche look like "mosaic" and the Ile Lacroix is "gorgeous" in colour. It is a pity he did not import, with these, Emma's poetic description of the Cathedral bell, "deep-toned, like a spirit speaking".[29] Hardy has nothing similar to glean from his own notebooks, except for a rather perfunctory mention of the 1875 Boat Race, when the tideway proved too narrow for the numerous barges anchored to watch it.[30]

The most vivid chapters of this manufactured and cryptic book, in fact, mark a decisive move in Hardy's married life. In mid-July 1875, after some unsuccessful house-hunting in Dorset, Emma and Hardy on Monday, 12 July, left London, stayed three nights in Bournemouth, and then went by boat to Swanage, where they were to live for the next ten months while he completed the novel. In the pretty West End Cottage, they were near enough Bockhampton for Emma to be introduced cautiously to the family. The most notable occasion, though not perhaps the first, was on 13 September, when Emma, Hardy, and his sisters Mary and Kate all went on a picnic to Corfe Castle. It was an expedition recorded by Emma as "a splendid day",[31] and she clearly got on well with Hardy's two schoolmistress sisters—Kate, following Mary, was preparing to go to Salisbury, and may have already been helping her as pupil-teacher at Piddlehinton School. What they thought of Emma, as they took their separate ways home, is not recorded, but there were later expeditions and letters were exchanged. The whole event was expanded by Hardy to furnish Ethelberta with a long expedition to Corfe, where she takes part in a meeting of a Historical Society. Swanage itself, and their seafaring landlord, Captain Masters, supplied all the more convincing local colour for these chapters of the novel. Bockhampton and Hardy's mother did not appear in any way, either in the novel or in his wife's diary, but he can hardly have held off the meeting at this time.

Hardy, in fact, records a good deal of the Swanage atmosphere at this time. He relished the sea-tales of their landlord, especially the grim ones of the seas at West Bay stripping their drowned victims in the powerful undertow, and the amusing reminiscences of smuggling and the outwitting of revenue men. He and Emma, before the stormy autumn and winter gales set in, also had a perfect day's sea-outing by steamer, the "Heather Bell", round the Isle of Wight, though Emma's sketch of Hardy on the boat shows a withdrawn slightly gloomy figure, like one of his own apprehensive heroes. Indeed, whether through marriage or not, he seems to have reverted to the old pessimistic state of his lonely days in London. As he described his hero,

He looked sad when he felt almost serene, and only serene when he felt quite cheerful. It is a habit people acquire who have had repressing experiences.

The hero's sister Faith, herself so recognizable as Mary Hardy, also comments on her brother's temperament,

> If I had to describe you I should say you were a child in your impulses and an old man in your reflections.

He himself later bursts out to her

> The only feeling which has any dignity or permanence or worth is family affection between close blood-relations.

Was he already regretting that he had to abandon or conceal these close blood-relationships through the pressures of marriage and popular fame? A poem written about himself and Emma at Bournemouth, *We Sat at the Window*, suggests that marriage had already begun to pall. The original line,[32] later changed,

> We were irked by the scene, by each other; yes,

sounds as if lack of sympathy was beginning to show, and that Emma's unthinking vitality was starting to grate on his thoughtful and surely often depressing melancholy. She came to irritate him, and he came to wear down her energy into self-defensive anger. Victorian reticence prevents any hint of their sexual compatibility; but Hardy's reversion to ineffective attitudes, and his dimly feeble portrait of his hero, might well show that he had failed himself in that aspect of marriage. At all events, there were no children; nor were there ever to be. The rough Hardys and the Hands of Puddletown, able to multiply their descendants at will, seemed to have produced, as he himself often so gloomily wrote and said, a final member who had no fortune or perhaps force in that direction.

It was perhaps at this point that Hardy decided to put all to the test with his one successful achievement, his writing and the position he had won by it in society. *The Hand of Ethelberta*, an enigma to critics, a puzzle to the reading public, a disappointment to its editor and publisher, and a stumbling-block to its talented illustrator, Du Maurier, was of great private importance to its author. In it, Hardy made his last gesture from the class to which he really belonged. He wrote out of his system the Hardy who was one of the people who toiled and suffered. From now onward, he surveyed such people as one who had escaped from their world. Their sufferings are no less intense, and he does not cease to portray them, but always now as one who has made his escape. The note of social protest, which had begun with *The Poor Man and the Lady*, is virtually dropped, its last flarings perhaps being Sol Chickerel's speeches to his sister. Hardy accepts the world in which he, as a novelist, must now move. Even as he accepts it, he satirizes it. In *The Hand of Ethelberta*, there is satire of the world of Leslie Stephen and the world of Emma, two aspects of Hardy's new official milieu. The curious tendency of almost every upper-class person in the novel to swear under his breath—even the mild hero whispers "an ancient exclamation", presumably of four letters—seems a direct satire on Stephen's behaviour. As for Emma, there is a significant early version of the expression in chapter 5, "fingers of a corpse". In the serial, it was "fingers of a woman who does nothing". Poor Emma's amateur novel, *The Maid on the Shore*, which she wrote at Swanage,[33] though it has moments of disorganized poetry, lacks the hard realities of a life that has been experienced at a basic level of human effort and suffering.

Hardy's farewell to the class in which he had been brought up, and his reluctant satire on the class he was now to enter, made this novel, as the critics found it, a "deliberate oddity".[34] It was, in fact, an oddity that was to pursue much of his subsequent life, the attempt to live in a world to which, like his self-portraying heroine, he did not really belong. In the world of letters and of society, he appeared strange and withdrawn, a man nursing an inner secret. In the world of his Dorset upbringing, he appeared, except to his close family, as one who had deserted them. From the second half of the 1870s, all mention of his cousins and relatives drops out of his notes and writings. A passing reference to his cousin James Sparks in 1879 seems to be the last mention of a near relative. He did not apparently communicate with Tryphena Sparks, even when in December 1877 she married "my old man",[35] Charles Frederick Gale of Topsham. He still kept in touch with her brother Nathaniel, who had also married hastily, earlier that year, Mary Hardy's student friend, Annie Lanham, just in time to legitimize her baby; but their correspondence was mainly on the subject of fiddles and cellos, of which Nathaniel, to supplement his meagre carpenter's wages, had become a repairer.[36]

Hardy found himself suppressing yet another part of his life. He had never ceased to think of himself as a poet, "anxious to get back to verse". Ethelberta had been, in part, a secret manifesto of his own poetry, and her "Metres by Me" a hope that his own verses, like hers, might gain popular success. Now that he was well known as a novelist, he would surely be able to get his poems, rejected ten years before, published at last. Hopefully, he took the idea to Leslie Stephen, and told him that he "planned some tragic poems".[37] To Hardy's chagrin, the editor seemed entirely indifferent and disinclined to encourage the idea. Stephen frankly did not want poems, but, after *Ethelberta*, another pastoral novel; in the event, he did not get one, for his prudish suspicions were aroused by the marital tangles that seemed to be developing in the early chapters of *The Return of the Native*. He declined to serialize it, and Hardy, though he continued as a friend, lost his only good literary adviser and editor. With Stephen's rejection of "tragic" poetry in mind, Hardy, asked for a "brief story", tried *The Gentleman's Maga-zine* with his comic poem, *The Bride-Night Fire*. It was printed in November 1875, Hardy's first published poem, but only after such cautious bowdlerization as made it hardly the same work. The heroine's "cold little buzzoms" become "her cold little figure", the hero, who "Made a back, horsed her up", is not allowed such an indecent way of rescuing her from the fire, and she is provided throughout with a chaperone, his old mother. Hardy had reason to feel cynical at his ruined handiwork; it was worse than no publication. So yet another prime passion of his life was driven underground.

Life for him now seemed to become full of concealments. Although Hardy introduced Emma to his sisters and brother, and eventually at last to his mother and father—they spent Christmas 1876 with his parents at Bockhampton—he seems to have taken pains that she should never know the personages of his Puddletown background. In March 1876 he moved her from Swanage to Yeovil, just over the Somerset border, to look for houses in North Dorset, where in May he saw cow-slips shining like "Chinese lanterns or glow-worms".[38] Then followed another holiday on the Continent, this time to Holland and the Rhine. The Hardys finally got their first home at Sturminster Newton, in Dorset certainly, but many miles distant from the area where many of his relatives still lived. Two of Emma's brothers visited them there;[39] but as far as can be made out, none of Hardy's relatives ever came. It is perhaps significant too that these eighteen months at Sturminster were remembered by Hardy as "their happiest days".[40] He had brought Emma into contact with as much of his past as he cared to show her; he had temporarily regained, even at a remove, his Dorset roots; and disillusion with her and the world that she came to stand for, had not yet fully set in, though the incident at Bournemouth had been a warning sign.

Yet from this time, Hardy shows evidence of the violence that his up-rooting from the past had done to his essential being. The settled sombreness of *The Return of the Native*, written at Sturminster, and the disorientated nature of all the actors in that story, show a man labour-ing under almost intolerable strain. It was this strain and fixed gloom that pursued him, like a haunted person, all the rest of his long life.

As for Emma, she was fixed too in the tragedy of two lives that, for no essential fault, were headed for personal disaster. The false glamour of their dramatic first meeting had concealed and disguised their deep-felt differences. Hardy was later to write poems regretting that he had ever uprooted her from the life and place where he found her. Even at this early time, though temporarily checked by the compromise of the Sturminster Newton idyll, the gulf was beginning to widen. Emma had begun to find that this obsessive, complicated, brooding mind could be unconsciously insensitive and accidentally cruel. She was nothing in herself unless she coincided with what was stirring in that tortuous process of his inner self. His vision of an epic of Napoleonic times, first conceived in 1874, and realized in *The Dynasts*, was a case in point. Hardy was pleased with her when she talked to the Waterloo veterans at Chelsea Hospital in June 1875;[41] he was angry with her when she became exhausted, exactly a year later, after he had tramped her all a long hot day over the battlefield itself.[42] His own obsessions, as much as her pathetic attempts to behave as she imagined a great writer's wife should, divided them. Yet she was no fool where her instincts were concerned. She suspected, if she did not fully know, the complications of his past. Her reactions to *Ethelberta* are noteworthy. "Too much about servants in it", she is alleged to have said;[43] and the inscribed copy her husband gave her remained uncut at her death.

Old and Young

A WELL-ESTABLISHED family tradition illustrates how Hardy cut himself off from his Dorset relatives. In the summer of 1885, Hardy and Emma moved into their newly-built house, Max Gate, on the south-east borders of Dorchester; but they did not mix with his people. When they went visiting, it was to the gentry. In the early 1890s, Hardy and his wife were enthusiastic in the craze for bicycling. One of the few happy photographs of Hardy shows him with a brand-new bicycle, and he continued riding into his eighties. A very frequent ride was to Turnworth, whose church Hardy had architected, and whose vicar shared the Hardys' passion for the protection of animals.[1] Hardy read the lessons there, and it was remembered how, after a summer bike-ride of nearly twenty miles, his balding head would steam gently as he stood at the lectern.[2] Their route lay through Puddletown; and another memory records how the Hardys would bicycle stiffly through the main street, looking neither to right nor to left. Cottage doors were full of his close relatives, the Hands, the Antells, and visiting Sparkses; but Hardy neither gave nor acknowledged greetings as he pedalled resolutely on with Emma.

Although he was allied with her in rejecting his ancestry, there was no sign now of any common bond between them. He was therefore doubly isolated; he had given up one life, and found another to be an illusion. Even the fact that they went to church together was a mockery. His early experiences had settled him in the belief that any supreme power must be ignorant of or indifferent to any form of human life. Emma, on the other hand, "had various experiences . . . all showing that an Unseen Power of great benevolence directs my ways".[3] To Hardy's evident dismay, she founded this belief on the narrowest form of sectarian Protestant prejudice. Even on their honeymoon in France, her low-church fears of sacerdotalism were confirmed by the sight of "priests walking about whose age can be known by their harshness & closeness of expression . . . concealed concentrated wickedness . . . like liquid become hard substance".[4] Grappling with the inexplicable mystery and tragedy of life, which he had experienced to the full in his youth, Hardy found himself tied to a religious bigot. In the 1880s, as he saw her ignorant, girlish charms diminish into gross middle age and incongruous chatter,[5] he shut his eyes and ears to her, and explored philosophies that could help him bear the shattering, suppressed happenings of his own early history.

In the decade from 1878 to 1887, his major published work, from *The Return of the Native* to *The Woodlanders*, shows a settled attempt to put his characters in a philosophical frame. One critic[6] says: "It takes a philosophical tinge of universality, for which we should seek vainly in the early writings." Yet though he added to his youthful reading of Mill, Spencer, and Comte the impressive trio of Spinoza, Schopenhauer, and Von Hartmann, his human problems remained. The novels, though fully "Wessex" still in setting and anecdote, lack some of the human feeling of his earlier work. They are great exercises to demonstrate the thesis that the universe is totally indifferent to men and women. He did not allow into his work the actual incidents that had caused his settled gloom, "as if enveloped in a leaden cloud", as he once described it.[7] These events of his youth were still too painfully near. His mother's poverty-stricken origins and relatives, his own ambitions and loss of faith, his fascination by his three girl-cousins, his delusive marriage-impulse, his virtual renunciation of poetry, and, the height of tragedy, the disasters in sex, drink, and suicide of the man called "my friend" were still too close to be the subject of fiction. He hugged them to him, with all that side of life he concealed from the world, taciturn in clubs, society, and tea-parties.

This could not last for ever. After ten years of suppression, the themes that had shaped his life began to force their way into his notebooks. On 28 April 1888 he wrote,[8] as subject for a story,

> a young man—"who could not go to Oxford"—His struggles and ulti-mate failure. Suicide. . . . There is something . . . the world ought to be shown, and I am the one to show it to them—

His own class-conscious struggles, the wasted ambition of his cobbler uncle, John Antell, who had died in 1878, and, more deeply, the tragedy of Horace Moule, were all beginning to surface. Then on 30 September he recalled that a relative of his mother, Rebecca Swetman, used to speak proudly of the past glories of the Hardy family, who, she be-lieved, owned land like his mother's ancestors, the Swetmans, in Woolcombe and Frome St. Quintin, which has a "Jude" brass.[9] In the week of 15 October, his mother recalled his paternal grandmother, Mary Head, telling stories of her girlhood and the time of the French Revolu-tion.[10] On 19 February 1889, thinking perhaps of his three Sparks girl-cousins, with their differing ages but striking facial likenesses, he wrote[11]

> The story of a face which goes through three generations or more, would make a fine novel or poem of the passage of Time. The differences in personality to be ignored.

Everywhere the buried themes were stirring. Even the memory of his schoolboy passion for Louisa Harding sent him, early in 1889, to a music shop on the site of Oxford Circus Station, where an old man sang to him, at his request, the words of Sheridan's "How oft, Louisa", but could not find the music which had haunted Hardy's youth.[12] As for the central tragedy of his present life, a loveless marriage, a note of 9 July read, "Love lives on propinquity, but dies of contact".[13] Yet there were fresh dawnings of hope too. On Christmas Day 1890, when he was "thinking of resuming 'the viewless wings of poesy' . . . new horizons seemed to open, and worrying pettinesses to disappear".[14]

The theme of what poverty meant to women, its power to blight well-aspiring lives, like those of young girls, was the first to break through his defences with such force that he had to write about it. It was, after all, the deepest-laid memory. His mother's family history was still vivid to him, for he did not give up his visits to the Bockhampton cottage, especially as his father, old and rheumatic, was now growing feeble, before his death in 1892. The place itself was alive with the old stories of woman's tragedy, his mother's at Melbury Osmond, his grandmother's in Berkshire. Mary Head of Fawley had become a symbol of the harshness of providence to a young girl. Losing her father in the year she was born, her mother at six, she had probably lodged with her uncle, Henry Head, churchwarden of the nearby Chaddleworth. If so, at only eleven she was involved in yet another family tragedy; for Henry Head's wife and two sons all died in the same year, 1783.[15] These reiterated blows of fate on one of his own ancestors turned Hardy's mind to the peasant superstition of some sort of family curse, a malignant, doomed heredity. Poverty and predestined family failure are part—though only part—of the novel he began to write in autumn 1888, *Tess of the d'Urbervilles*.

As many people have remarked, Hardy spoke about Tess Durbeyfield as if she were a real person. In a letter[16] in 1891, he regretted that "I have not been able to put on paper all that she is, or was, to me". On the other hand, he indulged in a good deal of deliberate mystification about her. In private conversations he confessed that the only physical model was a Dorset girl he had once seen on a cart, and that there was no exact original;[17] but he told Arthur Compton-Rickett that he had "built up" Tess from three women, a Weymouth waitress, from whom he took Tess's physique and appearance, and her character from two Dorchester girls.[18] The Antell family said that Tess in her life, adventures, and final death was "practically what happened to a relative".[19] This remarkable statement has never been followed up; if it were to be, it might well lead to Hardy's cousins, the family of William Hand of Melbury Osmond, who certainly show at least one illegitimate birth and considerable poverty.[20] It might also justify Hardy's confusing remark to an interviewer in 1892 that "Tess had a real existence".[21]

Yet the poverty and predestined tragedy of Tess seems to come from an earlier generation. The gang labour system, under which she suffers, had been controlled by the Gangs Act of 1868, and by the time Hardy wrote it was a thing of the past.[22] The steam threshing-machine, another cause of her suffering, first took the place of horse-power as early as 1803. Hardy was more probably drawing on ancestral memories. Even the weird tale, dredged up by Mary Hardy, about Farmer Head of Chaddleworth, who left his wife after their wedding night, may have contributed to Angel Clare's desertion of Tess after her bride-night revelation of her past doings with d'Urberville. In spite of references in the novel to "Victorian lucre" and the spectacular late nineteenth-century growth of Bournemouth, there is a primitive timelessness about the book. The end of Tess on the scaffold where she pays the penalty of the law, without reprieve, echoes Hardy's adolescent experience of the death of Martha Brown, and the harsher morality he had heard expressed in his youth.

It also must owe something to his abnormal interest in the hanging of women—in a sense, the fictional Tess was doomed by her creator—allied to the fact that, for all his temporary attractions to living women, the most moving symbol to him was a woman in death. One of these situations, with strange overtones, now occurred. In March 1890, during a train journey, he began to write on the subject of Tryphena Sparks,[23] whom he had not seen for many years, a poem beginning

> Not a line of her writing have I,
> Not a thread of her hair . . .

His memory, now searching the buried past, may have been prompted by the fairly recent deaths of two of Tryphena's sisters, Emma in 1884 and Rebecca in 1885.[24] What he did not realize till later was that Tryphena herself was dying when he wrote the lines. She was not quite forty. He felt as if his three girl-cousins had somehow closed their account with him. The fourth, Martha, was not indeed dead, but 8000 miles away in Queensland, looking after her own strong brood of children and her sister Emma's boys and girls. At all events, Hardy felt somehow free to symbolize his attachment to three sisters in his next work, *The Well-Beloved*. In a typical shift of fictional relationship, he made the three girls in the book not sisters of widely-spaced ages, as in real life, but three generations. His hero, Hardy himself thinly-disguised in his search from one woman to another for ideal beauty, falls in love at twenty-year intervals with three girls of the same family. There is even a hint of self-mockery, when the third girl, finding the hero has been the lover of her own grandmother and mother, innocently asks if he is old enough to have been her great-grandmother's lover too. Hardy drew a red herring across this autobiography by calling it a sketch of a temperament, letting it be known that he meant the artistic temperament of his sculptor hero: but it is a sketch of his own temperament in very realistic detail. Specially noteworthy are the portrayals of actual people in the fashionable society where Hardy now moved.[25] The actress Ellen Terry appears exactly as she appeared to Hardy in real life,[26] and so do many woman he knew. He treats his society acquaintances with the mixture of fascination and affected disdain that he felt for them, unable to stop staring at their décolletée beauty, and taking refuge from their attractions in a deliberate peasant rudeness and crude comment.[27] *The Well-Beloved*, in fact, is strikingly like *The Hand of Ethelberta*, a personal allegory carried to near-absurd lengths, and the same sort of puzzle was felt by the reviewers when it finally appeared, much later and heavily-revised, in volume form. They felt, obscurely, that there was something wrong with it. The wrongness was that it came uncomfortably near to self-revelation of some of the less attractive sides of Hardy's own character and physical make-up. In a letter replying to an unfavourable review in *The Academy*, Hardy stated that he had thought of the idea of the novel when young.[28] It would be more true to say that it was founded on his experiences when young, as *Ethelberta* had been, but wearing the heavy disguise that middle-age had taught him to adopt.

The serialization of *The Well-Beloved* in *The Illustrated London News* during 1892 does not seem to have aroused much attention. Yet the popular success of *Tess*, in spite of some violent attacks on its morality, made Hardy feel able to mount another assault on conventional society, and to release some of his oppressive, personal concealments. He was more than usually explicit about the literary origins of *Jude the Obscure*, though even more than usually reticent about some of its personal facets. He made notes for it in 1887 and onward, including the 1888 note, which has been quoted. As this would suggest, its first theme was that of a poor boy handicapped by social circumstances. This went back as far as *The Poor Man and the Lady*, and indeed much farther. The theme of suffering through poverty was so deeply associated with his Berkshire grandmother, Mary Head, that his hero was early called Jack Head, the actual name of a parish boy-relation of hers, who was, in real life as in the novel, a bird-scarer.[29] Even when he became Jude Fawley, his surname was the same as her birthplace. Jude the youth, dreaming of the spires of Oxford, haven of pure learning, is the self-taught Hardy, oblivious in his books to the coarse village life around him.[30] When Jude comes to Oxford as a young workman, another personal portrait takes over. This is John (known as "Jack") Antell, Hardy's self-taught cobbler uncle, who actually learnt enough Latin to open a "Latin school" in Puddletown, where he is even said to have taught the Squire's cricketing son. His fatal weakness for drink contributes to this picture of rural ambition and failure, which Hardy himself actually commemorated by composing an epitaph for his tombstone.

The second Mrs. Hardy, however, warned a correspondent that Jude was "only partly" based on John Antell, and herself later suggested the main model for the deeper shades of the character. This was, of course, the career of Horace Moule. The two sides of Jude, learning and intellect, contrasting with sex and drink, are Hardy's legacy from the tragic life and death of his great friend. Hardy saw the book as a series of such contrasts,[31] and Jude's correspond with the fatal battleground of Moule's temperament. In his previous published novel, Hardy had drawn Angel Clare's family, sometimes in unkind satire, from the Moules. Now, as if in expiation, he made his hero a fully sympathetic study of the terrible problems that had confronted and defeated his friend. His sensual attraction in the novel is Arabella, her name taken from the landlady of the Phoenix Inn, rendezvous for the Puddletown carrier's cart,[32] and her nature from Moule's Dorchester girl. His spiritual companion, herself ultimately just as fatal, is Sue Bridehead. The chief disaster in the book is when Jude's child by the former returns from Australia, where he has been brought up, and finally hangs both himself and Jude's children by Sue. The startling fact that Moule's own illegitimate child by the Dorchester girl was also brought up in Australia, and eventually hanged, is striking enough to make it clear that Hardy's hero owes much to Moule, besides his academic failures, his drink and depression, and virtual suicide. Such scenes as the drunken Jude reciting the Latin Creed to a scoffing pub audience are horribly reminiscent of what happened to Moule. The kind curate, who gives Jude fresh hope after this scene, may be taken from Moule's curate brother Frederick, who rescued him in such dilemmas. It would be a mistake to think of all the characters in this most carefully-constructed novel as personal portraits; but there is an even more probable identification of one of its most interesting characters, Phillotson, the middle-aged Berkshire schoolmaster who comes to teach in Dorset, and whose separation from Sue gets him into professional trouble. He may be based on the bachelor Mr. Holmes, schoolmaster of Athelhampton, under whom Tryphena Sparks had worked, a Berkshire man from a village near Fawley.[33] According to Tryphena, he too ran into some severe trouble in his fifties.[34]

Hardy's heroine, Sue Bridehead, was herself to be a schoolteacher, a symbol of class-emancipation in the 1860s, a suggestion that came, Hardy said, from "the death of a woman" in 1890—that is, the death of his former schoolteacher cousin Tryphena. In search of a realistic background for a rebel woman teacher, Hardy paid visits in 1891 first to Whitelands Training College at Putney,[35] then to Tryphena's old college at Stockwell,[36] and also to his own sisters' college at Salisbury. Jude and Sue were to be cousins, like himself and Tryphena, but, as another character remarks, they are more like brother and sister. It is worth noticing that he inscribed a copy of the completed book to his sister Mary,[37] and eventually set the scene of Sue's training in Mary's college, rather than at any of the others.

Sue's character, however, hung fire until the early summer of 1893, when it received a sudden new turn from Hardy's perpetual suscepti- bility to women. As if to illustrate his own allegory of The Well- Beloved, he became deeply attracted by Mrs. Florence Henniker, who seemed an 1890s reincarnation of the advanced woman on whom Sue was based. Together they went to the plays of Ibsen, cult-figure of emancipated thought. In the private language of their letters, Hardy became her Master Builder—he even took up church architecture again[38]—and she his Hilde Wangel, able to understand his "trollish" feelings.[39] Yet, as so often with Hardy, their relationship had what he called "the onesidedness"[40] of an illusion on his part. Far from being emancipated, she was not only conventionally married to a heavily- built military officer, but, to Hardy's horror, was an orthodox church- goer of High Church leanings. The scene in the novel where the innocent Jude, thinking Sue is wearing scent, discovers that it is the smell of incense from a church service she has just attended, almost certainly preserves some such moment of revelation. At all events, she became responsible for the final character of the heroine in Hardy's "hour- glass" construction of the novel. Sue begins freethinking and emanci- pated, but ends conventionally religious, while Jude passes through religion to utter unbelief, raging against marriage as an illustration of how "The letter killeth", the book's epigraph.

No one among Hardy's eventual readers was more shocked than his own wife. Though, according to her nephew,[41] it was the novel's general irreligion that alienated her, it was perhaps more the particular brand of religion adopted by the heroine that seemed such a personal outrage by her husband. To Emma, High Church was equivalent to the great enemy, Rome. It was this, as much as her husband's infatuation, that insured her well-attested disapproval of Mrs. Henniker.[42] She had even more cause for disapproval of Hardy's activities in ensuing years. Ever since he had felt 'the viewless wings of poesy' stirring again in 1890, Hardy began to write increasing numbers of poems, very often intensely personal. In 1898, 1901 and 1909, he published three volumes, Wessex Poems, Poems of the Past and the Present, and Time's Laughingstocks. To placate Emma, he tried in prefaces to pretend that none of these poems was personal, a transparent untruth; also scattered among them were many poems, also mainly personal, written in his youth. Exactly to whom most of these poems were addressed is still a matter of debate. It is not easy to detach poems which may refer to one of the Sparks sisters, or other early loves, from those more recently addressed to Florence Henniker or even to her namesake Florence Dugdale, whom she introduced to Hardy in 1904, to help with research for *The Dynasts*, and who ultimately became the second Mrs. Hardy. Some, dated in the early 1890s, may have been inspired plausibly either by Tryphena's death in 1890 or by Mrs. Henniker's advent in 1893. All, except one or two, had this in common; they were not about his wife.

Her protests were frequent and vigorous. Yet, if she had considered her husband's peculiar nature, she would have realized she had the last word over her rivals. She could die. When she did, in November 1912, his almost involuntary reaction to the death of a once-loved woman rose to a pitch it had never reached before. In the year following her death, he wrote a hundred poems to her. This astonishing feat by a seventy-two-year-old poet has often been remarked, praised and analysed. Even he himself seemed amazed at its vehemence, and tried to find reasons for it—"the mind goes back to the early times when each was much to the other—in her case and mine intensely much".[43] What was truly astonishing was the quality of the poems produced. Whenever the subject was Emma, whether in praise, regret, self-pity, self-reproach, or occasionally self-justification, his work takes on a new dimension of feeling, intensity, and emotional content. One cannot assess how much is due to the actual quality of the love these commemorate, but they seem to show, without doubt, that in retrospect his courtship of Emma was the great event of his early life, particularly in its exotic setting and circumstance. The unique gift of Hardy to associate place and person, the high point in his novels, is surpassed in this moving sequence of poems.

The outburst slackened after the first year of bereavement, and lessened after his remarriage in 1914 to Florence Dugdale. Other deaths produced their results to a minor degree. The death of his first, barely-known adolescent sweetheart, Louisa Harding, in 1913, brought its small clutch of wistful poems. A stronger impulse came from the death of his sister Mary in 1915. She had her poems too, in a deeper tone. His prose jottings also hint just how close their relationship had been. Even his mother, who had died in 1904, had not commanded such feeling. When he heard the verse he had long ago noted in his own prayer book read over Mary's grave, "I held my tongue and spake nothing: I kept silent, yea, even from good words", he commented, "That was my poor Mary exactly".[44] Ten years later, he wrote on her birthday, "She came into the world . . . And went out . . . And the world is just the same . . . not a ripple on the surface left".[45] It is not usually noticed that in the poem *Conjecture*, he brackets Mary with his two wives, as if he had been married to her too, and recalling the feeling between brother and sister in *Ethelberta*. One of his poems to her, *Molly Gone*, is as poignant as any other of the love-poems, especially in the typical broken rhythms of its final stanza:

> Where, then, is Molly, who's no more with me?
>   —As I stand on this lea,
> Thinking thus, there's a many-flamed star in the air
>   That tosses a sign
> That her glance is regarding its face from her home, so that there
>   Her eyes may have meetings with mine.

The same thought in one of his earliest poems, *The Imaginative Maiden*, confirms that there had been this lifelong sympathy between them, perhaps deeper in its way than any other love. Many poems suggested by her death, such as *Looking Across*, show him feeling more kinship with his dead family, and those he had known in youth, than those now around him. From childhood Mary had played Nekayah to his Rasselas.

Famous people came and went at Max Gate, including the then Prince of Wales; after a lunch of roast chicken, the bone the Prince had picked was appropriated by the gardener as a rustic trophy.[46] More and more, however, Hardy went back to the past and his youth for his real life. He rescued poems from his London years, he commemorated incidents from his youth in new poems, or in poems so personal that he had not dared publish them before. Many are mysterious colloquies with past women, so emotionally charged and yet so obliquely expressed that one can only guess at their meaning. The tragedy of Moule is crystallized, though not fully explained, in a poem that draws on details from their last meeting in Cambridge, *Standing by the Mantelpiece*. To the end, he was reliving his life in poetry. Outwardly, he was rich in honours and in material success. The child born in an isolated country cottage, the self-taught boy, died worth the modern equivalent of a million pounds. The process of cutting himself off from his family origins seemed complete; yet the poems, his inner life, tell a different story, a record of how the happenings of his young days were still as vivid and deeply-felt as when they had first occurred. Death brought Westminster Abbey, and his ashes in Poet's Corner. Yet even there, in the crowded, fashionable, and ill-organized service, so disliked by the surviving sister, Kate,[47] was a symbol of the stock they shared. In the reserved and ticketed seats, the daughter of a Dorset vicar, whose family were close friends of Hardy, found herself sitting next to an obvious tramp in ragged clothes. When she questioned him, he proved to know Hardy very well indeed.[48] In fact, he was probably a relative, one of the Hands of Melbury Osmond.[49] Kate Hardy herself already had the last word. While the ladies and gentlemen at Max Gate were making their important, national arrangements without consulting her, she had viewed the body, and gazed at the family face. She set it down in her diary:[50] "the same triumphant look on his face that all the others bore— but without the smile."

Appendix:

Hardy and Tryphena Sparks*

SINCE 1966, Hardy studies of all sorts have mentioned, in one way or another, a book published in that year under the title of *Providence and Mr. Hardy*. Some have dismissed it, some have accepted its claims, in part or on the whole. No one has quite been able to ignore it; for the thesis it sets out is biographically sensational. The young Thomas Hardy, according to this account, had a child by a very young girl, ostensibly his cousin, but really his niece. Apprised of this, he reproached himself (inaccurately) with the sin of incest. Guilt, atonement, and disillusion over this, it is said, lay at the bottom of all his work, and of his whole attitude to life. The story has been used in a sermon by a Bishop, in handbooks and companions to Hardy's works, in critical scholarly introductions, and has even found its way into a prize-winning modern novel. The theory has been canvassed with passionate intensity, for and against. It appeared in the colour supplement of a Sunday newspaper, and has passed, vaguely but persistently, into the popular conception of Hardy held by many general readers.

Yet perhaps the most extraordinary aspect of this whole bizarre affair is the nature of the book itself, and the fact that it ever could have been accepted, even at a superficial reading; for even to the ordinary non-specialist reader, the whole construction of the book must seem highly suspicious. It abounds in conditional sentences beginning "If . . ." and containing conditional verbs, such as "could have". *If* A was at a certain place at a certain time, she *could have* been seduced by B, and C *could have* been their child—and so on. It also deals with written documents in a quite arbitrary way. Those that fit the story are said to be true; those that do not are said to be forged or entered upon false information. All these conjectures are admitted, when they first appear, as conjectures only, but later in the book are treated as facts. Yet they obtained such a hold that in 1971 a quite serious critical work printed a photograph unequivocally captioned as being a portrait of the illegitimate son of Thomas Hardy and his girl-relative. [1]

The book, in fact, seems to have exercised some sort of hypnotic effect on many people's critical faculties. It is therefore important to see how it came into being, and to trace the different elements in it. In 1966, *Providence and Mr. Hardy* was published by Hutchinson, the authors' names being given as Lois Deacon and Terry Coleman. An explanation of the joint authorship is given in a preliminary "Author's Note" (though it does not say which author composed the note): "The original idea was Lois Deacon's, and she carried out, over several years, much the greater part of the necessary research. The

---

* This appendix is based on my previously printed article on this topic, by kind permission of Arthur Crook, formerly editor of *The Times Literary Supplement*.

writing is by Terry Coleman". This ignores the fact that the manuscript of much the same book had been submitted unsuccessfully to publishers "over several years" in Miss Deacon's name only. This version, however, was relatively incoherent in most of its arrangement and style. Certainly, the credit goes to Mr. Coleman for an extremely professional and skilful re-editing and re-writing of the whole and for the excellent provision and standardization of references.

Since Mr. Coleman modestly—perhaps too modestly—claims responsibility only for the actual writing, it is fair to study the ideas and research, to which he does not lay claim, as Miss Deacon's solely. These started, the note goes on to say, by a chance meeting in 1959 with someone who said, "my mother is a cousin [second cousin actually] of Thomas Hardy and her mother was once engaged to him". This was the original idea, which developed into the book published seven years later. The progress and expansion of all the ideas stemming from this statement can be divided fairly certainly into three main stages; in the survey that follows, however, one must recognize that these stages cannot be determined in a hard-and-fast way, and must sometimes have overlapped in time.

The first stage is fairly straightforward, and is an expansion of something already vaguely known. In 1940 Irene Cooper Willis, a friend of the second Mrs. Thomas Hardy, lawyer, executor, and trustee of Mrs. Hardy's estate, stated that when Hardy met his first wife, Emma Gifford, in 1870, he "broke off an understanding that there had been between him and a girl of his own countryside, and bestowed upon Emma the ring intended for the discarded maiden".[2] Twenty years later, Miss Cooper Willis confirmed this story, which, she said, she had had from the second Mrs. Hardy. As the result of her chance meeting, Miss Deacon in 1959 was introduced to Mrs. Eleanor Tryphena Bromell, then aged eighty. Mrs. Bromell was the daughter of Hardy's cousin Tryphena Sparks, who had married a man named Charles Gale. She confirmed that Tryphena Sparks was "the discarded maiden", with whom Hardy had once had an understanding. In conversations and letters she expanded the story, and in many ways gave it a new bearing. According to her, rather than an "understanding", there was an engagement of some years. Hardy did not merely "intend" the ring for Tryphena Sparks; he gave it to her. He still went on seeing her after he had met Emma Gifford in 1870, and it was Tryphena Sparks herself who sent him back the ring, after meeting her own future husband, Charles Gale, probably in 1873. Gale was said to have persuaded her to do this, and to marry him instead, on the grounds that she and Hardy were cousins. According to Mrs. Bromell, Hardy never saw Tryphena again; but when she died in 1890, after bearing Charles Gale four children, Hardy and his brother Henry visited her grave at Topsham in Devon, and placed a wreath on it. Her widowed husband refused to see Hardy on that occasion.

There seems little doubt that most of this story is true. It is difficult to say whether Mrs. Bromell ever actually spoke of a formal engagement between Tryphena Sparks and Thomas Hardy, but her own daughter did, and Mrs. Bromell did not demur when other people spoke of it in those terms. She herself was clear that Tryphena Sparks and Thomas Hardy had "walked out" for some time on the heath between their homes in Dorset, his at Higher

Bockhampton and hers at Puddletown. Miss Deacon did some further work on the rest of Tryphena's life, both before and after her marriage to Charles Gale, which took place on 15 December 1877, just over three years after Hardy's own marriage to Emma. In 1962 she published all this in a pamphlet.[3] This publication, despite a few aberrations, is reasonably accurate. Its only faults are a somewhat over-emphatic style—Hardy's association with Tryphena Sparks is called "an enduring and tragic love-story"—and an often arbitrary selection of dates. The "engagement" is dated precisely from late summer 1867 to early June 1872, though Mrs. Bromell never mentioned these times, and the latter date is contradicted by Miss Deacon herself in *Providence and Mr. Hardy*.[4] On the whole, however, the pamphlet is a useful small-scale work, and would have proved a valuable adjunct to any large-scale biography of Hardy. It is what may be called the first stage.

There were already signs, though, that Miss Deacon was not satisfied to leave it at that, and that her investigations had moved into a second stage, which was to elicit from Mrs. Bromell confirmation for ideas that had their sole origins in Miss Deacon's own mind. The chief of these was Miss Deacon's idea that Tryphena Sparks and Thomas Hardy had an illegitimate son. According to a friend, this was already a "surmise",[5] which she had confided to others, as early as September 1960, and probably much earlier. She had also selected, from loose photographs in the Gale family album, lent to her by Mrs. Bromell, the photograph of an unidentified boy; this selection seems to have been made quite at random. On 9 September 1960 she showed this photograph to Mrs. Bromell, who greeted it with the rather baffling remark, "Oh, that was a little boy who used to come and see Tryphena at Plymouth". Since Tryphena Sparks had moved from Plymouth, where she had been a schoolteacher, to Topsham when she married Charles Gale, her daughter (Mrs. Bromell) can never have seen the boy. The identification, even in such vague terms, must have been by hearsay only. In any case, it did not satisfy Miss Deacon's preconceived notion of an illegitimate son, and at various times during the next four years, she produced the same photograph, only to receive the same answer. It must be said that in spite of her ever-growing preconception, Miss Deacon did not act as an inquisitor, but always as a friend. She had also seen Mrs. Bromell's angry reaction in 1962 to another questioner, who had asked point-blank whether Hardy and Tryphena Sparks had had a child or not.[6]

In January 1964, however, Mrs. Bromell, then aged 85, was admitted to hospital, and died there just over a year later. Miss Deacon claims that for most of this year, Mrs. Bromell remained "in full command of her faculties, clear and lucid". According to official medical evidence, though, she suffered from cerebral atherosclerosis, primarily, with secondary epileptiform fits. Owing to this main condition of illness she was sometimes confused, and it was, of course, a condition that did not appear overnight, but was one of progressive deterioration. There are, in fact, signs of her being confused in answering questions as early as 1962. Although, again on the medical evidence, it is probable that her memory of the remote past could be reasonably accurate, it was noted that her condition did deteriorate still more during the latter part of her life in hospital.

By the middle of January 1965—actually only five or six weeks before her death—Mrs. Bromell was, as Miss Deacon herself admits, often confused and wandering in her thoughts. Up to this point she had spoken nothing of an illegitimate son of Hardy and Tryphena Sparks, and had always returned the same indeterminate answer about the portrait of the boy that Miss Deacon had selected. However, in three conversations on 17 January and on 7 and 10 February 1965, she spoke about this picture. She said it was "Hardy's boy" and that "he was a Sparks" and "he was a cousin". She gave his Christian name as Rantie or Randy, short for Randolph or Randal, and said he was also known as Henery. It may perhaps be some measure of her confused state of mind to remember that Hardy's wife, Emma Gifford, actually had a nephew with the unusual name of Randolph, and that Hardy himself had an uncle with the unusual name of Henery. Be that as it may, Mrs. Bromell went on to indicate that this boy was first of all brought up by Tryphena's sister, Rebecca, and then by Tryphena's brother Nathaniel, who lived in Bristol. Shown another random photograph of a youth, she said that this was the boy grown up, and that he had attended Tryphena's funeral. A fortnight after saying this, Mrs. Bromell died.

Mrs. Bromell died, it will be observed, without ever saying that Hardy and Tryphena Sparks had an illegitimate son. Once more, official medical authority states that it would be wise to treat unsupported statements made by her during the last few weeks of life with a degree of caution. Miss Deacon, however, regarded these last interviews as proof that her own preconception of an illegitimate son of Tryphena and Hardy was true. She had completed the second stage of her process, which was related to remarks made by Mrs. Bromell, regardless of the circumstances of health in which these remarks were made.

The third stage was to allow a number of other preconceptions, not connected in any way with Mrs. Bromell, nor with information given by her in her lifetime, to have free play. These included, among much else, arbitrary dates for the conception and birth of the alleged son, and a series of illegitimacies, unrecorded in any documents, to advance Miss Deacon's theory that Tryphena Sparks was not Hardy's cousin but really his niece.

This analysis of Miss Deacon's process into three stages will have made it clear that the major part of her story, the conception and birth of a child to Hardy by a young girl who was really his niece, was in what we have called her third stage, based entirely on her own imagination. It does not relate in any way to information given to her by Mrs. Bromell. This is important to note, since readers and scholars who have tried to deal with this question in the past decade have often tended to think it had some basis in something said by Mrs. Bromell. In view of this tendency, it must be emphasized that there is no evidence, either from Mrs. Bromell or from documents, for this third stage; or rather that it is based on a denial of all personal and documentary evidence—census returns, birth, marriage and death entries, and so on—that does not fit Miss Deacon's preconceived theories.

This general attitude towards evidence in her third stage can very easily be illustrated by one simple example. Miss Deacon attaches great importance to the conception of the alleged child in the late summer of 1867. "From weather records we know", she writes, "that 1867 was a year with a splendid Indian summer. . . . It was then in the late summer and long, hot autumn of 1867, that he [Hardy] and Tryphena . . . became lovers".[7] She associates this Indian summer with the line "Weeks and weeks we had loved beneath that blazing blue" of Hardy's poem *The Place on the Map*, and "the October month of wonderful afternoons" in *Tess of the d'Urbervilles*. Yet the plain truth is that such a summer in 1867 never existed. Far from consulting any weather records, as she claims, Miss Deacon cannot have looked at them. Nor, perhaps even more strangely, has any scholar. The weather at Weymouth, a few miles from Hardy's home, is given every day in *The Times*. 1867 was a wet year, with a rainfall above the average, and a bad summer. At Weymouth that August less than half the days had any blue sky at all, and there were only three days of continuous blue. Exactly the same was true of September. Finally, far from there being a long hot Indian summer, the October records show the reverse, as *The Times* duly noted. The month began by being very cold. The temperature on 4 October was only forty-one degrees. The record for the rest of the month reads:

> Overcast rain, cloudy, some blue sky rain, hail and cloud, rain and cloud, cloud some blue sky, overcast rain, overcast rain, fog and cloud, overcast, cloud, overcast and cloud, lightning thunder cloud, overcast cloud, overcast cloud, cloudy and rainy, rain and fog, fog and cloud, cloudy and overcast, cloudy some blue sky, cloudy some blue sky, cloudy blue then rain, cloudy and overcast, overcast mist and rain, overcast fog and mist.

Miss Deacon has invented the whole idea of a long, hot Indian summer in 1867. Indeed, she was unluckier than she could possibly have known. This year of 1867 ushered in a meteorological phenomenon, for which the highly-detailed *London Weather* by J. H. Brazell (Her Majesty's Stationery Office) has no explanation, though it records the facts. For the next forty years, including this year, there was an almost complete absence over the country of warm Octobers or Indian summers or whatever they may be called. The long hot summer of Hardy's wooing in 1867 exists only in Miss Deacon's imagination.

It may well be asked why Miss Deacon laid such emphasis on this particular (though, as it proves, non-existent) Indian summer; and the answer may be that, as is well known, both Hardy and his girl-cousin had watchful and powerful mothers. The alleged conception would have to take place out of doors. The point is, though, that the complete falsification of evidence, the statement that "from weather records we know", when, in fact, weather records cannot have been consulted, throws total doubt on all Miss Deacon's methods of "research" in this, the third stage of her investigations. Practically everything that can be checked in this third stage turns out to be guesswork, and when documents are cited, they often prove not to have been consulted. To take only one topic, Tryphena's education; she is said to have gone to College, to train as a teacher, in "autumn 1869", and College records are cited in evidence. In fact, the College records show that her date of entry was 28 January 1870. Her school as a child is described as "the school at Athelhampton . . . run by the *National Society for the Education of the Poor*", while a few lines later on the same page[8] it appears as "the Athelhampton school . . . run by the British and Foreign Bible Society". It is implied that educational records have been consulted; if they had, they would have shown that the second of these two contradictory statements is the true one. Finally, Tryphena is alleged to have been assisted to College by Mrs. Julia Augusta Martin, who had helped the very early stages of Hardy's own education. Mrs. Martin was a staunch Anglican, who had been hurt and angry that Hardy had eventually gone to a Nonconformist school. Tryphena's college was a Nonconformist foundation; it is therefore impossible that Mrs. Martin could assist her to such a place, where all the sponsoring bodies were composed of Nonconformists, as the records show. The so-called research into documents, claimed or implied by Miss Deacon, is pure invention.

What then about "Hardy's boy", elicited by Miss Deacon from Mrs. Bromell in the second stage of her investigations? It must be remembered again that official medical opinion states that, at the time of this particular questioning, it would be wise to treat unsupported statements made by Mrs. Bromell with a degree of caution. It is notable that the sole evidence for this boy's existence—for no birth, death, marriage, census, school, apprenticeship, or employment records have ever been found for him—depends largely on a statement made by Miss Deacon and a reply by Mrs. Bromell with no witnesses present.[9] Speaking of the home of Tryphena's brother Nathaniel in Bristol, where the boy was supposed to have been largely brought up, Miss Deacon said, "So that there were three boys there altogether", to which Mrs. Bromell is said to have replied, "Yes, two boys of his own and Hardy's boy as well". Does this have any supporting evidence, as medical opinion advises it should, before we accept its accuracy?

In point of fact, documents which are relevant to this question have appeared during the past few years. They consist of a section of Sparks family letters, to and from Bristol, dated at the precise time the "Hardy boy" is said to be living there. These are very full and unconstrained family letters, mentioning in one way or another every member of the family, and dealing with every kind of family matter, marriages, births, deaths, money troubles, illness, difficulties with in-laws, work, houses, emigration to Australia, the upbringing and education of children. In none is there the slightest mention of this boy being in the Bristol house; in fact, two boys only are always specifically mentioned, Nathaniel Sparks's sons, James and Nathaniel junior.

About 1883, Rebecca Sparks writes to Nathaniel Sparks's wife at Bristol.[10] She adds "Kiss my two good boys for me". There is no mention of the third boy (whom, incidentally, she is supposed to have brought up at an earlier stage). In October 1884, there is a letter,[11] to which one of the two Sparks boys has later added a note. He recalls that he and his brother played a practical joke on an interfering great-aunt, who tried to boss the Bristol home. He talks about "us two nippers", and says the joke—an attempt to blow up their great-aunt with gunpowder—was "not bad for two kids". There is no mention of any third nipper or kid in the household. Their mother, writing from Bristol in 1890,[12] speaks of bringing up two boys only, and having taught them both at home. Finally in 1896, in a very long and detailed letter to a nephew in Australia,[13] Nathaniel Sparks himself describes his Bristol household. He also mentions two boys only: "Jim is 19 years old now and Nat is 16 . . . both at the Art School." In short, one has either to imagine an extraordinary, concerted and elaborate conspiracy of silence by this very outspoken and voluble family, or to think these letters finally prove that the third child, "the Hardy boy", never existed. Far from supporting what is said to have been heard from a very ill and confused old lady on her death-bed, these letters contradict it.

The letters then disprove the second stage of Miss Deacon's story. Hardy's son is as much of a myth as the long, hot summer in which he is said to have been conceived. This is not to say that there is no truth in her first stage. With some reservations, as has been said, one can accept a great deal of her pamphlet published in 1962. Its chief fault, as has also been said, is the false emphasis that it places on Tryphena, the "enduring and tragic love-story". Hardy, as it now appears, knew and was attracted by a number of girls in his youth. Tryphena Sparks was one of a fairly long sequence, including her own older sisters, Rebecca and Martha. Hardy wrote many poems to many women in his lifetime; it would be unwise to identify any positively with Tryphena Sparks, except for the poems written in and about Weymouth in the year 1869–70, and the poem "Thoughts of Phena", written at the time of her death in 1890. She was certainly attractive, and Hardy was attracted by her. So was his cousin and hers, John Antell, who also wrote a moving little poem on her death. It would be wrong, in any case, to ascribe to any of these girls the whole nature and character of his later work, still less to see the special influence of Tryphena Sparks in numerous poems and novels. The making of a myth about Tryphena and Thomas Hardy, whether based on falsified evidence or unsupported evidence, has confused almost every critical account, biography, and handbook published in the past decade. It is in the hope of ending the confusion that this analysis has been made.

Abbreviations Used in the Notes

Bailey: J. O. H. Bailey, *The Poetry of Thomas Hardy: A Handbook and Commentary*, Chapel Hill, 1970.

Beatty: C. J. P. Beatty (ed.), *The Architectural Notebook of Thomas Hardy*, Dorchester, 1966.

Beatty (thesis): C. J. P. Beatty, *The Part Played by Architecture in the Life and Work of Thomas Hardy, with Particular Reference to the Novels.* Unpublished dissertation, University of London (External), 1964.

DCC: *Dorset County Chronicle.*

DCL: Dorset County Library.

DCM: Dorset County Museum.

DCRO: Dorset County Record Office.

DEE: *Dorset Evening Echo.*

Halliday: F. E. Halliday, *Thomas Hardy: his life and work*, Bath, 1972.

LTH: F. E. Hardy, *Life of Thomas Hardy*, I vol., London, 1962.

MTH: *Materials for the Study of the Life, Times and Works of Thomas Hardy*, 72 monographs, St. Peter Port, Guernsey, Toucan Press. Various dates from 1962.

Millgate: M. Millgate, *Thomas Hardy: His career as a Novelist*, London, 1971.

Munby: A. J. Munby, MS. Diaries, The Library, Trinity College, Cambridge.

NTHL: F. E. Hardy, typescript "Notes of Thomas Hardy's life . . . (taken down in conversations etc.)". DCM.

ORFW: E. Hardy and F. B. Pinion (eds.), *One Rare Fair Woman: Thomas Hardy's Letters to Florence Henniker, 1893–1922*, London, 1972.

Pinion: F. B. Pinion, *A Hardy Companion*, London, 1968.

Purdy: R. L. Purdy, *Thomas Hardy: A Bibliographical Study*, Oxford, Repr., 1968.

Rutland: W. R. Rutland, *Thomas Hardy: A Study of His Writings and Their Background*, Oxford, 1938; repr. New York, 1962.

SREH: E. Hardy and R. Gittings (eds.), *Some Recollections by Emma Hardy with Some Relevant Poems by Thomas Hardy*, Oxford, 1961; repr. New York, 1973.

Sparks: Photostats of letters of the Sparks family, in the possession of Anna Winchcombe, at Hardy's Cottage (originals in the possession of Ian Kennedy, Queensland).

THN: E. Hardy (ed.), *Thomas Hardy's Notebooks*, London, 1955.

TLS: *Times Literary Supplement.*

Weber: C. J. Weber, *Hardy of Wessex: his Life and Literary Career*, 2nd ed., New York and London, 1965.

Notes

1: YOUNG AND OLD, pp. 1–6

1. Cyril Clemens, 'My Chat with Thomas Hardy'. *Dalhousie Review*, April 1943.
2. R. L. Purdy, 'The Authorship of Hardy's Biography', TLS, 30 December 1960.
3. See, for example, F. R. Southerington, *Hardy's Vision of Man*, 250, for the totally fanciful suggestion that LTH, 214–215, is an elaborate and weird criticism by Hardy of his own father.
4. NTHL, DCM.
5. Some of these errors have been taken literally, with strange results. See Southerington, *Hardy's Vision of Man*, 248, who produces out of a simple mistype a theory that Hardy's mother had illegitimate children.
6. NTHL, 14.
7. Purdy, 266.
8. MTH, No. 6.
9. Weber, 42.
10. Note supplied by R. L. Purdy.
11. Sparks, No. 2, annotation.
12. Mary Hardy to Emma Hardy, 28 January 1881, DCM.
13. DCM.
14. Never R.A., as stated in *Providence and Mr. Hardy*, 196.
15. DCM.
16. MTH, No. 7.
17. Thomas Hardy to Arthur C. Benson, 8 May 1923. Maggs Bros. Catalogue, No. 664, 1938.
18. SREH, xiii.
19. ORFW, 54.
20. LTH, 255.
21. LTH, 253.
22. LTH, 378.

2: BOCKHAMPTON AND PUDDLETOWN, pp. 7–19

1. LTH, 215 and 8.
2. J. H. Antell, "Puddletown as Thomas Hardy knew it", DEE, 18 July 1973.
3. MS. accounts of will of Thomas Hardy (obit. 1837), DCM.
4. Census, Stinsford, 1841–71, DCL.
5. Probate of wills, Somerset House.
6. MTH, No. 53.
7. MTH, No. 44.
8. So described in most of the marriages of his children, Somerset House.
9. Elizabeth Hand to Mary Hand, 17 January 1842, Lock Collection, AI, DCL.
10. LTH, 8.
11. Melbury Osmond, Overseers of the Poor, Accounts, 1825–36, DCRO. The accounts for 1822–24 are missing, but the payment seems established.
12. Outdoor relief continued often after the Poor Law Act of 1834.
13. DCM. Hardy's idea that John Hardy had enough money to buy the land seems another instance of claiming a former importance. LTH, 8.
14. Census, Stinsford, 1841, DCL.
15. She was married in 1847 from the Bockhampton house.
16. Lock Collection, AI, DCL.
17. MTH, No. 22.

18. DCM.
19. Stinsford Parish registers, DCRO.
20. LTH, 13–15, 21–23.
21. NTHL, 6.
22. *Alumni Cantabrigiensis*. He later took Holy Orders.
23. THN, 65.
24. Lock Collection, A 10, DCL.
25. NTHL, 6–7.
26. THN, omitted in printed version.
27. LTH, 19.
28. THN, 127.
29. LTH, 15.
30. In DCM, with MS. note by Mary Hardy.
31. Evelyn Hardy, *Thomas Hardy*, 26–32, where Mrs. Martin's influence was first noted and discussed.
32. LTH, 16. Rutland, 25, 131, believes the books were given later, in 1850.
33. LTH, 18. Hardy says he was sent to the Dorchester school "after some postponements", which may refer to the Hertfordshire visit.
34. LTH, 19.
35. Churchwardens' accounts, Stinsford, DCRO.
36. Census, Stinsford, 1851, DCL.
37. NTHL, 8.
38. LTH, 102.
39. LTH, 6, 8, 18, 19.
40. Stinsford parish registers, DCRO. Hardy noted his baptism and his wife's without comment in a list of family information from the Stinsford registers, which he made in 1921 (omitted in the printed THN).
41. Renewal of lease to Thomas, James, and Thomas Hardy junior, DCM.
42. Modern Australian descendants of a John Hardy, claim relationship with Hardy. See *The Thomas Hardy Year Book, 1971*, 70–73.
43. Stinsford and Puddletown parish registers.
44. O. D. Harvey, *Puddletown*, 1968, reprinted 1971. The article "Arcadians in Dorset", *Daily Telegraph*, 30 April 1872, describing the new model village of Puddletown, is sometimes wrongly taken to describe the Puddletown that Hardy knew (as partly by Millgate, 100–102).
45. Puddletown, Population 1821, DCRO.
46. Puddletown, Church Rate Book, 1845–47, DCRO.
47. Preface to *Far From the Madding Crowd*, 1895 edition.
48. Lock Collection, A 1, DCL.
49. DCM.
50. Death certificate, Somerset House.
51. Census, Puddletown, 1851, DCL.
52. Florence Hardy to Alda, Lady Hoare, 30 July 1915, Stourhead Collection, Wiltshire County Archives.
53. Puddletown registers.
54. H. R. Haggard, *Rural England*, 1, 280.
55. *The Times*, 31 July 1846.
56. *The Times*, 4 February 1846.
57. LTH, 21.
58. H. W. Nevinson, *Thomas Hardy*, 13.
59. *Dorset County Chronicle*, bound volume for 1895, DCM.
60. MTH, No. 20.
61. DCM: omitted in the printed THN.
62. Literary Notebook III, f. 65, DCM.
63. Churchwardens' accounts, Stinsford, DCRO.
64. LTH, 420.
65. Mary Hardy to Thomas Hardy, 19 May 1864.
66. MTH, No. 20.
67. LTH, 248.

68. LTH, 15–16.
69. H. J. Moule to Thomas Hardy, 31 December 1883, DCM.
70. N. Flower, "Walks and Talks with Thomas Hardy", *Countryman*, xxxiv, 193.
71. Literary Notebook III, DCM.
72. LTH, 444.

3: DORCHESTER, pp. 20–30

 1. Differences between the typescript notes and the *Early Life* (Mrs. Hardy's copy), DCM, obscure the exact time of year.
 2. Halliday, 12.
 3. LTH, 20.
 4. C. J. Weber (ed.), *The Letters of Thomas Hardy*, 30.
 5. Newman and Pevsner, *The Buildings of Dorset*, 350–351.
 6. LTH, 21.
 7. Newman and Pevsner, op. cit., 423 and 448.
 8. LTH, 16 and 19.
 9. Millgate, 38, for an excellent account of Hardy's self-education.
10. DCM.
11. MTH, No. 8.
12. DCC, 19 January 1928.
13. MTH, Nos. 22 and 44.
14. MTH, No. 22.
15. Not 1845, as said by Halliday, 11, nor were the riots caused by Newman's secession to Rome.
16. LTH, 21.
17. LTH, 126.
18. THN, 82–83.
19. DCRO.
20. Mary Carpenter, *Our Convicts*, I, 224.
21. On the rear fly-leaf of Alphonse Mariette's *Half-Hours of French Translation*, Colby College Library, Waterville, Maine.
22. MTH, No. 22.
23. DCC, 19 January 1928.
24. LTH, 22.
25. DCM.
26. NLTH, 9; LTH, 24.
27. DCM.
28. Unpublished letter, Thomas Hardy to James Murray, 9 July 1903.
29. LTH, 23.
30. Millgate, 38.
31. LTH, 25.
32. DCM.
33. LTH, 25.
34. Stinsford parish registers, DCRO; Census, Stinsford, 1851, DCL.
35. LTH, 206.
36. Stinsford parish registers, DCRO.
37. ibid.
38. Census, Stinsford, 1851, DCL.
39. LTH, 26 and 219.
40. MTH, No. 15.
41. MTH, No. 43.
42. LTH, 23.
43. MTH, No. 44.
44. *The Times*, 3 August 1846.
45. LTH, 23.
46. MS. Diary of Albert Brett of Puddletown, 26 December 1864. DCRO.

47. LTH, 32.
48. DCM. Bailey, 259, prints this dream in full.
49. Christopher Hassall, *Edward Marsh*, 18–23.
50. DCM; LTH, 25.
51. LTH, 27; NTHL, 10.

4: APPRENTICESHIP, pp. 31–43

1. Purdy, 325.
2. LTH, 27–29.
3. D. Jackman, *300 Years of Baptist Worship at Dorchester, 1645–1945*.
4. W. P. Wreden, *Books from the Library of Thomas Hardy*, Nos. 12 and 31.
5. LTH, 33.
6. Purdy, 291–292. The second Mrs. Hardy's idea that this *was* the Clock article is, however, unlikely. Even at the advanced old age, in which he wrote his reminiscences, Hardy surely would not confuse a clock at Dorchester with a pump at Wareham. Part of Hardy's Clock essay probably survives in his first published novel, *Desperate Remedies*, xix, 4.
7. Purdy, 293.
8. Newman and Pevsner, *The Buildings of Dorset*, 178.
9. LTH, 29; MTH, No. 25.
10. MTH, No. 25.
11. DCM, various drafts.
12. Thomas Hardy (Personal) Scrapbook, DCM.
13. Elliott Felkin, "Days with Thomas Hardy", *Encounter*, XVIII (April 1962).
14. LTH, 19.
15. Reprinted in *The Thomas Hardy Year Book 1970*, 84–93.
16. LTH, 28–29.
17. MTH, No. 27.
18. H. G. C. Moule, *Memories of a Vicarage*, 55–57.
19. R. W. M. Lewis, *The Family of Moule*.
20. Harold Orel (ed.), *Thomas Hardy's Personal Writings*, 66.
21. *Standard*, 23 September 1873.
22. TLS, letter from Mary A. Blyth, 13 March 1969.
23. H. C. G. Moule, *Memories of a Vicarage*, 35.
24. DCM.
25. Wreden, op. cit.
26. LTH, 33.
27. LTH, 87.
28. cf. *Before My Friend Arrived*.
29. Bailey, 458.
30. *The Saturday Review*, III, 239–240.
31. *Tempora Mutantur*, A Memorial of the Fordington Times Society, 19–21.
32. Thomas Hardy, "Thomas William Hooper Tolbort", DCC, 14 August 1883.
33. DCM.
34. LTH, 32.
35. LTH, 28.
36. LTH, 215.

5: RELIGION, pp. 44–54

1. LTH, 36.
2. DCM.
3. The 1841 Census was imperfect in many details.
4. G. Kitson Clark, *The Making of Victorian England*, 148.
5. ibid., 151.
6. LTH, 112.

7. Owen Chadwick, *The Victorian Church*, II, 171–174.
8. H. Taine, *Notes on England*, trans. E. Hyams, 118.
9. LTH, 50.
10. Millgate, 37–38.
11. LTH, 34.
12. Information, Pamela Stewart, Assistant Diocesan Archivist.
13. DCM.
14. Owen Chadwick, *The Victorian Church*, II, 76.
15. ibid., 77–78.
16. LTH, 33.
17. Owen Chadwick, *The Victorian Church*, II, 3.
18. ibid., II, 83.
19. *Saturday Review*, XI, 211–212, 2 March 1861.
20. DCM, for all three books.
21. LTH, 29.
22. LTH, 18.
23. DCM.
24. G. Battiscombe, *John Keble*, 104–105.
25. ibid. 69.
26. DCM.
27. LTH, 38.
28. Also the lesson for the evening before his own birthday; but not, as wrongly said, marked for this reason, since he dates it in April.
29. DCM. Oddly called "that vicar" in MTH, No. 32, with other errors.
30. LTH, 7, n. 1.
31. LTH, 22.
32. *Alumni Oxoniensis*.
33. LTH, 29.
34. LTH, 29–30.
35. DCM.
36. LTH, 31.
37. LTH, 390–391.
38. DCM.
39. Letters of H. M. Moule to Thomas Hardy, DCM.
40. C. W. Moule to Thomas Hardy, 11 May 1873, DCM.

6: LONDON, pp. 55–65

1. LTH, 443.
2. DCM.
3. Sparks, Nos. 15 and 23.
4. Parish registers, Hemington, Somerset; Beatty, 113.
5. Sparks, Nos. 17 and 18.
6. MTH, No. 40.
7. DCM. Wrongly dated June in MTH, No. 32, which has many such errors.
8. MTH, No. 11.
9. LTH, 36.
10. Prayer book fly-leaf, and MS. list of Hardy's dwelling-places, DCM. He moved for a few weeks to No. 9 in the middle of the following February, *The Christian Year*, annotation, DCM.
11. LTH, 35.
12. Census, Hampstead, sub-district No. 9, 1861.
13. R. Blomfield, *Memoirs of an Architect*, 35.
14. ibid., 36.
15. ibid., 35–36.
16. Frederick Dolman, "An Evening with Thomas Hardy", *Young Man*, VIII (March 1894).
17. Purdy, 296.
18. Census returns, Dorchester, 1851, DCL.

19. LTH, 34.
20. H. Taine, *Notes on England*, trans. Hyams, 37–38.
21. Munby, *Diary*.
22. LTH, 41.
23. Munby, *Diary*.
24. Henry Mayhew, *London Labour and the London Poor*, vol. iv, ed. P. Quennell.
25. Munby, *Diary*.
26. Munby, *Diary*.
27. *Rogue's Progress: An Autobiography of 'Lord Chief Baron' Nicholson* (rep. 1965), 327-329.
28. Munby, *Diary*, vol. 23, ff. 28–29.
29. Mayhew, op. cit., 99.
30. Munby, *Diary*, vol. 26, ff. 42–49 and 93–94.
31. Munby, *Diary*.
32. LTH, 45.
33. LTH, 43–44.
34. *The Oxford Companion to the Theatre*.
35. LTH, 35 and 38.
36. Munby, *Diary*.
37. DCM.
38. LTH, 38 and 42.
39. See p. 12.
40. F. P. B. Martin, *A Memoir on the Equinoctial Storms of March–April 1850*, 3.
41. ibid., 91.
42. ibid., 2.
43. ibid., 4.
44. Information, Royal Geographical Society; P.O. Directory, 1860.
45. LTH, 41; Census, Stinsford, 1851; Will of F. P. B. Martin, Somerset House.
46. LTH, 41.
47. See above, p. 12.
48. LTH, 256.
49. Will of F. P. B. Martin.
50. Personal information, John Hardy Antell.
51. Hardy to Mary Hardy, 19 August 1862. I owe this unprinted passage to a note from R. L. Purdy.
52. Munby, *Diary*, vol. 14, ff. 94.
53. Sparks, No. 2, annotation.
54. DCM.
55. NTH, 54–55.
56. Middle Temple records.
57. LTH, 38.
58. Beatty, 1.
59. Purdy, 293.
60. Halliday, 22.
61. He was still at Kilburn on 18 February. Prayer book annotation. DCM.
62. Prayer book, DCM.
63. Census returns, St. Stephen's, 1861.
64. R.I.B.A., Nominations for Fellowships, 1876, f. 38.
65. J. Kingsgate, "*Tess* and Thomas Hardy, New Facts about His Life in London". *Graphic*, cxii, 5 September 1925, 377.

7: SELF-HELP, pp. 66–75

1. Munby, *Diary*, vol. 23, ff. 141–142.
2. LTH, 37–38.
3. Beatty, 159–160.
4. DCM.
5. DCM.

6. Munby, *Diary*.
7. LTH, 37.
8. DCM.
9. Newman and Pevsner, *The Buildings of Dorset*, 131.
10. A. P. Webb, *A Bibliography of the Works of Thomas Hardy*, 41; Purdy, 159.
11. Beatty, 133.
12. Rutland, 35.
13. DCM.
14. Moule to Hardy, 2 March 1863; *Saturday Review*, 21 February and 7 March 1863.
15. Moule to Hardy, 2 July 1863, DCM.
16. DCM.
17. LTH, 48.
18. Literary Notebook I, DCM.
19. LTH, 345.
20. Moule to Hardy, 21 February 1864, DCM.
21. LTH, 40.
22. C. Holland, *Thomas Hardy*, 54, Rutland, 26, Beatty, 16; unconvincingly discussed in *The Thomas Hardy Year Book, 1972–1973*, 42–43.
23. LTH, 257. Beatty, 16, while accepting the Radcliffe Chapel legend, shows surprise at no evidence of a visit in Hardy's notebook.
24. Marlborough College Register.
25. Deacon and Coleman, *Providence and Mr. Hardy*, quotation from letter by H. G. C. Moule, 95.
26. D. A. Winstanley, *Later Victorian Cambridge*, 210 and 214.
27. Moule to Hardy (? June 1867), DCM.
28. See p. 37.
29. DCM.
30. LTH, 40.
31. MS. Diary of Arthur Brett, DCRO.
32. LTH, 56.
33. Mary Hardy to Thomas Hardy (MS. fragment), 19 May 1864, DCM.
34. *Descriptive Catalogue of the Grolier Club Centenary Exhibition of the Works of Thomas Hardy* (1940), No. 10.
35. DCM.
36. Moule to Hardy, 21 February 1864, DCM.
37. Goldwin Smith, *Does the Bible Sanction Slavery?*
38. Munby, *Diary*, vol. 24, ff. 85–96.
39. Christopher Hibbert, *Garibaldi and his Enemies*, 341.
40. ibid., 342.
41. Prayer book, MS. annotation, DCM.
42. MTH, No. 32, which states, on no evidence, that he was suffering from "nervous exhaustion".
43. Nairn and Pevsner, *The Buildings of England: Sussex*, 435.
44. Munby, *Diary*, vol. 23, ff. 40–43.
45. Beatty, 162.
46. ibid., 69.
47. D. Drew Cox, "The Poet and the Architect", *Agenda* (Spring–Summer, 1972), 57.

8 POETRY, pp. 76–87

1. DCM. Partly described by Evelyn Hardy, "Hardy and the Phrenologist", *John O'London's Weekly*, LXIII (26 February 1954).
2. Rutland, 111.
3. Information from the present tenant.
4. Orel, 168.
5. DCM, where poems of this type are ticked in the Index.
6. DCM.

7. By Weber, 52, who cites no evidence, and E. Hardy, 76, who wrongly dates this volume as being published in 1867.
8. LTH, 53.
9. Pinion, 215–217.
10. Rutland, 15, n. 1.
11. DCM.
12. Purdy, 297.
13. Pinion, 213.
14. Quoted Weber, 50, from "Barrie Reviews Hardy", *The Literary Digest* (2 February 1929), 22.
15. ORFW, 14.
16. Grolier, No. 4.
17. Partly described by Phyllis Bartlett, 'Hardy's Shelley', *Keats–Shelley Journal*, IV, (Winter 1955), who however confuses this volume with the two described by Barrie.
18. Rutland, 15.
19. Rutland, 13.
20. LTH, 49.
21. David Garnett (ed.), *Letters of T. E. Lawrence*, 193.
22. Pinion, 121–122.
23. Rutland, 71.
24. *Saturday Review*, xvi, 562–563, 24 October 1863.
25. LTH, 47.
26. One must, I think, accept Hardy's statement that his revision to his own early poems consisted only of "the mere change of a few words or the rewriting of a line or two", LTH, 47. The few available MSS. seem to bear this out.
27. DCM.
28. *Wessex Poems*, preface.
29. DCM. This marking and others in the Coleridge were first noted by E. Hardy, 75–76.
30. DCM.
31. Hardy, perhaps mischievously, gives her the christian name, Amelia, of one of his two spinster aunts (Amelia and Sarah Sparks) to whose cottage in Dorchester he went for his schoolboy lunches.
32. Originally, "laughter" for "gladness" made this even more obscure.
33. See Rutland, 266, who says it "suggests a club".
34. 1865 edition, DCM. It occurs in *The Hind and the Panther*.
35. Dated 1867 and "W.P.V." (by Hardy in the Wessex Edition). Hardy left this address in July of that year.
36. The MS. of *Wessex Poems*.

9: LOSS OF FAITH, pp. 88–99

1. Bailey, 611.
2. LTH, 50.
3. LTH, 330.
4. LTH, 264.
5. LTH, 51–52.
6. LTH, 50.
7. Prayer book, DCM.
8. *The Christian Year*, DCM.
9. LTH, 39 and 52.
10. DCM; LTH, 370.
11. Lock Collection, DCL.
12. Munby, *Diary*, 22 November 1865.
13. LTH, 272.
14. *At a Bridal*; the original of line 14, afterwards altered.
15. V. H. Collins, *Talks with Thomas Hardy . . . 1920–1922*, 23.
16. King's College, London, Evening Classes, Winter Session, 1865–6. King's College Archives.

17. Thomas Hardy to the Principal, King's College, 19 June 1926, King's College, London, Library.
18. Colby College Library, Waterville, Maine.
19. Purdy, 297.
20. *The Christian Year*, DCM; Beatty, 11–12.
21. LTH, 55.
22. Bailey, 199; Purdy, 143.
23. *Memoirs of Mark Pattison*, introduction by Jo Manton, xix.

10: FIRST NOVEL, pp. 100–110

1. Wreden, No. 19.
2. 9th Baron Digby of Sherborne to Mary Hardy, 27 May 1867; Lock Collection, B10, and Mary Hardy's sketch book, Lock Collection, H, DCL.
3. *The Times*, weather records for Weymouth, August–October 1867. The exceptionally fine hot summer, claimed by the authors of *Providence and Mr. Hardy*, and in numerous pamphlets by Lois Deacon, is a pure fiction, and not based on any records at all. See my "Thomas Hardy and Tryphena Sparks", TLS, 27 April 1973.
4. John Hardy Antell, "Puddletown as Thomas Hardy Knew It", DEE, 18 July 1973.
5. LTH, 56.
6. Actually current for some thirty years before, though not in Hardy's copy of J. R. M'Culloch, *Principles of Political Economy* (1825).
7. LTH, 59; Purdy, 275.
8. Best discussed by Rutland, 111–133.
9. As suggested by Evelyn Hardy, 88.
10. DCM.
11. LTH, 48.
12. 'Thomas Hardy and a Royal Occasion', *The Times*, 21 November 1963.
13. George Brereton Sharpe to Thomas Hardy, 21 January 1868, Lock Collection, B 1 and 2, DCL.
14. Sparks, No. 23.
15. LTH, 330.
16. DCM, where Hardy's copy is the 1867 edition.
17. LTH, 61.
18. NTH, 28, where it is mistranscribed.
19. LTH, 62.
20. LTH, 57–58.
21. S. Nowell-Smith (ed.), *Letters to Macmillan*, 129–130.
22. Charles Morgan, *The House of Macmillan*, 91.
23. LTH, 59.
24. Purdy, 275.
25. LTH, 61–63.
26. Purdy, 329.
27. See p. 72.
28. Education: Reports, Commissioners, 1868/9, xx. British Museum.
29. O. D. Harvey, *Puddletown (Thomas Hardy's Weatherbury)*, 27–28.
30. Puddletown School (Girls) Log-book, entries for April and August 1867.
31. F. G. Walcott, *The Origins of Culture and Anarchy*, 95–96.
32. Education: Reports, Commissioners, 1867, xxii.
33. As argued by F. R. Southerington, *Hardy's Vision of Man*, 261.
34. Education: Reports, Commissioners, 1868/9, xx.
35. Personal information, Miss Catherine Shepherd, Mrs. Hawkins's granddaughter.
36. Who only taught at "National" schools; see the announcement of Mary Hardy's death, *Dorset County Chronicle*.
37. Sparks, No. 2.
38. *Dorset County Chronicle*, 10 December 1868.
39. Plymouth Day Schools (Girls) Log-book, f. 292, Plymouth City Library.

40. Sparks, No. 2.
41. ibid., and census returns, Portesham, 1871, DCL.
42. Census returns, Portesham, 1871.
43. LTH, 57–58.
44. DCM.
45. Quoted Purdy, 242, with photograph of MS. on the opposite page.

11: TRYPHENA AND THE SPARKSES, pp. 111–125

1. See p. 90.
2. See particularly, *Providence and Mr. Hardy*.
3. Sparks, No. 9.
4. He is described as journeyman on his wife's death certificate.
5. Sparks, No. 10.
6. Death certificate, Somerset House.
7. Sparks, No. 18.
8. P.O. Directories.
9. Sparks, No. 2, annotation.
10. The poem *Unrealized* from *Time's Laughingstocks*.
11. Sparks, No. 2, annotation.
12. Sparks No. 1. Annotated much later as being to her brother James in London, it is clearly, from internal evidence, to Nathaniel in Somerset.
13. Entry Lists, College of Sarum St. Michael, Salisbury.
14. Certificates of Marriage and Birth, Somerset House.
15. Archives, College of Sarum St. Michael, Salisbury.
16. W. M. Payne, *Dial*, XXII, 16 May 1897.
17. Sparks, No. 2, annotation by Nathaniel Sparks junior; mistranscribed in *Dorset: A County Magazine*.
18. Earlier dates, as proposed in *Providence and Mr. Hardy*, are purely fictitious, and often produced by the falsification of documents. See my "Thomas Hardy and Tryphena Sparks", TLS, 28 April 1973.
19. Census returns, Stinsford, 1871.
20. Permissions for Faculties, Diocese of Salisbury, Diocesan Record Office, Salisbury.
21. Beatty (thesis), Appendix 1, 120.
22. Reproduced Beatty, 27.
23. Pinion, 369.
24. LTH, 65.
25. MS. table of places and dates, I. C. Willis's copy of LTH, DCM.
26. DCL.
27. With possibly the draft of a poem afterwards revised, *At a Seaside Town in 1869*, and *In the Vaulted Way* (dated in MS. 1870).
28. NTH, 33–34.
29. Manchester College, Oxford, MS.
30. Sparks, No. 2.
31. Irene Cooper Willis, MS., Colby College.
32. MTH, No. 3.
33. See p. 35.
34. *Dorset County Chronicle*, 28 October 1869.
35. ibid., March 1868.
36. Thomas J. Graham, *Modern Domestic Medicine*, 657–658 and 660.
37. Marriage certificate, Somerset House.
38. P.O. Directories, confirmed by birth certificates, 1870.
39. Sparks, No. 13.
40. DCM.
41. F. B. Pinion, *Notes and Queries*, November 1972, 430–431.
42. Census, Athelhampton 1871, DCL.
43. Reports of British and Foreign School Society, 1870 and 1871.
44. *Dorset County Chronicle*, 10 July 1866.

45. Report of the British and Foreign School Society, 1872, which tabulates the progress of students in the previous two years. The authors of *Providence and Mr. Hardy*, consulting the wrong report, give a totally inaccurate account of her entry.
46. Quoted in M. Sturt, *The Education of the People*.
47. Personal information, John Hardy Antell.
48. Archives, Stockwell College of Education.
49. LTH, 64.
50. DCM.
51. Chapter 1, verses 6, 7, and 18; chapter 2, verse 10.
52. LTH, 64.
53. Census, Stinsford, 1871. DCL.
54. Mary Hardy's sketch book, Lock Collection, H, DCL; and Archives, College of Sarum St. Michael, Salisbury.
55. LTH, 65.
56. LTH, 84.
57. Millgate, 381.
58. Personal information, Mary A. Blyth, Horace Moule's grand-niece.
59. Census, Fordington, 1871, DCL.
60. Literary Notebook IV, f. 31, DCM.
61. LTH, 64.
62. Beatty, 27.

12: EMMA AND THE GIFFORDS, pp. 126–37

1. Bishop's transcripts, St. Paul's parish, Bristol Archives Office.
2. SREH, 17. His late matriculation, aged 34 (*Alumni Oxoniensis*) may indicate failure in some previous profession.
3. Matthews Bristol Directories and Bristol 1812 Poll Book, Bristol Central Library.
4. SREH, 4, 14, 15, 18.
5. SREH, 22.
6. Probate of Wills, Somerset House.
7. SREH, 16–17.
8. Loose fragment of family memoirs by Emma Hardy, DCM.
9. Bristol Archives Office and Bristol Central Library.
10. *Felix Farley's Bristol Journal*, 7 April 1832, Bristol Central Library.
11. Bailey, 388, oddly confuses Emma herself with the spectre, applying the adjective "mirthless" in stanza 4 to her. Apart from the fact that this reading makes nonsense of the whole poem, the original word was "shadowless", which suggests a supernatural figure.
12. Irene Cooper Willis, MS. covering note to Selection of Letters to Emma Hardy, DCM.
13. "Some Notes on the Hardys", MS. by I. C. Willis, c. 1937, DCM.
14. DCM.
15. MS. Note to Selection of Letters to Emma Hardy, DCM.
16. Purdy, 11.
17. Emma Hardy's Diary, DCM.
18. Helen Catherine Holder to Emma Hardy, 28 November 1882, DCM.
19. Archives, Warneford Hospital.
20. Death certificate, Somerset House.
21. *Dictionary of National Biography*.
22. Probate of Wills, Somerset House.
23. *Felix Farley's Bristol Journal*, 1830, Bristol Central Library.
24. Gifford family papers.
25. I owe this suggestion to Dr. Ida Macalpine.
26. *The Times* index of bankrupts, 1860–80, does not show his name.
27. Death certificate, Somerset House.
28. MS. annotation, letter of Walter Gifford to Emma Hardy, DCM.
29. Hardy to Manager, Accident Dept., The London Assurance, draft, DCM.

30. Death certificate, Somerset House.
31. Lilian Gifford to Thomas Hardy, 27 November 1913, DCM.
32. Gifford family information.
33. ORFW, 155.
34. As said by Bailey, 387, who has not observed that Kate Gifford's letter of 25 November is simply a sympathetic reply to Hardy's of 23 November, repeating his words.
35. Archives, Warneford Hospital.
36. MS. Note to Selection of Letters to Emma Hardy, DCM.
37. Henry Gifford, "Thomas Hardy and Emma", *Essays and Studies 1966*.
38. ibid., 113. Letter conjecturally dated in 1911.
39. ibid., 115.
40. Letter from C. W. Moule to Emma Hardy, 1911, DCM.
41. SREH, 50, 51.
42. MTH, Nos. 5 and 17. She also wrote to the local press advocating bloomers, and sometimes wore a pair herself, MTH, No. 22.
43. Carl J. Weber, *Dearest Emmie*, 45.
44. MTH, No. 20.
45. A. Pretor to Emma Hardy, 1898, DCM.
46. Letter by Gordon Gifford, TLS, 1 January 1944.
47. ORFW, Preface 2.
48. ORFW, 29.
49. A. P. Watt to Emma Hardy, 10 January 1894, DCM.
50. Irene Cooper Willis, "Some Notes", DCM.
51. As thought by Millgate, 119.
52. SREH, 53.
53. *The Times*, weather reports, 1870.
54. SREH, 50.
55. Preface to new edition of *A Pair of Blue Eyes*, March 1895.
56. LTH, 74–75.
57. SREH, 50.
58. SREH, 7; Henry Gifford, op. cit., 114.
59. In his corrections to her own manuscript account, SREH, 52.
60. Census returns, Stinsford, 1871.
61. MS. curriculum vitae of E. H. Gifford in the possession of Henry Gifford.
62. SREH, 18–19.
63. Barbara Stephen, *Emily Davies and Girton College*, chapter viii.
64. SREH, 16, 20.

13: DESPERATE REMEDIES, pp. 138–48

1. LTH, 75.
2. Beatty, 27–29.
3. LTH, 75.
4. See p. 100.
5. S. M. Ellis, "Thomas Hardy: Some Personal Recollections", *Fortnightly Review*, N.S., cxxii (1928), 395.
6. W. L. Phelps, *Autobiography with Letters*, 391, 394.
7. Charles Morgan, *The House of Macmillan*, 93–94.
8. Phyllis Bartlett, "Hardy's Shelley", *Keats–Shelley Journal* IV (Winter 1955), 18.
9. Pinion, 165.
10. Beatty (thesis), Appendix 1. "Manston", the villain's surname, is a village nearby.
11. *Desperate Remedies*, 276–277, not 95–96, as said by Purdy, 98.
12. Charles Morgan, *The House of Macmillan*, 93–94.
13. Millgate, 32.
14. The cutting of an interview, in which this remark appears, is annotated by Hardy "(largely faked)". DCM.
15. Edmund Gosse, "Thomas Hardy's Lost Novel", *Sunday Times*, 22 January 1928.
16. Thomas Hardy, Obituary of Mary Hardy, DCC.

17. Purdy, 329.
18. LTH, 76.
19. LTH, 76.
20. Birth certificates, Somerset House.
21. NTH, 29.
22. LTH, 78.
23. Still less that Moule met her, as invented in *Providence and Mr. Hardy*.
24. About 9 August was the usual date. Archives, Stockwell College.
25. SREH, 56, n. 1.
26. LTH, 155–157.
27. *The Times*, 5 July and 4 August 1870.
28. Moule to Hardy, undated note, DCM.
29. Prayer book, DCM.
30. Wreden, No. 153.
31. DCM.
32. NTH, 31.
33. NTH, 32, where it is mistranscribed.
34. Bible, DCM. MTH, No. 32 quotes more than he actually marked.
35. NTH, 32, where it is mistranscribed.
36. LTH, 78.
37. LTH, 83.
38. Report of the British and Foreign School Society, 1872.
39. LTH, 83.
40. Purdy, 4–5. Hardy afterwards claimed (LTH, 83) that Tinsley had altered his terms for the worse; this seems untrue.
41. LTH, 84.
42. Sparks, No. 2.
43. Thomas Hardy to Miss Thomson, 22 February 1898(?). Christie's Sale Catalogue, 12 July 1972.
44. Bible, DCM, Isaiah, xiv, 16, wrongly transcribed verse 23 in MTH, No. 32.
45. NTH, 33.
46. LTH, 84.
47. Cyril Clemens, "My Chat with Thomas Hardy", *Dalhousie Review*, April 1943, 90.

14: UNDER THE GREENWOOD TREE, pp. 149–59

1. The reviewer had decided to use this pronoun as a matter of convenience.
2. LTH, 84.
3. Millgate, 36.
4. DCM.
5. LTH, 84.
6. SREH, 56, n. 1.
7. Beatty, 28–29.
8. LTH, 79.
9. LTH, 85.
10. Beatty, 21 and 33.
11. Beatty, 42, 56, 86.
12. Millgate, 45–48.
13. The paste-in of the MS. (DCM) seems to show this, rather than that he was intended first as a publican in *Under the Greenwood Tree*, as thought by Millgate, 53.
14. S. M. Ellis, "Thomas Hardy: Some Personal Recollections", *Fortnightly Review*, N.S., cxiii (1928), 397.
15. Triffy was her home name.
16. Morgan, op. cit., 95–97.
17. Weber, 65.
18. LTH, 59.
19. Purdy, 11.

20. LTH, 86.
21. Sparks, No. 2, annotation.
22. Her own daughter's evidence on this is full of contradiction; but its most coherent part is positive that Tryphena's eventual husband saw the ring. MTH, No. 3.
23. Personal information, John Hardy Antell.
24. Sparks, No. 15, annotation.
25. Purdy, 332.
26. Beatty, 2.
27. Moule to Hardy, 17 April 1872, DCM.
28. LTH, 88; Purdy, 332.
29. Purdy, 332.
30. Purdy, 332–333.
31. LTH, 89–90.
32. DCM, inscribed Thomas Hardy 1873.

15: A PAIR OF BLUE EYES, pp. 160–70

1. TLS, 13 March 1969, letter from Mary A. Blyth.
2. Administrations, Somerset House.
3. SREH, 57.
4. SREH, 16.
5. LTH, 91.
6. Not relations, as wrongly noted in SREH, 43, note 2.
7. DCM.
8. Florence Dugdale to Edward Clodd, 3 July 1913, Brotherton Library Collection, Leeds.
9. Bailey, 407–408.
10. V. H. Collins, *Talks with Thomas Hardy*, 26.
11. Bailey, 350, but who then, contradicting Hardy's own identification, thinks she was leaning on a nearby signpost, thus destroying the point of the whole poem.
12. Bailey, 351, believes this to be a reference "no doubt, to Emma's mental eccentricities", but this itself seems very doubtful.
13. MTH, No. 31.
14. Emma Hardy to Rebekah Owen, 24 April 1899, Colby College Library, quoted Bailey, 23.
15. NTH, 38.
16. NTH, 39.
17. Purdy, 333.
18. Bible, DCM.
19. Millgate, 75.
20. S. M. Ellis, op. cit.
21. MTH, 31–32.
22. Census, Stinsford, 1851, DCL, where the deafness is recorded.
23. Millgate, 62.
24. H. C. G. Moule, *Memories of a Vicarage*, 35.
25. Personal information, Mary A. Blyth.
26. Presumably copied by Hardy from one of his numerous volumes of general information; it is, in fact, a popular fallacy. See *Nouvelle Biographie Générale*, tome 39, Paris, 1862.
27. Millgate, 62.
28. LTH, 32.
29. LTH, 73.
30. Millgate, 67.
31. Moule to Hardy, May (?) 1873, DCM.
32. Hardy actually took the *height* from Beeny, but most of its other characteristics from Pentargan Cliff a little further south, as convincingly shown by Denys Kay-Robinson, *Hardy's Wessex Re-appraised*, 249–250.

16: FAR FROM THE MADDING CROWD, pp. 171–78

1. Purdy, 333.
2. ibid., 7.
3. ibid., 12.
4. ibid., 336–337.
5. LTH, 96.
6. Sparks No. 10 and annotation.
7. NTH, 39; not South Hill, as wrongly transcribed.
8. NTH, 42.
9. NTH, 40.
10. Accepted by Hardy's own family as the original of Bathsheba. See Kate Hardy's Diary, 24 July 1930, Lock Collection, H. 10, DCL.
11. Granvile D. Hill to Catherine Hawkins, 12 October 1865.
12. Catherine Hawkins to Miss Hill, 23 January 1866.
13. Sparks, No. 19, annotation.
14. Sparks, No. 18.
15. The death of William Keats, tranter, by which he dates it, had occurred two years earlier, in August 1870. MTH, No. 51.
16. J. I. M. Stewart, *Thomas Hardy*, 89–90.
17. NTH, 38.
18. NTH, 42.
19. John Hutton to Thomas Hardy, DCM.
20. As thought by Millgate.
21. John Hutton to Thomas Hardy, 29 April 1873, DCM.
22. Buttery Accounts, Queens' College, Cambridge University Library.
23. TLS, 27 January 1969 *et seq*.
24. DCM.
25. LTH, 93.
26. LTH, 93–94.
27. SREH, 60.
28. *Midnight on Beechen*, 187–, i.e. Beechen Cliff, just south of Bath.
29. Purdy, 16.

17: MOULE, pp. 179–86

1. *Cambridge Chronicle*, 27 September 1873.
2. DCM.
3. Not against the description of Hallam, as said by Evelyn Hardy, TLS, 29 January 1969.
4. By Bailey, 33, n. 8.
5. The two entries of "Moule" in Hardy's Bible (DCM) seem to refer to texts used by the Reverend Henry Moule.
6. NTH, omitted in printed text.
7. I owe all that follows on this topic to the unpublished notes of R. L. Purdy, taken down in 1933 in conversations with Florence Hardy at Max Gate.
8. See chapter 20.
9. DCM.
10. Bailey, 57.
11. Plymouth Day School's (Girls) Log-book, f. 294.
12. DCM.
13. Manuscript Room, Cambridge University Library.
14. As well argued by Millgate, 84–85, and 372, n. 15.
15. Information and note, R. L. Purdy.
16. See p. 15.
17. As put forward in *Providence and Mr. Hardy*, 192–193.

18. Bailey, 279, connects this with a boy, not consulting the MS.
19. MS., *Satires of Circumstance*, DCM.
20. See Appendix.

18: SUCCESS AND MARRIAGE, pp. 187–97

1. LTH, 100.
2. Not 1864, as said by Bailey, 282, who anyway confuses this with Stephen's resignation of his tutorship in 1862.
3. Noel Annan, *Leslie Stephen*, 66n.
4. LTH, 96.
5. NTH, 43, 44.
6. NTH, 44, where "fringe" is mistranscribed as "finger".
7. MTH, No. 20.
8. Cancelled draft pages, DCM.
9. Cancelled draft pages, DCM.
10. Purdy, 338.
11. Purdy, 15.
12. Purdy, 337; Millgate, 79–94, for a good account of Stephen's influence.
13. Millgate, 372, n. 11.
14. LTH, 99.
15. See p. 183.
16. C. J. Weber, 'Ainsworth and Thomas Hardy', *Review of English Studies*, XVII (April 1941), 193–200.
17. Hardy's copy of a book called *Manly Exercises* is inscribed "Thomas and Henry Hardy, Professors of Boxing", DCM.
18. Weber, 94.
19. LTH, 98.
20. NTH, 48.
21. SREH, 53.
22. The date is conjectural, but the London weather then corresponds with Hardy's description in F. W. Maitland, *Life and Letters of Leslie Stephen*.
23. F. W. Maitland, *Life and Letters of Leslie Stephen*, 273.
24. Viola Meynell (ed.), *The Best of Friends: Further Letters to Sydney Carlyle Cockerell*.
25. LTH, 98, 100.
26. LTH, 97.
27. Purdy, 337.
28. LTH, 99.
29. *The Opportunity: For H.P.*
30. Emma Hardy's Diary, DCM.
31. SREH, 60.
32. Thomas Hardy to Henry Hardy, 18 September 1874, DCM.
33. Emma Hardy's Diary, DCM, where the entry, though heavily crossed out, seems to be decipherable as this address.

19: ETHELBERTA, pp. 198–212

1. Emma Hardy's Diary, ff. 1–3, DCM.
2. ibid., f. 5, DCM.
3. ibid., ff. 20–21, DCM.
4. ibid., ff. 38–41, DCM.
5. ibid., f. 52, DCM.
6. ibid., f. 71, DCM.
7. *Saturday Review*, 16 January 1892.
8. Merryn Williams, *Thomas Hardy and Rural England*, 135.
9. Purdy, 339.
10. John Hutton to Hardy, 23 December 1874, DCM.

11. Purdy, 335.
12. Emma Hardy's Diary, attached to end-paper, DCM.
13. John Hutton to Hardy, 23 December 1874, DCM.
14. LTH, 101–102.
15. Kate Hardy's Diary, 12 January 1928, Lock Collection, N. 10, DCL.
16. Kate Hardy's Diary.
17. MTH, No. 20.
18. Purdy, 19.
19. LTH, 105–106.
20. LTH, 76.
21. He uses the expression twice. See Orel, 58 and 127.
22. Gordon S. Haight, *George Eliot*, 302.
23. LTH, 146. Hardy advocated "This as a matter of *policy*, without which no religion succeeds in making way".
24. Henry Gifford, "Thomas Hardy and Emma", *Essays and Studies 1966*, 113–114.
25. Baptisms, Melbury Osmond, DCRO.
26. LTH, 98.
27. Jo Manton, *Sister Dora*, 162, n. 31.
28. Sparks, No. 13.
29. Emma Hardy's Diary, ff. 6 and 9, DCM.
30. *The Times*, 22 March 1875.
31. Emma Hardy's Diary, ff. 89–92, DCM.
32. MS. version.
33. SREH, 90–91.
34. *Saturday Review*, 6 May 1876.
35. Sparks, No. 3.
36. Sparks, No. 23.
37. F. W. Maitland, *Life and Letters of Leslie Stephen*, 276.
38. LTH, 109.
39. Emma Hardy's Diary, DCM.
40. LTH, 111.
41. LTH, 106.
42. Emma Hardy's Diary, DCM.
43. C. J. Weber, *Hardy's Love Poems*, 43.

20: OLD AND YOUNG, pp. 213–22

1. ORFW, 57 and 82.
2. Guide to Turnworth Church.
3. SREH, 60–61.
4. Emma Hardy's Diary, DCM.
5. DCM.
6. Rutland, 85.
7. LTH, 176.
8. LTH, 207–208.
9. LTH, 214; information, Clare Gittings.
10. LTH, 215.
11. LTH, 217.
12. LTH, 219.
13. LTH, 220.
14. LTH, 230.
15. Chaddleworth parish registers, Berkshire County Archives.
16. Millgate, 267.
17. Personal information, Miss Mary Stickland. See also J. Henry Harper, *The House of Harper*.
18. A. Compton-Rickett, *I Look Back: Memories of Fifty Years*, 176–186.
19. MTH, No. 20.

20. Parish Records, Melbury Osmond, DCRO.
21. Millgate, 401, n. 11.
22. E. Royston Pike, *Human Documents of the Victorian Golden Age*, 217.
23. LTH, 224.
24. Sparks, Nos. 18, 19, 20.
25. Well described by Millgate, 299–303.
26. LTH, 232.
27. ORFW, 8, for an instance of such rudeness.
28. Millgate, 303.
29. Churchwardens' Accounts, Chaddleworth, Berkshire County Archives.
30. LTH.
31. LTH, 272–273.
32. Baptisms, All Saints, Dorchester, and P.O. Directory, Dorset, 1867, DCRO.
33. Census, Athelhampton, 1871, DCL.
34. Sparks, No. 4.
35. LTH, 235.
36. LTH, 236–237.
37. Purdy, 91.
38. In the restoration, August 1893–May 1894, of West Knighton Church, as first pointed out by Beatty, 30–34.
39. ORFW, 28.
40. ORFW, 5 and 23.
41. Letter by Gordon Gifford, TLS, 1 January 1944.
42. See chapter 12.
43. Hardy to Edward Clodd, 13 December 1912, British Museum, quoted Bailey, 25.
44. LTH, 371.
45. LTH, 430.
46. Personal information, Mrs. Dubben of Sydling.
47. Kate Hardy's Diary, Lock Collection, DCL.
48. Personal information, Miss Mary Stickland.
49. MTH, No. 34.
50. Kate Hardy's Diary, Lock Collection, DCL.

APPENDIX: HARDY AND TRYPHENA SPARKS, pp. 223–29

1. F. R. Southerington, *Hardy's Vision of Man*, opposite page 136.
2. "Thomas Hardy", an unpublished signed typescript, Colby College Library.
3. MTH, No. 3.
4. *Providence and Mr. Hardy*, 22.
5. MTH, No. 71.
6. Southerington, op. cit., 262.
7. *Providence and Mr. Hardy*, 75 and 31.
8. ibid., 39.
9. ibid., 189.
10. Sparks, No. 16.
11. Sparks, No. 17.
12. Sparks, No. 20.
13. Sparks, No. 23.

List of Sources

A. MANUSCRIPT
Antell, G. S. Family papers.
Antell, J. H. Family papers.
Berkshire County Record Office. Berkshire parish registers, etc.
Bristol Record Office. Parish registers, Bishops' transcripts, etc.
Cambridge University Library. Buttery accounts, Queens' College. Diaries of H. C. G.
    Moule.
College of Sarum St. Michael, Salisbury. Archives.
Dorset County Library. Lock Collection. Letters, etc.
Dorset County Museum. Hardy Collection. Letters, etc.
Dorset County Record Office. Dorset parish registers, etc.
Gifford, Henry. Gifford family papers.
Hardy's Cottage, Higher Bockhampton. Photostats of Sparks family letters.
Hawkins, the Misses. Letters of Catherine Hawkins.
Hemington, Somerset. Parish registers.
King's College, London. Archives.
Murray, K. M. E. Unpublished letters of Thomas Hardy to James Murray.
Plymouth (City of) Public Libraries. Log Books 1872–77, Plymouth Public Free School
    (for Girls), Cobourg Street, Plymouth.
Probate of Wills, Somerset House.
Public Record Office. Census Returns, 1841–71.
Puddletown School. Log Books.
Registers of Births, Marriages, Deaths. General Registry.
Royal Institute of British Architects. Archives.
Salisbury Diocesan Record Office. Faculties, Bishops' transcripts.
Stockwell College of Education. Archives.
Trinity College, Cambridge, Library. Diaries of A. J. Munby.
Warneford Hospital, Oxford. Case Books.

B. TYPESCRIPT
Beatty, C. J. P., "The Part Played by Architecture in the Life and Work of Thomas
    Hardy, with Particular Reference to the Novels". Unpublished dissertation,
    University of London (External), 1964.
Hardy, F. E., "Notes of Thomas Hardy's Life . . . (taken down in conversations, etc.)".
    Dorset County Museum. Hardy Collection.

C. PUBLISHED
Alumni Cantabrigienses.
Alumni Oxoniensis.
Annan, Noel, *Leslie Stephen*, London, 1951.
Anon., *Thomas Hardy from Behind*, Dorchester, 1965.
Antell, John H., "Puddletown as Thomas Hardy Knew It", *Dorset Evening Echo*,
    18 July 1973.
Bailey, J. O., *The Poetry of Thomas Hardy: A Handbook and Commentary*, Chapel Hill,
    1970.
Barnard, H. C., *A Short History of English Education, 1760–1944*, London, 1947.
Bartlett, Phyllis, "Hardy's Shelley", *Keats–Shelley Journal*, IV, 15–29.
Battiscombe, G., *John Keble*, London, 1963.
Beatty, C. J. P. (ed.), *The Architectural Notebook of Thomas Hardy*, Dorchester, 1966.
Bevington, M. M., *The Saturday Review. 1855–68*, Cambridge, 1941.
Blomfield, Sir Arthur, *Memoirs of an Architect*, London, 1932.
Bristol City Library, *Poll Books, Directories*, etc.

Brooks, Jean R., *Thomas Hardy: The Poetic Structure*, London, 1971.

Brown, Douglas, *Thomas Hardy*, London, 1961.

Chadwick, Owen, *The Victorian Church*, 2 vols., London, 1970.

Clark, G. S. R. Kitson, *The Making of Victorian England*, Oxford, 1960.

Clemens, Cyril, "My Chat with Thomas Hardy", *Dalhousie Review*, April 1943.

Colby Library Quarterly, *A Descriptive Catalogue . . . of the Works of Thomas Hardy*, Waterville, Maine, 1940.

Collins, V. H., *Talks with Thomas Hardy*, New York, 1928.

Compton-Rickett, A., *I Look Back: Memories of Fifty Years*, London, 1933.

Cox, D. Drew, "The Poet and Architect", *Agenda*, Spring–Summer 1972.

Cox, J. S. (gen. ed.), *Materials . . . for a Life of Thomas Hardy*, 72 vols. St. Peter Port, Guernsey, 1962–.

    (ed.), *The Thomas Hardy Year Book*, 1970–.

Deacon, Lois and Coleman, Terry, *Providence and Mr. Hardy*, London, 1968.

Dolman, Frederick, "An Evening with Thomas Hardy", *Young Man*, VIII, March 1894, 74–79.

Ellis, S. M., "Some Personal Recollections of Thomas Hardy", *Fortnightly Review*, N.S. CXXIII, March 1928, 393–406.

Falk, Bernard, *The Naked Lady*, London, 1934.

Felkin, Elliott, "Days with Thomas Hardy: from a 1918–1919 diary", *Encounter*, XVIII, April 1962, 27–33.

Flower, Newman, *Just As It Happened*, New York, 1950.

    "Walks and Talks with Thomas Hardy", *The Countryman*, XXXIV, Winter 1966, 193–195.

Haight, G. S., *George Eliot*, Oxford, 1968.

Gifford, Henry, "Thomas Hardy and Emma", *Essays and Studies*, N.S. XIX (1966), 106–121.

Gosse, Edmund, "Thomas Hardy's Lost Novel", *Sunday Times*, 22 January 1928.

Graham, Thomas J., *Modern Domestic Medicine*, 13th edn., London, 1864.

Guerard, Albert J., *Thomas Hardy, The Novels and Stories*. Oxford, 1959.

Haggard, H. Rider, *Rural England*, 2 vols., London, 1902.

Halliday, F. E., *Thomas Hardy: His Life and Work*, Bath, 1972.

Hardy, Evelyn, "Hardy and the Phrenologist", *John O' London's Weekly*, 26 February 1954.

    "Some Unpublished Poems by Thomas Hardy", *London Magazine*, III (1956), 28–39.

    Thomas Hardy: A Critical Biography. London, 1954.

    "An Unpublished Poem by Thomas Hardy", *Times Literary Supplement*, 2 June 1966; and Robert Gittings (eds.), *Some Recollections by Emma Hardy*, Oxford, 1961; and F. B. Pinion (eds.), *One Rare Fair Woman: Letters of Thomas Hardy to Florence Henniker*, London, 1973.

Hardy, Florence E., *The Early Life of Thomas Hardy: 1840–1891*, London, 1928.

    The Later Years of Thomas Hardy: 1892–1928, London, 1930.

    The Life of Thomas Hardy: 1840–1928, London, 1962.

    (*The Life* is a one-volume publication of *The Early Life* and *The Later Years*. All, except the last few years, was really written by Hardy himself.)

Hardy, Thomas, "Death of Miss Mary Hardy", *Dorset County Chronicle*, 2 December 1915.

Harvey, O. D., *Puddletown, the Weatherbury of "Far from the Madding Crowd"*, Dorchester, 1968.

Hawkins, Desmond, *Thomas Hardy*, London, 1950.

Hibbert, Christopher, *Garibaldi and his Enemies*, London, 1965.

Holland, Clive, "My Walks and Talks in Wessex with Thomas Hardy", *John O'London's Weekly*, 30 March 1951.

Howe, Irving, *Thomas Hardy*, London, 1967.

Hynes, Samuel, *The Pattern of Hardy's Poetry*, Chapel Hill, 1961.

Jackman, Douglas, *300 Years of Baptist Witness in Dorchester, 1645–1945*, Dorchester, 1945.

Jones, Bernard (ed.), *The Poems of William Barnes*, 2 vols., Fontwell, 1963.

Kay-Robinson, Denys, *Hardy's Wessex Re-Appraised*, Newton Abbot, 1972.

Kingsgate, J. " *Tess* and Thomas Hardy, New Facts about his Life in London", *Graphic*, CXII, 5 September 1925.

Lewis, R. W. M., *The Family of Moule of Melksham, Fordington, and Melbourne*, Privately printed (1938).

M'Culloch, J. R., *Principles of Political Economy*, Edinburgh, 1825.

Maitland, F. W., *The Life and Letters of Leslie Stephen*, London, 1906.

Manton, Jo, *Sister Dora: A Life of Dorothy Pattison*, London, 1971.

   (ed.), *Memoirs of Mark Pattison*, Fontwell, 1969.

Martin, F. P. B., *A Memoir on the Equinoctial Storms, March–April 1850*. Privately printed, 1852.

Meynell, Viola (ed.), *Friends of a Lifetime: Letters to Sydney Cockerell*, London, 1940.

Miller, J. Hillis, *Thomas Hardy: Distance and Desire*. Cambridge, Mass. 1970.

Millgate, Michael, *Thomas Hardy, His Career as a Novelist*, Bodley Head, 1971.

Morgan, Charles, *The House of Macmillan*, London, 1943.

Morrell, Ray, *Thomas Hardy, The Will and the Way*, Kuala Lumpur, 1943.

Moule, H. C. G., *Memories of a Vicarage*, 1931.

Nevinson, H. W., *Thomas Hardy*, London, 1941.

Newman, J. and Pevsner, N., *The Buildings of Dorset*, London, 1972.

Orel, Harold (ed.), *Thomas Hardy's Personal Writings*, Kansas, 1966.

Phelps, W. L., *Autobiography and Letters*, Oxford, 1939.

Pike, E. Royston, *Human Documents of the Victorian Golden Age*, London, 1969.

Pinion, F. B., *A Hardy Companion*, London, 1968.

Purdy, R. L., *Thomas Hardy: A Bibliographical Study*, Oxford, 1954, rep. 1968.

   "The authorship of Hardy's Biography", TLS, 30 December 1960.

Reports of the British and Foreign School Society.

Rutland, W. R., *Thomas Hardy: A Study of his Writings and Their Background*, London, 1938, New York, 1962.

Smith, Goldwin, *Does the Bible Sanction Slavery?* Oxford, 1863.

Smith, S. Nowell (ed.), *Letters to Macmillan*, London, 1967.

Smith, W. Sylvester, *The London Heretics, 1870–1914*, London, 1967.

Southerington, F. R., *Hardy's Vision of Man*, London, 1971.

Stephen, Barbara, *Emily Davies and Girton College*, London, 1937.

Stewart, J. I. M., *Thomas Hardy*, London, 1971.

Taine, H. trans. Hyams, E., *Notes on England*, London, 1957.

Walcott, Fred G., *The Origins of Culture and Anarchy*, London, 1970.

Webb, A. P., *A Bibliography of the Works of Thomas Hardy*, London, 1916.

Weber, Carl J., *Hardy of Wessex*, London, 1940; rev. and repr. 1965.

   (ed.), *"Dearest Emmie"*, London, 1953.

   (ed.), *Hardy at Colby*, Waterville, Maine, 1936; *Hardy and the Lady from Madison Square*, Waterville, Maine, 1952.

   (ed.), *The Letters of Thomas Hardy*, Waterville, Maine, 1954.

Webster, H. C., *On a Darkling Plain: The Art and Thought of Thomas Hardy*, Chicago, 1947.

Williams, Merryn, *Thomas Hardy and Rural England*, London, 1972.

Winstanley, D. A., *Later Victorian Cambridge*, Cambridge, 1947.

Wreden, W. P., *Books from the Library of Thomas Hardy*, New York, 1938.

D. MAGAZINES, NEWSPAPERS, PERIODICALS

Academy
Athenaeum
Cornhill Magazine
Daily News
Daily Telegraph
Dorset County Chronicle
Daily Evening Echo
Englishwoman's Journal
Felix Farley's Bristol Journal
Frazer's Magazine
Gentleman's Magazine

Illustrated London News
London Review
Morning Post
Pall Mall Gazette
Saturday Review
Spectator
Standard
Sunday Times
The Times
Times Literary Supplement

ACKNOWLEDGEMENT OF QUOTATIONS

Extracts from the novels of Thomas Hardy and from his *Collected Poems*, and quotations from *The Life of Thomas Hardy* by Florence Hardy are reprinted by permission of the Trustees of the Hardy Estate, Macmillan, London and Basingstoke, and the Macmillan Company of Canada Limited.

Index